FUNDAMENTALS of WEB APPLICATIONS

Using .NET

and XML

ISBN 0-13-041790-4

90000

9 780130 417909

The Integrated .NET Series from Object Innovations and Prentice Hall PTR

C#

- Introduction to C# Using .NET
  Oberg

- Application Development Using C# and .NET
  Stiefel/Oberg

VISUAL BASIC

- Introduction to Visual Basic Using .NET
  Wyatt/Oberg

- Application Development Using Visual Basic and .NET
  Oberg/Thorsteinson/Wyatt

VISUAL C++

- .NET Architecture and Programming Using Visual C++
  Thorsteinson/Oberg

WEB APPLICATIONS

- Fundamentals of Web Applications Using .NET and XML
  Bell/Feng/Soong/Zhang/Zhu

PERL

- Programming PERL in the .NET Environment
  Saltzman/Oberg

FUNDAMENTALS of WEB APPLICATIONS Using .NET and XML

ERIC BELL • HAO "HOWARD" FENG
EDWARD L. W. SOONG • DAVID ZHANG
SHIJIA "SAM" ZHU

Prentice Hall PTR, Upper Saddle River, NJ 07458
www.phptr.com

Library of Congress Cataloging-in-Publication Data

Fundamentals of Web applications using .NET and XML / Eric Bell ... [et al.].
    p. cm.
  Includes index.
  ISBN 0-13-041790-4
    1. Web site development. 2. Application software--Development. 3. Microsoft.net frame-
work. 4. Internet programming. 5. XML (Document markup language). I. Bell, Eric.

TK5105.888 .F86 2002
005.2'76--dc21   2002016978

Editorial/Production Supervision: *Argosy*
Acquisitions Editor: *Jill Harry*
Marketing Manager: *Dan DePasquale*
Manufacturing Buyer: *Maura Zaldivar*
Cover Design: *Anthony Gemmellaro*
Cover Design Direction: *Jerry Votta*
Interior Series Design: *Gail Cocker-Bogusz*
Editorial Assistant: *Sarah Hand*
Project Coordinator: *Anne R. Garcia*

© 2002 Prentice Hall PTR
A Division of Pearson Education, Inc.
Upper Saddle River, NJ 07458

Prentice Hall books are widely used by corporations and government agencies for training, marketing, and resale.

The publisher offers discounts on this book when ordered in bulk quantities. For more information, contact Corporate Sales Department, phone: 800-382-3419; fax: 201-236-7141; email: corp-
sales@prenhall.com
Or write: Corporate Sales Department, Prentice Hall PTR, One Lake Street, Upper Saddle River,
NJ 07458

Product and company names mentioned herein are the trademarks or registered trademarks of
their respective owners.

Printed in the United States of America

10 9 8 7 6 5 4 3 2 1

ISBN 0-13-041790-4

Pearson Education LTD.
Pearson Education Australia PTY, Limited
Pearson Education Singapore, Pte. Ltd
Pearson Education North Asia Ltd
Pearson Education Canada, Ltd.
Pearson Educación de Mexico, S.A. de C.V.
Pearson Education—Japan
Pearson Education Malaysia, Pte. Ltd

To this great country, land of freedom and opportunity

CONTENTS

▼ CHAPTER 9   **SOAP Client and XML**   **335**

A new computing model, which breaks down the boundaries of business integration, is emerging. In it, data will be exchanged freely and applications will interoperate seamlessly across the Internet. Based on XML Web Services, this new model will bring our Internet-based economy to a new plateau. Microsoft .NET, with a compelling set of new technologies, is a platform for building, deploying, operating, and integrating these XML Web Services.

Fundamentals of Web Applications Using .NET and XML, part of the Prentice Hall/Object Innovations .NET series, is intended as a practical introduction to the fundamentals of .NET Web technologies for experienced programmers who are not necessarily familiar with .NET, to learn the basics of programming Web applications with .NET. It reviews the basics of current Web technologies; introduces .NET architecture; describes the major .NET Web technologies, ASP.NET, ADO.NET, Web Services, and XML programming; and explores advanced topics such as SOAP, Object Remoting, system interoperability, and the future of Web technology. A case study shows the .NET Web and XML technologies creating a new model of business.

The book also provides practical guidance on moving to .NET technology for readers with programming skills such as VB, C/C++, JScript, and Java, who may or may not have Web programming experience.

Organization

Fundamentals of Web Applications is structured to make it easy for you to find what you need to know. The first part, which should be read by everyone, begins with an introduction to Web sites in a .NET world (Chapter 1). It explains the paradigm shift from applications and products to the new concepts and practice of Web Services. Next comes a guided tour of .NET Framework, the infrastructure for all applications and services in the .NET environment (Chapter 2). As its greatest contribution to the industry, .NET Framework removes the distinction between traditional software development and Web development. Chapter 3 explores the programming environment of .NET Framework in which. You can find detailed descriptions and examples for learning this a major breakthrough in cross-language interoperability. In this environment, object-oriented programming capabilities, including inheritance and polymorphism, have broken the barriers between languages. The chapter attempts to explain why .NET Framework is very desirable for the development of large-scale distributed systems and Web applications.

The second part of this book covers the major features of .NET programming using ASP.NET, ADO.NET, Web Services, and XML. Chapter 4, a very thorough write-up about ASP.NET, the Active Server Pages for .NET Framework, its benefits by comparing ASP.NET with ASP, the new features like the Web Forms programming model, and server controls. Using a comprehensive Web site example, we show you how to build and deploy ASP.NET applications, as well as handle issues that affect real-world Web applications, such as session state and security. Finally, we take a quick look at the syntax of ASP.NET and the migration path from ASP. Chapter 5 takes a look at the major task of any software development—accessing data for both stand-alone and Web-based applications. ADO.NET, the Active Data Objects for .NET Framework, offers a consistent and scalable solution for access to various data sources. You will also find its benefits in interoperability, maintainability, programmability, and performance. Chapter 6 explores the core of this new computing model, Web Services, including how services are built and how they are accessed from clients. Chapter 7 explains Extensible Markup Language (XML), and provides sample programs. By this point you should have a fairly good understanding of Web application development using the .NET platform.

The third part of the book gets into more advanced Web programming in a .NET environment, Object Remoting, the Simple Object Access Protocol (SOAP), and interoperating with other platforms. It shows you how to build client/server applications based on the Object Remoting facility to make create distributed systems that are flexible and powerful (Chapter 8). Chapter 9 is for those of you who do not want to rely on XML but to build SOAP-based client applications directly. Of course, SOAP will help you to bridge various platforms to allow Windows and non-Windows applications to communicate effectively over the Internet. Is Microsoft's interoperability support for open system too good to be true? Chapter 10 will show you how this seemly impossible task, using SOAP, Universal Description, Discovery, and Integration (UDDI), and Web Services Description Language (WDSL), is accomplished.

Chapter 11, the fourth part, demonstrates the ultimate goal of this book—Web programming with .NET. This case study chapter offers you the chance to everything you have learned into practice. It shows you a clean and simple way to create a Web-based distributed application over the Internet using .NET and XML.

The last part has a rich set of reference materials. Appendix A is a Web technology primer for programmers who do not have Web programming experience. It can also serve as a quick reference for more experienced programmers. Appendix B discusses Visual Basic for.NET Framework and compares the old VB and the new VB. (For more information on VB.NET, please consult *Introduction to Visual Basic Using .NET* and *Application Development Using Visual Basic and .NET*.) The C# appendix (Appendix C) could have been a chapter by itself, but because the main topic of this book is not programming language, we made it an appendix. (For more in-depth study, please refer to *Introduction to C# Using .NET* and *Application Development Using C# and .NET* in the series.) You can also learn about what's new in JScript in Appendix D. The last appendix (Appendix E) introduces Visual Studio.NET, the latest incarnation of Microsoft's popular Visual Studio development environment. The new Visual Studio has many features that make application development easier and more pleasant. Learning it will equip you for programming with .NET.

Sample Programs

The only way to learn a programming language is to read and write many, many programs, including some of reasonable size. This book provides many small programs that illustrate pertinent features of Web programming in isolation, where they are easy to understand.

There is also a major case study, which illustrates how to program Web applications using .NET and XML. The case study is essential to understanding the topic.

The sample programs are provided in a self-extracting file. When the file is expanded, a directory structure is created, rooted in **c:\OI\Web**. The sample programs are in directories **Chap1**, **Chap2**, and so on. The sample programs for other books in the Prentice Hall/Object Innovations .NET series are located in their own directories under **c:\OI**, so all the .NET examples from all books in the series will be located in a common area as you install them.

Web Site

The Web site for the Prentice Hall/Object Innovations .NET series is

www.objectinnovations.com/dotnet.htm

A link is provided at that Web site for downloading the sample programs for this book.

Acknowledgments

We are grateful to Dr. Anna Janghong Chang and Ms. Patsy Man-Ling Huang for their active participation in the early planning stages of the book. Their interest and enthusiasm helped our project get off the ground. They spearheaded our development on ASP.NET and ADO.NET, and helped us complete the work.

The book owes its origin to Charlie Ferebee, who proposed the book to our publisher and created the first outline. Charlie attended our planning meetings and helped our book project get under way. We are also grateful to Mike Meehan, who showed us the ropes in book publishing. Our acquisitions editor Jill Harry has been most supportive throughout the project.

Our series editor, Dr. Bob Oberg, has given us this writing opportunity and memorable experience. We thank him for his guidance and support. Our thanks also go to Jonathan Levinson and Peter Lu for taking time from their tight schedules to review our manuscript and make valuable suggestions.

Certainly, we are indebted to Barbara Badgley, Qingyan Wang, Lily Soong, Qiyuan "Wendy" Wu, and Su Zhu, for their behind-the-scenes help, encouragement, ideas, suggestions, and support. Howard's first baby boy was born right before the publishing of this book. We thank him for his patience.

About this Series
Robert J. Oberg, Series Editor

Introduction

The Integrated .NET Book Series from Object Innovations and Prentice Hall PTR is a unique series of introductory and intermediate books on Microsoft's important .NET technology. These books are based on proven industrial-strength course development experience. The authors are expert practitioners, teachers, and writers who combine subject-matter expertise with years of experience in presenting complex programming technologies such as C++, MFC, OLE, and COM/COM+. These books *teach* in a systematic, step-by-step manner and are not merely summaries of the documentation. All the books come with a rich set of programming examples, and a thematic case study is woven through several of the books.

From the beginning, these books have been conceived as an *integrated whole*, and not as independent efforts by a diverse group of authors.. The initial set of books consists of three introductory books on .NET languages and four intermediate books on the .NET Framework. Each book in the series is targeted at a specific part of the important .NET technology, as illustrated by the diagram below.

		C# Learning Pathway	VB.NET Learning Pathway		
.NET Language Introductions	Programming PERL in the .NET Environment	**Introduction to C# Using .NET**	Introduction to Visual Basic Using .NET		
Intermediate .NET Framework Titles		Application Development Using C# and .NET	Application Development Using Visual Basic and .NET	.NET Architecture and Programming Using Visual C++	Fundamentals of Web Applications Using .NET and XML

Introductory .NET Language Books

The first set of books teaches several of the important .NET languages. These books cover their language from the ground up and have no prerequisite other than programming experience in some language. Unlike many .NET language books, which are a mixture of the language and topics in the .NET Framework, these books are focused on the languages, with attention to important interactions between the language and the framework. By concentrating on the languages, these books have much more detail and many more practical examples than similar books.

The languages selected are the new language C#, the greatly changed VB.NET, and Perl.NET, the open source language ported to the .NET environment. Visual C++ .NET is covered in a targeted, intermediate book, and JScript.NET is covered in the intermediate level .NET Web-programming book.

Introduction to C# Using .NET

This book provides thorough coverage of the C# language from the ground up. It is organized with a specific section covering the parts of C# common to other C-like languages. This section can be cleanly skipped by programmers with C experience or the equivalent, making for a good reading path for a diverse group of readers. The book gives thorough attention to the object-oriented aspects of C# and thus serves as an excellent book for programmers migrating to C# from Visual Basic or COBOL. Its gradual pace and many examples make the book an excellent candidate as a college textbook for adventurous professors looking to teach C# early in the language's life-cycle.

Introduction to Programming Visual Basic Using .NET

Learn the VB.NET language from the ground up. Like the companion book on C#, this book gives thorough attention to the object-oriented aspects of VB.NET. Thus the book is excellent for VB programmers migrating to the more sophisticated VB.NET, as well as for programmers experienced in languages such as COBOL. This book would also be suitable as a college textbook.

Programming Perl in the .NET Environment

A very important part of the vision behind Microsoft® .NET is that the platform is designed from the ground up to support multiple programming languages from many sources, and not just Microsoft languages. This book, like other books in the series, is rooted in long experience in industrial teaching. It covers the Perl language from the ground up. Although oriented toward the ActiveState Perl.NET compiler, the book also provides excellent coverage of the Perl language suitable for other versions as well.

Intermediate .NET Framework Books

The second set of books is focused on topics in the .NET Framework, rather than on programming languages. Three parallel books cover the .NET Framework using the important languages C#, VB.NET, and Visual C++. The C# and VB.NET books include self-contained introductions to the languages suitable for experienced programmers, allowing them to rapidly come up to speed on these languages without having to plow through the introductory books. The fourth book covers the important topic of web programming in .NET, with substantial coverage of XML, which is so important in the .NET Framework.

The design of the series makes these intermediate books much more suitable to a wider audience than many similar books. The introductory books focus on languages frees up the intermediate books to cover the important topics of the .NET Framework in greater depth. The series design also makes for flexible reading paths. Less experienced readers can read the introductory language books followed by the intermediate framework books, while more experienced readers can go directly to the intermediate framework books.

Application Development Using C# and .NET

This book does not require prior experience in C#. However, the reader should have experience in some object-oriented language such as C++ or Java™. The book could also be read by seasoned Visual Basic programmers who have experience working with objects and components in VB. Seasoned programmers and also a less experienced reader coming from the introductory C# book can skip the first few chapters on C# and proceed directly to a study of the Framework. The book is practical, with many examples and a major case study. The goal is to equip the reader with the knowledge necessary to begin building significant applications using the .NET Framework.

Application Development Using Visual Basic .NET

This book is for the experienced VB programmer who wishes to learn the new VB.NET version of VB quickly and then move on to learning the .NET Framework. It is also suitable for experienced enterprise programmers in other languages who wish to learn the powerful RAD-oriented Visual Basic language in its .NET incarnation and go on to building applications. Like the companion C# book, this book is very practical, with many examples, and includes the same case study implemented in VB.NET.

.NET Architecture and Programming Using Visual C++

This parallel book is for the experienced Visual C++ programmer who wishes to learn the .NET Framework to build high-performing applications. Unlike the C# and VB.NET book, there is no coverage of the C++ language itself, because C++ is too complex to cover in a brief space. This book is specifically for experienced C++ programmers. Like the companion C# and VB.NET books, this book is very practical, with many examples, and includes the same case study implemented in Visual C++.

Fundamentals of Web Applications Using .NET and XML

The final book in the series provides thorough coverage of building Web applications using .NET. Unlike other books about ASP.NET, this book gives attention to the whole process of Web application development. The book incorporates a review tutorial on classical Web programming, making the book accessible to the experienced programmer new to the Web world. The book contains significant coverage on ASP.NET, Web Forms, Web Services, SOAP, and XML.

Web Sites in a .NET World

If you want to learn how to use .NET to build Web sites, to control remote applications, and to learn about the platform through hands-on examples, you have the right book in your hands. .NET is coming to a computer near you soon; it's going to be big. Inevitably, it will be on every Windows computer.

To help you get started building Web sites using .NET, this book covers the technology from one end to the other. But before you begin hacking away (beginning with Chapter 2), this chapter sets out to show you what changes will take place and why. This chapter discusses

- *The distributed nature of .NET*
- *Comparisons between today's Web and the .NET Web*
- *New notions like* experiences

Web sites can and will be built differently than they are today. Before you begin your journey a little direction may help you. If you want to jump into the technologies, you can go right to Chapter 2.

1.1 Integrated Web Sites

Web sites before .NET largely operate independently of each other. But some Web sites are different. By integrating parts of other Web sites into themselves, they form partnerships. One can see this in most Web portals, such as Yahoo (*www.yahoo.com*) and Snap (*www.snap.com*), where weather reports and news articles are available. These portals license or own the services, which are Web sites themselves, to enrich the content of the portals. Call it integration or collaboration or simply working together, this kind of "distributed computing" has benefits. This is integrating pieces of one Web site into another and getting them to work together, stitching pages together instead of merely hyperlinking pages. .NET is all about getting Web sites to work together and realizing these benefits.

Collaboration of this type is more involved than one might think. Aside from the technical details of melding two or more sites together, various business details have been put into place. Services have to be arranged and provided, and the portals have to consume the services in specific ways. Finally, presentation has to be seamless.

For Web developers, integrating pages or parts of pages from different sites may not be everyday work, but most developers can do it with some effort. But there is no common framework for integrating two or more sites together, and there are no standards, no well-known tool kits, and no books on the subject. Integrating multiple Web sites is still a do-it-yourself affair.

1.1.1 Collaboration

The first issue is to agree on a working definition of *collaboration*. The dictionary definition is simply "working with others." Networking computers is often thought of as making the computers work together, but networking by itself doesn't do this. Networking provides pathways through which computers can share data—and that is all that networking does. Computers working together implies that each participating computer is contributing to a conversation, intentionally driving the tasks at hand to their completion.

Collaboration involves *intentionally* working together, which means that the collaborators, in a distributed fashion, are processing tasks. Each computer provides what another computer needs as part of the tasks they perform. This kind of collaboration between computers is one form of distributed computing. Distributed computing theory and practice has filled books and is beyond what this book intends to explore. Distributing the work to build a Web site or Web application over several computers is one form of distributed computing. An effective mechanism to foster this in the computer information technology community had been missing until the

.NET initiative. All forms of distributed computing are not met by .NET, but the most critical one—the mechanism to stitch applications together to form one cohesive application—is met. This much of distributed computing is present in .NET and we shall call it *collaboration* between computers.

Now that we have a working definition of collaboration, why do we want it? If you accept the concept of collaboration just presented then the reason to want it is the benefits we get. But what are they? First, using two or more computers at once to solve a problem is better use of the computers. So much of a computer's time is often just idling that we can make better use of it.

Second, deciding how to break up a problem for distributed processing has been difficult. It takes some work to break problems up between computers, so the process has not been practical. .NET reworks the problem by supplying a framework that provides incentives for the pieces of solutions to appear before they are needed. Deciding how to break up a problem is addressed in a different way. Don't envision a problem and break it up, envision what you want, find the pieces, and form the solution. Use inside-out thinking.

Third, outsourcing parts of your site means that someone else will worry about the upkeep of those parts. This is simple economics.

1.1.2 The Costs of Collaboration

The price for collaboration of this kind is adopting .NET. This means committing yourself to this platform, and learning the tools, kits, and servers that support it. The learning curve is a bit steep across the spectrum of products that make up .NET. The class library is large, languages have been invented or changed to suit it, and there are new tools to learn and use and new servers to integrate. This book addresses all of these issues.[1] Servers are addressed in terms of their use rather than in terms of managing them. ASP.NET, for instance, is technology supported by Internet Information Server (IIS) and SQL Server (Microsoft's industrial-strength database server), so our chapter on ASP.NET will get you up and running without getting into the details about managing IIS. While this kind of commitment can be predicted, it needs to be stated because .NET's success depends on people adopting the changes. Microsoft is making an effort to attract developers to this platform and is making .NET attractive for companies to deploy, but the human cost is there nevertheless.

---

[1] See Chapter 2, "Fundamentals of .NET," and Chapter 3, "The Programming Environment of .NET Framework," for a discussion on the class library. A class library is a large set of prewritten code that you must use to take advantage of .NET. See Appendices B, C, and D for information about C#, managed C++, VB.NET, and JScript.NET.

1.1.3 Experience

The word *experience* has been drafted by Microsoft to become jargon. Literature suggests that .NET will herald a new era in software ease-of-use that will enrich people's lives at work or play with new experiences.

At this time, computers don't hide the fact that you have to know how to operate them. Like a pilgrim visiting a shrine you have to go to the computer, learn its ways, and take what you can from it. A typical desktop computer can run thousands of programs if they are available, and you have to learn how to operate each to get any benefit from them. This ranges from different commands for similar operations among different packages to the work required to manage your hard disk. Computers demand that users bend to their needs rather than the other way around.

People generally want computers to do more of the work. Saving a Web page in a browser illustrates this point. First you must select the menu item to save the page, then you select the location for the page and possibly rename the page. This is a common pattern of behavior of most software. Once you are past being a computer novice, you accept this repeated behavior and perform it with little thought. If you have to hunt around on your hard disk for a place to store the Web page, you could be clicking or keying quite a bit. The real annoyances occur when you save several documents and have to hunt the disk for the same folder each time to save the next page in. The program doesn't remember where you just stored the previous document. This is a poor experience.

The experiences you understand as a user of the Web are important to you. The word *experience*—to directly observe events—is now jargon. Microsoft uses *experience* to express "how you perceive events," which is slightly different. We programmers provide experiences for users through our software. A *.NET experience* is the conscious attention paid to how users work with software. The same package can provide different experiences by its presentation, how it works, its speed of operation, and more.

There has always been a push to make personal computers easier to use. Making the details of using Web sites less noticeable is a continuing process. Ultimately, we want the details to disappear completely. The less you have to think about the technology the more effective it is. This is why people new to computers generally feel uneasy if not afraid. A computer is utterly foreign to any experience they may have ever had. Novice computer users spend most of their time mentally translating what they want into what the computer needs. It is a lot of work and it is an error-prone process.

A good experience is one that meets the expectations of users. If you have to think hard about how to use a site, you are less likely to use it. Working with a site has to be relatively easy. Experiences are part of the .NET push even if you won't find support for them yet. The .NET platform as of yet has no tools, APIs, or programming mechanisms supporting or deploying experiences. There is little literature that you can refer to that can guide you, but this term is cropping up in different places and will become common. Tools will probably merge to support creation, maintenance, and deployment of experiences.

1.1.4 Site-to-Site Collaboration

In order to make collaboration between Web sites work there have to be standard mechanisms in place. Our lives are littered with devices that don't cooperate or collaborate with each other because there are no mechanisms allowing them to. Successful technology seems to flourish when it can be part of something else and that is made better if there are standards for them to follow.

HyperText Markup Language (HTML) was one of the first mechanisms that allowed everyone to join the party, building Web pages all over the world. And underlying HTML is HyperText Transfer Protocol (HTTP), the protocol Web servers use to communicate. HTML is intended to describe how to present data but does not provide ways to work with data. For example, money means different things to you and me, or a date is written one way by me and another way by you. Enter Extensible Markup Language (XML), a standard becoming nearly as ubiquitous as HTML. XML is a general way to describe data.

The meaning of data and our intentions for its use can get very complicated. XML is a specification for storing it, for transmitting it, and for using it. Where HTML's strength is its ability to show data, XML's strength is in describing the data.

XML alone does not solve all the data problems we encounter with Web sites. XML is a general specification for data that is customized for each use. Each site uses XML its own way and this is intentional. How then do we get two sites to talk to each other? By agreeing to use even more standards. .NET is centered on standards to get sites and applications to talk to each other.

1.1.5 The .NET Solutions

There are several challenges to designing and building Web sites that depend on XML. Three of these are discussed here. The first challenge is the availability of tools for processing XML. Before .NET, we would have needed to obtain an XML coding tool that understood XML structure, an XML parser, and an XML generator.[2] These would have been integrated into our development environments and products. These are costly and time-consuming activities.

---

[2] A parser reads and digests matter for the computer to make use of. XML parsers read XML into the computer. A generator in this context is software that creates and emits matter for other computers. XML generators create XML to be sent elsewhere.

Microsoft is building XML into all its server products and many client products, which is part of the answer. The .NET strategy has a clear XML component to it, wherein all servers have to be XML capable and tools for XML processing have to be available. All of their servers in one way or another read and write XML in a way that is suitable for each. This gives XML the ubiquity it needs to be fundamental to the architecture of .NET.

The second challenge is a management issue. Programmers, software architects, and others make choices about which products to use when building sites. Web sites have been built largely from programmers coding the site together. Reducing the coding effort by buying and integrating prebuilt code is less common.

As .NET-compatible components become available, buying and integrating components will be more widespread than it is now. XML is underlying such decisions. "Does the component send its data in XML format?" and other questions will be routinely asked when programmers design sites. When components answering these questions are found, they will be used in lieu of programming. Web sites will likely be constructed from XML-based components as .NET gains acceptance. Building a Web site from components is not new but not widespread either. Those components that are available today tend to be lower level, handling small chores rather than larger pieces of business. Because of .NET, a market will develop for .NET components (Web services), just as an ActiveX[3] components market developed.

The third challenge is getting Web services to be commonplace. Within a company the barriers to making this happen are fewer than the barriers between companies. An intranet can be mandated into existence. If companies want to create one within their own walls they can. Conversely, when unrelated companies provide Web services for sale, client companies that would buy the services will have to be convinced that collaborating is practical and profitable. Until these objections are overcome, Web services will not be commonplace.

The existing and emerging standards are laying much of the groundwork for collaboration to take place.

1.2 Comparing Visions

The World Wide Web today is filled with different kinds of sites and applications. To discuss this in terms of .NET, let's categorize these sites loosely as online brochures, support sites, online stores, applications, and services.

---

[3] ActiveX is a set of technologies that create components out of bits of code. Having premade components on hand when building applications means faster time to delivery and better products because less coding is required.

1.2.1 Conventional Online Brochures

A brochure site is really a computerized pamphlet. It's made by handcrafting each page and hyperlinking these pages together. These sites are the granddaddy of all sites, being nothing more than HTML and Dynamic HTML (DHTML). These sites are created by businesses and people to serve a simple purpose, which is to advertise something. Files are often available for download, and hyperlinks to other sites are common and they rarely use outsourced services. A Web server like IIS is all that is needed to drive this site.

Pages are created to communicate different thoughts by weaving graphics and text together. Simply linking pages provides navigation between pages. The typical navigation scheme consists of a row of links. Usually the major links appear across the top of each page and minor ones down the left side. Content appears on the remaining space on the pages. Content is embedded in the pages or is dynamically placed in the stream of page data sent to the reader's browser.

A typical brochure will have a home page that provides the principal identity of the site and several pages of content. In this way the pages are electronic versions of a print brochure.

Maintaining this site, and keeping links up-to-date and the content fresh is often a burden. Engaging content is provided once when the site is built but never again, except when the site undergoes a makeover. Companies whose basic business is not online leave their Web presence as an afterthought. This makes sense because there were no standards to foster building online brochures any other way. Enter .NET.

1.2.2 .NET Online Brochures

Taking for granted that a .NET brochure site could be built the same as a conventional one, the interesting benefit of .NET for online brochures comes in the form of improved maintenance and content. Since .NET fosters building not only Web sites but also Web services, tasks performed by remote Web sites can be integrated into your site and content for your site can be provided by another site. Furthermore, various service providers can even provide parts of your site.

A simple two-page brochure site with a static home page and static page touting your service could have its content updated. This way, your site could become more compelling for visitors to revisit and be more economical to maintain.

To illustrate this, let's consider a two-page site for an investment firm, a home page and a page describing the company's specific offerings. Both pages are, in conventional terms, unchanging from day to day. There is no in-house crew of Web programmers busily updating the Web pages every day or even periodically, because Web page production is not the firm's business.

They don't change their paper brochures every day and they don't change their Web site every day. There is no model in place to do this. Enter .NET.

A site built with ASP.NET, in this case the investment firm's site, can be quickly changed once to allow an outsourcing company supplying content to provide pieces of the pages with new content as agreed to. While this scenario can and has happened before now, .NET makes doing so more practical. This will yield a more abundant supply of services and eventually cost advantages to using them.

The bundling and integration capabilities of .NET are significant. Being promoted by the world's largest company and pushed to the hilt is going to make the introduction of .NET an important historical event.

1.2.3 Conventional Support Sites

Support sites or self-help sites are a bit more sophisticated than brochure sites. Often a support site develops from a brochure site. New features, like the ability to create e-mail messages, have discussions with other users of the site, and upload files for distribution, are added through a Common Gateway Interface (CGI), which executes programs on the Web server. Simple CGI such as executables and scripts running in Perl or JScript (see Appendix A) as well as sophisticated CGI in the form of Active Server Pages (ASP) (see Appendix A), go beyond using a mere Web server and add mail and database servers. Programming this kind of site takes more knowledge and tools.

Visitors focus on the knowledge they can glean from the site and the services the site provides. One example is e-mail that is generated right on the site. The visitor is presented with an e-mail form that will generate an e-mail message to the operators of the site. Another example is customizing content for the visitor. On a typical programmer's site where discussion groups, code samples, tutorials, and articles can be found, the site organizes this information for the visitor. By offering a few page links or by asking the visitor to fill out a form, the site can produce specific content for the visitor. To make this happen, CGI is used extensively beyond HTML and DHTML.

For an example of a support site using CGI, consider a site that has a large collection of code samples for programmers to download and use. There are many sites like this on the Web servicing every conceivable computer language and technology. In our example site, a visitor could search the site for a sample of code that creates a menu on a page. The visitor notices that the code is in JScript, which is fine because he is comfortable with JScript. He downloads it, customizes it, and puts it into his Web site. The visitor's site then has a snazzy menu that his visitors can use. This is the conventional support site. To create a more interactive mechanism or to provide more features may entail significant programming by the support site personnel that is not cost-effective. Enter .NET.

1.2.4 .NET Support Sites

Let's focus on .NET-ifying this site. The code samples that are stored on the support site are unformatted text residing in files. It would be more useful if the support site could customize the code samples before our visitor downloads them. Why? Because the means of customizing the code is built into the support site, our visitor will have less to do, an appealing benefit for the visitor. But setting up each code sample to participate in customization could be very expensive because each sample is different from the next in scope, work, and interface. How do you automate customization?

Automating customization starts with using XML to wrap the sample code. How much we use XML to wrap the code is another matter, perhaps down to individual syntactic elements like words within the sample. Once samples have been wrapped in appropriate XML, the other part of automating customization is creating a process on the site that generates the customized sample. One way to accomplish this is by questioning the user about his intentions based on the XML used to wrap the sample. Answers to questions would map to the XML, and this process could then create the unique version of the code.

While we have moved the work of customizing the code from the programmer visitor to the site, the question of cost comes up. What are the benefits to the support site of doing this? Isn't this going to be more expensive for the support site to set up and maintain?

This is a choice between first-time cost and life-cycle cost for the support site. When the code samples are instrumented up front (the first-time cost), the utility of the sample and reusability of the sample increases at a lowered long-term expense (life-cycle cost). That is, it's cheaper in the long run. Also, it is the business of the site to attract and keep visitors. If two support sites had the same code samples to offer and one customized them for you, which would you visit?

How was the customization processor built? Was the custom programming written to any standards? If it is written in a .NET environment it will be written as a Web service with two benefits. One, the framework exists to do this already, which makes the job easier. Two, as a service, the processor becomes reusable to a wider range of applications, first to the support site and later to other consumers as the need or opportunity arises.

If the visitor's tools understand how to use Web services and the site publishes Web services, then it's natural to connect the visitor's tool to the site's service. This kind of collaboration is just beginning to be demonstrated.

Once the Web service connection is made between the visitor's tool, in this case Visual Studio .NET, and the support site, the Web service can be employed on behalf of the visitor. This means less work for the visitor, and we expect better results. An added benefit is that as the support site changes the code sample from time to time, older versions of the code snippet deployed can be made to match the version on the support site with less work. Visual Studio.NET might learn of an update for the code at the support site, bring it down, and integrate it all automatically.

The collaborative mechanism employed will do most of the work. Taking this one step further, once the customized snippet is deployed in the visitor's Web application, changes to the support site's code could be integrated directly into the visitor's application without the need for programmer intervention at all. This extensive kind of collaboration is not yet available but it's only a matter of time before it will be.

1.2.5 Conventional Online Stores

Online stores are familiar to most users of the Internet. These sites represent the most sophisticated uses of the Web that people commonly interact with. Commerce sites tend to use the most technology, have more diversified requirements, and need to evolve to fulfill many goals. Online stores generally encompass the look and feel of a brochure site, a support site, and a commerce site. Online stores show the visitor the products the merchant sells, let the visitor collect items for purchase in a shopping cart, order the products in real time, process the order for shipment, and even allow the visitor to arrange the return of purchased merchandise. Store sites differ from the first two categories in their dependence on state information and the experience the site incorporates.

These sites are generally goal-oriented. This goal-orientation is called a pipeline: As you move through the site you advance along the pipeline. You select products, indicate whether they are gifts, choose how they should be shipped, and finally pay for them. There is an order to things on these sites. Stores have been using components to build with from their beginning. Viewed this way, the typical components of an online store are

- Product catalog
- Shopping cart
- Real-time credit-card purchasing
- Real-time order processing
- Return merchandise authorization

Each component has a protocol to follow to communicate data to other components on the site. The total interaction between these components is the store.

The very first commercial use of XML may have been in online stores. Being able to describe data is one of the principal functions of an online store. Another way to think of a store is as an inventory management business. It may appear to you that the store is selling shoes, but in their minds they are managing inventory. The seduction of XML is significant. Once you embed XML in with your data, it's natural to use XML for communicating the data throughout the site.

Critical to the success of any store is controlling costs, and one way to do this is to connect front-end operations to back-end operations. A typical example is connecting the cash register to the accounts receivable system. XML makes this more doable if all the systems "speak" XML.

Sites that have XML embedded in this way have had to roll their own schemas,[4] inventing how to use XML to their advantage. If they had the advantage of standard schemas and well-known uses, they could have leveraged existing work to increase capability, decrease cost, and increase reliability or time to market.

1.2.6 .NET Online Stores

Online stores represent some of the most fertile ground for immediate use of .NET technology. First, .NET servers have XML firmly embedded in their fiber so interfacing front-line operations will be smoother.

Second, sites will be made from integrating components, which we call Web services. The plug-and-play structure we enjoy with hardware becomes available for Web development too. Vendors offering XML-based services that have standard interfaces with different cost-benefit relationships will enable site builders to change services as easily as they can change a video card in a computer.

Lastly, internal company use of services to support the stores will be the most likely place this becomes accepted practice. The barriers will be the lowest and problems most manageable. Perhaps the first intercompany collaboration that will be successful will be the purchasing functions that Electronic Data Interchange (EDI) handles between large companies. Large companies could invest in EDI, a private protocol, for certain kinds of purchasing. With IP technology, EDI is steadily being replaced, and today XML is the underlying data format. However, switching and swapping partners even when they all use XML is not an easy matter since the schema and its meaning have to be agreed to by all parties. While a reasonable goal, this still requires human intervention, and the cost of setting up all the interactions between parties can be high. .NET with SOAP, WSDL, and UDDI may be the answer to lowering the first-cost issue. Chapters 6, 9, and 10 cover the details of these protocols, but the gist here is that from a pool of services, UDDI will allow you to find the one you are after, specify the interchange with WSDL, and communicate through SOAP, which encapsulates your XML data.

With plug-and-play components used to construct online stores, we refine the *experience* for both the stores and the shoppers; that is, online stores will be better places to shop. This all comes with a price and will only

---

[4] A schema is a definition of what should be interpreted and how to interpret it. For example, the schema that includes a definition for money would know the difference between the numbers $3.56 and 0.01E-3.

happen if the technology continues to mature and vendors have incentives to innovate.

Eventually we will see catalogs of Web services from merchants who will provide online store functions. We then select each piece of the store: a product catalog, shopping cart, and real-time purchasing piece. To make this work we integrate the pieces using a meta-service that contains and organizes other services. Such a meta-service has not yet been invented, and until it has, programs will have to stitch Web services together. This is the state of the art of .NET.

1.2.7 Conventional Web Applications

Web applications are nothing more than a desktop or server application made available through the Web. Create a few Web forms, add processing functions on a server, and you have a Web application. This is a light treatment of the amount of work necessary to make a professional Web application, but in simple terms this is what is involved. Although they are Web sites, we call them applications in deference to the workflow they provide. An example of a Web application is an accounting package that can handle sales, payables, receivables, payroll, and more. Such an accounting package available over the Web would be available for any computer and browser. This is a great reason to make the package Web-enabled.

The other side of the coin is worth mentioning too. First, because the user's data resides on the provider's systems, the user would have to be able to trust the provider, the application would have to be available at all times, and adequate security measures would have to be taken to protect the data. Second, if the provider goes out of business or stops supporting the application, it may not be an easy matter to transfer data from their systems to another. While this is true of applications the user hosts, too, at least the decision to stop is controlled by the user. Third, if a payment or quality of service issue arises and the provider suspends the service until the issue is settled, the user would again lose access to the data. Other issues exist but these are significant enough for now.

1.2.8 .NET Web Applications

The .NET version of Web applications needs to be explained in two parts. First, aside from the advancement Windows forms bring (see Chapter 5) to creating applications faster than before, standards once again play an important role to making Windows forms even more prevalent. Using XML to describe the data and SOAP to glue services together, applications can be built better, faster, and more cheaply than before.

The second part is data ownership. Applications will consist of remote services integrated together. If services could be located on user computers as well as remote provider servers, then the data could reside on the user's computers as well. We currently conceptualize systems in multiple tiers, so there is no great leap in theory about this. The user interface and the business rules can be on the service provider's hosts and the data can be on the user's hosts. When the provider makes available business rules services that talk to the user's data services, most of these problems go away.

To illustrate, imagine you browse to the application site located somewhere on the Internet. When you sign in, the provider's host establishes contact with your locally running data service. Once all the pieces are connected, the business rules are run on the provider's site but the data stays on your side. When you're done, all the connections are broken and you still have your data. At this writing, .NET hasn't got facilities for making services local or for wiring up providers to users in this fashion. If this is viable, this facility will appear.

1.2.9 Conventional Services

Service sites are like application sites except that they have little if any front end to browse to. They have, if you will, no home page. They are meant to be part of another application, which is much of what .NET is about already. Service sites exist today and are readily used in some circles. Service sites come in all sizes and levels of complexity, with little or no standards to provide interoperability. Each company's service follows its own usage plan. Although many follow standards, there is no widespread agreement on them.

An example of a service that is widely available and used is delivery of news articles. Companies scan the Web for news articles that they can group together, make searchable, and deliver on demand to a consumer. Some providers make the articles available in a wide variety of formats, most of them XML variants. To integrate news articles into your site, you have to find one of these providers, make an agreement with them, select a format, and weave them into a page. To the extent that XML is already a format of choice for services, there are conventions and standards in place.

1.2.10 .NET Services

A .NET service is a .NET Web Service. Companies have been struggling with this for several years. How do you make services available, reusable, and ubiquitous? With the acceptance of XML, SOAP, WSDL, and UDDI, Web services are not only possible but also practical.

1.3 Experiences

Now we move to the collaboration between people and sites. When you browse sites do you consider how you feel and think? Try an experiment: Find two sites that fit two categories and noodle around them for a little bit. Start with a brochure site, then follow up with an online store site. Do it now if you have a mind to. Notice how you feel and think. Do you sense the shift in your thinking when you move from one kind of site to the other? It's no mystery: The goal of a brochure site is to get you to jump from one page to another to read, watch, or listen to the content. You cover as much of the site as interests you because you are in control. An online store is different. You are guided through the experience by an unseen hand that wants you to find products, put them into the shopping cart, and pay for the items. We generally don't give this much thought unless the site is hard to use. In a brochure site the links may not stand out, so we don't know what to click; in an online store site the shopping cart may be constructed so that we don't feel comfortable or know whether we have purchased something. We call this difference the experience.

Sites have been constructed to give users different experiences intentionally. If the site provides an experience that is similar to the real-world experience, the user is comfortable and confident. As architects and programmers we strive to create this feeling in the user. The technologies we employ, such as Web servers and coding tools, do not aid in this process. They are just so much of the background to be pulled and pushed by the efforts of the programmers. The success of the site—the experience—depends on the people who created the site and the technology they employed.

Let's suggest a different scenario.

1.3.1 Experiences in Web Services

The notion of an *experience* is relatively new and provides us with the means to understand the world on the Web differently than before. .NET offers some improvement in conceptualizing new experiences and, ultimately, to creating new experiences. However, .NET does not provide a specific solution; rather, it provides some of the critical pieces. More work will be needed to make experiences commonplace. To this end, the first and most important inroad to creating sophisticated experiences is Web services. You will read more about Web services later in this book, but for now let's focus on what Web services are and what using them may mean.

A Web service is the programmatic interface for an application made available over the Web. You expose your application, others expose theirs, and we all can use each other's applications to build bigger and better applications. Said another way, Web services are the latest Remote Procedure

Calls (RPCs), invoking procedures, functions, or methods of other applications over networks.

If you standardize the way you expose applications over a network and we all use the standard, then it follows that a client application using one or more Web services could switch services at the drop of a hat when a better one comes along. Better services rolled out over time mean better client applications when the client can easily change the service it uses. We all know a common example of this—dial-up Internet access. Our computers can use anyone's dial-up service because of a standard network mechanism built into the computer—a TCP/IP stack and the PPP connection protocol. Changing the provider is often no more complicated than choosing a sign-on name and password. Poof! You've changed your service; you've changed your experience.

To explore notions of experience further, three terms are introduced: *deep experiences*, *shallow experiences*, and *sensations*. *Deep experiences* are Web applications performing sophisticated work on your behalf with little interaction from you. You probably cannot guess at the amount of work being done and yet the results are expected and feel ordinary. An e-commerce shopping cart is a deep experience because it is so common at this point. Except when implemented badly, Web users can shop using the shopping cart mechanism and expect certain results every time at every shopping cart. *Shallow experiences* also have a considerable amount of work performed on your behalf, yet more of the process is visible to you. You have to interact more with the Web application so that in the end you get the results that you expect but you feel that the computers have not done as much of the work. The dial-up example is a shallow experience. Lastly, *sensations* are the components that make up experiences. Clicking any button on a Web page carries with it a sensation in the overall experience of the page. All of this terminology is new and not well agreed upon.

1.3.2 Shallow Experience

We can divide up a shallow experience into three sensations. A sensation is a part of an experience. One or more sensations make up an experience. In the case of dial-up Internet service, there are three sensations: the client sensation, the provider's sensation, and the medium connecting the two.

Providers like AOL, MSN, Earthlink, or, in days gone by, CompuServe and Delphi, could not expect that their customer's computers would have a TCP/IP (the software needed to connect you to the Internet) stack installed nor have the right client application or dial-up application to access their servers. Installation disks for AOL seemed to fall out of everything including cereal boxes for a while. These disks would ensure that a potential customer could dial up and get online. The customer's sensation was made simpler by these disks. The sensation each provider supplied was basically the same.

The provider's sensation was installing enough servers and modems to meet the demand and advertising like mad. For some this worked, for others it didn't. Lastly the medium sensation was the public telephone company that interestingly enough shaped the other two sensations in this shallow experience. It was through their standards and requirements that dial-up Internet access became a reality.

There are other important pieces to this experience like the modem manufacturers and other vendors, but to keep this simple we have confined ourselves to these three.

1.3.3 Evolving to Deep Experiences

Cable modems, DSL, and faster Internet access/service did not change the Internet experience from a shallow to a deep one. The same providers (more or less) are there, we as customers are still the same, and a medium is still required and still transparent to us. We now have full-time connectivity to the Internet, but otherwise, the home cable modem is every bit like the analog modems of five years ago. The home computer is basically the same. The service provider may now be a cable company instead of an ISP down the street, but it is still just a provider. Things have changed, but not dramatically.

First, what has changed is that our connection to the Internet is always on. Not only can you sit down in front of your computer and surf the Web immediately, you can also access your computer when you are away from home.

Second, your IP address appears to be fixed rather than changing, which was standard with dial-up connections. Even rebooting your machine does not change the IP address generally. (There are times when it changes but those occurrences are few and far between.) A fixed and stable address means you can reach your machine all the time at the same address.

Always-on also means you face security issues that you didn't generally before. With an always-on computer it's tempting for crackers to try and abuse your machine. This is unlikely but still a threat.

Finally, with the increase in Internet speed and access, how you use your machine has changed. For example, you can download large amounts of data from the Internet. Even if you used to do this at work, you probably did not consider doing it at home before. More changes in attitude and use can be found if you look for them.

The sensations that make up your experience have indeed changed. As newer technology is introduced to you, you will find uses for some of it. This changes your experience, too.

Why did the cable companies permit you a new experience? They did so because they wanted to gain acceptance and market share. It's just that simple. The experience that you have with the ISP and all the vendors who are part of these activities has changed. Internet access, once a shallow experience involving you in many steps, is now a deep experience. You are asked for little, and the computers do most of the work—the way in which you get what you want is more commonplace than ever before.

1.3.4 Deep Experience

Now that your home Internet access is a deep experience, what will happen? The modem you use is leased and every month you pay a leasing fee. At the time you started the service there was no way that you could buy the modem and save the leasing fee. Modems were linked to the cable company's technology and were not offered openly for sale. Perhaps recently you received an offer in the mail from your cable company to buy a modem, return your leased one, and pay less per month for the service. You would pay once for the modem and over its lifetime save money. How do you do this? You go online, pay for the modem, and days later the modem arrives in the mail. The instructions with the modem tell you to browse to a certain Web page and fill out a form with information about your account and the modem. Once the page is submitted, the next page tells you to power down the computer, switch modems, and reboot. You do so, and no more than 15 minutes later, your new modem is tearing up the cable line—bits flying back and forth.

Self-installing the modem through a Web page is called self-provisioning. You might say, "I provisioned the modem," meaning you established the service and got your old account up and running with the equipment. Originally, the leased cable modem required a serviceman to come out and handle the provisioning. Today you can handle it. It's not just a Web page and little coding, it's a whole lot more.

Once Internet access service is provisioned, it has to be mediated or billed. Mediation comes after provisioning and has always been a people-intensive activity for companies. Not anymore—the experience has changed! After you self-provisioned your new modem, mediation was put into place automatically as part of the process.

Self-service here is radically different than self-service at a gas pump. At a gas pump all that is happening is the person who pumps the gas is you, not the service attendant. Cable services like Internet access and equipment provisioning, where the user performs the provisioning is very much a leap forward. First, you can do this at any time—you do not have to schedule an appointment for service and wait for the serviceman. Second, you can stop the process at any point without penalties. Third, you can tailor the experience through the choices the provisioning page gives you, such as changing the account information at the same time. You save time, you are in control, and you elected to do this.

This entailed many changes on the cable company's part. We want this kind of experience and they meant it for the people at large. Gas stations changed the experience for themselves. It takes people longer to get gas at a self-service pump, and it inconveniences them more than when attendants pumped the gas; it takes less time to self-provision cable services and it is more convenient.

1.3.5 Implementing Experiences

With proper support for experiences, such as products to create and build them, experiences will evolve and possibly come into their own as a product. The pressure from the marketplace at all times to find better solutions to problems should kick in here in the near future. The problem of fitting Web sites to the needs of users will see more solutions with time. Experiences are one solution to this problem. So what can be done to embrace experience notions and integrate them into your site?

To answer this we start with a specific illustration of the problem. There is a Web site that, among other things, provides up-to-date reviews of laptop computers. Every available laptop is reviewed on this site. One can find prices, specifications, and reviews, including reviews provided by other visitors to the site.

This site groups the laptops in a few different ways to make it easier for you to look at the material. For example, you can compare laptops by speed and performance through a benchmark program each laptop must run.

The current site provides you with comparison charts of all the data deemed relevant. These charts can run on for pages. The site provides some of these numbers in ways that cannot be readily used. One such number is the battery size in each laptop: You may want to know the battery life relevant to your needs, but battery size does not help you understand how long the battery lasts. This is a mismatch—the provider of information wants to provide one thing and the receiver of the information wants something else.

We're not taking pot shots at Web sites, just observing what sites provide and how the sites do so—in other words, the experience these sites provide.

What is the expectation, therefore, from the Web site that reviews laptops? Let's agree on what the expectation from this site is. Then we'll talk about what could have been done. To do so, let's use an analogy. Recast this research into a telephone call to a vendor of laptop computers. The conversation might have been a fact-finding mission, where several questions would cut to the heart of the matter important to the caller. The caller might ask, "What is the battery life of the laptop?", "How heavy is the laptop?", and "How much does the laptop retail for?" Your questions might be different, but these are a good illustration.

These few questions form an experience that works and has worked for a very long time. State-of-the-art Web-site building practices foster a different experience. Sites are built to show as much information as possible in a few ways. This forms a pattern that can be repeated with other products reviewed on the site. These patterns create a Web site that can grow, be maintained, and provide valuable information for visitors, but at a cost to the visitor in time and effort—valuable commodities that are wasted by Web sites all the time. How can this experience, which wastes time and doesn't service needs directly, be made into a better experience? Enter .NET!

Let's propose the following:

1. Create an XML schema for representing product review information. Make it detailed and expect to change it over time. This is perfect for XML.

2. Encourage every laptop vendor to use the schema and publish a Web service with this information. The review site can go to the vendor sites, get the laptop data frequently, and post the most up-to-date data and more data than ever before.

3. Provide other ways to filter and retrieve the data on the review site. Again, Web services should be created that explore the data in more ways. The Web site the visitors go to becomes a front-end application to these Web services. As a start, expect that every visitor will ask questions about laptops based on keywords. One Web service would accept keywords and build on-the-fly queries based on keywords using the XML data gleaned from the vendors. Provide other Web services that compare and contrast the data. Then a visitor can drill down to get the information he or she wants rather than what is merely provided. This suggests that fewer drill-downs would be required and that makes for an added benefit.

This is nothing more than the business model currently in place for laptop makers when they supply hardware drivers. Every time a laptop operating system changes, the maker of the laptop would supply the hardware drivers for that operating system. Similarly, hardware makers of add-on products for the laptops could also provide drivers for their products if they want their add-on product to be used in the laptop with the operating system. Doesn't it make sense for the information about the laptop to be provided by the makers of the laptops in the exact same way they provide drivers? The only reason they haven't done this is that they had no reason to. Now they do—and it's called the *experience*.

The experience you have researching a laptop could be remarkably different and much better. This is only a first cut at improving the experience a visitor can have with .NET as long as experience is integrated into the design of Web sites.

1.4 Building and Maintaining a Web Site

Now we tour a typical Web site and look at today's site-building practices. Next we look at .NET practices and give you the chance to compare them. The sites we have already categorized cover a range of possibilities, each requiring some or all of what we now discuss. A site plan includes some or all of these features:

Pages

- Entry page or pages
- Content pages

Services

- Access control
- Provisioning
- Mediation
- Others

Production

- Staging
- Integration
- Deployment
- Maintenance

1.4.1 Pages

Web sites are made up of pages and require at least one entry page, commonly called a home page. Other entry pages are possible, too, and are provided to bypass the home page if circumstances permit. A typical example is the sign-in page of Microsoft's Hotmail application. When you sign in to your Hotmail account, you face a sign-in page asking for your e-mail address and password. If you have already signed in today but have left the site temporarily, you face a partial sign-in page asking for your password only.

The remainder of the site consists of content pages that typically make up the bulk of sites on the Web. For Hotmail this means your mailbox and e-mail processing pages, as well as links to other applications like a calendar and Microsoft's Messenger application. These pages are all generated on the fly and represent what is currently state of the art.

Creating pages is left up to you. Your operating system or computer platform does not dictate what tools you use. If you build on Windows platforms there are dozens of tools for creating pages or entire sites. You can mix and match technologies if you want to put the time into making them work together.

1.4.2 Services

Services are reusable functions Web sites incorporate to form complete functionality. The first of these is access control, also known as authentication. At Hotmail, this is the sign-in page.

Successfully signing in entitles you to roam selected pages or have run of the site privileges. Creating the sign-in and sign-out pages and their coordinating security comes about through a mixture programming, databases, and standards.

Each site typically has its own homegrown access control. Microsoft has provided Passport (*www.passport.com*) as its first .NET Web Service. Their intention is to have the whole world use Passport as access control for all Web sites. This .NET Web Service demonstrates what may be the present level of capability and a first glimpse of the future.

Provisioning is connecting a device, service, or product into the billing system so that transactions can be made. Even if billing is not the goal, provisioning still takes place all the time. Merely registering at a Web site so that you may use it is provisioning; you are self-provisioning an account on that site. Sister to provisioning is mediation or billing. Once the device, service, or product is provisioned, use of the Web site generates billing or other information. For example, every time you use Hotmail, Microsoft knows that you have used it, how many e-mails you composed, what addresses you received mail from, and which you sent mail to.

1.4.3 Production

The last set of activities is production, which is composed of staging, integration, and deployment. Staging is how and where you build the development version of your site, application, or service. You may build it on the production machine or you may use a separate machine. There is a programming environment you have to set up and make available to developers and others.

Next, integration is weaving pieces of your site together, including what is needed from your operating system.

Deployment takes the staged site files and moves them into production. Often this is no more complicated than copying the staged site to the production machine(s). It can get more complicated if you need to make adjustments to page links, change privileges, employ services, and so on.

Some Web site building tools help you manage staging and deployment environments. Sometimes you are left to create your own rules and mechanisms to stage the site and then deploy it.

Integrating outside services into your product requires thought about scaling and uptime, among other issues. If you have a Web farm (two or more Web servers collaborating to provide your site), the programming must incorporate session and state information so your site can run on multiple hosts. Uptime for your hosts can vary, once again requiring additional management in the code that takes this into account. Some products exist today to help with this. For Windows NT, Microsoft Transaction Server (MTS) provides some ability to orchestrate Web farms scaling and availability. MTS can provide multithreading (running the pieces of your site in parallel) capability in a managed way for Web site components. Another product, ClusterCats, a clustering package used to create farms, handles scaling issues raised here.

Once the code has been staged and ultimately deployed, long-term maintenance has to be considered. How will changes to the product be made? How will knowledge be transferred from the developers to the maintainers? These questions and others are handled by each company in its own way. Sometimes they are not handled at all.

This is in brief how Web products are built today.

1.4.4 Building and Maintaining with .NET

.NET tools and servers are designed to help you build forms-based applications and to supply services to other sites.

Using .NET-only tools and products means thinking about what you are doing in a different way than you would if you were building with the tools we use today. Microsoft is making available tools to create code and platforms to run the code, and is weaving them together. While this is being done, standards are being promoted so that other vendors can add to these products, and the industry can grow.

To build a significant Web site, you must first divide it up into constituent pieces or subsystems, which will eventually be integrated. You need sign-in and sign-out functions, which are tied to access control,[5] then the functions that your site performs, integrated with a means of storing and retrieving data. If you provide advertising space, a mechanism to add this into your site must be provided and the business deals fostering this have to be made. Online commerce is mixed into the pages, and those business deals have to be worked out as well. Ties to back-end systems have to be woven in where appropriate and data conflicts resolved. Site architecture issues such as staging versus production platforms and hardware in lieu of software (like firewalls) have to be worked in.

Tools have been changed with .NET. The CLR underpinnings along with a class-based framework mean your programmers have to learn this technology if they are to make an effective contribution. Working with .NET means having specific choices for tools rather than being able to use the universe of existing ones.

Microsoft is providing a number of servers to support .NET, starting with operating systems, which they are throwing all of their weight behind.

---

[5] Every user is privileged to use parts of a Web site. Some users have access to more parts than others.

Existing servers such as SQL and Exchange (a mail server) are already using XML. Revamped servers like the Commerce server now have a broader appeal due to their new missions and have XML integrated into them. New servers like Content Management and BizTalk are directly aimed at solving basic business needs that have always required mixing and matching products and considerable programming on your part.

1.4.5 Implementing .NET

What choices do you make in implementing .NET? What is the spectrum of investment to use this technology? What are the human costs?

First, using .NET means that you produce Web services or consume them, switch to C# or relearn Visual Basic or C++, and embrace other technologies. There are many new technologies to consider embracing. Updating your skills is required every once in a while, but .NET may require more than you expected.

Second, there are philosophy components of .NET that can easily get overlooked because this is all new. To this end, this chapter has tried to bring out some aspects of .NET that are not technical.

To implement .NET, start with a small project and an evangelistic team. Don't plunge into this with all resources changing at once. This is good advice whenever you adopt new technology, and in the .NET case it's the best advice possible. Unlike other changes to our industry, .NET is so big and new we don't know all its pitfalls yet.

It is an evolving process for Microsoft and it is one for you too.

1.4.6 Migrating to .NET

For a company to employ .NET it needs to schedule and coordinate four activities:

1. Provide technical and business-side training for .NET

2. Integrate and deploy .NET servers

3. Migrate Visual Basic to VB.NET, C++ to Managed C++ or C#, and Java to C#

4. Create Web services and develop with .NET technologies and standards

Bringing .NET servers into a company will be a challenge, and success depends on the current configuration and paths for change. For staple servers like Web servers and databases, IIS and SQL Server are fairly simple to install. If the company has other servers, the challenges will be significant. This book does not cover migration issues to any extent. The number of these servers, their capacity, and their arrangement should be studied before they are deployed companywide. For developers, a minimum number of server machines are needed. They could be outfitted this way:

- One machine hosts IIS and SQL Server.
- A second machine hosts other .NET servers, like Application server and BizTalk.

In this way, a small team could explore .NET without impacting other teams and at minimal cost.

Web services are one of the critical technology shifts of .NET. Instead of architecting stand-alone applications and packages of library code, developers create small, usable services, exposing them through the Web service framework.

You can integrate .NET standards by modify existing methodologies used to build software. Why methodologies? If the Rational Unified Process is your methodology and you use Rational Rose to document and generate code, Rose has to match the .NET technology, and at this time it doesn't. This will be more work for you, but it is necessary. Somewhere in everyone's methodology is a set of standards used to design and deploy solutions, so methodology is a good place to start integrating .NET.

Where data is formatted in a proprietary way, use XML with published schemas (see *www.schema.net* for instance) rather than inventing your own. XML provides a means to make data more usable by more applications. It is self-documenting up to a point, extensible as all get-out, and represents the future. By employing existing schemas, you exploit work performed by others and possibly help a standard emerge. If no schema does what you want and you cannot recast your needs into one, invent one.

When you are connecting components and applications, use SOAP to wrap the data. This is an emerging standard, it is already defined, and it's part of the .NET suite of standards.

Learn about the .NET technologies and integrate them into your platforms. Learning about .NET is complicated and has to be respected. You can learn about an isolated piece of .NET and still be profitable, but if you intend to engineer solutions you have to learn about more than pieces. You have to do more than copy solutions from this book and others.

An example is the BizTalk server. BizTalk is a transaction platform that supports short- and long-term transactions. It has a visual tool to develop the transaction pipeline for your business needs and is integrated tightly with XML. You can map data coming in and data going out. These features make BizTalk an exciting server for managing line-of-business activities. You might implement the same kind of functionality using several servers, some of which will be homemade. This is a build-versus-buy question, and this time the choice should be buy. To implement only a part of BizTalk you would have to use a queuing server,[6] a transaction monitor,[7] and a lot of your own code.

Lastly, migrate your deployment languages if you can. Not only are there Microsoft-created languages that you may use, other CLR-based languages are appearing. Using a CLR-based language affords you smooth integration into the .NET SDK (Software Development Kit). These languages will force you to rethink your approaches to solving problems using this SDK. Some synergy can be expected over time to justify the effort.

1.5 Unanswered Challenges

There are many issues that have not been addressed by .NET yet that remain as significant challenges to broad use of this technology. Here are four: availability, confidentiality, provisioning, and mediation.

1.5.1 Availability

When a consumer company uses a vendor's Web service they expect the service to be always available. If this is not the case, then an agreement reached ahead of time should specify the uptimes and the amount of time the service is available, so the consumer company can work this into their product or service. On the other hand, if 24/7 uptime is expected, which is generally the case, any glitch in this level of performance would be bad. The Internet today suffers from general unavailability at times where routed[8] paths disappear due to equipment failure and from latency[9] problems, again due to routing.

If a Web service is unavailable for a period of time or is slow in performing, the perception of the consumer is the product is poor or bad. This won't do.

Can we expect that the Internet in time will outgrow these problems and that availability will no longer be an issue? There may be no way that the Internet will increase its availability in both path stability and minimizing latency. However, a guarantee of service is needed that may never exist. To support this, consider data compression and available bandwidth.

Will we ever have big enough data connections so that there would be no need to compress data? It seems that we should get to that point. The

---

[6] A server that stores messages and data to be forwarded when appropriate.
[7] A server that manages database queries, ensuring that each gets appropriate time to be fulfilled.
[8] Fundamental to the Internet is automatic routing, the connection forming a path between two computers.
[9] The delay from the time data is transmitted to the time it is received. At some point in time, if the latency is too large, data is either retransmitted or lost completely.

Internet 2 is right around the corner and is possibly the solution to this problem. The likely scenario is that we always use bandwidth to capacity. The larger the connection, the more we want to pass through it. When the connection doubles in size, we want to send triple the amount of data. Yesterday, it was a chore to send pictures through slow modems; today it's a chore to get real-time streaming video across cable modems. Tomorrow, who knows? Availability as uptime or latency is another view of compression and bandwidth. Perhaps it isn't possible to build an Internet that provides the basic guarantee needed. What then?

The availability problem is between companies, not within a company. A vendor has to provide a service to a consumer and bill for it. If the service is unavailable at times, it may not even be used. Web services may be relegated to intracompany use if this continues. What is needed is remotely supplied Web services that can be downloaded to hosts needing such guarantees and made into local Web services. In other words, the services must be able to be detached from the provider. Just as ActiveX components and Java applets may be downloaded to a Web site visitor, so should Web services be downloadable. Perhaps we will call this detachable Web services. The difference between ActiveX or Java applets and detachable Web services is that the download is between servers not from server to browser.

Part of the infrastructure for doing this will have to include mediation so that the provider is appropriately compensated. The benefits of this go beyond stabilizing access to the service. This also solves the confidence problem.

1.5.2 Confidentiality

The second benefit detachable Web services give the user is confidence their data is private. Companies are unlikely to entrust their data to every service vendor that comes along. Some outsourcing goes on today where company data is sent to a vendor, but this occurs with specific conditions that seem to satisfy the need for confidentiality. Detachable Web services are one way to provide this trust.

Of course another way is to guarantee that the company's data is encrypted en route to the remote Web service. Both methods would suffice in solving this problem. While encryption is integrated into .NET, it doesn't currently provide for confidentiality as presented here.

1.5.3 Provisioning

Provisioning is one of two necessary components to have a market emerge in Web services. By *market* we mean that companies voluntarily produce products and others voluntarily consume those products. If there is no market, intercompany Web services will never thrive.

What is taking place is a roll-your-own approach by companies wanting to provide Web services. They are working through the necessary procedures and providing their own mechanisms for allowing services to be provisioned. This is creating confusion in the marketplace. Standards would solve this problem; all players can use the standards. When we don't see standards for implementing technology, the technology is slow to be accepted, if at all. The question remains, how can you use a Web service without standards? If no standard provisioning mechanism is in place, will there even be vendors?

Today, the push is on to create master vendors, businesses that aggregate various services from vendors and provide a one-stop shop. As such, these master vendors will be able to create agreements encompassing provisioning that can make the market work. However, innovation will be slowed dramatically because of the built-in buffer such arrangements create. For example, if your company has plans to create a number of services for general sale, you will have to find a master vendor, work through agreements, work through technology issues allowing them to provide a market for you, and then provide the service. On the consumer side, potential customers of your service will be dealing with these master vendors, not you. Your ability to react to your customers' needs will be compromised, and both you and they will be locked into using the master vendor. Some of the promise of your services will be lost.

An alternative is to work out standard mechanisms for managed provisioning and self-provisioning that are part of the .NET framework.

1.5.4 Mediation

A close relative of provisioning is mediation or billing for the service. All arguments put forth about provisioning apply here as well. Once the service has been provisioned for use, it has to be billed. Billing is a complex matter. Just think about any issue you've ever experienced personally with a bill that went awry and you may see some of the problems.

To create a robust market for Web services, you must have a standard mechanism to bill for the service. Just as SOAP is an evolving standard to create Web services and UDDI is a standard to locate a service, we need a standard for billing.

1.6 The Next Five Years

In order to see five years into the future, try one last experiment. Let's wipe the slate clean and restart the personal computer revolution from scratch. Pretend it is 1981 and IBM has just released the first mass-market personal computer with 16MB of memory, one floppy disk, and a network card. The only difference is that the Internet exists as it does today, with all the appliances that we currently use: wireless-enabled PDAs, mobile phones, e-mail, and so on. Personal computers are new.

Why would a computer need more storage than a floppy disk? Why would it need more memory? Those designing a computer would make it into a general-purpose device to handle all the odds and ends kind of applications that dedicated appliances do not handle. The computer would use the network to provide access to applications, to store data, and generally to do all its work. This was the idea behind the Networked Computer (NC) workstations in the press a few years ago when Java looked like it was the next killer app. The difference between that vision and the one presented here is that .NET offers the same opportunity and perhaps a more compelling delivery vehicle. Java has shortcomings that .NET may not have. Networked computers depended on Java running on desktop computers and appliances. Promises about performance and capability were not lived up to, and these computers faded away. .NET is asking to do the same thing in essence as the NC movement but is not using lightweight desktop computers. It is using layers of software, with all the souped-up hardware that can be imagined. In this respect the two visions differ dramatically. What is remarkable is the distributed aspect of .NET, which is downplayed but still very much at the heart of what Microsoft is doing. A computer that gets all of its software from the network is an appealing idea, but this is not the XML vision that .NET is currently fostering. XML is data-oriented and involves getting your data anywhere or having data customize your software on the fly. Network computers were a complex vision in which the data as well as the applications which manipulated the data were sent across the network. This too is a difference.

Network computers would support software and data anywhere a network connection existed. .NET computers, on the other hand, support only data where the software and network connection exists. The NC vision meant that cheaper and more versatile devices could provide the things you wanted from more places. While NC lost its battle, the .NET vision may evolve into this. If it does, an even bigger leap forward is in store.

Why? Imagine a handheld device giving you the same information that your desktop computer does, all because of .NET. The program you run on your desktop would be no different from the one you run on your handheld device.

Summary

This chapter started off with the mission to show you what a .NET world may look like. Microsoft has created a platform, tools, and theories about what we should do and how to do it for the near future. XML is the dominant technology threading all of .NET together. It provides a means for connecting legacy systems, current applications, and future projects. The core belief that you provide your application as a Web service that employs standards is our goal now.

Microsoft as of yet does not communicate the .NET vision clearly, and because it's not clear it isn't compelling either. This may be because they don't know themselves what the vision really is or they don't care to at this time. It is an open vision that time will firm up for us all. Regardless of which it really is, this chapter has made an attempt to present .NET as a step toward allowing software publishers to deliver services rather than products. Products require maintenance, become overly engineered to users, and do not collaborate well with each other. Services, on the other hand, can evolve behind the scenes, invisibly, because they reside with the provider. This requires shifts in our thinking as purchasers and in the thinking of those who provide the services.

There are problems and challenges to .NET, some of which are the availability of the service, the confidentiality of the data, and the ability not only to find a service but to contract for it. Microsoft has not demonstrated that these challenges are being considered, let alone solved.

This book will give you a clear understanding of the platform, languages, and technologies, with many usable examples.

Fundamentals of .NET

Microsoft's .NET Framework is an open language platform for Web development. Its aim is to provide an abstract machine for professional developers, covering both traditional and Web-oriented applications.

This chapter takes you on a guided tour of the wonderful world of .NET Framework. We first take a look at its major components and the environment for application development. Then we discuss the technical aspects, including assemblies, application domains, and run-time hosts; they play a key role in facilitating a flexible, yet powerful, programming environment for Web development.

2.1 Overview

As a new computing platform, .NET Framework is designed to simplify application development in the highly distributed environment of the Internet. It has two main components: Common Language Runtime and the .NET Framework class library.

Common Language Runtime is the foundation of .NET Framework. It provides core services for code execution, such as verification and compilation, as well as memory management and thread management. In addition, it enforces strict safety and accuracy of the code. The concept of code management is a fundamental principle of the run time. Code that targets the run time is known as *managed code*, while code that does not target the run time is known as *unmanaged code*.

.NET Framework provides an object-oriented programming environment. Its class library is a comprehensive collection of reusable classes that support development of traditional command-line applications, graphical user interface (GUI) applications, and Web-based distributed applications, based on the latest innovations of ADO.NET, ASP.NET, and Web Services.

In this section, we discuss the features of the components and the benefits to application development. The technical aspects of .NET Framework are covered in the following sections.

2.1.1 Common Language Runtime

Common Language Runtime supports multiple programming languages, including C# (C Sharp), Visual Basic, JScript, and C++ with the managed extensions, as well as third-party support for other languages, including COBOL, Perl, and Eiffel. For each hardware platform on which Common Language Runtime runs, a just in time (JIT) compiler is supplied. Therefore, a program that was developed in one platform can be executed on another.

Common Language Runtime provides software developers with a programming environment that supports cross-language interoperability. In this environment, applications and components developed in different languages can communicate and interact with each other, and their behaviors can be tightly integrated. You may define a class in one language and then, using a different language, derive a class from the original language or call a method on it. You may also pass an instance of a class to a method on another class that is written in a different language.

During code compilation, verification processes are carried out whereby the managed code is examined against the metadata in order to make sure it is *type-safe*. The verification processes ensure that Microsoft Intermediate Language (MSIL) code has been correctly generated.

Before managed code is executed, it is awarded degrees of trust, depending on factors that include its origin, such as the Internet, enterprise network, or local computer. That is, the privileges of the managed code are well controlled regarding sensitive operations like file access.

During the execution of managed code, Common Language Runtime manages the memories through a garbage collection mechanism. When an object is no longer accessed, its memory is automatically released and a cleanup routine is invoked to do housekeeping. Thus, reference counters need not to be maintained and memory leaking can be avoided.

Common Language Runtime allows you to write applications that can perform multiple tasks independently. Tasks that could hold up other tasks can execute on a separate thread, a process known as *free threading*. Free threading allows you to write applications that are more scalable and more responsive to user input because you can cause complicated tasks to run on threads that are separate from your user interface.

Under Common Language Runtime, "DLL hell" problems have been resolved. "DLL hell" problems occur when multiple applications attempt to share a common component like a dynamic link library (DLL). They usually occur when one application installs a new version of the shared component that is not backward compatible with the version already on the machine. Although the application that has just been installed works fine, existing applications that depended on a previous version of the shared component may no longer work. The managed codes are self-describing and their versioning is enforced so that "DLL hell" problems can be avoided. We come back to this topic later in this chapter.

2.1.2 .NET Framework Class Library

The .NET Framework class library is a collection of reusable classes that tightly integrate with Common Language Runtime. These classes are types from which your own managed code can derive functionality. For example, the .NET Framework collection classes implement a set of interfaces, which you can use to develop your own collection classes. Your collection classes will then be seamlessly integrated with the classes in .NET Framework.

As you would expect from a base class library, the .NET Framework types enable you to accomplish a range of common programming tasks, including tasks such as string management, data collection, database connectivity, and file access. In addition to these common tasks, the class library includes types that support a variety of specialized development scenarios. Listed below are a few of them.

- Console classes for applications based on standard I/O
- Windows Forms classes for graphical user interface (GUI)
- Network-related classes for networking at various layers
- ASP.NET and Web Services classes for Web-based distributed applications
- ASP.NET and Web Forms classes for programmable Web pages
- ADO.NET classes for scalable and consistent access to various data sources
- XML-related classes for text-based data exchange between applications

The next section briefly discusses these scenarios.

2.1.3 Application Development

In its simplest form, an application under .NET Framework can be implemented as a console program that is based on standard I/O on your workstation, i.e. keyboard and display screen.

Under .NET Framework, the GUI programming is supported by Windows Forms, a programming model for developing Windows client applications that combines the simplicity of the Visual Basic 6.0 programming model with the power and flexibility of the Common Language Runtime. Windows Forms takes advantage of the versioning and deployment features of Common Language Runtime to offer reduced costs for development, deployment, and maintenance, as well as higher application robustness over time.

Windows Forms offers full support for quickly and easily connecting to Web Services as well as the ADO.NET data model. It also takes full advantage of the security features of the Common Language Runtime. This means that Windows Forms can be used to implement everything from an untrusted control running in the browser to a fully trusted application installed on a user's hard disk.

.NET Framework supplies a simple yet complete solution for networked applications in managed code. The class library for networking programming with .NET Framework has been designed based on a layered model of computer networks. It provides classes at various layers of the network, each of which enables applications to access the network with the control of the specific level. The spectrum of classes covers all the levels that are needed for development of Web and Internet applications, from fine-grained control over the socket to a generic request-response model. You may work at a highest layer that is suitable to your goals, making your development much more effective and efficient.

At the top level of the network abstraction of .NET Framework, the request-response model provides a simple way to access resources on the Web. This functionality is significant not only because of the large share of Web traffic going over the HTTP protocol today, but also because of the increasing volume of non-Web traffic carried by the HTTP protocol, such as SOAP. At the next level down in the network abstraction, transport layer protocol (TCP or UDP) is used. Classes at this level give you the flexibility to work with all the application protocols that are not limited to HTTP. Finally, Socket, the lowest level of the network abstraction, is a handyman's tool whereby sophisticated client and/or server applications can be developed.

Web Services represent an important evolution in Web-based technology that simplifies Web-based distributed application to a great extent. Web Services consist of reusable software components designed to be consumed by client applications over the Internet. As a result, Web Services technology is rapidly moving application development and deployment into the highly distributed environment of the Internet.

.NET Framework also provides a collection of classes and tools to aid in the development and consumption of Web Services applications. At the server site, Web Services can be easily defined and tested. On the other hand, proxy objects may be automatically created at the client site with downloaded specification.

Web Services are built on standards such as SOAP (a remote procedure-call protocol), XML (an extensible data format), and Web Service Description Language (WSDL). .NET Framework conforms to these standards to promote interoperability with non-Microsoft solutions.

If you develop and publish your own Web Services, .NET Framework provides a set of classes that conform to all of the underlying communication standards, such as SOAP, WSDL, and XML. Using those classes enables you to focus on the logic of your service, without worrying about the communications infrastructure required by distributed software development.

Web Forms is a scalable programming model of the run time that can be used on the server to dynamically generate Web pages. It gives you the ability to create and use reusable UI controls that can encapsulate common functionality and thus reduce the amount of code that you have to write. It allows developers to structure their page logic in an orderly fashion and allows development tools to provide strong WYSIWYG design support for pages.

ASP.NET is the hosting environment for both Web Services and Web Forms applications. Web Forms and Web Services use Internet Information Server (IIS) as the publishing mechanism for applications, and they have a collection of supporting classes in .NET Framework.

2.2 Inside .NET Framework

This section discusses the infrastructure of .NET Framework, including managed execution processes, multilanguage execution environment, Microsoft Intermediate Language, JIT compilation, and program execution.

2.2.1 Managed Execution Processes

Under Common Language Runtime, execution of managed code includes the following steps:

- You write your programs using one or more languages that are supported by the run time.
- The compliers translate your source code into Microsoft Intermediate Language (MSIL), which is a CPU-independent set of instructions that can be efficiently converted to native code. In addition, *metadata* is created that provides information on the types and references in your code and makes the managed code self-describing.

- Before the MSIL code can be executed, .NET Framework just in time (JIT) compilers convert it to native code that runs on the underlying hardware platform.
- The native code is finally executed. Common Language Runtime provides the infrastructure that enables execution to take place, as well as a variety of services that can be used during execution.

2.2.2 Multilanguage Execution Environment

To obtain the benefits provided by Common Language Runtime, you must use one or more language compilers that target the run time, such as Visual Basic, C#, Visual C++, JScript, or one of many third-party compilers such as a Perl or COBOL.

Because it is a multilanguage execution environment, the run time supports a wide variety of data types and language features. The language compiler you use determines which run-time features are available, and you design your code using those features. Your compiler, not the run time, establishes the syntax your code must use. The Common Type System defines the supported types in Common Language Runtime and specifies how they interact with each other. A *type* defines allowable values and the operations that can apply to the values.

If your component must be completely usable by components written in other languages, your component's exported types must expose only language features that are included in common language specification (CLS).

Common language specification is a set of rules intended to support cross-language interoperability. These rules apply only to items that are exposed for use by those written by other programming languages. In particular, they apply only to types that are visible in assemblies other than those in which they are defined, that is, to types that have members accessible from outside its assembly, such as public classes and public methods.

2.2.3 Microsoft Intermediate Language (MSIL)

When generating managed code, the compiler translates your source code into Microsoft Intermediate Language (MSIL), which is a CPU-independent set of instructions that can be efficiently converted to native code. MSIL includes instructions for loading, storing, initializing, and calling methods on objects, as well as instructions for arithmetic and logical operations, control flow, direct memory access, exception handling, and other operations. Before code can be executed, code in MSIL must be converted into CPU-specific code by a JIT compiler that is discussed in the next subsection.

When a compiler produces MSIL, it also produces metadata. Metadata describes the types in your code, including the definition of each type, the signatures of each type's members, the members that your code references, and other data that the run time uses at execution time. The MSIL code and the metadata are contained in a portable executable (PE file) that is based on and extends the published Microsoft PE and Common Object File Format (COFF) used historically for executable content. This file format, which accommodates MSIL or native code as well as metadata, enables the operating system to recognize Common Language Runtime images. The presence of metadata in the file along with the MSIL enables your code to describe itself, which means that there is no need for type libraries or Interface Definition Language (IDL). The run time locates and extracts the metadata from the file as needed during execution.

2.2.4 JIT Compilation

Before codes in Microsoft Intermediate Language (MSIL) can be executed, it must be converted by a .NET Framework just in time (JIT) compiler to native code, which is CPU-specific code that runs on the same computer architecture as the JIT compiler. Because the run time supplies a JIT compiler for each hardware platform it supports, the same set of MSIL code can be JIT-compiled and executed on any supported platform. Therefore, a code file in MSIL is called a *portable executable file.*

JIT compilation takes into account the fact that some code might never get called during execution. Rather than using time and memory to convert all the MSIL code in a portable executable to native code, it converts the MSIL code as it is needed during execution and stores the resulting native code so that it is accessible for subsequent calls. The loader creates and attaches a stub to each of a type's methods when the type is loaded. On the initial call to the method, the stub passes control to the JIT compiler, which converts the MSIL code for that method into native code and modifies the stub to direct execution to the location of the native code. Subsequent calls of the JIT-compiled method proceed directly to the native code that was previously generated, reducing the time it takes to JIT-compile and execute the code.

As part of compiling MSIL code to native code, code must pass a verification process unless an administrator has established a security policy that allows code to bypass verification. Verification examines MSIL code and metadata to find out whether the code can be determined to be type-safe, which means that it is known to access only the memory locations it is authorized to access. Type safety is necessary to ensure that objects are safely isolated from each other and are therefore safe from inadvertent or malicious corruption. It also provides assurance that security restrictions on code can be reliably enforced.

The run time relies on the fact that the following statements are true for code that is verifiably type-safe:

* A reference to a type is strictly compatible with the definition of the type.
* Only appropriately defined operations may be invoked on an object.

- Identities are what they claim to be.
- Memory locations and methods can be accessed only through properly defined types.
- MSIL code has been correctly generated.

During the verification process, MSIL code is examined in an attempt to confirm that the code can access memory locations and call methods only through properly defined types. For example, code cannot allow an object's fields to be accessed in a manner that allows memory locations to be overrun. Additionally, verification inspects code to see whether the MSIL code has been correctly generated, because incorrect MSIL could lead to a violation of the type-safety rules.

2.2.5 Execution

Common Language Runtime provides both the infrastructure that enables managed execution to take place and a variety of services that can be used during execution. Before a program can be executed, it must be compiled to processor-specific code. MSIL code is JIT-compiled when it is called for the first time and then executed. The next time the method is executed, the existing JIT-compiled native code is executed. The process of JIT-compiling and then executing the code is repeated until execution is complete.

During execution, managed code receives services such as automatic memory management, security, interoperability with unmanaged code, cross-language debugging support, and enhanced deployment and versioning support.

2.3 Assemblies

Assemblies are the building blocks of .NET Framework applications; they form the fundamental unit of deployment, version control, reuse, activation scope, and security permissions. An *assembly* is a collection of types and resources that are built to work together and form a logical unit of functionality. An assembly provides Common Language Runtime with the information it needs to be aware of type implementations. To the run time, a type does not exist outside the context of an assembly.

2.3.1 Assembly Functions

Assemblies are fundamental units of programming with the .NET Framework. They contain codes that the run time executes.

As fundamental units, assemblies form boundaries in various senses. First, assemblies form *security boundaries*. They are the units at which permission is requested and granted. Second, assemblies form *type boundaries*.

Every type's identity includes the name of the assembly in which it resides. Third, assemblies form *reference scope boundaries*. The manifest of an assembly contains metadata that is used to resolve types and satisfy resource requests. It specifies the types and resources that are exposed outside the assembly. The manifest also enumerates other assemblies on which it depends. A managed code cannot be executed without it. Finally, assemblies form *version boundaries*. An assembly is the smallest unit for versioning in Common Language Runtime; all types and resources in the same assembly are versioned as a unit. The assembly's manifest describes the version dependencies you specify for any dependent assemblies.

Assemblies also serve as deployment units. When an application starts, only the assemblies the application initially calls must be present. Other assemblies, such as localization resources or assemblies containing utility classes, can be retrieved on demand. This allows applications to be kept simple and thin when they are initially downloaded.

2.3.2 Assembly Benefits

Assemblies are designed to simplify application deployment and to solve versioning problems that can occur with component-based applications, including the "DLL hell" problems that we discussed earlier in this chapter. Many deployment problems have been solved by the use of assemblies in .NET Framework. Because they are self-describing components that have no dependencies on registry entries, assemblies enable zero-impact application installation. They also simplify uninstalling and replicating of applications.

Without .NET Framework, versioning problems may occur with Windows applications, because

- Versioning rules cannot be expressed between components of an application and enforced by the operating system. The traditional approach relies on backward compatibility. That is, interface definitions must be static, once published, and a single piece of code must maintain backward compatibility with previous versions. Furthermore, code is typically designed so that only a single version of it can be present and executing on a computer at any given time.
- Moreover, there is no way to maintain consistency between sets of components that are built together and the set that is present at run time.

These two versioning problems combine to create DLL conflicts, or "DLL hell," where installing one application can inadvertently break an existing application because a certain software component or DLL was installed that was not fully backward compatible with a previous version. Once this situation occurs, there is no support in the system for diagnosing and fixing the problem.

Microsoft Windows 2000 began to address these problems. It enables you to create client applications where the dependent .dll files are located in the same directory as the application's .exe file. Windows 2000 can be configured to check for a component in the directory where the .exe file is located before checking and/or searching other paths. This enables components to be independent of components installed and used by other applications. Furthermore, Windows 2000 locks files that are shipped with the operating system in the System32 directory so they cannot be inadvertently replaced when applications are installed.

Common Language Runtime uses assemblies to continue this evolution toward a complete solution to DLL conflicts.

To ultimately solve versioning problems, as well as the remaining problems that lead to DLL conflicts, the run time uses assemblies so that the developers specify version rules between different software components. In addition, assemblies provide the infrastructure that enforces versioning rules and allows multiple versions of a software component to be run simultaneously, or in a side-by-side fashion.

In the rest of the section, we will consider how this solution is realized.

2.3.3 Assembly Contents

In general, an assembly can consist of four elements:

- The assembly manifest, which contains assembly metadata
- Type metadata
- Microsoft Intermediate Language (MSIL) code that implements the types
- A set of resources

Only the assembly manifest is required, but either types or resources are needed to give the assembly any meaningful functionality.

There are several ways to group these elements in an assembly. You can group all elements in a single physical file or, alternatively, place the elements of an assembly in several files.

The structure of a single-file assembly, MySingleFileAssmbly, is shown in Figure 2-1. As can be seen, all the components of this assembly are in **MySingleFileAssembly.dll**.

A multiple-file assembly is composed of files that can be modules of compiled code, resources, or other files required by the application. You may create a multiple-file assembly when you want to combine modules written in different languages and to optimize downloading an application by putting seldom-used types in a module that is downloaded only when needed.

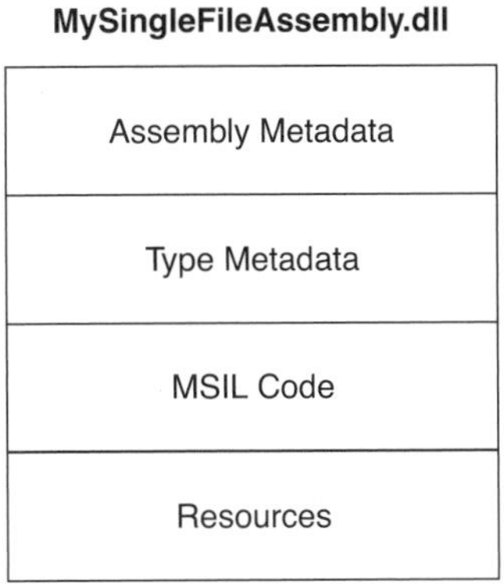

MySingleFileAssembly.dll

Assembly Metadata
Type Metadata
MSIL Code
Resources

Figure 2-1   *A single-file assembly.*

The structure of a multiple-file assembly, MyMultipleFileAssembly, is shown in Figure 2-2. Note that files that make up a multiple-file assembly are not physically linked by the file system. Rather, they are linked through the assembly manifest, and the run time manages them as a unit.

In this figure, the utility code is in a different module as a separate file, **MyUtility.netmodule**, and a large resource file is in its original file, **MyPicture.jpg**. .NET Framework downloads a file only when it is referenced; keeping infrequently referenced code in a file separate from the application optimizes code download.

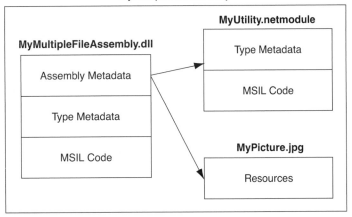

Figure 2-2   *A multiple-file assembly.*

Each assembly's manifest performs the following functions:

- Enumerates the files that make up the assembly.
- Governs how references to the assembly's types and resources map to the files that contain their declarations and implementations.
- Enumerates other assemblies on which the assembly depends.
- Provides a level of indirection between consumers of the assembly and the assembly's implementation details.
- Renders the assembly self-describing.

In the example in Figure 2-2, all three files belong to an assembly, as described in the assembly manifest contained in **MyMultipleFileAssembly.dll**. To the file system, they are three separate files. Note that the file **MyUtility.netmodule** was compiled as a module because it contains no assembly information. When the assembly was created, the assembly manifest was added to **MyMultipleFileAssembly.dll**, indicating its relationship with **MyUtility.netmodule** and **MyPicture.jpg**.

An assembly manifest contains all the metadata needed to specify the assembly's version requirements and security identity, as well as all metadata needed to define the scope of the assembly and resolve references to resources and classes. The assembly manifest can be stored in either a PE file (with suffix .exe or .dll) with Microsoft Intermediate Language (MSIL) code or in a stand-alone PE file that contains only assembly manifest information.

Table 2-1 shows the information contained in the assembly manifest, including the assembly name, version number, culture, and strong name that makes up the assembly's identity. An assembly may be signed with a strong name and later referenced by that name. An assembly is created with a strong name using one of the following methods:

Table 2-1	*Contents of assembly manifest*
Information	**Description**
Assembly name	A text string specifying the assembly's name.
Version number	A major and minor version number, and a revision and build number. The run time uses these numbers to enforce version policy.
Culture	Information on the culture or language the assembly supports. This information should only be used to designate an assembly as a satellite assembly containing culture- or language-specific information. (An assembly with culture information is automatically assumed to be a satellite assembly.)
Strong name information	If the assembly has been given a strong name, the manifest contains the public key from the publisher.

Table 2-1	Contents of assembly manifest, continued
Information	**Description**
List of all files in the assembly	A hash of each file contained in the assembly and a file name. Note that all files that make up the assembly must be in the same directory as the file containing the assembly manifest.
Type reference information	Information used by the run time to map a type reference to the file that contains its declaration and implementation. This is used for types that are exported from the assembly.
Information on referenced assemblies	A list of other assemblies that are statically referenced by the assembly. Each reference includes the dependent assembly's name, assembly metadata (version, culture, operating system, and so on), and public key, if the assembly is strong-named.

You may add or change some information in the assembly manifest by using assembly attributes in your code. You may also change version information and informational attributes, including Trademark, Copyright, Product, Company, and Informational Version.

2.3.4 Assembly Security Considerations

When you build an assembly, you can specify a set of permissions that the assembly requires to run. Optional permissions can be granted by the security policy set on the computer where the assembly will run.

At load time, the assembly's evidence is used as input to security policy. Security policy is established by the enterprise and the computer's administrator as well as by user policy settings, and determines the set of permissions that is granted to all managed code when executed. Security policy can be established for the publisher of the assembly, for the Web site and zone that the assembly was downloaded from, or for the assembly's strong name. For example, a computer's administrator can establish security policy that allows all code downloaded from a Web site and signed by a given software company to access a database on a computer, but that does not grant access to write to the computer's disk.

2.3.5 Assembly Versioning

Common Language Runtime facilitates versioning at the assembly level. The specific version of an assembly and the versions of dependent assemblies are recorded in the assembly's manifest. The default version policy for the run time is that applications run only with the versions they were built and tested with, unless overridden by explicit version policy in configuration files, such as the application configuration file, the publisher policy file, or the computer's administrator configuration file. In addition, versioning is done only on assemblies with strong names.

The run time performs several steps to resolve an assembly-binding request. First, the original assembly reference is checked in order to determine which version of the assembly is to be bound. Second, all the applicable configuration files are checked so as to apply version policy. Third, which referenced assemblies and their versions are to be bound to the calling assembly are identified. Finally, all the appropriate assemblies are located.

Each assembly has two distinct ways of expressing version information:

- The assembly's version number, which, along with the assembly name and culture information, is part of the assembly's identity. This number is used by the run time to enforce version policy and plays a key part in the type resolution process at run time.
- An informational version, which is a string that represents additional version information included for informational purposes only.

Each assembly has a version number as part of its identity. As such, two assemblies that differ by version number are considered by the run time to be completely different assemblies. This version number is physically represented as a four-part number with the following format:

```
<major version>.<minor version>.<build number>.<revision>
```

For example, version 1.5.1254.0 indicates 1 as the major version, 5 as the minor version, 1254 as the build number, and 0 as the revision number.

The version number is stored in the assembly manifest along with other identity information, including the assembly name and public key, as well as information on relationships and identities of other assemblies connected with the application. When an assembly is built, the development tool records dependency information for each assembly that is referenced in the assembly manifest. The run time uses these version numbers, in conjunction with configuration information set by an administrator, an application, or a publisher, to load the proper version of a referenced assembly. The run time distinguishes between regular and strong-named assemblies for the purposes of versioning. Version checking only occurs with strong-named assemblies.

The informational version is a string that attaches additional version information to an assembly for informational purposes only; this information is not used at run time. The text-based informational version corresponds to the product's marketing literature, packaging, or product name and is not used by the run time. For example, an informational version could be "Common Language Runtime Version 1.0" or ".NET Control SP 2."

2.3.6 Assembly Location

For most .NET Framework applications, assemblies that make up an application are located in the application's directory, in a subdirectory of the application's directory, or in the global assembly cache (if the assembly is shared). You can override where the run time looks for an assembly by using the **<codeBase>** element in a configuration file. If the assembly does not have a strong name, then the location specified using the **<codeBase>** element is restricted to the application directory or a subdirectory. If the assembly has a strong name, the **<codeBase>** element can specify any location on the computer or on a network.

2.3.7 Side-by-Side Execution

Side-by-side execution is the ability to run multiple versions of the same assembly simultaneously. Common Language Runtime provides the infrastructure that allows multiple versions of the same assembly to run on the same computer, or even in the same process.

Code that is capable of side-by-side execution has greater flexibility and provides compatibility with previous versions. Components that can run side by side do not have to maintain strict backward compatibility. For example, consider a class MyClassX that supports side-by-side execution. An incompatibility is introduced between versions 1 and 2. Callers of MyClassX that express a dependency on version 1 will always get version 1, regardless of how many subsequent versions of MyClassX are installed on the computer. A caller gets version 2 only if it specifically upgrades its version policy.

Support for side-by-side storage and execution of different versions of the same assembly is an integral part of versioning and is built into the infrastructure of the run time. Because the assembly's version number is part of its identity, the run time can store multiple versions of the same assembly in the global assembly cache and load those assemblies at run time.

There are two types of side-by-side execution: running on the same computer and running in the same process.

In side-by-side execution that runs on the same computer, multiple versions of the same application run at the same time without interfering with each other. An application that supports side-by-side execution on the same computer demands careful coding. For example, consider an application that uses a file at a specific location for a cache. The application must either handle multiple versions of the application accessing the file at the same time or the application must remove the dependency on the specific location and allow each version to have its own cache.

To successfully run side by side in the same process, multiple versions cannot have any strict dependencies on process-wide resources. Side-by-side execution in the same process means that single applications with multiple dependencies can run multiple versions of the same component, and Web servers and other hosts can run applications with possibly conflicting dependencies in the same process.

Although the run time provides you with the ability to create side-by-side applications, side-by-side execution is not automatic. You still must take great care in the code when creating applications intended to run side by side.

2.4 Application Domains

Operating systems and run-time environments typically provide some form of isolation between applications. This isolation is necessary to ensure that code running in one application cannot adversely affect other, unrelated applications.

Application domains provide a secure and versatile unit of processing that Common Language Runtime can use to provide isolation between applications. Application domains are typically created by run-time hosts, which are responsible for bootstrapping Common Language Runtime before an application is run.

This section explains how to use application domains to provide isolation between applications.

2.4.1 What Are Application Domains?

Historically, process boundaries have been used to isolate applications running on the same computer. Each application is loaded into a separate process, which isolates the application from other applications running on the same computer.

The applications are isolated because memory addresses are process-relative; a memory pointer passed from one process to another cannot be used in any meaningful way in the target process. In addition, you cannot make direct calls between two processes. Instead, you must use proxies, which provide a level of indirection.

Managed code must be passed through a verification process before it can be run (unless the administrator has granted permission to skip the verification). The verification process determines whether the code can attempt to access invalid memory addresses or perform some other action that could cause the process in which it is running to fail to operate properly. Code that passes the verification test is said to be type-safe. This ability allows Common Language Runtime to provide as great a level of isolation as process boundaries, at a much lower performance cost.

Application domains provide a secure and versatile unit of processing that Common Language Runtime can use to provide isolation between applications. You can run several application domains in a single process with the same level of isolation that would exist in separate processes, but without incurring the additional overhead of making cross-process calls or switching between processes. The ability to run multiple applications within a single process dramatically increases server scalability.

Isolating applications is also important for application security. For example, you can run controls from several Web applications in a single browser process in such a way that the controls cannot access each other's data and resources.

The isolation provided by application domains has the following benefits:

- Faults in one application cannot affect other applications. Because type-safe code cannot cause memory faults, using application domains ensures that code running in one domain cannot affect other applications in the process.

- Individual applications can be stopped without stopping the entire process. Using application domains enables you to unload the code running in a single application. However, you cannot unload individual assemblies or types; only a complete domain can be unloaded.

- Code running in one application cannot directly access code or resources from another application. Common Language Runtime enforces this isolation by preventing direct calls between objects in different application domains. Objects that pass between domains are either copied or accessed by proxy. If the object is copied, the call to the object is local. That is, both the caller and the object being referenced are in the same application domain. If the object is accessed through a proxy, the call to the object is remote. In this case, the caller and the object being referenced are in different application domains. Cross-domain calls use the same remote call infrastructure as that used by calls between two processes or between two machines. As such, the metadata for the object being referenced must be available to both application domains to allow the method call to be JIT-compiled properly. If the calling domain does not have access to the metadata for the object being called, the compilation may fail with an exception of type **System.IO.FileNotFound**.

- The behavior of code is scoped by the application in which it runs. In other words, the application domain provides configuration settings such as application version policies, the location of any remote assemblies it accesses, and information about where to locate assemblies that are loaded into the domain.

- Permissions that are granted to code can be controlled by the application domain in which the code is running.

2.4.2 Application Domains and Assemblies

You must load an assembly into an application domain before you can run the application. Running a typical application causes several assemblies to be loaded into an application domain. By default, Common Language Runtime loads an assembly into the application domain containing the code that references it. In this way, the assembly's code and data are isolated to the application using it.

If multiple domains in a process use an assembly, all domains referencing the assembly may share its code but not its data. This reduces the amount of memory used at run time. An assembly is said to be domain-neutral when all domains in a process may share its code. The host decides whether to load assemblies as domain-neutral when it loads Common Language Runtime into a process.

There are three options for loading domain-neutral assemblies:

- Load no assemblies as domain-neutral, except mscorlib, the core library of .NET Framework, which is always loaded domain-neutral. This setting is called single domain because it is commonly used when the host is running only a single application in the process.
- Load all assemblies as domain-neutral. Use this setting when there are multiple application domains in the process, all of which run the same code.
- Load strong-named assemblies as domain-neutral. Use this setting when running more than one application in the same process.

When you decide whether to load assemblies as domain-neutral, you must make a trade-off between reducing memory use and performance. The performance of a domain-neutral assembly is slower if that assembly contains static data or static methods that are accessed frequently. Access to static data or methods is slower because of the need to isolate applications. Each application domain that accesses the assembly must have a separate copy of the static data or method, to prevent references to objects in static variables from crossing domain boundaries. As a result, Common Language Runtime contains additional logic to direct a caller to the appropriate copy of the static data or method. This extra logic slows down the call.

An assembly is not shared between domains when it is granted a different set of permissions in each domain. This can occur if the host sets an application domain-level security policy. Assemblies should not be loaded as domain-neutral if the set of permissions granted to the assembly is to be different in each domain.

2.4.3 Application Domains and Threads

Application domains form an isolation and security boundary for managed code. Threads are the operating system construct used by Common Language

Runtime to execute code. At run time, a managed code is loaded into an application domain and is run by a particular operating system thread.

There is no one-to-one correlation between application domains and threads. Several threads can be executing in a single application domain at any given time and a particular thread is not confined to a single application domain. That is, threads are free to cross application domain boundaries; a new thread is not created for each application domain.

At any given time, every thread is executing in one application domain. The run time keeps track of which threads are running in which application domains. You can locate the domain in which a thread is executing at any time by calling the **Thread.GetDomain** method.

2.5 Run-Time Hosts

Application domains are usually created and manipulated programmatically by *run-time hosts*.

Common Language Runtime has been designed to support a variety of different application types, from Web server applications to applications with a traditional, rich, Windows user interface. Each type of application requires a run-time host to start it. The run-time host loads Common Language Runtime into a process, creates the application domains within the process, and loads user code into the application domains.

.NET Framework ships with a number of different run-time hosts, including those listed in Table 2-2.

Table 2-2	Run-time Hosts
Run-time Host	**Description**
ASP.NET	Loads the run time into the process that is to handle the Web request. ASP.NET also creates an application domain for each Web application that will run on a Web server.
Microsoft Internet Explorer	Creates application domains in which to run managed controls. The .NET Framework supports the download and execution of browser-based controls. The run time interfaces with the extensibility mechanism of Microsoft Internet Explorer through a mime filter to create application domains in which to run the managed controls. By default, one application domain is created for each Web site.
Shell executables	Invokes the run-time host code to transfer control to the run time each time an executable is launched from the shell.

Microsoft also provides a set of APIs for writing your own run-time hosts.

Summary

.NET Framework is an open language platform for Web development. Its aim is to provide an abstract machine for professional developers, covering both traditional IT applications and Web-oriented applications. As its greatest contribution to the industry, it removes the distinction between traditional software development and Web development. So far, many Web applications have been created in an ad hoc fashion. Under .NET Framework, however, Web applications can be development in a systematic way. Meanwhile, traditional software development may also take advantage of .NET Framework.

In the following chapters, we get into details regarding the good features of .NET Framework, including cross-language interoperability, networking programming, ASP.NET, ADO.NET, and Web Services.

The Programming Environment of .NET Framework

As a major breakthrough, cross-language interoperability is supported under the .NET programming environment. Therefore, the first half of this chapter concentrates on this topic. We first consider the concept of cross-language interoperability, then discuss the cross-language features of the programming in detail. Next, a set of programs that explore these features are presented. These sample programs cover simple console programs, Windows programs, and ASP.NET pages. Components that are developed in various languages are integrated to provide incorporated services.

.NET Framework also provides programmers with a rich library of classes whereby they can build applications effectively and efficiently. In this chapter, the base classes for networking are presented, with examples of the request-response model, socket programming, and server development.

3.1 Cross-Language Interoperability

With the increasing use of distributed systems, interoperability has become a major issue in software development. A number of approaches have been developed to address this issue:

- Representation standards, like External Data Representation (XDR) and Network Data Representation (NDR), define the format for data exchange between various platforms.

- Architecture standards, like Distributed Computing Environment's (DCE) Remote Procedure Call (RPC), Common Object Request Broker Architecture (CORBA), and Microsoft's Component Object Model (COM), allow for calling methods across boundaries between computers, processes, and languages.
- Language standards, like ANSI C, permit distribution of source code across compilers and machines.
- Standard environment for execution, like Java Virtual Machine (JVM), allow the same code to run on different physical machines.

Although these approaches provide significant benefit to software developers, none of them break the barrier between various languages. *Cross-language interoperability* refers to a schema that allows classes and objects in one language to be used in another language seamlessly, not just to a standard calling model, such as COM and CORBA, which permits methods of remote classes to be called as an alien.

.NET Framework provides software developers with a programming environment that supports cross-language interoperability. In this environment, applications and components developed in different languages can communicate and interact with each other, and their behaviors can be tightly integrated. You may define a class in one language and then, using a different language, derive a class from the original one or call a method on it. You may also pass an instance of a class to a method on another class that is written in a different language. It is obvious that cross-language integration of classes and objects is a very desirable feature for programmers, especially for the developers of distributed Web applications.

In order to support cross-language integration, the following components are mandatory for a programming environment:

- A *type system* that defines the types found in the supported programming languages
- A *metadata system* that stores metadata on the types at compile time and then queries the information at run time
- A *common language specification* that describes the design rules for a class library and supported languages for their interaction
- A *debugger* with cross-language capability

In the following section, we discuss how cross-language interoperability is supported in .NET Framework.

3.2 The Programming Environment

This section describes the programming environment of .NET Framework, including the supported languages, common type system, metadata system, common language specification, debugger, classes, and class library.

3.2.1 Supported Languages

Currently, .NET Framework supports four languages. You may use them immediately after you have installed .NET Framework SDK. These are

- *Visual Basic (Version 7.0 or VB.NET)*. If you are a Visual Basic programmer, you may notice that it has more object-oriented features than before. The following benefits may be particularly interesting to you:
    - Performance improvement
    - The ability to easily use components developed in other languages
    - Extensible types provided by a class library
    - A broad set of language features

    The new features of VB.NET are discussed in Appendix A.
- *C++ with Managed Extension*. If you are a Visual C++ programmer, you may write managed code using the managed extensions to C++, which provide you with the benefits of a managed execution environment while giving you access to powerful capabilities and expressive data types that you are familiar with. You might find the following run-time features especially compelling:
    - Cross-language integration, especially cross-language inheritance
    - Automatic memory management, which manages object lifetime so that reference counting is not necessary in order to avoid memory leaking
    - Self-describing objects with metadata, which make using IDL unnecessary
    - The ability to compile once and run on any CPU and operating system that supports Common Language Runtime
- *C# (C Sharp)*. C# is a new development language introduced as a part of .NET Framework. It combines the low-level functionality of Visual C++ with the productivity of a higher-level language like Visual Basic. C# allows the programmers to take full advantage of Common Language Runtime, including cross-language integration, cross-language execution, cross-language exception handling, and garbage collection. In C#, object-oriented applications can be built in fewer lines of code so that the possibility of introducing errors can be reduced. An introduction to C# for C++ and Java Programmers is given in Appendix B.
- *JScript (JScript.NET)*. Improvements in JScript.NET include true compiled code, typed and type-less variables, classes, packages, cross-language support, and access to .NET Framework. It allows for

enhanced execution speed, compile-time and run-time type-checking, and more self-documenting codes. In addition, JScript.NET can be used to implement Web Services (see Chapter 6). The new features of JScript.NET are discussed in Appendix D.

In addition, third-party packages are available to support more languages, such as COBOL, Perl, and Eiffel. However, these packages are beyond the scope of this book.

3.2.2 Common Type System

Common Type System defines the supported types in Common Language Runtime and specifies how they interact with each other. A *type* defines allowable values and the operations that can apply to the values. The types in .NET Framework include *classes*, *interfaces*, and *values*. Because Common Type System supports object-oriented as well as functional and procedural programming languages, it deals with two kinds of entities: *objects* and *values*.

Values are simple bit patterns for things like integers and floats; each value has a type that describes both the storage that it occupies and the meaning of the bits in its representation. Values are intended for representing the corresponding objects in programming like C, and also for representing nonobjects in languages like C++.

An object is self-typing; that is, its type is explicitly stored in its representations. It has an identity that distinguishes it from all other objects, and it has slots that store its members, which may be either values or objects.

The built-in types listed in Table 3-1 are an integral part of Common Type System, being built into .NET Framework. Also listed are the corresponding data types in the supported languages, including Visual Basic, C#, and the managed extension for C++.

| Table 3-1 | Built-In Types | | | |

Common Types	Description	Visual Basic	C#	Managed Extension for C++
Byte	An 8-bit unsigned integer	Byte	byte	char
SByte	An 8-bit signed integer	*Not supported*	sbyte	signed char
Int16	A 16-bit signed integer	Short	short	short
Int32	A 32-bit signed integer	Integer	int	int or long
Int64	A 64-bit signed integer	Long	long	__int64

| Table 3-1 | Built-In Types, continued |

Common Types	Description	Visual Basic	C#	Managed Extension for C++
UInt16	A 16-bit unsigned integer	*Not supported*	ushort	unsigned short
UInt32	A 32-bit unsigned integer	*Not supported*	uint	unsigned int or unsigned long
UInt64	A 64-bit unsigned integer	*Not supported*	ulong	unsigned __int64
Single	A single-precision (32-bit) floating-point number	Single	float	float
Double	A double-precision (64-bit) floating-point number	Double	double	double
Object	The base type of the class hierarchy	Object	object	Object*
Char	A Unicode character (a 16-bit character)	Char	char	__wchar_t
String	An immutable, fixed-length string of Unicode characters	String	string	String*
Decimal	A 96-bit decimal value	Decimal	decimal	Decimal
Boolean	A Boolean value (true or false)	Boolean	bool	bool

The data types in the supported languages are mapped to the corresponding common types when the source codes are compiled. The integration of software components written in various languages can be supported at run time because all the components understand the common types.

New types, either values or objects, are introduced into the Common Type System via type declarations expressed in metadata.

3.2.3 Metadata System

In the traditional programming environment, compiled components can communicate with each other only through a binary interface. Cross-language interaction and/or cross-language integration are made difficult by the conflicting protocols for defining and storing data. In .NET Framework, metadata serves as part of the solution to these problems.

Metadata is a structured way of representing all the information that Common Language Runtime uses to locate and load class, lay out instances in memory, resolve method invocations, translate MSIL code into native code, enforce security, and set up run-time context boundaries. Many key benefits of .NET Framework stem from the use of metadata. It provides a common frame of reference that allows for communication between Common Language Runtime, compilers, debuggers, and codes that have been compiled into MSIL.

Metadata is stored in the components themselves and makes them self-describing. The information stored as metadata in the component includes the following:

- Description of the .NET Framework portable executable or assembly of the component
- Identity, such as name and version
- Types exported
- Dependency; that is, any other assembly on which it depends
- Security permission needed to run
- Description of types
- Name, visibility, base class, and interface implemented
- Members, including methods, fields, properties, events, and nested types
- Attributes
- Additional descriptive elements that modify types and members

The self-describing components contain all the information they need to interact with each other. The metadata always reflects the actual situation of the compiled code. This architecture has therefore eliminated the need for IDL files, type libraries, or any external method of component reference. .NET Framework components do not even require registration with the operating system.

3.2.4 Common Language Specification

Common language specification (CLS) is a set of rules intended to support cross-language interoperability. These rules, however, apply only to items that are exposed for use by those written in other programming languages. In particular, they apply only to types that are visible in assemblies other than those in which they are defined, that is, to types that have members accessible from outside their assembly, such as public classes and public methods.

We show examples of CLS-compliant code when we discuss application development under the programming environment of .NET Framework.

3.2.5 Debugger

Common Language Runtime allows its debugger to understand multilanguage application so that the programmer may step through programs written in different languages.

The .NET SDK debugger uses *solutions* to associate source files and the applications being debugged. A solution is created automatically when you open a compiled application and its associated source file or files. The next time you debug the same application, you can open the solution instead of having to load the source file and the compiled application separately.

3.2.6 Classes

In object-oriented programming, a class defines the operations that the object can perform (methods) and defines the variables that hold the state of the objects (fields).

Table 3-2 and Table 3-3 show characteristics of both classes and their members in .NET Framework.

Table 3-2	*Class Characteristics*
Class Characteristic	**Meaning**
Sealed	You cannot derive another class from this one.
Implements	The class fulfills the contract specified by one or more interfaces.
Abstract	You cannot create an instance of the class. If you want to use it, you must derive another class from it.
Inherits	Indicates that instances of the class can be used anywhere the base class is specified. A derived class that inherits from a base class can use the implementation of any virtual methods provided by the base class, or the derived class can override them with its own implementation.
Exported or not exported	Indicates whether a class is visible outside the assembly.

Table 3-3	*Member Characteristics*
Member Characteristic	**Meaning**
Abstract	This virtual method has no implementation. If you inherit from the class that it is a member of, you must implement this member if you want to instantiate the derived class.
Private	Accessible only from within the same class as the member or within a nested class.
Family	Accessible from within the same class as the member and from subtypes that inherit from it.
Assembly	Accessible only from within the assembly that contains the member's implementation. .NET applications are partitioned into one or more assemblies, which establish the visibility scope for types at execution time.
Family and Assembly	Accessible only from classes that qualify for both family and assembly access.
Public	Accessible from any class.
Final	You cannot override this virtual method in a derived class.
Overrides	The virtual method's implementation replaces the implementation supplied by a member of the class from which it derives.
Static	The member belongs to the class it is defined on, not to a particular instance of the class; the member exists even if the class is not instantiated, and it is shared among all instances of the class.
Overloads	The method has the same name as another member defined in the same type, but it differs in some way from the other method(s) with the same name; for example, its parameter types, the order of parameter types, or the calling convention might be different.
Virtual	The method can be implemented by a subclass and can be invoked either statically or dynamically. If dynamic invocation is used, the type of the instance that is used to make the call at run time determines which implementation of the method to call, instead of the type known at compile time.
Synchronized	The run time ensures that only one thread of execution at a time can access the implementation. This characteristic can be applied to static methods as well as instance and virtual methods.

3.2.7 Class Library

.NET Framework provides programmers with a class library that helps speed up and optimize the development processes. All the types in the class library are CLS-compliant so as to support cross-language interoperability.

These types are named using a dot-syntax scheme that represents a naming hierarchy. This technique is employed in order to group related classes logically so that they may be searched and referenced more efficiently. For example, class **System.Net.Sockets.TCPListener** is used to create a network server process that listens to connections from TCP clients. The part of the name up to the last dot, in this case **System.Net.Sockets**, is often referred to as the namespace, and the last part, in this case **TCPListener**, is the class name. This naming syntax is simply a notation and has no effect on the accessibility of the class.

The root namespace for the types in .NET Framework is the **System** namespace that includes 24 second-level namespaces. The following list shows the categories of functionality that are covered and the namespaces in each category:

- Component Model:
  System.CodeDom
  System.ComponentModel
- Configuration:
  System.Configuration
- Data:
  System.Data
  System.Xml
  System.Xml.Serialization
- Framework Services:
  System.Diagnostics
  System.DirectoryService
  System.Messaging
  System.ServiceProcess
  System.Timer
- Globalization and Localization:
  System.Globalization
  System.Resources
- Network:
  System.Net

- Common Tasks:
  System.Collections
  System.IO
  System.Text.RegularExpressions
  System.Threading
- Reflection:
  System.Reflection
- Graphic User Interface:
  System.Drawing
  System.Windows.Forms
- Run-time Infrastructure Services:
  System.Runtime.CompilerService
  System.Runtime.InteropServices
  System.Runtime.Remoting
  System.Runtime.Serialization
- .NET Framework Security:
  System.Security
  System.Security.Cryptography
- Web Services:
  System.Web
  System.Web.Services

Therefore, .NET Framework supplies a rich set of base classes that allow the programmers to build applications of various kinds effectively and efficiently. Later in this chapter, we discuss network programming with .NET Framework to demonstrate the power and versatility of the programming environment.

In addition, there is a class under namespace **System** that corresponds to the built-in data types discussed earlier, such as **System.Int16**, **System.Int32**, **System.Int64**, **System.String**, and **System.Object**. **System.Object** is the root of the inheritance hierarchy of all the classes in .NET Framework.

The reference documentation for the types in .NET Framework provides an overview of each type, along with a formal description of its members (including parameters and return values). Reflecting the cross-language interoperability of the programming environment, the description contains the syntax for all the supported languages.

Using the class library, we build applications of various kinds in the rest of this chapter, as well as in the following chapters.

3.3 Console Programs That Say "Hello!"

Let us start with a very simple example: building an application that says "Hello" to you. It facilitates a simple dialogue between you and the standard I/O device of your PC, that is your screen and keyboard, or *Console* in the terminology of .NET Framework. Because we are working in a programming environment with cross-language interoperability, we can implement this application in multiple languages, including Visual Basic, C++ with managed extension, and C#.

3.3.1 Required Tools

Once you have installed .NET Framework, you need to check directory **%windir%\Microsoft.net\Framework\v1.0.bbbb**, where **bbbb** is the final build number. The files listed in Table 3-4 must be under this directory. Moreover, this directory should also be included in your path.

Table 3-4	*The Required Files*
File	**Comment**
bc.exe	Compiler for VB.NET
cl.exe	Compiler for C++ with managed extension
csc.exe	Compiler for C#
mscorlib.dll	Core library of .NET Framework
Other .dll files	Libraries that are used in this book

Moreover, this directory should also be included in your path.

3.3.2 Required Classes and Methods

In order to build such an application, it is necessary for us to access the standard I/O device, or Console. Class **System.Console**, or more specifically, the following methods in the class library are needed for this task: **System.Console.Write**, **System.Console.ReadLine**, and **System. Console.WriteLine**.

In addition, method **Concat** of class **System.String** is needed for string concatenation as well.

The required classes are defined as:

CONSOLE

Description
This class provides access to the standard input, standard output, and standard error streams.

Inheritance
Object => Console (System.Console is directly derived from **System.Object)**

Syntax
Table 3-5 lists the syntax of **Console** class in Visual Basic, C#, and the managed extension for C++.

Table 3-5	**Console** Class
Language	**Syntax**
Visual Basic	`NotInheritable Public Class Console`
C#	`public sealed class Console`
C++	`public __gc __sealed class Console (`__gc indicates that this class is in the managed extension.)

Requirements (Required namespaces and assemblies)

Namespace: System
Assembly: mscorlib.dll

Class System.String is defined as:

STRING

Description
This class represents an immutable string of characters.

Inheritance
`Object => String`

Syntax
Table 3-6 lists the syntax of **String** class in Visual Basic, C#, and the managed extension to C++.

Table 3-6	**String** *Class*
Language	**Syntax**
Visual Basic	NotInheritable Public Class Console
	Implements IComparable, ICloneable, IConvertable
C#	public sealed class Console: IComparable, ICloneable, IConvertable
C++	public __gc __sealed class String: IComparable, ICloneable, IConvertable

Requirements

Namespace: System
Assembly: mscorlib.dll

The required methods are defined as:

CONSOLE.READLINE()

Description
This method reads the next line of characters from **Console.In**, which is set to the system's standard input stream by default. *(The keyboard)*

Syntax
Table 3-7 lists the syntax of **Console.ReadLine()** method in Visual Basic, C#, and the managed extension to C++.

Table 3-7	**Console.ReadLine()** *Method*
Language	**Syntax**
Visual Basic	Public Shared Function Read() As String;
C#	public static int Read();
C++	public: static int Read();

Return Value
The next line from the input stream, or null if the end of the input stream has already been reached.

As for methods System.Console.Write, System.WriteLine, System.String.Concat, each of them has several overloaded versions and listed below are only those we are going to use:

CONSOLE.WRITE(STRING)

Description
This method writes a string to Out that is set to the system's standard output stream by default. *(The screen)*

Syntax

Table 3-8 lists the syntax of Console.Write(String) method in Visual Basic, C#, and the managed extension to C++.

Table 3-8	**Console.Write(String)** Method
Language	**Syntax**
Visual Basic	Overloads Public Shared Sub Write(ByVal value As String)
C#	public static void Write(string value);
C++	public: static void Write(String* value);

Parameter

The string to write.

CONSOLE.WRITELINE(STRING)

Description

This method writes a string with a new line appended to its end, to Out that is set to the system's standard output stream by default.

Syntax

Table 3-9 lists the syntax of Console.WriteLine(String) method in Visual Basic, C#, and the managed extension to C++.

Table 3-9	**Console.WriteLine(String)** Method
Language	**Syntax**
Visual Basic	Overloads Public Shared Sub WriteLine(ByVal value As String)
C#	public static void WriteLine(string value);
C++	public: static void WriteLine(String* value);

Parameter

The string to write.

STRING.CONCAT(STRING, STRING, STRING)

Description

This method creates a new string from the concatenation of three strings.

Syntax

Table 3-10 lists the syntax of **String.Concat(String, String, String)** method in Visual Basic, C#, and the managed extension to C++.

Table 3-10	*String.Concat(String, String, String)* Method
Language	**Syntax**

Visual Basic	```Overloads Public Shared Sub Concat(```
	``` ByVal value0 As String,```
	``` ByVal value1 As String,```
	``` ByVal value2 As String,```
	```) As String```

C#	```public static void String Concat(```
	``` string value0,```
	``` string value1,```
	``` string value2```
	```);```

C++	```public: static void String* Concat(```
	``` String* value0,```
	``` String* value1,```
	``` String* value2```
	```);```

Parameter

value0	The first string.
value1	The second string.
value2	The third string.

Return Value

The new string that is the concatenation of the input strings.

Now, we are ready to write our programs.

3.3.3 C++ Program

Following is the program written in C++ with managed extensions. The file name is **Hello.cpp**.

```
// Hello.cpp
#using <mscorlib.dll>

using namespace System;

void main() {
    // prompt for input
    Console::Write("Your name, please: ");

    // read the response
    String* name = Console::ReadLine();
```

```
    // write the greeting and identify myself
    Console::WriteLine(String::Concat(
L"Hello, ",
name,
L"!"
));
    Console::WriteLine(String::Concat(
        L"This is a greeting ",
        L"from a program ",
        L"written in C++.")
    );
}
```

This program begins with **#using <mscorlib.dll>** in order to incorporate the assembly of the required core library, i.e. **mscorlib.dll**. Note that **#include** and **#using** are different because the former simply incorporates the source code rather than the pre-built library as does the latter.

As you know, this program uses class **Console** under namespace **System**. The **#using** statement only tells the compiler *where* to find the required classes, but not *what* the required classes are. Statement **using namespace System** specifies the namespace in which the required classes are located.

Here comes the main block of the program, **void main() { ... }**. It follows the syntax of C++. Command line arguments may also be used here, even though we do not include them in this simple example.

Statement **Console::Write("Your name, please: ")** prints a string on the screen so as to prompt for your input. Note that the difference between **Write()** and **WriteLine()** is that the latter outputs an **"\n"** in the end of the string while the former does not. Note that C++ uses double colon "::" to reference object members.

Then, **Console::ReadLine()** is called for you to type your name. This method returns the string you typed when you hit [**Enter**].

Finally, **String::Concat()** is invoked by the concatenation of its input strings so as to generate the output string as the argument of **Console:: WriteLine()**. Here, specifying **L** in front of a string tells the compiler to encode the string in Unicode. If you omit the **L**, the program will still compile but the string will be encoded in ASCII. At run time, this string will be converted into Unicode, so the performance will be degraded. It is therefore recommended that Unicode string always be used during the coding.

The command for compiling this program looks like this:

```
cl /CLR HelloCPP.cpp /link /entry:main
```

The switch **/CLR** is mandatory; it tells the compiler to create managed code. Also important is **/entry:main**, which specifies the entry point of the program.

Because of the complexity of the command, it is recommended that a batch file be created for compilation. This batch file, **build.bat**, looks like this:

```
cl /CLR %1CPP.cpp /link /entry:main
```

Thus, the executable can be generated in the following way:

```
>build Hello

>cl /CLR hello.cpp /link /entry:main
Microsoft (R) 32-bit C/C++ Optimizing Compiler Version
13.00.9030 for CLR
Copyright (C) Microsoft Corp 1984-2000. All rights
reserved.

hello.cpp
Microsoft (R) Incremental Linker Version 7.00.9030
Copyright (C) 1992-2000 Microsoft Corporation. All rights
reserved.

/out:helloCPP.exe
/entry:main
hello.obj

>
```

Then we may run the program:

```
>HelloCPP
Your name, please: David Zhang
Hello, David Zhang!
This is a greeting from a program written in C++.

>
```

In these dialogues, what the program says is shown in boldface.

3.3.4 C# Program

This is the program written in C#. The file name is **Hello.cs**.

```
// Hello.cs
using System;

class MainApp {
    // Entry point of the program
    public static void Main() {
        // prompt for input
        Console.Write("Your name, please: ");
```

```
// read the response
    String name = Console.ReadLine();

// write the greeting and identify myself
    Console.WriteLine(String.Concat(
        "Hello, ",
        name,
        "!")
    );
    Console.WriteLIne(String.Concat(
        "This is a greeting ",
        "from a program ",
        "written in C#.")
    );
    }
}
```

While this program is very similar to the C++ version, you may have noticed some differences:

- The structure of the program is different. Very much like Java, a class has to be defined in a piece of C# program and its entry is defined as **public static void Main()** method.
- The core library mscorlib.dll is loaded implicitly; there is no need to specify it.
- C# supports the period as a scope resolution operator, which allows the same syntax in object member referencing as that in the class library, such as **Console.Write()**.

In addition, **Console.WriteLine("Hello, " + name + "!")** also works for C# as a replacement of **Console.WriteLine (String.Concat ("Hello, ", name, "!"))**. However, that does not work for C++ with managed extension. Therefore, it is a good practice to use the classes in the .NET Framework library as much as possible.

The command for compiling this program is simple:

```
csc /out:HelloCS.exe /t:exe Hello.cs
```

You may also create a batch file **build.bat**:

```
csc /out:%CS.exe /t:exe %1.cs
```

Thus, the executable can be generated in the following way:

```
>build hello
```

```
>csc /out:HelloCS.exe /t:exe Hello.cs
Microsoft (R) Visual C# Compiler Version 7.00.9030 [CLR
version 1.00.2204.21]
Copyright (C) Microsoft Corp 2000. All rights reserved.

>
```

Then we may run the program:

```
>HelloCS
Your name, please: David Zhang
Hello, David Zhang!
This is a greeting from a program written in C#.

>
```

3.3.5 Visual Basic Program

This is the program written in Visual Basic. The file name is **Hello.vb**.

```
' Hello.vb
Imports System
Public Module modmain
    Private name As String

    ' prompt for input
    Sub Main()
        ' prompt for input
        Console.Write("Your name, please: ")

        ' read the response
        name = Console.ReadLine()

        ' write the greeting and identify myself
        Console.WriteLine(String.Concat( _
            "Hello, ", _
            name, _
            "!" _
        ))
        Console.WriteLIne(String.Concat( _
            "This is a greeting ", _
            "from a program ", _
            "written in C#." _
        ))
    End Sub
End Module
```

The structure of the Visual Basic program is remarkably different from the C# and C++ with managed extension programs. In addition, **Imports** is the keyword for incorporating namespaces rather than **using**. As a final point, do not forget the underscore (_) when you break a line.

The command for compiling this program is:

```
vbc Hello.vb /out:HelloVB.exe /t:exe
```

You may also create a batch file **build.bat**:

```
vbc %1.vb /out:%1VB.exe /t:exe
```

Thus, the executable can be generated in the following way:

```
>build hello

>vbc Hello.vb /out:HelloVB.exe /t:exe
Microsoft (R) Visual Basic.NET Compiler version 7.00.9030
for Microsoft (R) .NET Framework Common Language Runtime
version 1.00.2204.21
Copyright (C) Microsoft Corp 2000. All rights reserved.

>
```

Then we may run the program:

```
>HelloVB
Your name, please: David Zhang
Hello, David Zhang!
This is a greeting from a program written in Visual Basic.

>
```

3.4 Components That Say "Hello!"

Now we want to write components in various languages to explore the following features of .NET Framework:

- Cross-language integration, that is, the inheritance and invocation of classes that break the boundaries between languages
- Method overriding or polymorphism in this environment

3.4.1 Base Class

First, we write a base class in a language, say in C#. Its file name is **CompBase.cs**.

```
// CompBase.cs
using System;

namespace CompBase {
    // base class
    public abstract class Hello {
        // language in which this program is written
        private String lang = "Unknown";

        // abstract method to be implemented
        public abstract String Greeting(String name);

        // methods to access the property
        public String GetLang() {
```

```
                    return lang;   •
            }
            public void SetLang(String l) {
                    lang = l;
            }
        }
}
```

This is an abstract class because its method **Greeting()** is abstract, that is, yet to be implemented.

The following command compiles this program and creates the **CompBase.dll** file for the base class.

```
csc /out:CompBase.dll /target:library CompBase.cs
```

Next, we write components with classes that derived from the base class and implement its abstract method.

3.4.2 Component as a Derived Class in C#

This is the component program written in C#. Its file name is **CompCS.cs**.

```
// CompCS.cs
using System;
using CompBase;

namespace CompCS {
    public class HelloCS : Hello {
            // The constructor sets the language property.
            public HelloCS() {
                    base.SetLang("C#");
            }
            // implement the abstract method in the base
            // class
            public override String Greeting(String name) {
                    return String.Concat("Hello, ", name, "!");
            }
        }
}
```

The following command compiles this program and creates the **CompCS.dll** file for the component.

```
csc /r:CompBase.dll /out:CompCS.dll /target:library ⇓
CompCS.cs
```

3.4.3 Component as a Derived Class in Visual Basic

This is the component program written in Visual Basic. Its file name is **CompVB.vb**.

```
' CompVB.vb
Imports System
Imports CompBase

Namespace CompVB
    Public Class HelloVB
    Inherits CompBase.Hello
        ' New() is a constructor that sets the language
        ' property
        Public Sub New()
            MyBase.New
            MyBase.SetLang("Visual Basic")
        End Sub

        ' implement the abstract method in the base class
        Overrides Function Greeting(name As String) ⇓
            As String
            Greeting = String.Concat( ⇓
                "Hello, ", name, "!!")
        End Function
    End Class
End Namespace
```

The following command compiles this program and creates the **CompVB.dll** file for the component.

```
vbc CompVB.vb /out:CompVB.dll /r:CompBase.dll /t:library
```

3.4.4 Component as a Derived Class in C++

This is the component program written in C++ with a managed extension. Its file name is **CompCPP.cpp**.

```
// CompCPP.cpp
#using <mscorlib.dll>
#using <CompBase.dll>

using namespace System;
using namespace CompBase;

namespace CompCPP {
    __gc public class HelloCPP : public Hello {
        public:
            // The constructor sets the language
            // property
```

```
                        HelloCPP() {
                                SetLang("C++");
                        };

                        // implement the abstract method in
                        // the base class
                        String* Greeting(String* name) {
                                return String::Concat(
                                        "Hello, ",
                                        name,
                                        "!!!"
                                );
                        }
                };
        };
```

The following command compiles this program and creates the
CompCPP.dll file for the component.

```
cl /CLR /c CompCPP.cpp
link -noentry -dll /out:CompCPP.dll CompCPP
```

3.5 Client Programs of the Components

Now we are ready to use the components we have just developed. In this
section, we use console programs in various languages.

3.5.1 Console Program in C#

This is the client program written in C#. Its file name is **ClientCS.cs**.

```
// ClientCS.cs
using System;
using CompBase;
using CompCS;
using CompVB;
using CompCPP;

class MainApp {
    public static void Main() {
        Console.Write("Your name, please: ");
        String name = Console.ReadLine();

        // define an array of base class objects
        CompBase.Hello[] myHello = new Hello[3];

        // populate the array with objects of the
        // derived classes
```

```
myHello[0] = new CompCS.HelloCS();
myHello[1] = new CompVB.HelloVB();
myHello[2] = new CompCPP.HelloCPP();

// loop over the array of objects
for (int i = 0; i < 3; i++) {
        Console.WriteLine();

        // methods that implemented in the
        // derived classes will be invoked
        Console.WriteLine( ⇓
                myHello[i].Greeting(name));
        Console.WriteLine(String.Concat(
                "This is a greeting from a program ⇓
                        written in ",
                myHello[i].GetLang(),
                ".")
        );
}
}
}
```

In the statement **Console.WriteLine(myHello[i].Greeting(name))**, polymorphism allows the methods implemented in the derived classes to be invoked to realize the desired behavior of the program.

The following commands compile this program:

```
csc /r:CompBase.dll;CompCS.dll;CompVB.dll;CompCPP.dll ⇓
/out:ClientCS.exe ClientCS.cs
```

Note that the libraries of the components need to be indicated as references.

Now let's run this program:

```
>ClientCS
Your name, please: David Zhang

Hello, David Zhang!
This is a greeting from a program written in C#.

Hello, David Zhang!!
This is a greeting from a program written in Visual Basic.

Hello, David Zhang!!!
This is a greeting from a program written in C++.

>
```

As you can see, the number of exclamation points in the greetings indicates that the desired versions of method **Greeting()** have been called. In addition, method **GetLang()** implemented in the base class obtains the correct language properties.

3.5.2 Console Program in Visual Basic

This is the client program written in Visual Basic. The file name is ClientVB.vb.

```
' ClientVB.vb
Imports System

Imports CompBase
Imports CompCS
Imports CompVB
Imports CompCPP

Public Module modmain
    Private name As String
    Sub Main()
        Dim Count As Integer

        Console.Write("Your name, please: ")
        name = Console.ReadLine()

        ' define an array of base class objects
        Dim MyHello(3) As CompBase.Hello

        ' populate the array with objects of the derived
        ' classes
        MyHello(0) = New CompCS.HelloCS
        MyHello(1) = New CompVB.HelloVB
        MyHello(2) = New CompCPP.HelloCpp

        ' loop over the array of objects
        For Count = 0 To 2
            Console.WriteLine()
            ' methods that implemented in the derived
            ' classes will be invoked

    Console.WriteLine( _
        myHello(Count).Greeting(name) _
    )
            Console.WriteLine(String.Concat( _
                "This is a greeting from a program ⇓
                    written in ", _
                myHello(Count).GetLang(), _
                ".") _
            )
        Next
    End Sub
End Module
```

In the statement **Console.WriteLine(myHello(Count).Greeting (name))**, polymorphism allows the methods implemented in the derived classes to be invoked to realize the desired behavior of the program.

The following commands compile this program:

```
vbc ClientVB.vb /r:CompBase.dll /r:CompCS.dll ⇓
    /r:CompVB.dll /r:CompCPP.dll /out:ClientVB.exe ⇓
    /t:exe
```

Note that the libraries of the components need to be indicated as references.

Now let's run this program:

```
>ClientVB
Your name, please: David Zhang

Hello, David Zhang!
This is a greeting from a program written in C#.

Hello, David Zhang!!
This is a greeting from a program written in Visual Basic.

Hello, David Zhang!!!
This is a greeting from a program written in C++.

>
```

As you can see, the number of exclamation points in the greetings indicates that the desired versions of method **Greeting()** have been called. In addition, method **GetLang()**, which is implemented in the base class, obtains the correct language properties.

3.5.3 Console Program in C++

This is the client program written in C++ with managed extension. The file name is **ClientCPP.cpp.**

```
// ClientCPP.cpp
#using <mscorlib.dll>
using namespace System;

#using "CompBase.dll"
#using "CompCS.dll"
#using "CompVB.dll"
#using "CompCPP.dll"

void main() {
    Console::Write("Your name, please: ");
    String* name = Console::ReadLine();

    // define an array of base class objects
```

```
CompBase::Hello* myHello[] = new CompBase::Hello*[3];

// populate the array with objects of the derived
// classes
myHello[0] = new CompCS::HelloCS();
myHello[1] = new CompVB::HelloVB();
myHello[2] = new CompCPP::HelloCPP();

// loop over the array of objects
for (int i = 0; i < 3; i++) {
    Console::WriteLine();

    // methods that implemented in the derived classes
    // will be invoked
    Console::WriteLine(myHello[i]->Greeting(name));
    Console::WriteLine(String::Concat(
        L"This is a greeting from a program ⇓
            written in ",
        myHello[i]->GetLang(),
        L".")
    );
}
}
```

In the statement **Console.WriteLine(myHello[i]->Greeting(name))**, polymorphism allows the methods implemented in the derived classes to be invoked to realize the desired behavior of the program.

The following commands compile this program

```
cl /CLR ClientCPP.cpp /link /entry:main /out:ClientCPP.exe
```

Note that the libraries of the components have been included in the program so that they do not need to be indicated in the command line.

Now let's run this program:

```
>ClientCS
Your name, please: David Zhang

Hello, David Zhang!
This is a greeting from a program written in C#.

Hello, David Zhang!!
This is a greeting from a program written in Visual Basic.

Hello, David Zhang!!!
This is a greeting from a program written in C++.

>
```

As you can see, the number of exclamation points in the greetings indicates that the desirable versions of method **Greeting()** have been called. In addition, method **GetLang()**, which is implemented in the base class, obtains the correct language properties.

3.5.4 Windows Program

.NET Framework supports window-based applications. Now, let us move our "Hello!" application to a Windows environment. The name of the program in Visual Basic is **ClientWin.vb**:

```
' ClientWin.vb
Imports System
Imports System.Collections
Imports System.WinForms
Imports CompCS
Imports CompVB
Imports CompCPP
Imports CompBase

Public Module modmain
    ' Return and New Line
    Private Const vbCrLf as String = CChar(13) & CChar(10)

    Public Class Client
    Inherits Form
        Private components As _
            System.ComponentModel.Container
        Private Button2 As System.WinForms.Button
        Private Button1 As System.WinForms.Button
        Private Label1 As System.WinForms.Label
        Private Label2 As System.WinForms.Label
        Private TextBox1 As System.WinForms.TextBox

        ' Constructor that initialize the form
        Public Sub New()
            MyBase.New
            InitForm
        End Sub

        ' Clean up
        Overrides Overloads Public Sub Dispose()
            MyBase.Dispose
            Components.Dispose
        End Sub

        ' Entry point; shared by all the instances
        Shared Sub Main()
            Application.Run(New Client)
        End Sub
        Private Sub InitForm()
            ' Allocate all the controls
```

```
Me.components = New _
      System.ComponentModel.Container
Me.Button1 = New Button
Me.Button2 = New Button
Me.Label1 = New Label
Me.Label2 = New Label
Me.TextBox1 = New TextBox

' Close button
Button1.SetLocation(200, 240)
Button1.TabIndex = 1
Button1.Text = "&Close"
Button1.SetSize(75, 23)
AddHandler Button1.Click, _
      New System.EventHandler( _
            AddressOf Me.Button1_Click)

' Hello button
Button2.SetLocation(120, 240)
Button2.TabIndex = 2
Button2.Text = "&Hello"
Button2.SetSize(75, 23)
AddHandler Button2.Click, _
      New System.EventHandler( _
            AddressOf Me.Button2_Click)

' Area to show the greeting
Label1.SetLocation(10, 60)
Label1.TabIndex = 0
Label1.TabStop = False
Label1.Text = ""
Label1.SetSize(272, 232)

' Prompt text
Label2.SetLocation(10, 10)
Label2.TabIndex = 0
Label2.TabStop = False
Label2.Text = "Your Name Please: "

' User input
TextBox1.SetLocation(120, 10)
TextBox1.TabIndex = 0
TextBox1.TabStop = False
TextBox1.MaxLength = 25
TextBox1.TextAlign = _
      HorizontalAlignment.Left
TextBox1.Text = ""

' Title of the window
Me.Text = "ClientWin"
```

```
                    ' Show the result
                    Me.Controls.Add(Button1)
                    Me.Controls.Add(Button2)
                    Me.Controls.Add(Label1)
                    Me.Controls.Add(Label2)
                    Me.Controls.Add(TextBox1)
            End Sub

            ' Close the window
            Private Sub Button1_Click( _
            ByVal sender As System.Object, _
            ByVal e As System.EventArgs)
                    Me.Close
            End Sub

            ' get the greeting
            Private Sub Button2_Click( _
            ByVal sender As System.Object, _
            ByVal e As System.EventArgs)
                    Dim Count As Integer
                    ' define an array of base class objects
                    Dim MyHello(3) As CompBase.Hello
                    ' populate the array with objects of the
                    ' derived classes
                    MyHello(0) = New CompCS.HelloCS
                    MyHello(1) = New CompVB.HelloVB
                    MyHello(2) = New CompCPP.HelloCpp
                    Label1.Text = ""
                    ' loop over the array of objects
                    For Count = 0 To 2
                    ' methods that implemented in the
                    ' derived classes will be invoked
                    Label1.Text = Label1.Text & _
                    mHello(Count).Greeting(TextBox1.Text) & _
                            vbCrLf
                    Label1.Text = Label1.Text & _
                    "This is a greeting from a program in "
                    Label1.Text = Label1.Text & _
                            myHello(Count).GetLang() & _
                            vbCrLf & vbCrLf
                    ' method GetLang() was implemented in the
                    ' base class
                    Next
            End Sub
        End Class
    End Module
```

In .NET Framework, the Windows Forms library is located in **System.Windows.Forms** namespace. In this program, class **Client** is derived from **System.WinForms.Form**. The entry point of the program is **Main()**, which creates an instance of Client and the constructor of Client is invoked whereby the following controls are created on the form. In addition, the Click events of Button1 and Button2 are associated with their handlers. Table 3-11 describes all the controls in this program.

Table 3-11   *Controls in the Windows Program*

Control	Text	Function	Event
Button1	Close	End the application.	Click
Button2	Hello	Get the greetings from the Components.	Click
Label1	Your name please:	Prompt for user input.	
Label2		Show the greetings from the Components.	
TextBox1		Get the user input.	

This form-based scheme makes Windows programming much more straightforward.

In the Click event handler of Button2, i.e. subroutine **Button2_Click**, polymorphism allows the methods implemented in the derived classes to be invoked so that the desired behavior of the program can be realized.

The following commands compile this program.

```
vbc ClientWin.vb /reference:System.dll, ⇓
Microsoft.Win32.Interop.dll, ⇓
System.WinForms.dll,System.IO.DLL, ⇓
System.Data.DLL, ⇓
System.drawing.dll, ⇓
CompCS.dll,CompVB.dll,CompCPP.dll, ⇓
CompBase.dll /out:ClientWin.exe /t:exe
```

Note that the libraries of the components need to be indicated as references.

Run this program and you may see a window like the one in Figure 3-1.

As you can see, the number of exclamation points in the greetings indicates that the desired versions of method **Greeting()** have been called. In addition, method **GetLang()**,which is implemented in the base class, obtains the correct language properties.

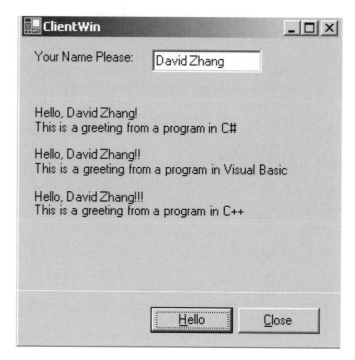

Figure 3-1   *Windows program as the client of the components.*

3.5.5 ASP.NET Page

One of the most attractive features of .NET Framework is that the same code may be used in ASP.NET. Chapter 5 is dedicated to ASP.NET. The following is a simple example of an ASP.NET page program in C# that accesses our "Hello!" components. The file name is **ClientASP.aspx**.

```
<!-- ClientASP.aspx. -->

<%@ Page Language="C#" %>
<%@ Import Namespace="CompBase" %>
<%@ Import Namespace="CompCS" %>
<%@ Import Namespace="CompVB" %>
<%@ Import Namespace="CompCPP" %>

<html>
<script language="C#" runat=server>
void Submit_Click (Object sender, EventArgs EvArgs) {
```

```
  CompBase.Hello[] myHello = new Hello[3];
  myHello[0] = new CompCS.HelloCS();
  myHello[1] = new CompVB.HelloVB();
  myHello[2] = new CompCPP.HelloCPP();
  Result.Text = "";
  for (int i = 0; i < 3; i++) {
    Result.Text = Result.Text +
        myHello[i].Greeting(name.Text) +
        "<br>" +
        "This is a greeting from a program in " +
        myHello[i].GetLang() +
        "<br><br>";
  }
}
</script>
<body>
<h3>ClientASP</h3>
<form runat="server">
Your name please: <asp:TextBox id="name" Text=15
    runat="server"/>
<input type="submit" OnServerClick="Submit_Click"
    Value="Hello" runat="server"/>
<p><asp:Label id="Result" runat="server"/>
</form>
</body>
</html>
```

Both user input and result presentation are dealt with in the same page. When the user types in his or her name and hits the Submit button, the server side routine, **Click_Submit()**, retrieves the greetings from the components and writes them on the Result label in the same form. In this routine, polymorphism allows the methods implemented in the derived classes to be invoked so that the desired behavior of the program can be realized.

In order to run this program, you need Microsoft Internet Information Server (IIS). .NET Framework must be installed after IIS has been installed.

The directory where **ClientASP.aspx** is located may be configured as a virtual directory of the IIS on your PC. It will serve as the entry point of the application. This directory should have a subdirectory *bin*, where the library files, namely **CompBase.dll**, **CompCS.dll**, **CompVB.dll**, and **CompCPP.dll**, are located.

Suppose that the virtual directory is called test. Then, you may reach this page via *localhost/test/ClientASP.aspx*. It is shown in Figure 3-2.

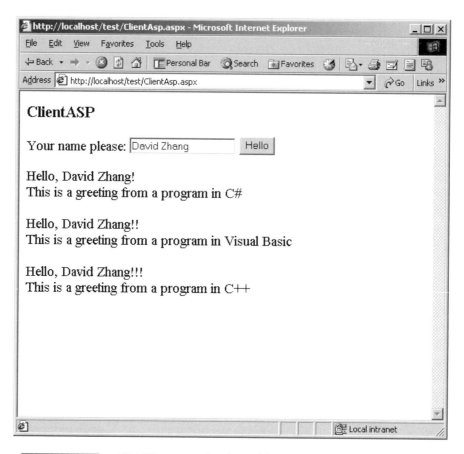

Figure 3-2 *ASP.NET page as the client of the components*

3.6 Network Programming

In the previous sections, we explored the cross-language interoperability of the programming environment with .NET Framework. In addition, .NET Framework also provides programmers with a rich set of base classes. Using these classes, you can create applications of various categories effectively and efficiently. In this section, we discuss network programming with .NET Framework and show how powerful and versatile the programming environment is.

.NET Framework supplies a simple yet complete solution for networked applications in managed code. The class library for networking programming with .NET Framework has been based on a layered model of computer networks. It provides classes at various layers of the network, each of which enables applications to access the network with the control of the specific level. The spectrum of the classes has covered all the levels that are needed for development of Web and Internet applications, from fine-grained control over the socket to a generic request-response model. You may work at the highest layer suitable for the goals of your application, so your development is much more effective and efficient. It may also expand so as to allow you to continue to work with your applications as the Internet evolves.

In this section, all the programs are written in C#. As shown in the previous sections, it would be easy to translate them into other supported languages. In these programs, localhost, your own PC, is used as much as possible so as to make it convenient for you to run the programs. It is not difficult to run them in a local area network with multiple PCs.

3.6.1 Request-Response Model

At the top level of the network abstraction in .NET Framework, the request-response model provides a simple way to access resources on the Web. This functionality is significant not only because of the large share of Web traffic today going over the HTTP protocol, but also because more and more non-Web traffic is carried by the HTTP protocol, such as SOAP.

System.Net.WebRequest and **System.Net.WebResponse** are the abstract base class for the request-response model of .NET Framework. Applications can use them in a protocol-agnostic manner. That is, the application works with instances of the base class, while the specific protocol-specific descendent classes deal with the details of the requests and responses.

Applications should never create the **WebRequest** or **WebResponse** objects. The **WebRequest** objects are always created with the **System.Net. WebResponseFactory** class. The **WebResponse** objects are created with a method of **WebRequest** class, such as **System.Net.WebRequest. GetResponse()**.

In order to read data from the network, an instance of **System. IO.Stream** is created by using **WebResponse;System.Net. WebResponse. GetResponseStream()**.

A **System.IO.StreamReader** object is in turn created on the stream, and method **System.IO.StreamReader.Read()** is used for reading the data.

This program is based on the request-response model. Its file name is **ReqResp.cs**.

```
//ReqResp.cs
using System;
using System.Net;
using System.IO;
using System.Text;
```

```
class MainApp {
    public static void Main() {
            // prompt for user input, e.g.
            // http://localhost/test/ClientASP.aspx
            Console.Write("URL, please: ");
            String url = Console.ReadLine();

            // create a WebRequest object
            WebRequest rq = WebRequestFactory.Create(url);

            // get the corresponding WebResponse object
            WebResponse rp = rq.GetResponse();

            // get the StreamReader
            StreamReader sr = new StreamReader(
                // Stream of the respone
                rp.GetResponseStream(),
                // Encoding to be used
                Encoding.ASCII
            );

            // a buffer to read the stream
            int len = 1024;
            char[] buf = new char[1024];

            // read it
            int n = sr.Read(
                buf,           // buffer to hold the data read
                0,             // index to the buffer
                len            // length of data to be read,
                               // i.e. size of the buffer
            );
            // keep reading when there is more data
            while (n > 0) {
                Console.Write(buf, 0, n);
                n = sr.Read(buf, 0, len);
            }
            sr.Close();
    }
}
```

The following command compiles this program:

```
csc /r:System.Net.dll;System.IO.dll ReqResp.cs
```

Then we may run this program to get the data for page **ClientASP.aspx**, which the server actually transmits to your PC.

```
> ReqResp
URL, please: http://localhost/test/ClientASP.aspx
<html>
<body>
<h3>ClientASP</he>
<form name="ctrl5" method="post" action="ClientASP.aspx"
id = "ctrl5"/>
<input type="hidden" name="_VIEWSTATE"
value="YTB6MTM3NTI4MDMxM19fX3g=9c8c9e6f"/>
<p>
<span id="Reslut"></span>
</form>
</body>
</html>
```

It is interesting to compare the source and actual data of this page.

3.6.2 TCP Client

At the next level down in the network abstraction of .NET Framework, transport layer protocol (TCP) or UDP is used. Classes at this level give you the flexibility to work with all the varieties of the application protocols that are not limited to HTTP.

Class **System.Net.Sockets.TcpClients** is used for programming at this level. The **System.Net.Sockets.TcpClients.GetStream()** method returns a stream for reading data from the network. In addition, class **System.Net.DNS** deals with network addresses, host names, and end points.

This is the program that accesses the date and time service on port 13 of the given server using **TCPClient** class. Its file name is **TCPClient.cs**.

```
//TCPClient.cs:

using System;
using System.Net;
using System.Net.Sockets;
using System.IO;
using System.Text;

class MainApp {
  public static void Main() {
      TcpClient tcpc = new TcpClient();
      // buffer for reading data
```

```
byte[] buf = new byte[256];

// prompt for server name
Console.Write("Server name, please: ");
String svrn = Console.ReadLine();

// verify the given server name
if (Dns.GetHostByName(svrn) == null) {
    Console.WriteLine(String.Concat(
        "Cannot find ",
        svrn)
    );
    return;
}

// open connection to the clock service on server
try {
    tcpc.Connect(svrn, 13);
}
catch (SocketException ) {
    Console.WriteLine(String.Concat(
        "Cannot connect to ",
        svrn,
        ".")
    );
    return;
}

// get the stream to read data
Stream s = tcpc.GetStream();

// read the data and present it
int n = s.Read(buf, 0, buf.Length);
String ServerData =  ⇓
    Encoding.ASCII.GetString(buf);
Console.WriteLine(String.Concat(
    "Received: ",
    n,
    " bytes: ")
);
Console.WriteLine(ServerData);

// close the connection
tcpc.Close();
    }
}
```

The following command compiles this program:

```
csc /r:System.Net.dll;System.IO.dll TCPClient.cs
```

Then we may run this program to get the date and time from a server.

```
>TCPClient
Server name, please: localhost
Received: 19 bytes:
05/12/2001 14:16:13

>
```

If there is no date-time service on your PC, you may try to reach a UNIX server. Later in this section, you will build such a server yourself.

3.6.3 Socket Programming

Socket is the lowest level of the network abstraction of .NET Framework. Its services are supported by class **System.Net.Sockets.Socket**. Socket also provides **Send()** and **Receive()** methods whereby data can be written to, and read from, the network.

The following program reads the data of the default Web page of a given server using **Socket** class. Its file name is **Socket.cs**.

```csharp
//Socket.cs:
using System;
using System.Net;
using System.Net.Sockets;
using System.IO;
using System.Text;

class MainApp {
    public static void Main() {
        // prompt for the server name
        Console.Write("Server name, please: ");
        String svrn = Console.ReadLine();

        // request for the default page
        String Get = String.Concat(
            "GET / HTTP/1.1\r\nHost: ",
            svrn,
            "\r\nConnection: Close\r\n\r\n"
        );
        // convert it into ascii
        Byte[] ByteGet = Encoding.ASCII.GetBytes(Get);
        // buffer for reading data
        Byte[] ByteRecv = new Byte[1024];

        // get the endpoint as a parameter to
        // create a new socket
        IPHostEntry a = Dns.Resolve(svrn);
```

```
IPEndPoint e = new ⇓
        IPEndPoint(a.AddressList[0], 80);

// string builder for hold data block
// whose size is unknown
StringBuilder b = new StringBuilder();

// create a new socket
Socket s = new Socket(
        /* AddressFamily.AfINet,
        SocketType.SockStream,
        ProtocolType.ProtTCP */
        AddressFamily.InterNetwork,
        SocketType.Stream,
        ProtocolType.Tcp
);

// connect to the server
try {
  s.Connect(e);
}
catch (SocketException ) {
        Console.WriteLine("Cannot connect to {0}",
                svrn);
        return;
}

// send the request
s.Send(ByteGet, ByteGet.Length, 0);

// read the data
int n = s.Receive(ByteRecv, ByteRecv.Length, 0);
b.Append(String.Concat(
        "Default HTML page on ",
        svrn,
        ":\n")
);
// append to the string
b.Append(
        Encoding.ASCII.GetString(ByteRecv, 0, n)
);

// keep reading when there is more data
while (n > 0) {
        n = s.Receive(
                ByteRecv,
                ByteRecv.Length,
                0
            );
        b.Append(
```

```
                    Encoding.ASCII.GetString(⇓
                        ByteRecv, 0, n)
                );
        }
        // present the default page
        Console.Write(b.ToString());
    }
}
```

The following command compiles this program:

```
csc /r:System.Net.dll;System.IO.dll Socket.cs
```

Then we may run this program. When you specify the name of an HTTP server at the prompt, you get the source of its home page.

3.6.4 TCPListener and Server Programming

At the socket level, class **System.Net.Sockets.TcpListener** is available for server programming. It may listen on a specific port and it provides the designated services when a connection request is accepted.

The following program provides data and time services using **TcpListener** class. Its file name is **Server13.cs**.

```
//Server13.cs:
using System;
using System.Net.Sockets;
using System.IO;
using System.Text;

class MainApp {
    public static void Main() {
        // a new listener on port 13
        TcpListener myListener = new TcpListener(13);

        // start listening
        myListener.Start();

        // keep working until you hit ^C
        while (true) {
            // wait until a connection request is
            // accepted
            Socket mySocket = ⇓
                myListener.AcceptSocket();

            // the data to be sent
            DateTime now = DateTime.Now;
            String strDateLine = String.Concat(
                now.ToShortDateString(),
                " ",
```

```
                        now.ToLongTimeString()
            );

            // log the event
            Console.WriteLine(String.Concat(
                strDateLine,
                ": request from ",
                mySocket.RemoteEndPoint)
            );

            // convert it into ascii
            Byte[] byteDateLine = ⇓
                Encoding.ASCII.GetBytes(
                    strDateLine.ToCharArray()
            );
            // send it
            mySocket.Send(
                byteDateLine,
                byteDateLine.Length,
                0
            );
        }
    }
}
```

The following command compiles this program:

```
csc /r:System.Net.dll;System.IO.dll Server13.cs
```

Now you may run the program to start your service. Then you may use the program **TCPClient** and access this service.

```
>TCPClient
Server name, please: localhost
Received: 19 bytes:
05/12/2001 14:16:13

>
```

At the server site, this activity is logged.

```
>Server13
05/12/2001 14:16:13: request from 127.0.0.1:1991
```

You may hit ^C to stop its service.

Summary

This chapter explored the programming environment of .NET Framework. In this environment, object-oriented programming capabilities, including inheritance and polymorphism, have broken the barriers between languages. That makes .NET Framework very desirable for the development of large-scale distributed systems and Web applications.

ASP.NET

*A*SP.NET is a Web development platform that provides the services developers need to build Web applications. While ASP.NET is
largely syntax-compatible with ASP, it provides a brand-new programming model and infrastructure that enables powerful applications. In short, it is more than a new version of its predecessor,
ASP.

In this chapter, we introduce ASP.NET and demonstrate its
benefits by comparing ASP.NET with ASP. Then we introduce the
new Web Forms programming model, as well as server controls
that are newly introduced in ASP.NET. Using a comprehensive
example for a complete Web site, we show you how to build and
deploy ASP.NET applications, as well as handle issues that affect
real-world Web applications, such as session state and security.
Finally, we take a quick look at the syntax of ASP.NET and the
migration path from ASP. In some areas, Microsoft did not make
ASP.NET backward compatible with ASP. However, this is not necessarily a bad thing.

Web Services is one of the most important concepts under
.NET. It provides programmable application logics with common
Web standards and protocols, such as HTTP and XML. ASP.NET
makes creating and exposing Web Services an easy job. We defer
the detailed discussion of Web Services to Chapter 6.

4.1 Overview

ASP.NET is compiled Common Language Runtime code running at the server side. It offers built-in language support for three .NET-compatible languages: C#, Visual Basic, and JScript. Furthermore, all of .NET Framework is available to any ASP.NET application. Developers can easily access the benefits of these technologies, which include not only a managed Common Language Runtime environment but also features like type safety and inheritance.

ASP.NET provides better performance than ASP because ASP.NET code is compiled instead of interpreted. ASP.NET not only takes advantage of performance enhancements found in .NET Framework and Common Language Runtime, it has also been designed to offer significant performance improvements over ASP and other Web-development platforms.

ASP.NET has been designed to work with WYSIWYG (What You See Is What You Get) HTML editors and other programming tools, such as Microsoft Visual Studio.NET (VS.NET). With built-in features such as drag-and-drop server controls and automatic deployment, VS.NET is a powerful development tool for Web applications and an excellent choice for professional developers.

The examples in this chapter help explain different aspects of programming ASP.NET. In order to run these example programs, you will need to have Internet Information Services (IIS) installed on your system. IIS comes with Windows 2000 Server by default. You can access the documentation on IIS through Internet Explorer via the URL *http://localhost*, which will redirect you to the starting IIS documentation page, as illustrated in Figure 4-1.

The management tool for IIS is the Internet Services Manager, which you can find under Administrative Tools in the Control Panel. Figure 4-2 shows the main window of the Internet Services Manager, where you can start or stop the default Web server for IIS. The default home directory for this Web server is *\Inetpub\wwwroot* on the drive where Windows is installed.

All the example programs for this chapter, including the comprehensive example, are in the chapter folder, *Chap4*. You can access Web pages stored at any location on your hard drive by creating a virtual directory. The easiest way to create a virtual directory is from Windows Explorer. Right-click over the desired directory, choose Sharing..., select the Web Sharing tab, click on the Add button, and enter the desired alias, which will be the name of the virtual directory. For example, Figure 4-3 illustrates creating an alias *Chap4*, or virtual directory, for the folder *C:\OI\Web\Chap4*. You should perform this operation now based on how the examples are installed on your own system.

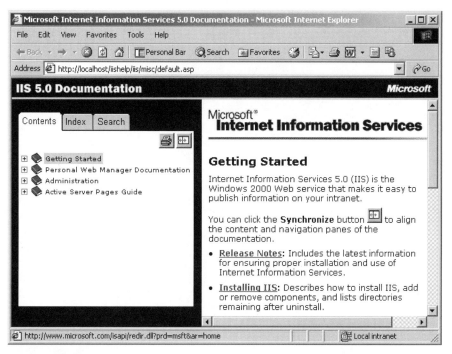

Figure 4-1   *IIS documentation.*

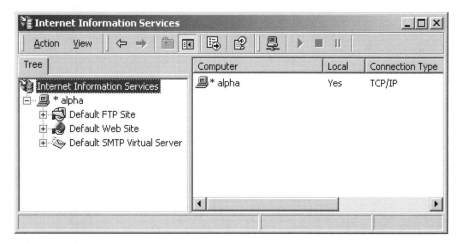

Figure 4-2   *Internet Services Manager.*

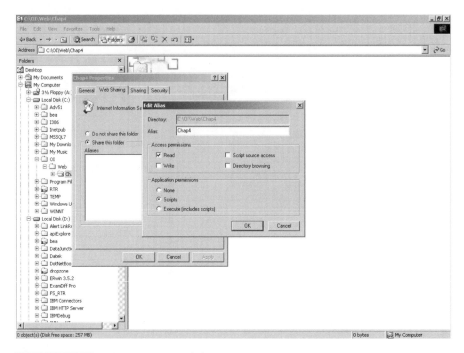

Figure 4-3   *Creating a virtual directory.*

4.2 Features of ASP.NET

Over the past few years, ASP has provided tremendous benefits to Microsoft Web developers, as a fast and efficient way to develop dynamic Web applications. When Microsoft rolled out the new .NET platform, it also upgraded ASP into a new version: ASP.NET.

One of the design goals for ASP.NET was to make the new platform backward compatible with previous versions of ASP. However, it became clear during development of the product that total backward compatibility would not be possible if ASP.NET was going to become a powerful, robust environment for next-generation Web application development. Therefore, a decision was made to relax the compatibility requirement in order to create a superior development and deployment environment.

Even though there are many differences between ASP and ASP.NET, developing new ASP.NET code does not break existing ASP applications, because ASP.NET uses the **.aspx** extension and provides syntax compatibility with existing ASP pages. The bottom line is that ASP and ASP.NET code can coexist even on the same IIS server instance. On the other hand, migrations from ASP to ASP.NET are trivial under most circumstances. We cover some migration details in Section 4.6.

4.2.1 Coding in ASP.NET versus ASP

In order to better understand the architectural differences between ASP and ASP.NET, let's look at a simple example, Echo Hello, and compare the old to the new way of developing the same functionality.

The functional requirement for our example is straightforward: Our Web page needs to take an input string, which is the name of a person, and echo back a greeting with this person's name. We can create the ASP application **Hello.asp** using either Visual InterDev 6.0 or a text editor. Here is the source code for this simple ASP application, which consists of some HTML along with dynamic script code written in VBScript.

```
<!-- Hello.asp -->
<%@ Language=VBScript %>
<HTML>
<HEAD>
<META NAME="GENERATOR" Content="Microsoft Visual Studio 6.0">
</HEAD>
<BODY>
<form action="Hello.asp" method="post">
<P>Your name: <INPUT id=text1 name=txtName></P>
<P><INPUT id=submit1 type=submit value=Echo name=submit1></P>
</form>
<%
If Len(Request.Form("txtName")) > 0 Then
Response.write "Hello, " & Request.Form("txtName")
End If
%>
</BODY>
</HTML>
```

The processes for deploying ASP and ASP.NET applications are identical. First, we need to make sure that the default Web server for IIS is started. Then, we can create a virtual directory that maps to the folder where the application is located. For example, if **Hello.asp** is located under C:\OI\Web\Chap4\Hello, we can create a virtual directory using Internet Services Manager and map a virtual directory name such as **SampleASP** to C:\OI\Web\Chap4\Hello. Finally, we can access our application via the URL *localhost/SampleASP/Hello.asp*. Figure 4-4 shows the greeting echoed when we type in a name and click on the Echo button.

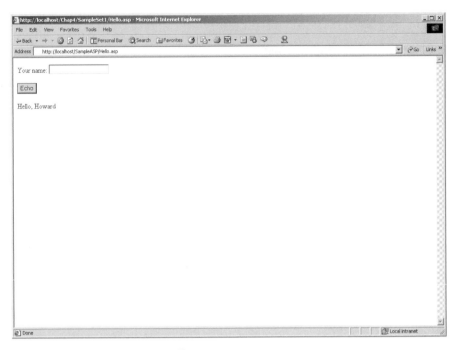

Figure 4-4   *Running the **Hello.asp** greeting program.*

We can implement the same functionality as that of **Hello.asp** using ASP.NET. The following is the code listing for **Hello.aspx**, which is the counterpart of Echo Hello under ASP.NET:

```
<!-- Hello.aspx -->
<%@ Page Language="C#" %>
<HTML>
<HEAD>
    <%-- Code %>
    <SCRIPT RUNAT="SERVER">
    protected void cmdEcho_Click(object Source, EventArgs e)
    {
        lblGreeting.Text="Hello, " + txtName.Text;
    }
    </SCRIPT>
</HEAD>
<BODY>
<%-- Content %>
<FORM RUNAT="SERVER"><b>Your name:</b> 
<asp:textbox id=txtName Runat="server"></asp:textbox>
<p><asp:button id=cmdEcho onclick=cmdEcho_Click Text="Echo"
```

```
runat="server" tooltip="Click to echo your name">
</asp:button></p>
<asp:label id=lblGreeting runat="server"></asp:label>
<P></P>
</FORM>
</BODY>
</HTML>
```

This code produces the same execution result shown in Figure 4-4. We make the text box prompt "Your name:" bold in this and subsequent versions of ASP.NET code to distinguish it from ASP. Even though this ASP.NET application seems awfully simple, it reveals a few key features of this new language that do not appear in ASP:

- *Compiled Code.* ASP.NET applications can be written in any .NET language that runs on top of the Common Language Runtime, including C#, VB.NET, and C++ with managed extensions. Because this code is compiled, it offers better performance than ASP pages with code written in an interpreted scripting language such as VBScript.

- *Server Controls.* ASP.NET provides a significant innovation known as server controls. These controls have special tags such as **<asp:textbox>** in **Hello.aspx**. Server-side code interacts with these controls, and the ASP.NET run time generates straight HTML that is sent to the Web browser. The result is a programming model that is easy to use, yet produces standard HTML that can run in any browser. We review various types of server controls, including Web Form controls, in Section 4.4.

- *Code and Content Separation.* ASP script code tends to intersperse with the content (HTML), as shown in sections surrounded by **<%** and **%>** in **Hello.asp**. Since designers of HTML content and developers of ASP script may not be the same group of people, it is desirable to separate the code and content in a meaningful way.

ASP.NET provides two ways to separate the code and content: The server code can be isolated within a single **<script runat="server"> ... </script>** block, or, even better, it can be placed within a code-behind page. We discuss code-behind pages later in this chapter. If you would like to see an example right away, you can examine the second ASP.NET sample program **HelloCodebehind.aspx**, with server code in the file **HelloCodebehind.aspx.cs**.

4.2.2 ASP.NET and Common Language Runtime

As mentioned in the previous section, ASP has been limited to interpreted, scripting languages such as VBScript and JScript. On the other hand, the .NET programming environment supports a variety of languages choices, including

VB.NET, C#, JScript, and even C++. All these languages are compiled and offer the potential for performance enhancement of ASP.NET applications.

Web application development can directly benefit from this multiple language support offered by .NET Common Language Runtime as well. Not only does ASP.NET provide more language choices for developers, and thus a further reach, it also allows a deeper level of integration. It is possible for Web applications that are based on ASP.NET to integrate with applications or components that are developed in any language supported by .NET. For example, we could have a C#-based Web page that references objects built in Visual Basic.NET.

Here is a sample ASP.NET Web application, Travel Destination, which is written in Visual Basic.NET and saved in a file named **exampleVB.aspx**. It is a simple Web page that provides a list of tourist destination options and prints the user's choice.

```
<!-- exampleVB.aspx -->
<%@ Page Language="VB" %>
<html>
<head>
<link rel="stylesheet"href="example.css">
</head>
<body>
<form action="exampleVB.aspx">
 <h3> Name: <input name="Name"      ⇓
 type=text value="<%=Request.QueryString("Name")%>"> ⇓
 Destination:
 <select name="Destination" size=1>
 <%
 Dim I As Integer
 Dim Values(4) As String
 Values(0) = "Destination"
 Values(1) = "Boston"
 Values(2) = "New York"
 Values(3) = "Orlando"
 Values(4) = "Seattle"

 For I = 0 To Values.Length - 1
 %>
 <% If (Request.QueryString("Destination") _  ⇓
  = Values(i)) %>
  <option selected>
 <% Else %>
  <option>
 <% End If %>
 <%=Values(i)%>
  </option>
  <% Next %>
  </select>
  </h3>
```

```
<input type=submit name="Lookup" value="Lookup">
<p>
 <% If ((Not Request.QueryString("Name") = Nothing) _ ⇓
    And(Not Request.QueryString("Destination") _ ⇓
    = "Destination")) %>

    <%=Request.QueryString("Name") %>,
    you chose to travel to
    <%=Request.QueryString("Destination") %>

 <% Else If ((Not Request.QueryString("Lookup") _⇓
    = Nothing) And _ ⇓
    (Request.QueryString("Name") = Nothing)) %>

    Please try again!

 <% Else If ((Not Request.QueryString("Lookup") _⇓
    = Nothing) And _ ⇓
    (Request.QueryString("Destination") _⇓
    = "Destination")) %>
    Please try again!
 <% End If %>
</form>
</body>
</html>
```

In this code, you probably noticed that an object **Request** is used. We discuss it in detail in Section 4.3.4. The following is a C# version of the same Web application, **exampleCS.aspx**, which produces the output shown in Figure 4-5.

```
<!-- exampleCS.aspx -->
<%@ Page Language="C#" %>
<html>
   <head>
      <link rel="stylesheet"href="example.css">
   </head>
   <body>
      <form action="exampleCS.aspx">
         <h3> Name: <input name="Name" ⇓
         type=text ⇓
         value="<%=Request.QueryString["Name"]%>">
         Destination:
         <select name="Destination" size=1>
      <%
        String [] values = { "Destination", "Boston", ⇓
       "New York", "Orlando", "Seattle" };
        for (int i=0; i<values.Length; i++) {
      %>
      <option <% if (Request.QueryString["Destination"] ⇓
```

```
== values[i]) { Response.Write("selected"); } %>>
  <%=values[i]%>
</option>
<% } %>
      </select>
      </h3>
      <input type=submit name="Lookup" value="Lookup">
      <p>
      <% if ((Request.QueryString["Name"] != null) ⇓
      && (Request.QueryString["Destination"] ⇓
      != "Destination")) { %>
        <%=Request.QueryString["Name"] %>, ⇓
       you chose to travel to ⇓
       <%=Request.QueryString["Destination"] %>
      <% } else if ((Request.QueryString["Lookup"] ⇓
      != null) ⇓
      && (Request.QueryString["Name"] == null)) { %>
        Please try again!
      <% } else if ((Request.QueryString["Lookup"] ⇓
      != null) ⇓
      && (Request.QueryString["Destination"] ⇓
      == "Destination")) { %>
        Please try again!
      <% } %>
    </form>
  </body>
</html>
```

4.2.3 Other ASP.NET Features

Although the World Wide Web is built on standards, the unfortunate fact of life is that browsers are not always compatible to one another and each could have special features. A Web page designer, then, has the unattractive options of either writing to a lowest common denominator of browser or writing special code for different browsers. Server controls help remove some of this pain. ASP.NET takes care of browser compatibility issues when it generates code for a server control. If the requesting browser is high-end, the generated HTML can take advantage of these features, otherwise the generated code will be vanilla HTML. In short, ASP.NET takes care of detecting the type of browser.

Compared to ASP, extending basic functionality of ASP.NET Web pages is much easier. In order to reference complex business logic from ASP, we need to build COM objects, which are challenging even for seasoned developers. On the other hand, creating a component for ASP.NET under the .NET platform does not require extra effort compared to normal programming. ASP.NET lets the Web application access component DLLs from its own **\bin**

Figure 4-5   *Output of both **exampleVB.aspx** and **exampleCS.aspx**.*

folder and it supports easy, side-by-side component installation. Section 4.5.1 offers an example of such component deployment, where we add references to two .NET DLLs for hotel and customer business modules. For those of you who have been through DLL hell, this is probably very refreshing.

Besides the facility provided by .NET and key features previously mentioned, ASP.NET itself provides a number of infrastructure services, including state management, security, configuration, caching, and tracing.

Session/state management is essential to every Web-based application. Since HTTP is a stateless protocol, if a user enters information in various controls on a form and sends this filled-out form to the server, the information will be lost if the form is displayed again, unless the Web application provides special code to preserve this state. ASP.NET makes this kind of state preservation totally transparent. There are also convenient facilities for managing other session states and application states.

We will cover the infrastructure services of ASP.NET, including examples of Web application configuration, in Section 4.5.

4.3 Web Forms

The ASP.NET Web Forms page framework is a scalable programming model that can be used on the server to dynamically generate Web pages. It allows the creation of dynamic, programmable Web pages as part of an overall Web application. The ASP.NET Web Forms framework simplifies and empowers the development of Web applications in the following ways:

- Enables a rich design-time experience. The Web Forms framework supports reusable User Interface controls that can encapsulate common functionality, thus reducing the amount of code that ASP.NET developers have to write. Furthermore, Visual Studio.NET provides a rapid application development (RAD) experience for creating and managing Web Forms.
- Allows complete separation of HTML markup from application logic so that "spaghetti" code can be avoided. The application logic, or code behind the page, is compiled and designed to provide much better performance.
- Provides an event-based programming model on the server similar to the forms-based development paradigm found in Microsoft Win32-based development tools such as the Visual Basic development platform.
- Supports a rich and highly functional set of server controls and .NET components that offer a consistent and type-safe object model. In addition, the framework naturally lends itself to extensibility through custom and third-party components.

ASP.NET Web Forms pages are text files with an **.aspx** file name extension. Any HTML page could be renamed to have this extension, making it accessible and with results identical to the original. Thus Web Forms are upwardly compatible with HTML pages.

4.3.1 Web Forms and Page Class

In a typical multitiered Web application, a Web Form itself resides in the presentation layer. A Web Form usually consists of two components:

- The visual content or presentation, typically specified by HTML elements
- Code that contains the application logic for interacting with the visual elements

It is the application logic code that makes a Web Form special. This code can either be in a separate file (having an extension corresponding to a .NET language, such as **.cs** for C# code), or else it can be in the **.aspx** file, within a **<script runat="server"> ... </script>** block. When your page is invoked on the Web server, the application logic code runs and dynamically generates the output for the page.

In order to better understand the architecture of a Web Form, let's take a look at the code behind version of our Echo Hello example. **HelloCodebehind.aspx** specifies the visual content of this example.

```
<!-- HelloCodebehind.aspx -->
<%@ Page Language="C#" Src="HelloCodebehind.aspx.cs"
Inherits= MyWebPage %>
<HTML>
  <HEAD>
  </HEAD>
<BODY>
<FORM RUNAT="SERVER"><b>Your name:</b> 
<asp:textbox id=txtName Runat="server"></asp:textbox>
<p><asp:button id=cmdEcho onclick=cmdEcho_Click Text="Echo"
runat="server" tooltip="Click to echo your name">
</asp:button></p>
   <asp:label id=lblGreeting runat="server"></asp:label>
<P></P>
</FORM>
</BODY>
</HTML>
```

The application logic code (written in C#) is in file **HelloCodebehind.aspx.cs**:

```
// HelloCodebehind.aspx.cs

using System;
using System.Web;
using System.Web.UI;
using System.Web.UI.WebControls;

public class MyWebPage : System.Web.UI.Page
{
   protected TextBox txtName;
   protected Button cmdEcho;
   protected Label lblGreeting;

   protected void cmdEcho_Click(object Source, EventArgs e)
   {
      lblGreeting.Text="Hello, " + txtName.Text;
   }
}
```

As you can see, our original ASP.NET code from **Hello.aspx** has been reorganized into two files. **HelloCodebehind.aspx.cs** contains a custom class that derives from the **System.Web.UI.Page** class. All namespaces related to Web Forms are under **System.Web**. Support for server controls such as text boxes and buttons is under the namespace **System.Web.UI. WebControls**.

The **MyWebPage** object, which we derive from the **Page** object, holds all server controls found on a requested page, including text boxes and buttons. When **HelloCodebehind.aspx** is requested, ASP.NET dynamically instantiates a class for this **.aspx** file, whether it contains .NET code or only HTML text. As a result, the **.aspx** page that contains a **MyWebPage** object is compiled as an executable and cached in server memory. This executable is also responsible for returning dynamically generated HTML back to the client.

The process described above is quite different from the ASP process, where HTML code is interleaved with VBScript or JScript code. In that case, the HTML response to the client is generated as the server interprets the ASP file and its included files (if any) line by line. (We examine the internal workflow for ASP.NET pages in the next section.)

As a result, our business logic, even though extremely simple, has been separated from the HTML presentation code. This allows further division of labor for some large software development organizations: HTML designers can dedicate their effort solely to the look and feel of the Web site, while application developers can focus on implementing business logic. Another benefit of this arrangement is that it allows third parties to develop their own HTML GUI designers to integrate with .NET, and these designers do not have to recognize specific .NET languages.

4.3.2 ASP.NET Page Processing

Processing a page is a cooperative endeavor between the Web server, the ASP.NET run time, and your own code. Under ASP.NET, a Web Forms page is processed by both browser client and server. The browser is responsible for presenting the form, and the server processes server controls and code behind. We cover some of the highlights of page processing, and you can consult the .NET Framework documentation for a complete description.

4.3.2.1 PAGE LIFE CYCLE

Under ASP.NET, for each action that requires processing, the form must be posted to the server, processed, and returned to the browser. This sequence is referred to as a round trip.

We can get an in-depth understanding of the Web Forms architecture by following the life cycle of our simple Echo Hello application. We will follow the code behind version, **HelloCodebehind.aspx**, for its complete life cycle. Here are the steps of the interaction:

1. User requests the **HelloCodebehind.aspx** Web page in the browser.

2. Web server compiles the page class from the **.aspx** file and executes it, creating HTML, which is sent to the browser. (In Internet Explorer you can see the HTML code from the menu View | Source, while in Netscape Navigator it is View | Page Source.) Note that the server controls are replaced by straight HTML.

```
<!-- HelloCodebehind.aspx -->

<HTML>
  <HEAD>
  </HEAD>
<BODY>
<form name="ctrl0" method="post"
action="HelloCodebehind.aspx" id="ctrl0">
<input type="hidden" name="__VIEWSTATE"
value="dDwxMzc4MDMwNTk1Ozs+" />
<b>Your name:<b>  <input name="txtName" type="text"
id="txtName" />
<p><input type="submit" name="cmdEcho" value="Echo"
id="cmdEcho" title="Click to echo your name" /></p>
    <span id="lblGreeting"></span>
<P></P>
</form>
</BODY>
</HTML>
```

3. The browser renders the HTML, displaying the simple form shown in Figure 4-6. This is the first time the form is displayed. The text box is empty and there is no greeting message displayed.

4. The user types in a name, such as Howard, and clicks the Echo button. The browser recognizes that the Submit button has been clicked. The method for the form is "post" and the action is **"HelloCodebehind.aspx"**. We thus have what is called a postback to the original **.aspx** file.

5. The server now performs processing for this page. This time an event was raised by the user clicking the Echo button, and an event handler in the **MyWebPage** class is invoked.

```
protected void cmdEcho_Click(object Source, EventArgs e)
{
    lblGreeting.Text="Hello, " + txtName.Text;
}
```

6. The server interacts with server controls using property notation. The **Text** property of the **TextBox** server control **txtName** is used to read the name submitted by the user. A greeting string is composed and assigned to the **Label** control **lblGreeting**, again using property notation.

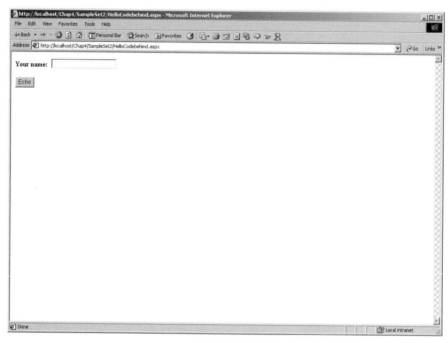

Figure 4-6   *The form for the Echo Hello application when displayed for the first time.*

7. The server again generates straight HTML for the server controls and sends the whole response to the browser. Here is the HTML:

```
...
<form name="ctrl0" method="post"
action="HelloCodebehind.aspx" id="ctrl0"><input
type="hidden" name="__VIEWSTATE"
value="dDwxMzc4MDMwNTk1O3Q8O2w8aTwyPjs+O2w8dDw7bDxpPDU+Oz47b
Dx0PHA8cDxsPFRleHQ7PjtsPEhlbGxvLCBIb3dhcmQ7Pj47Pjs7Pjs+Pjs+P
js+" />
<b>Your name:</b>  <input name="txtName" type="text"
value="Howard" id="txtName" /><p><input type="submit"
name="cmdEcho" value="Echo" id="cmdEcho" title="Click to
echo your name" /></p>
<span id="lblGreeting">Hello, Howard</span>
...
```

8. The browser renders the page and a greeting message is displayed, as shown in Figure 4-7. Meanwhile, the server can unload the **HelloCodebehind.aspx** page from the memory.

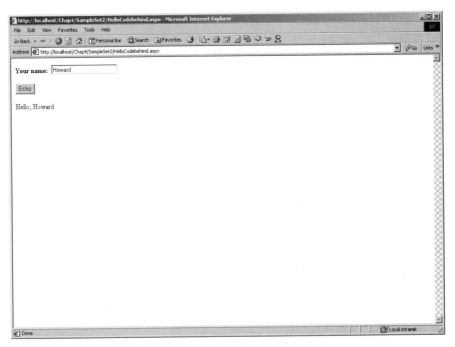

Figure 4-7   *A greeting message is displayed after an ASP.NET page round trip.*

There is one point worth noting in the page round trip, which is the concept of the page state. As we know that the HTTP protocol itself is stateless, the Web server intrinsically treats client requests from steps 1 and 4 as no different. However, the second client request is a postback that requires the pair to retain the information about prior client request(s) in order to proceed.

To solve this problem, ASP.NET uses a hidden control named ViewState to store information such as values in form fields and the state of user controls, which makes ASP.NET stateful. We discuss in detail how ASP.NET keeps track of session and state information in Section 4.5. The following are HTML code segments that show the content of ViewState in steps 2 and 7:

```
...
<input type="hidden" name="__VIEWSTATE"
value="dDwxMzc4MDMwNTk1Ozs+" />
...
```

```
...
<input type="hidden" name="__VIEWSTATE"
value="dDwxMzc4MDMwNTk1O3Q8O2w8aTwyPjs+O2w8dDw7bDxpPDU+Oz47b
Dx0PHA8cDxsPFRleHQ7PjtsPEhlbGxvLCBIb3dhcmQ7Pj47Pjs7Pjs+Pjs+P
js+" />
...
```

You may be wondering how to write code to process these bizarre strings of ViewState. Fortunately, neither the browser nor the user of the Web page has to deal with ViewState directly because the Web server handles the interpretation.

4.3.2.2 WEB FORMS EVENTS

At first glance, the event model for Web Forms appears to be quite similar to that of traditional client forms or client-based Web applications. The big difference is that most Web Forms events are raised on the client and get processed on the server, while in a client-based application, events are raised and handled on the client.

Fortunately, the Web Forms framework handles virtually all of the mechanics of capturing, transmitting, and interpreting the event, and hides the complexity from developers. Therefore, even though the underlying mechanism is somewhat different, we can still create event-handling methods in the same way we create them for traditional client forms.

There are a couple key aspects that are worth noting in the event model of Web Forms:

- *Intrinsic Event Set.* Since most of the real-world applications have much more complex user interfaces than Echo Hello, and round trips to the server are expensive, events do not automatically initiate a round trip to the server. Server controls provide what is known as an *intrinsic event set* of events that automatically cause a postback to the server. These intrinsic events usually are limited to click-type events, while events such as typing characters in a text box do not cause immediate postbacks to the server. Instead, these events are cached until the next postback event to the server.

- *Postback vs. Nonpostback.* By default, change events to server controls such as typing characters in a text box do not cause a postback to the server. However, you can specify that a change event cause an immediate form post by setting its **AutoPostBack** property to true. There is also an **IsPostBack** property in the **System.Web.UI.Page** class, which indicates whether the page is being loaded in response to a client postback, or being loaded and accessed for the first time.

A number of events could be raised on the server as part of the normal processing of a page. These events are actually defined in the **Control** base class (**System.Web.UI** namespace) and are available to server controls through inheritance:

- *DataBinding* occurs when the server control binds to a data source.
- *Disposed* occurs during the last stage of the server control life cycle of an ASP.NET page, when a server control is garbage collected.

- *Init* is the first step in the page's life cycle and occurs when the page is initialized. There is no view state information for any of the controls at this point.
- *Load* occurs when the controls are loaded into the page. View state information for the controls is now available.
- *PreRender* occurs just before the controls are rendered to the client. Normally this event is not handled by a page, but it is important for customizing your own server controls.
- *Unload* occurs when the controls are unloaded from the page. At this point it is too late to write your own data to the output stream.

Figure 4-8 shows the order of execution for these selected key events when they are raised by the page. Along with these events, Figure 4-8 also illustrates the most commonly used stages of page processing, when they occur, and what usually happens at each stage.

An example Web Forms page can help you gain some hands-on experience with the event model of Web Forms. We extend one of our earlier examples, Travel Destination, to handle various page events. The new example, **exampleEvents.aspx**, provides handlers for a number of page events, including **Page_Init** and **Page_Load**. In addition, we replace all straight HTML elements with their counterparts from ASP.NET server controls. Using the **Response** property, we can show the values for all server controls within the handlers of each event.

```
<!-- exampleEvents.aspx -->
<%@ Page Language="C#" Debug="true" %>
<HTML>
<HEAD>
 <SCRIPT RUNAT="SERVER">
public void Button1_ServerClick(object sender,
           System.EventArgs e)
{
  if ((TextBox1.Text.Length > 0)
    && (DropDownList1.SelectedItem.Text != "Destination"))
 greetingTxt.Text=TextBox1.Text
        + ", you chose to travel to "
        + DropDownList1.SelectedItem.Text;
  else
 greetingTxt.Text="Please try again!";
}

private void Page_Init(object sender, EventArgs e)
{
  Response.Write("Page_Init<br>");
  Response.Write("Name = " + TextBox1.Text + "<br>");
  Response.Write("Destination = " +
       DropDownList1.SelectedItem.Text + "<br>");
```

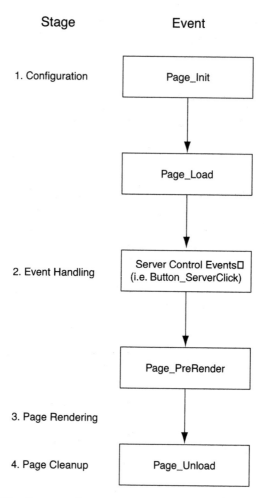

Stage	Event
1. Configuration	Page_Init
2. Event Handling	Server Control Events (i.e. Button_ServerClick)
3. Page Rendering	Page_PreRender
4. Page Cleanup	Page_Unload

Figure 4-8 *Stages and common events in processing an ASP.NET page.*

```
      Response.Write("greetingTxt = " + greetingTxt.Text
            + "<br><br>");
}

private void Page_Load(object sender, System.EventArgs e)
{
   // Put user code to initialize the page here
   Response.Write("Page_Load<br>");
   Response.Write("IsPostBack = " + IsPostBack + "<br>");
   Response.Write("Name = " + TextBox1.Text + "<br>");
   Response.Write("Destination = " +
         DropDownList1.SelectedItem.Text + "<br>");
   Response.Write("greetingTxt = " + greetingTxt.Text
         + "<br><br>");
}

private void Page_PreRender(object sender,
            System.EventArgs e)
{
   // Put user code to test the page here
   Response.Write("Page_PreRender<br>");
   Response.Write("Name = " + TextBox1.Text + "<br>");
   Response.Write("Destination = " +
   DropDownList1.SelectedItem.Text + "<br>");
   Response.Write("greetingTxt = " + greetingTxt.Text
         + "<br><br>");
}

private void Page_Unload(object sender, System.EventArgs e)
{
   // The page has finished rendering
   // and is ready to be discarded
   // Response.Write("Page_Unload<br>");
}

</SCRIPT>
</HEAD>
<BODY>
<FORM id="Form1" method="post" runat="server">
<P>
 
<asp:label id="Label1" runat="server" Font-Bold="True">
Name:</asp:label>
<asp:textbox id="TextBox1" runat="server"></asp:textbox>
<asp:label id="Label2" runat="server" Font-Bold="True">
Destination:</asp:label>
<asp:DropDownList id="DropDownList1" runat="server">
 <asp:ListItem ⇓
 Value="Destination">Destination</asp:ListItem>
```

```
    <asp:ListItem Value="Boston">Boston</asp:ListItem>
    <asp:ListItem Value="New York">New York</asp:ListItem>
    <asp:ListItem Value="Orlando">Orlando</asp:ListItem>
    <asp:ListItem Value="Seattle">Seattle</asp:ListItem>
</asp:DropDownList>
</P>
<P>
<asp:button id="Button1" text="Lookup"
onClick="Button1_ServerClick"
runat="server"/>
</P>
<P>
<asp:Label id="greetingTxt" runat="server"></asp:Label>
</P>
</FORM>
</BODY>
</HTML>
```

When we access the page for the first time, all controls are either empty or filled with a default value, which in the case of an HTML select list is **Destination**. **IsPostBack** is **false** as this page is retrieved for the first time.

Now we type in a name and select a non-default destination, such as Boston, then submit the form by clicking the Lookup button. The page is re-rendered with the following output from event handlers:

```
Page_Init
Name =
Destination = Destination
greetingTxt =

Page_Load
IsPostBack = True
Name = Howard
Destination = Boston
greetingTxt =

Page_PreRender
Name = Howard
Destination = Boston
greetingTxt = Howard, you chose to travel to Boston
```

Within **Page_Init**, none of the controls are populated because view state is not available at page initialization. During **Page_Load**, **Name** and **Destination** are populated as a result of user input, but **greetingTxt** is not, since the click event handler has not yet been invoked. **IsPostBack** is **true**. In **Page_PreRender**, all controls are populated.

Now enter a new name, Bob, and the destination New York and click Lookup again. Again, the controls have no data during **Page_Init**.

Page_Load provides a more interesting picture: **Name** and **Destination** are repopulated with new data, while the view state provides cached data for **greetingTxt**. Figure 4-9 shows the browser output after the Lookup button has been clicked a second time with new input data.

You may wonder what happens during the **Page_Unload** event. We actually provided some code for the **Page_Unload** event, but it is commented out. In **Page_Unload**, all HTML output has been streamed to the client; therefore the **Response** property is out of scope. The following is the exception if we try to use **Response** to print out information in **Page_Unload**:

```
[HttpException (0x80004005): Response is not available in this
context.]
    System.Web.UI.Page.get_Response() +63
...
```

Even though you cannot use the **Response** property of a Web page, the **Page_Unload** event is still important because you could use it to release expensive resources, including files and database connections, to help .NET garbage collection.

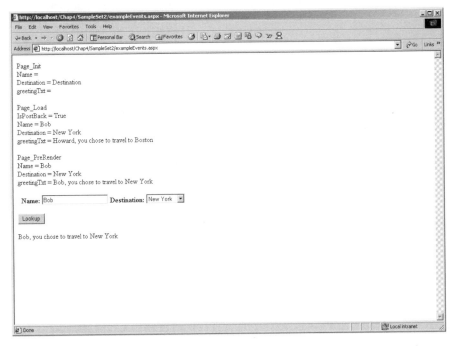

| **Figure 4-9** | *Browser output after Lookup has been clicked a second time and with new input data.* |

4.3.3 Page Directive and Tracing

An **.aspx** file may contain a page directive that defines various attributes, which control how ASP.NET processes the page. A page directive contains one or more attribute/value pairs of the form

```
attribute="value"
```

enclosed in

```
<@ Page ... @>
```

Our example program **HelloCodebehind.aspx** illustrates an **.aspx** page that does not have any code. A code-behind file, **HelloCodebehind.aspx.cs**, is specified using the **Src** attribute. Several other attributes are also illustrated.

```
<!-- HelloCodebehind.aspx -->
<%@ Page Language="C#" Src="HelloCodebehind.aspx.cs"
Inherits=MyWebPage %>
...
```

- *Src.* This attribute identifies the code-behind file.
- *Language.* This attribute specifies the language used for the page. The code in this language may either be in a code-behind file or in a SCRIPT block within the same file. Values can be any .NET-supported language, including C# and VB.NET.
- *Inherits.* This directive specifies the page class from which the **.aspx** page class will inherit.
- *Debug.* This attribute indicates whether the page should be compiled with debug information. If **true**, debug information is enabled and the browser can provide detailed information about compile errors. The default is **false**.
- *ErrorPage.* This attribute specifies a target URL to which the browser will be redirected in the event of an unhandled exception occurring on the page.
- *Trace.* This attribute indicates whether tracing is enabled. A value of **true** turns tracing on. The default is **false**.

ASP.NET provides extensive tracing capabilities. Merely setting the **Trace** attribute for a page to **true** will cause trace output generated by ASP.NET to be sent to the browser. In addition, you can output your own trace information using the **Write** method of the **TraceContext** object, which is obtained from the **Trace** property of the **Page**.

The page **HelloTrace.aspx** illustrates the use of tracing in place of writing to the **Response** object.

```
<!-- HelloTrace.aspx -->
<%@ Page Language="C#" Debug="true" Trace = "true" %>
<HTML>
<HEAD>
 <SCRIPT RUNAT="SERVER">
protected void cmdEcho_Click(object Source, EventArgs e)
{
   lblGreeting.Text="Hello, " + txtName.Text;
}
protected void Page_Init(Object sender, EventArgs E)
{
   Trace.Write("Page_Init<br>");
   Trace.Write("txtName = " + txtName.Text + "<br>");
   Trace.Write("lblGreeting = " + lblGreeting.Text +
               "<br>");
}
...
```

Figure 4-10 shows the browser output after a request for the page; you probably need to scroll down to see the complete page. Notice that the trace output is shown *after* the form, along with trace information that is generated by ASP.NET itself.

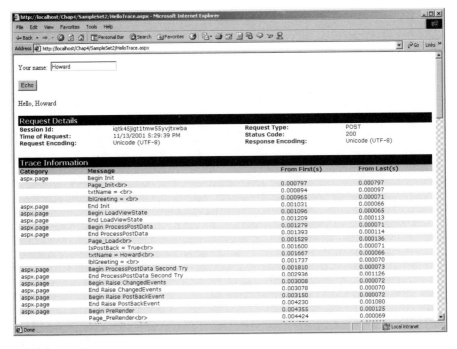

Figure 4-10   *Trace information shown as Web browser output.*

4.3.4 HttpRequest and HttpResponse Classes

The Web Forms architecture is built on top of a more fundamental processing architecture, which may be called request/response. Understanding request/response is important to your overall grasp of ASP.NET. In addition, there are certain programming situations where request/response is the natural approach.

4.3.4.1 HTTPREQUEST CLASS

The **HttpRequest** class is commonly used to read the various HTTP values that are sent by a client during a Web request. These HTTP values are what a classical CGI program uses to respond to a Web request and are the foundation upon which higher-level processing is built. Table 4-1 shows selected public instance properties of **HttpRequest**. **HttpRequest** is mapped to the **Request** property of the **Page** class.

Table 4-1   Public Instance Properties of **HttpRequest**

Property	Meaning
AcceptTypes	Gets a string array of client-supported MIME accept types.
ApplicationPath	Gets the ASP.NET application's virtual application root path on the server.
Browser	Gets information about the requesting client's browser capabilities.
ContentEncoding	Gets the character set of the entity-body.
ContentLength	Specifies the length, in bytes, of content sent by the client.
ContentType	Gets the MIME content type of the incoming request.
Cookies	Gets a collection of cookies sent by the client.
Form	Gets a collection of form variables.
Headers	Gets a collection of HTTP headers.
HttpMethod	Gets the HTTP data transfer method (such as GET, POST, or HEAD) used by the client.
InputStream	Gets the contents of the incoming HTTP entity body.
IsAuthenticated	Gets a value indicating whether the user has been authenticated.
Params	Gets a combined collection of QueryString, Form, ServerVariables, and Cookies items.
Path	Gets the virtual path of the current request.

Table 4-1	Public Instance Properties of *HttpRequest*, continued
Property	**Meaning**
PathInfo	Gets additional path information for a resource with a URL extension.
PhysicalApplicationPath	Gets the physical file system path of the currently executing server application's root directory.
PhysicalPath	Gets the physical file system path corresponding to the requested URL.
QueryString	Gets the collection of HTTP query string variables.
RequestType	Gets or sets the HTTP data transfer method (GET or POST) used by the client.
ServerVariables	Gets a collection of Web server variables.
TotalBytes	Gets the number of bytes in the current input stream.
Url	Gets information about the URL of the current request.
UrlReferrer	Gets information about the URL of the client's previous request that linked to the current URL.
UserAgent	Gets the raw user agent string of the client browser.
UserHostAddress	Gets the IP host address of the remote client.
UserHostName	Gets the DNS name of the remote client.
UserLanguages	Gets a sorted string array of client language preferences.

There are a number of useful collections that are exposed as properties of **HttpRequest** directly. The collections are of type **NamedValueCollection** (in **System.Collections.Specialized** namespace). For example, the following code extracts values for the QUERY_STRING and HTTP_USER_AGENT server variables using the **ServerVariables** collection.

```
string strQuery =
   Request.ServerVariables["QUERY_STRING"];
string strAgent =
   Request.ServerVariables["HTTP_USER_AGENT"];
```

A common task in many low-level Web programming techniques, such as Common Gateway Interface (CGI), is to extract information from controls on a form. In HTML, controls are identified by a **name** attribute, which can be used by the server to determine the corresponding value. The way form data is passed to the server depends on whether the form uses the HTTP GET method or the POST method.

With GET, the form data is encoded as part of the query string. The **QueryString** collection can then be used to retrieve the values. With POST, the form data is passed as content after the HTTP header. The **Form** collection can then be used to extract the control values. You could use the value of the REQUEST_METHOD server variable (GET or POST) to determine which collection to use.

The **HttpRequest** object is also available in ASP via the same method (the **Request** property), but ASP.NET made some changes in a few areas:

- **HttpRequest** now exposes more server variables directly as members of the **HttpRequest** object. For example, we can conveniently retrieve the HTTP_USER_AGENT string via the **UserAgent** property, instead of using the code listed above to extract values for the HTTP_USER_AGENT server variable.

- There is more than one way to access collections such as **QueryString** and **ServerVariables.** There is a new collection called **Params**, which is a combined collection of **ServerVariables**, **QueryString**, **Form**, and **Cookies**.

- A new **Browser** property is added to directly expose the **Browser Capabilities** component from ASP, which was stored in the BROWSCAP.INI file.

4.3.4.2 HTTPRESPONSE CLASS

The **HttpResponse** class encapsulates HTTP response information that is built as part of an ASP.NET operation. The Web Forms page framework uses this class when it is creating a response that includes writing server controls back to the client. Your own server code may also use the **Write** method of the **Response** object to write data to the output stream, which will be sent to the client. We have already seen many illustrations of **Response.Write** in several prior examples.

The **HttpResponse** class has another useful method, **Redirect**, which enables server code to redirect an HTTP request to a different URL. Redirecting without passing any data is simple—all you have to do is call the **Redirect** method and pass the URL. An example of such usage would be a reorganization of a Web site, where a certain page is no longer valid and the content has been moved to a new location. You can keep the old page live simply by redirecting traffic to the new location.

A more interesting case involves passing data to the new page. One way to pass data is to encode it in the query string while preserving HTTP conventions. The class **HttpUtility** provides a method **UrlEncode**, which will properly encode an individual item of a query string. You must then properly construct the new redirect URL by appending the original URL with the query string with a "?" and separating items (data in name-value pair format) of the query string with "&". An example of constructing such a redirect URL is given in Section 4.5.

4.3.4.3 REQUEST/RESPONSE PROGRAMMING IN ASP.NET

The best way to illustrate how request/response programming works in ASP.NET is through examples. A simple ASP.NET page, **Factorial.aspx**, displays the factorial for an input integer. The following is the code listing for **Factorial.aspx**, which contains mostly mathematical "magic":

```
<!-- Factorial.aspx -->
<%@ Page Language="C#" Trace="true"%>
<script runat="server">
protected void Page_Load(object sender, EventArgs e)
{
   string strQuery =
           Request.ServerVariables["QUERY_STRING"];
   Response.Write("QUERY_STRING = " + strQuery + "<br>");
   string strAgent = Request.UserAgent;
   Response.Write("HTTP_USER_AGENT = " + strAgent
                  + "<br>");
   int length = Request.ContentLength;
   Response.Write("ContentLength = " + length + "<br>");
   string strCount = Request.Params["txtCount"];
   int count = Convert.ToInt32(strCount);
   int fact = 1;
   for (int i = 1; i <=count; i++)
   {
      fact *= i;
   }
   Response.Write(fact + "<br>");

}
</script>
```

One page, called **GetFactorial.aspx**, submits the request using HTTP GET, while another page, named **PostFactorial.aspx**, submits a similar request using HTTP POST. The user interface is identical for both pages, as shown in Figure 4-11.

Here is the HTML for **GetFactorial.aspx**. Except for the **@Page** directive that turns tracing on, it is straightforward HTML. The code for **PostFactorial.aspx** is almost identical except for the form method, which is "post" instead.

```
<!-- GetFactorial.aspx -->
<%@ Page Trace = "false" %>
<html>
<head>
</head>
<body>
<P>This program will print factorial for an integer</P>
<form method="get" action = Factorial.aspx>
Input integer:
```

```
<INPUT type=text size=2 value=4 name=txtCount>
<P></P>
<INPUT type=submit value=Factorial name=cmdFactorial>
</form>
</body>
</html>
```

The **form** tag has attributes specifying the method (GET or POST) and the action that points to **Factorial.aspx**. You can launch **GetFactorial.aspx** and click on the Factorial button. You will then see some HTTP information printed by **Factorial.aspx**, followed by the factorial. When tracing is turned on (trace directive to be **true**), details about the request are displayed by ASP.NET. Figure 4-12 illustrates the output from this GET request.

You can see that form data is encoded in the query string, and the content length is 0. If you scroll down on the trace output, you will see a lot of information. For example, the master collection of **ServerVariables** is shown, which contains everything you need to know about the last GET request, using an input of 4.

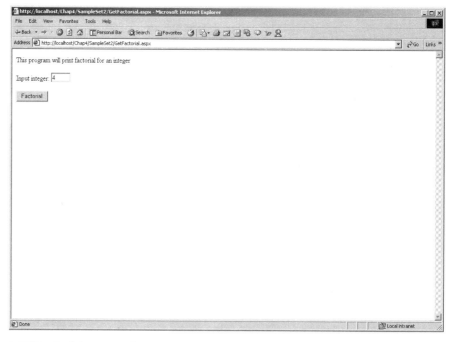

Figure 4-11 *Form for calculating the factorial for an integer.*

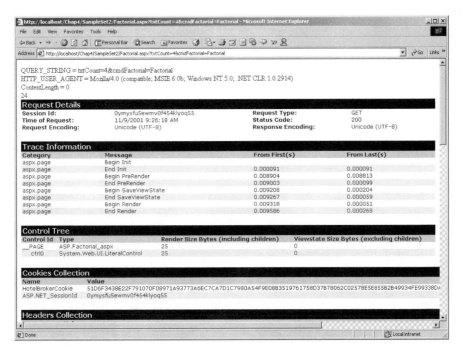

Figure 4-12   *Output from a GET request from **GetFactorial.aspx**.*

Then you can execute **PostFactorial.aspx** and click on the Factorial button. Everything should look similar to what was produced by **GetFactorial.aspx**. Figure 4-13 illustrates the output from this POST request, using an input of 5.

For the HTTP POST request, the query string is empty while the content length is 33. This is different from GET since a POST request transfers its query data via the HTTP request body. The form data is passed as part of the content, following the HTTP header information. If you scroll down on the trace output, you will see that there is a new collection named **Form**, which is used by ASP.NET to provide access to the form data in the case of a POST method.

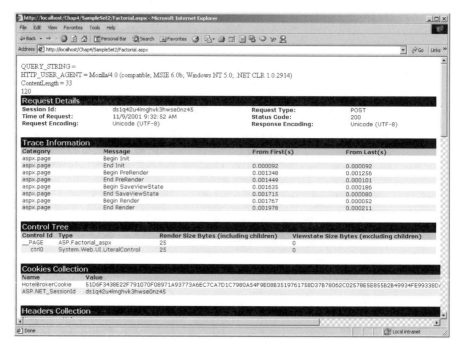

Figure 4-13   *Output from a POST request from **PostFactorial.aspx**.*

4.4 Server Controls

As we have seen in several previous examples, ASP.NET page developers can use ASP.NET server controls to program Web pages besides the **<% %>** code blocks. One of the most important innovations in ASP.NET is the concept of server controls. They provide an event-driven model that is startlingly similar to Windows GUI programming and encapsulates browser dependencies.

Another critical success factor for ASP.NET is the tight integration of server controls with Visual Studio.NET (VS.NET). Inside VS.NET, a Web developer can drag and drop any server controls that are available from ASP.NET or even third parties, and code a Web page just like a Visual Basic Windows Form. Microsoft certainly brings the WYSIWYG Web programming to a new height.

There are two broad categories of server controls under ASP.NET: HTML server controls, which are defined within the **System. Web.UI.HtmlControls** namespace, and Web controls, which are defined under the **System.Web.UI.WebControls** namespace. HTML server controls provide equivalent functionality to standard HTML controls, with server-based processing. We cover these controls in Section 4.4.1.

There are four key groups of server controls available under the category of ASP.NET Web controls:

- *ASP.NET Validation Controls.* These controls automatically create client-side script so browsers can perform validation on the user's machine before a postback, allowing for much more interactive and user-friendly pages. They can also work on the server as a fallback mechanism. We look at these controls in Section 4.4.2.
- *ASP.NET Web Form Controls.* Web Form controls provide equivalent functionality to normal HTML form elements, such as a text box and a submit button, *and* other HTML tags, such as hyperlinks. Even though Web Form controls seem redundant to existing HTML server controls, .NET Framework creates these new controls to support a consistent object model with standard sets of properties, which provide a better design time experience with VS.NET. We discuss these controls in Section 4.4.3.
- *ASP.NET Rich Controls.* Rich controls are relatively elaborate and were created for special purposes, such as the Calendar and Ad Rotator. We briefly go over an example of rich controls in Section 4.4.4.
- *ASP.NET List Controls.* List controls are provided to build lists, either data bound or not. As it might be easier for you to grasp the concept of a list after we introduce ADO.NET, we discuss examples of list controls in the final case study in Section 11.4 of Chapter 11.

4.4.1 HTML Controls

HTML server controls provide equivalent functionality to standard HTML controls, except that they run on the server. In fact, the only way to distinguish an HTML server control from an ordinary HTML control on a Web page is the presence of the **runat="server"** attribute.

Here are two HTML controls and both are INPUT controls. The second control is of type **password**. The first control is a server control.

```
<INPUT id=txtUserId

style="WIDTH: 135px; HEIGHT: 22px" type=text size=17
runat="server"></P>

<INPUT id=""

style="WIDTH: 138px; HEIGHT: 22px" type=password size=17
name=txtPassword>
```

You work with HTML server controls in a manner similar to the Web Forms server controls we've used already. In the server-side code you access the control through a control variable that has the same name as the **id** attribute. However, since we are dealing with HTML controls, there are some differences. For example, you access the string value of the control not through the **Text** property but through the **Value** property. Here is some code that uses the value entered by the user for the **txtUserId** control.

```
lblMessage.Text = "Welcome, " + txtUserId.Value;
```

The advantage of HTML controls for the experienced Web programmer is that they match HTML controls closely, so that their knowledge of the details of HTML control properties and behavior carries over to the ASP.NET world. However, this is also the disadvantage for HTML controls, as they carry over all the quirks and inconsistencies of HTML. For example, rather than have two different controls for the somewhat different behaviors of a text box and a password control, HTML uses the INPUT control in both cases, distinguishing between the two with the **type=password** attribute. Web controls, in contrast, are freshly designed with an internal consistency. Besides, as we will see in Sections 4.4.2 through 4.4.4, there is a much greater variety to Web controls.

4.4.1.1 CREATING AN ASP.NET WEB APPLICATION USING VS.NET

If you have not tried out VS.NET by now, it is probably a good idea to read Appendix E now. As we mentioned before, VS.NET is a powerful development tool for Web applications. For ASP.NET development, it combines WYSIWYG HTML editing, drag-and-drop server controls, easy debugging, and automatic deployment. You can certainly write ASP.NET code using a regular text editor, as we have done so far, but it is easier to program server controls with VS.NET. Here are the steps for creating an ASP.NET Web application under VS.NET:

1. In Visual Studio select the menu File | New | Project...

2. In the New Project dialog box choose "Visual C# Projects" as the project type and "ASP.NET Web Application" as the template.

3. Enter "MyServerControls" as the name of your project. For the location enter an HTTP path to a folder on your server machine. The default will be the IIS home directory \Inetpub\wwwroot. If you have made C:\OI\Web\Chap4 into a virtual directory with alias Chap4, you can enter the path *localhost/Chap4/MyServerControls*, as illustrated in Figure 4-14. In this way you create a brand new directory and avoid overwriting any existing code directories.

4. Click OK. The project files will then be created in C:\OI\Web\ Chap4\MyServerControls. The corresponding VS.NET solution **MyServerControls.sln** will be created under My Documents\Visual Studio Projects\MyServerControls.

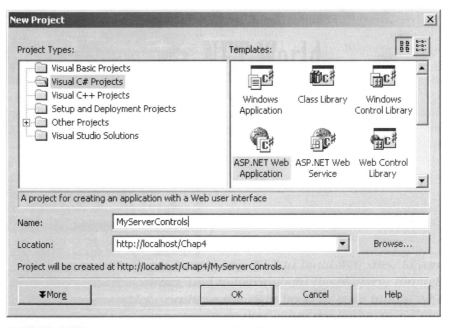

Creating a Visual Studio ASP.NET Web application project.

At this point, you should have a blank yet complete ASP.NET project automatically generated for you, as shown in Figure 4-15. There are several pregenerated files in the new project, including **global.asax**, **web.config**, and **WebForm1.aspx**. We start with the last, **WebForm1.aspx**.

WebForm1.aspx is a default Web Form for any new ASP.NET project under VS.NET, and it adopts the code-behind style by default. You may want to rename it (**WebForm1** really does not sound very informative) and replace or augment it with your own code. For example, we can swap in the code for **HelloCodebehind.aspx**, set it as start page, and execute the ASP.NET application with no problem. The only difference is that this Web page can be launched from VS.NET as well.

4.4.1.2 HTML CONTROLS IN VISUAL STUDIO

It is easy to work with HTML controls in Visual Studio.NET. When we have an ASP.NET project such as **MyServerControls.sln** open in VS.NET, the Toolbox of VS.NET shows a palette of HTML controls. You can access these HTML controls through the HTML tab under the Toolbox window. Figure 4-16 shows some of the HTML controls in the Visual Studio Toolbox.

You can drag HTML controls as well as Web controls onto a form. You have the option of using **FlowLayout** or **GridLayout**. The default is

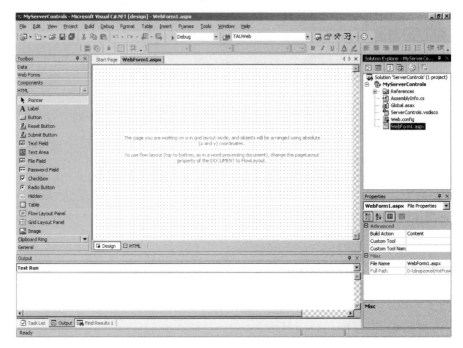

Figure 4-15   *A newly created ASP.NET project under Visual Studio.NET.*

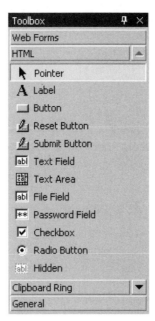

Figure 4-16   *HTML controls in the Visual Studio Toolbox.*

GridLayout, which enables absolute positioning of controls on a form. **FlowLayout** is the simplest layout, resulting in elements positioned in a linear fashion. You can set the layout mode through the **pageLayout** property of the form. In our example in Section 4.4.1.3 we use **FlowLayout** for the two INPUT controls and their associated labels.

The default choice for HTML controls is not to run at the server. To make an HTML control into a server control, right-click on it in the Form Designer. Clicking on "Run As Server Control" toggles back and forth between running on the server and not running on the server. You can inspect the **runat** property in the Properties panel, but you cannot change it there.

4.4.1.3 EXAMPLE OF HTML CONTROLS

Let's look at an example of HTML controls. If you have made C:\OI\Web\Chap4\ServerControls into a virtual directory with alias ServerControls under another virtual directory of Chap4, you can enter the path *localhost/Chap4/ServerControls/WebForm1.aspx* for all of the server control examples in Section 4.4, including the example of HTML controls. **WebForm1.aspx** provides a choice of four:

- HTML Controls (one link in this set)
- Validations (six links in this set)
- Web Form Controls (one link in this set)
- Rich and List Controls (one link in this set)

Follow the link to HTML controls and you will come to a page called **Login.aspx**, illustrated in Figure 4-17.

There is a text box for entering a user ID and a password control for entering a password. Both of these controls are HTML INPUT controls, as shown previously. The text box runs at the server, and the password control is an ordinary HTML control. Clicking the Login button (implemented as a Windows Forms **Button** control) results in very simple action. There is one legal password, which is hardcoded as "77." The button event handler checks for this password. If the password is legal, it displays a welcome message; otherwise it displays an error message.

```
private void Login_Click(object sender, EventArgs e)
{
   if (Request.Params["txtPassword"] == "77")
      lblMessage.Text = "Welcome, " + txtUserId.Value;
   else
      lblMessage.Text = "Illegal password";
}
```

Since the password control is *not* a server control, there is no server control variable available for accessing the value. Instead, we must rely on more fundamental techniques, such as using the **Params** collection.

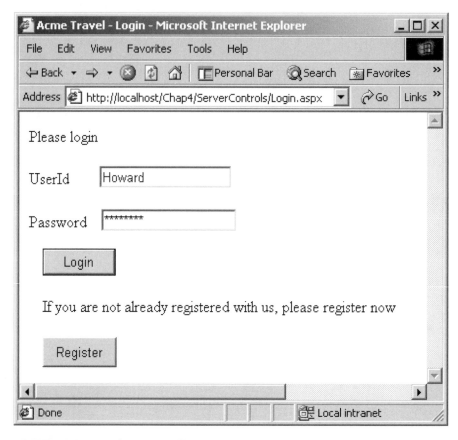

Figure 4-17   *A login page illustrating HTML server controls.*

4.4.2 Validation Controls

In theory, for the rest of Section 4.4, all of the server controls that we talk about belong to Web controls (a.k.a. Web Forms controls), which are under the **System.Web.UI.WebControls** namespace. However, in practical sense, because these server controls belong to several groups that provide distinctive sets of functionality, we discuss them separately in groups.

A very convenient category of control is the group of validation controls. One of the most common tasks for Web page development is to validate input values that the user supplies. With validation controls, you can associate one or more of them with a server control whose input you want to validate. The following validation controls are available in ASP.NET:

- **RequiredFieldValidator**
- **RegularExpressionValidator**
- **RangeValidator**

- **CompareValidator**
- **CustomValidator**

There is also a **ValidationSummaryControl** that can provide a summary of all the validation results in one place.

Validation controls are very flexible. An interesting feature of validation controls is that they can run on either the client or the server, depending on the capabilities of the browser. On the client side, these controls can automatically create client-side script, such as JavaScript, for browsers[1] to perform validation on the user's machine before a postback. This allows for much more interactive and user-friendly pages. If the browser does not support client-side validation, the validation will be done only on the server.

A validation control itself can display an error message if the validation is not passed. Alternatively, you can check the **IsValid** property of the validation control. If none of standard validation controls does the job for you, you can even implement a custom validation control.

4.4.2.1 REQUIRED FIELD VALIDATION

A very simple and useful kind of validation is to check whether the user has entered information in required fields. Our page for the **Required-FieldValidator** server control example provides such an illustration. Starting from the **ServerControls\WebForm1.aspx** page and following the link for "ValidationRequired," you come to **validationRequired.aspx**. The screen-shot in Figure 4-18 shows the result of entering an employee ID, password, and first name, but leaving the Last Name text box blank. When you click the Submit button, you will see a red error message next to the Last Name text box.

The First Name and Last Name text boxes each have an associated **RequiredFieldValidator** control. **ControlToValidate** must be set to the ID of the control that is to be validated and **ErrorMessage** must be specified. When you submit the form, the validator control will check whether information has been entered in its associated control. If not, the specified error message will be displayed. Here is the section of **validationRequired.aspx** that implements this:

```
...
<tr>
<td class="smallFieldBold" nowrap>
 First Name:
</td>
<td>
 <input type="text" id="firstName" runat="server">
</td>
```

---

[1] Right now, only Internet Explorer versions 5 and up are supported. Other browser support may be available in the future.

```
<td>
 <asp:requiredfieldvalidator controltovalidate="firstName"
 errormessage="First Name is required."
 runat="server">First Name is required.
 </asp:requiredfieldvalidator>
</td>
</tr>
<tr>
<td class="smallFieldBold" nowrap>
 Last Name:
</td>
<td>
 <input type="text" id="lastName" runat="server">
</td>
<td>
 <asp:requiredfieldvalidator controltovalidate="lastName"
 errormessage="Last Name is required." runat="server">Last
 Name is required.
 </asp:requiredfieldvalidator>
</td>
</tr>
 . . .
```

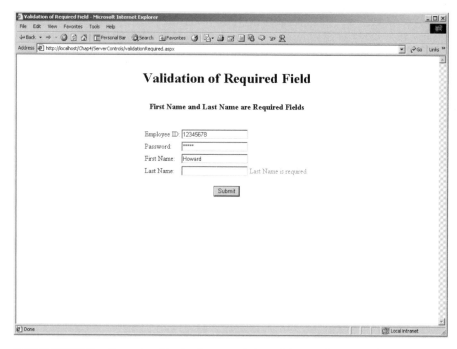

Figure 4-18   *Example of ASP.NET controls for validation of required field(s).*

Internet Explorer supports client-side validation using JavaScript. You can verify that ASP.NET generates suitable JavaScript by looking at the generated source code in the browser (View | Source).

4.4.2.2 REGULAR EXPRESSION VALIDATION

The **RegularExpressionValidator** control provides a very flexible mechanism for validating string input. It checks whether the string is a legal match against a designated regular expression. Following the link for "ValidationExpressed" (**validationExpressed.aspx**), you will find our example illustrating regular expression validations for the Employee ID and Password fields. The requirements are that the employee ID consist only of letters and digits, which can be specified by the regular expression **[A-Za-z0-9]+**, while the password can contain the symbols **@#$%** besides letters and digits.

The following properties should normally be assigned for a **RegularExpressionValidator** control:

* **ValidationExpression** (the regular expression, not surrounded by quotes)
* **ControlToValidate**
* **ErrorMessage**

You can try this validation out on page **validationExpressed.aspx** by entering a string for Employee ID that contains a nonalphanumeric character, as shown in Figure 4-19.

4.4.2.3 OTHER VALIDATION CONTROLS

RangeValidator and **CompareValidator** are two other built-in validators from ASP.NET, which are similar to **RequiredFieldValidator** and **RegularExpressionValidator**. You can follow the links to both examples from the **ServerControls\WebForm1.aspx** page. The following code segment shows how age verification is done on **validationRange.aspx**:

```
...
<tr>
<td class="smallFieldBold" noWrap>
Age
</td>
<td>
<asp:textbox id="age" runat="server"></asp:textbox>
</td>
<td>
<font color="red">
 <asp:rangevalidator id="rangeAge" runat="server"
 MinimumValue="11" MaximumValue="99"
 ControlToValidate="age" Type="Integer"
 ErrorMessage="Minimum is 11 and Maximum is 99.">
```

```
</asp:rangevalidator>
<asp:label id="msgAge" runat="server"></asp:label>
</font>
</td>
</tr>
...
```

CustomValidator is very practical when validation is too complex for any of the standard methods. The screenshot of **validationCustom.aspx**, illustrated in Figure 4-20, shows the result of entering an integer in the **ServerValidate** and **ClientValidate** text boxes. When you click the Submit button, you will see a red error message displayed next to the corresponding text box(es) if the input integer is not an even number.

ControlToValidate must be set to the Web Forms control ID for the control that is to be validated. When validation is done on the server, **OnServerValidate** must be set to the function **ServerValidation** to check whether the number is an even integer. Accordingly, when validation is done on the client, **ClientValidationFunction** must be set to the function **ClientValidation** as well. The following code segment shows a

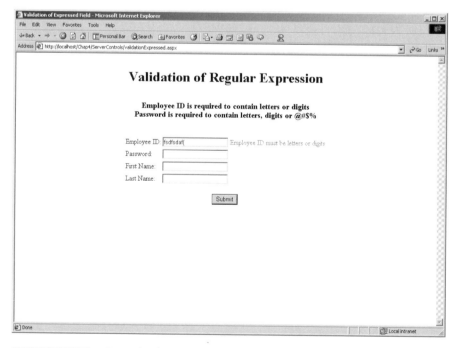

Figure 4-19   *Example of ASP.NET controls for validation of regular expressions.*

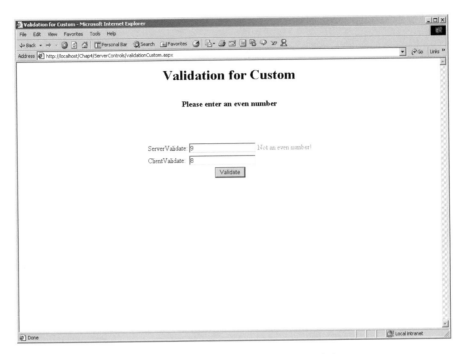

Figure 4-20   *Example of ASP.NET controls for custom validation.*

CustomValidator control on **validationCustom.aspx**, as well as the
server validation function from **validationCustom.aspx.cs**:

```
<asp:CustomValidator id="CustomValidator1"
runat="server" ControlToValidate="Text1"
OnServerValidate="ServerValidation" Display="Static"
ForeColor="red" ErrorMessage="Not an even number!" />


protected void ServerValidation (object source,
ServerValidateEventArgs args)
{
  try
  {
     int i = int.Parse(args.Value);
     args.IsValid = ((i%2) == 0);
  }
  catch
  {
     args.IsValid = false;
  }
}
```

4.4.3 Web Form Controls

When we talk about Web *Form* controls (instead of Web *Forms* controls), we are referring to a group of server controls that have HTML **<form>** counterparts. As we mentioned briefly in Section 4.4.1, ASP.NET not only provides a set of HTML server controls that just mirror the standard HTML controls, such as **<INPUT>**, it also creates a set of new controls:

- All Web Form controls adhere to an abstract and strongly typed object model, while standard HTML controls do not. Web Form controls are more abstract than HTML server controls, in that their object model does not necessarily reflect HTML syntax. This can make programming Web pages more predictable even without extensive HTML background.
- Every Web Form control has a uniform and structured interface so that third-party vendors for Integrated Development Environment (IDE) can easily build tools to take advantage of these new controls. All Web Form controls belong to **System.Web.UI.WebControls** namespace. Table 4-2 provides a partial list of all key Web Form controls under ASP.NET.

Table 4-2	*Mappings for Key Web Form Controls and Their HTML Counterparts*
Web Form Control	**HTML Tags**
`<ASP:Button>`	`<input type = "button">`
`<ASP:HyperLink>`	`<a>`
`<ASP:TextBox>`	`<input type = "text">, <input type = "password"> or <textarea>`
`<ASP:Label>`	`<span>`
`<ASP:Panel>`	`<div>  <ASP:Image> <img>`
`<ASP:CheckBox>`	`<input type = "checkbox">`
`<ASP:ImageButton>`	`<input type = "image">`
`<ASP:RadioButton>`	`<input type = "radio">`
`<ASP:Table>`	`<table>`
`<ASP:TableRow>`	`<tr>`
`<ASP:TableCell>`	`<td>`
`<ASP:DropDownList>`	`<select>`

All ASP.NET server controls, including Web Form controls, are declared within the tags that contain a **runat="server"** attribute/value pair, such as **<form runat="server">**, **<asp:TextBox runat="server">**,

<asp:DropdownList runat="server">, **<asp:CheckboxList runat="server">**, and **<asp:RadioButton runat="server">**. These server controls keep the client-side data in the hidden form field between round trips to the server. There are no client-side scripts needed for the client.

When you have an ASP.NET project open under VS.NET, its Toolbox shows a palette of Web Form controls, similar to that of HTML controls. You can access these Web Form controls through the Web Forms tab under the Toolbox window. In order to try our example for Web Form controls, you can follow the "Web Controls" link on the **ServerControls\WebForm1.aspx** page to **webFormControl.aspx**.

Operations for **webFormControl.aspx** are fairly straightforward: After you enter your name, destination, ticket class, and preferred menu, click the Submit button. The confirmation message will display at the bottom of the page. When you click the Reset button, the Web page will be reset to the default. Figure 4-21 shows the scenario for the user who chooses to travel to Chicago, with an economy-class ticket and a meal preference of chicken.

In this example, we used a few Web Form controls: **name** as **asp:textbox**; **destination** as **asp:dropdownlist**, where the travel destination is selected; **Radio1** through **Radio3** (**asp:RadioButton**) in **ticketClassGroup**

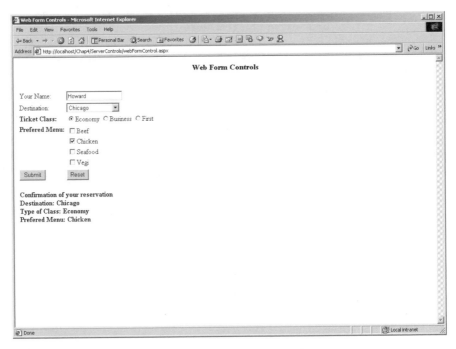

Figure 4-21   *Example of ASP.NET Web Form controls.*

for picking the ticket class; **menu** (**asp:CheckBoxList**) for choosing the meal preference; and **submit** and **reset** buttons (**asp:button**) for form submission. The following code segments from **webFormControl.aspx.cs** show the actions behind these two submission buttons and corresponding processing for various Web Form controls involved.

```
using System;
using System.Collections;
using System.ComponentModel;
using System.Data;
using System.Drawing;
using System.Web;
using System.Web.SessionState;
using System.Web.UI;
using System.Web.UI.WebControls;
using System.Web.UI.HtmlControls;

namespace ServerControls
{
 /// <summary>
 /// Summary description for webFormControl.
 /// </summary>
 public class webFormControl : System.Web.UI.Page
 {
    protected System.Web.UI.WebControls.TextBox name;
    protected System.Web.UI.WebControls.RadioButton ⇓
                                    Radio1;
    protected System.Web.UI.WebControls.RadioButton ⇓
                                    Radio2;
    protected System.Web.UI.WebControls.RadioButton ⇓
                                    Radio3;
    protected System.Web.UI.WebControls.Label msgDropdown;
    protected System.Web.UI.WebControls.Label msg;
    protected System.Web.UI.WebControls.CheckBoxList menu;
    protected System.Web.UI.WebControls.DropDownList ⇓
                                    destination;
    protected System.Web.UI.WebControls.Button submit;
    protected System.Web.UI.WebControls.Button reset;
    protected System.Web.UI.WebControls.Label msgCheckbox;

    ...
    protected void SubmitBtn_Click(Object Sender,
                            EventArgs e)
    {
       if (Radio1.Checked)
       {
```

```
        msg.Text = "<BR>Type of Class: " + Radio1.Text;
    }
    else if (Radio2.Checked)
    {
        msg.Text = "<BR>Type of Class: " + Radio2.Text;
    }
    else if (Radio3.Checked)
    {
        msg.Text = "<BR>Type of Class: " + Radio3.Text;
    }
    string s = "<br>Preferred Menu: ";
    for (int i=0; i < menu.Items.Count; i++)
    {
        if ( menu.Items[ i ].Selected )
        {
            s = s + menu.Items[i].Text;
            if (i < menu.Items.Count -2)
            {
                s = s + " ";
            }
        }
    }
    msgCheckbox.Text = s;
    string msg3 = "<br>Confirmation of your
        reservation" + "<br>Destination: " ;
    for(int j=0; j < destination.Items.Count; j++)
    {
        if(destination.Items[j].Selected == true)
        {
            msg3 += destination.Items[j].Text;
        }
    }
    msgDropdown.Text = msg3;
}

protected void ResetBtn_Click(Object Sender,
                              EventArgs e)
{
    name.Text = "";
    msg.Text = "";
    msgCheckbox.Text = "";
    msgDropdown.Text = "";
    for(int k=0; k < menu.Items.Count; k++)
    {
        menu.Items[k].Selected = false;
    }
    destination.Items[0].Selected = true;
```

```
        for(int m=1; m < destination.Items.Count; m++)
        {
            destination.Items[m].Selected = false;
        }
        Radio1.Checked = true;
        Radio2.Checked = false;
        Radio3.Checked = false;
    }
    ...
    }
}
```

4.4.4 Rich Controls

Rich controls, which can have quite elaborate functionality, are another category of Web Forms controls. The Calendar control, for example, provides an
easy-to-use mechanism for entering dates on a Web page. Follow the
"Calendar" link on the **ServerControls\WebForm1.aspx** page to see our
sample server control page, as shown in Figure 4-22.

    On this page the user can select a date on the Calendar control. The
SelectedDate property then contains the selected date, as an instance of the
DateTime structure. You can work with this date by handling the
SelectionChanged event. In our example page, the event handler displays
the date as a string in a text box.

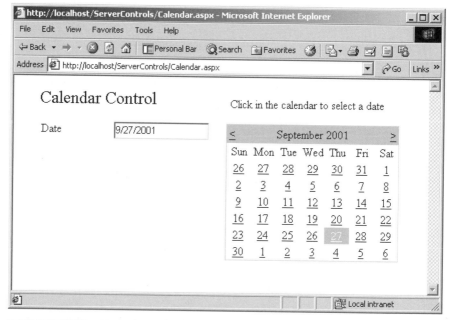

Figure 4-22   *Using the Calendar control to select a date.*

```
private void Calendar1_SelectionChanged(object sender,
                                        System.EventArgs e)
{
   txtDate.Text =
      Calendar1.SelectedDate.ToShortDateString();
}
```

4.5 ASP.NET Web Applications

We have examined the fundamentals of ASP.NET and created some simple ASP.NET pages. In this section, we demonstrate how to use VS.NET to create more comprehensive Web applications.

Everything we do in this section could also be accomplished using only the .NET Framework SDK and regular text editors, but our work becomes much easier when using VS.NET. Forms Designer of VS.NET makes it an easy job to create Web Forms by dragging controls from a palette. We can add event handlers for controls in a manner very similar to the way event handlers are added in Windows Forms. In fact, the whole Web application development process takes on much of the rapid application development (RAD) characteristics typical of Visual Basic.

In Section 4.5.1, we go over a comprehensive Web site example that models business activities for a member of a travel agency union. The travel agency union (TAU) is a federation of travel agencies in which each member shares some common services. In our comprehensive case study in Chapter 11, we go over how to implement and integrate all these common services using .NET. Right now, we focus on building one union member's Web site using ASP.NET; we refer to this member as TAUM for simplicity.

In our example, the union member's Web site provides hotel reservation services for its customers and allows them to reserve hotel rooms in advance. In Sections 4.5.2 through 4.5.4, we elaborate on specific features of ASP.NET Web applications, such as configuration, session, and state, using code from the TAUM Web site as examples.

4.5.1 Building the TAUM Web Site Using Visual Studio.NET

To illustrate the detailed steps for building ASP.NET applications using VS.NET, we divide the coding tasks for the TAUM Web site into three major steps. First, we configure the VS.NET and IIS environment to accommodate the TAUM Web site. Meanwhile, we build a couple of supporting libraries to supply the back end for this site. Second, as version 1 of the TAUM Web site, we build a two-page Web site that provides a hotel reservation framework.

Finally, we showcase a full-blown implementation of the TAUM Web site (version 2) for hotel reservations.

4.5.1.1 CONFIGURING THE TAUM WEB SITE

Before getting started you may wish to check, and possibly change, your VS.NET Web server connection setting. The two options are File share and FrontPage. If you are doing all your development on a local computer, you might find File share faster and more convenient. To access this setting, select the menu Tools | Options..., then choose Web Settings under Projects. You can set the Preferred Access Method by using a radio button, as illustrated in Figure 4-23.

4.5.1.2 BUILDING SUPPORTING LIBRARIES

The core of the TAUM Web site consists of two ASP.NET Web pages. The first Web page allows the user to see a list of hotel choices grouped by their locations; the user can submit reservation preferences, including check-in time and length of stay. The second Web page allows the user to list or cancel his or her existing reservations. Therefore, there are needs to create a database back end to manage the data for the TAUM Web site and support the operations of these Web pages.

In this chapter, we simplified the implementation of the back end and implemented a few C# classes that can hold the data in memory using data

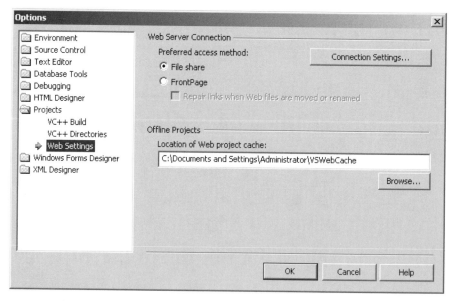

Figure 4-23   *Configuring the Web server connection preferred access method.*

structures such as **ArrayList**. Obviously, these mechanisms will not preserve the application data when the TAUM Web site application is stopped or swapped out of the memory, but they do illustrate the features of ASP.NET.

There are two types of data that we need to keep track in the TAUM Web site:

- Hotel-related data, including locations (cities), hotel names, and reservation details.
- Customer-related data, including login information. The ability to keep track of user information in the ASP.NET session and state is a key feature of ASP.NET, as well as a fundamental requirement for real-world electronic commerce applications.

Drop-down list boxes are used to show cities and hotels. Selecting a city from the first drop-down box will cause the hotels in that city to be shown in the second drop-down box. We obtain the hotel information from the **Hotel.dll** component, and we use data binding to populate the list boxes. The **Hotel.dll** component we need is in the folder TAUMGui\Hotel\ bin\Debug. It is relative to the root of the virtual directory Chap4, which we set up at the beginning of the chapter. **Customer.dll**, containing customer information, is under the folder TAUMGui\Customer\bin\Debug.

We can take a brief look at the code for the **Hotel.dll** component. **HotelBroker.cs** is one of the objects that we build to serve the back end functionality for managing hotel-related data. The following is an excerpt of its code segments:

```
// HotelBroker.cs

namespace TAUMLib
{
 using System;
 using System.Collections;

 ...
 public class HotelBroker : Broker, IHotelInfo,
                            IHotelAdmin, IHotelReservation
  {
    private const int MAXDAY = 366;
    private const int MAXUNIT = 10;
    private ArrayList cities;
    public HotelBroker() : base(MAXDAY, MAXUNIT)
    {
       cities = new ArrayList();
       AddHotel("Boston", "Marriott", 200, 250.00M);
       AddHotel("Boston", "Sheraton", 250, 125.00M);
       AddHotel("Boston", "Yankee", 150, 95.00M);
       AddHotel("New York", "Motel 88", 500, 70.00M);
       AddHotel("New York", "Ritz Carlton", 500, 480.00M);
```

```
            AddHotel("Orlando", "Magical", 150, 200.00M);
            AddHotel("Orlando", "Travelodge", 200, 65.00M);
            AddHotel("Orlando", "New Bates", 150, 135.00M);
        }
    ...
    public ArrayList GetHotels(string city)
    {
        ArrayList list = new ArrayList();
        for (int i = 0; i < NumberUnits; i++)
        {
            Hotel hotel = (Hotel) units[i];
            HotelListItem item;
            if (city == hotel.City)
            {
                item.City = hotel.City;
                item.HotelName = hotel.HotelName;
                item.NumberRooms = hotel.NumberRooms;
                item.Rate = hotel.Rate;
                list.Add(item);
            }
        }
        return list;
    }
    ...
```

In this code segment, you can see that we populate the in-memory "database" with some hard-coded hotel choices. If you are interested, you may want to try replacing these components using ADO.NET after reading Chapter 5. **GetHotels** is a method that the front-end ASP.NET Web page can use to populate server controls such as a drop-down list for all available hotels in a given city.

Hotel.dll and **Customer.dll** components are built from two Visual C# projects so that they can be easily incorporated into our TAUM Web site as independent modules. We go over the detailed steps for this in Section 4.5.1.3. You can use the **TAUMGui** Windows Forms application to exercise these two components.

4.5.1.3 TAUM WEB SITE VERSION 1

In Version 1 we provide a simple two-page Web site. On the first page, **HotelReservations.aspx**, users can make reservations, and on the second page, **ManageReservations.aspx**, they can manage their reservations. We have hard-coded our first customer as "John Doe," who has customer ID 1. Assume that you install the TAUM Web site source code from this book under C:\OI\Web; there should be two subdirectories, Version1 and

Version2, under C:\OI\Web\TAUMWebsite. We use the Version1 subdirectory in this version. Here is the detailed procedure to get Version 1 of the TAUM Web site working:

1. Create an ASP.NET Web application called **TAUMWeb**. If you have made C:\OI\Web\Chap4 into a virtual directory with alias Chap4, you can enter *localhost/Chap4/TAUMWeb* for the path. The project files will then be created in a brand new directory, C:\OI\Web\Chap4\ TAUMWeb. The corresponding VS.NET solution **TAUMWeb.sln** will be created under My Documents\Visual Studio Projects\TAUMWeb.

2. Add the supporting libraries **Hotel.dll** and **Customer.dll**. Copy **Hotel.dll** and **Customer.dll** from TAUMGui\Hotel\bin\Debug and TAUMGui\Customer\bin\Debug, respectively, to TAUMWeb\bin. In your **TAUMWeb** project, add references to **Hotel.dll** and **Customer.dll**. In addition, you can merge Visual C# projects for **Hotel.dll** and **Customer.dll** so that any updates to them can be done easily within the same **TAUMWeb** solution.

3. Import the two ASP.NET pages or build their UI using Form Designer. The easiest way to do this is to delete **WebForm1.aspx** from the **TAUMWeb** project and copy all **.aspx** and C# files as well as **Global.asax** from C:\OI\Web\TAUMWebsite\Version1 to the project directory C:\OI\Web\Chap4\TAUMWeb. Then we can import all these files to the **TAUMWeb** project. Of course, you can always build the ASP.NET pages from scratch using VS.NET Form Designer, and the WYSIWYG design experience is also excellent. Figure 4-24 shows how the **TAUMWeb** project should look like at this point in the VS.NET environment.

4. Initialize the **HotelBroker** and bind data to the ASP.NET Web pages. If you copied the code from C:\OI\Web\TAUMWebsite\Version1, then the code change here and in step 5 is already done for you. However, it is still important to know how these two steps are done. First, we need to add code to **Application_Start** in **Global.asax**, to instantiate **HotelBroker** and **Customers**, which produces some of the original default values for the **TAUMWeb** Web application in Version 1.

```
using System;
using System.Collections;
using System.ComponentModel;
using System.Web;
using System.Web.SessionState;
using TAUMLib;

namespace TAUMWeb
{
```

```
/// <summary>
/// Summary description for Global.
/// </summary>
public class Global : System.Web.HttpApplication
{
    protected void Application_Start(Object sender,
                                    EventArgs e)
    {
        HotelState.hotelBroker = new HotelBroker();
        HotelState.customers = new Customers();
        ArrayList array =
            HotelState.customers.GetCustomer(1);
        CustomerListItem cust =
            (CustomerListItem) array[0];
        HotelState.user.FirstName = cust.FirstName;
        HotelState.user.LastName = cust.LastName;
        HotelState.user.HotelCustomerId = 1;
        HotelState.user.EmailAddress = cust.EmailAddress;
    }
    ...
```

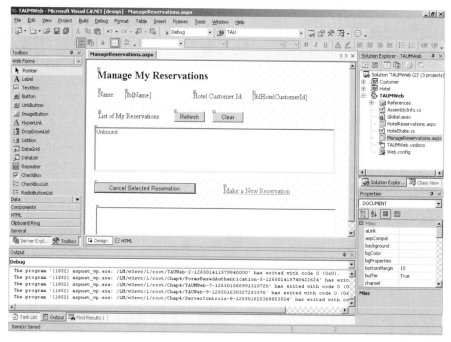

Figure 4-24   The ASP.NET Web application project: **TAUMWeb**.

Next we populate the first drop-down list in the **HotelReservations** class with city data, which can be obtained by the **GetCities** method of **HotelBroker**. We make use of the data binding capability of the **DropDownList** control. .NET Framework provides a number of data-binding options, which can facilitate binding to data obtained through a middle-tier component. A very simple option is binding to an **ArrayList**. This option works perfectly in our example, because we need to populate the drop-down list of cities with strings, and the **GetCities** method returns an array list of strings.

All we need to do to populate the **listCities** drop-down list is to add the following code to the **Page_Load** method of the **HotelReservations** class. The following code also shows how to populate the second drop-down list with hotel data using a similar procedure and a helper method, **BindHotels**.

```
private void Page_Load(object sender,
                    System.EventArgs e)
{
    // Put user code to initialize the page here
    if (!IsPostBack)
    {
        hotelBroker = HotelState.hotelBroker;
        ArrayList cities = hotelBroker.GetCities();
        listCities.DataSource = cities;
        ArrayList hotels =
            hotelBroker.GetHotels((string)cities[0]);
        BindHotels(hotels);
        DataBind();
        txtDate.Text =
            DateTime.Today.ToShortDateString();
        InitCustomer();
    }
}
private void BindHotels(ArrayList hotels)
{
    ArrayList hotelNames = new ArrayList(hotels.Count);
    foreach(HotelListItem hotel in hotels)
    {
        hotelNames.Add(hotel.HotelName.Trim());
    }
    listHotels.DataSource = hotelNames;
}
```

5. Finally, for the **HotelReservations** class, we implement the feature that selecting a city causes the hotels for the selected city to be displayed. We can add an event handler for selecting a city by

double-clicking on the **listCities** DropDownList control. Alternatively, in the Properties window you can click on the button to see all the events for the control. You can then double-click on the event. The second method allows you to add a handler for *any* event of the control. The first method is a shortcut for adding a handler for the primary event. Here is the code for the **SelectedIndexChanged** event.

```
private void listCities_SelectedIndexChanged(
                           object sender,
                           System.EventArgs e)
{
string city = listCities.SelectedItem.Text;
ArrayList hotels = hotelBroker.GetHotels(city);
BindHotels(hotels);
DataBind();
}
```

The start page for the application is **HotelReservations.aspx**. Figure 4-25 shows this page in Internet Explorer, after a reservation has been booked at the Marriott Hotel in Boston.

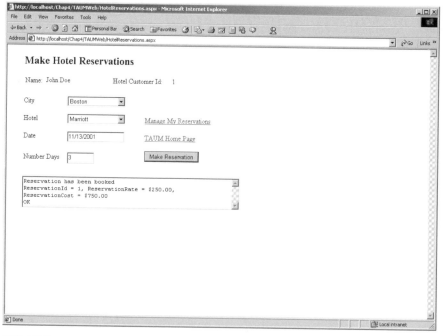

Figure 4-25 *Hotel reservations page of TAUM Web site.*

6. The second page for the application is **ManageReservations.aspx**. The following is the code listing for a helper method to show the reservations in the list box on **ManageReservations.aspx**.

```
private void ShowReservations()
{
    int id = Convert.ToInt32(lblHotelCustomerId.Text);
    ArrayList array =
        hotelBroker.FindReservationsForCustomer(id);
    if (array == null)
    {
        return;
    }
    ClearReservations();
    foreach (ReservationListItem item in array)
    {
        string rid = item.ReservationId.ToString();
        string hotel = item.HotelName;
        string city = item.City;
        string arrive = item.ArrivalDate.ToString("d");
        string depart =
            item.DepartureDate.ToString("d");
        string number = item.NumberDays.ToString();
        string str = rid + "\t" + hotel + "\t"
            + city + "\t" + arrive + "\t" + depart
            + "\t" + number;
        listReservations.Items.Add(str);
    }
}
```

Now all the detailed steps for completing the first version of the TAUM Web site are done. Figure 4-26 shows the **ManageReservations.aspx** page in Internet Explorer, after reservations have been booked for Boston, New York, and Orlando.

4.5.1.4 TAUMLIB COMPONENTS

Version 1, even though beautifully done, is not a full-function Web site. In the full-blown implementation of our TAUM Web site, which is our Version 2, a customer must register, providing a user ID, name, and e-mail address. Subsequently, the user can log in by providing just the user ID and interact with the Web site to perform various activities including hotel reservations.

In order to achieve this functionality, we need to construct some library components, which are under **TAUMLib** namespace. The Version2 subdirectory contains the code for the **TAUMLib** components.

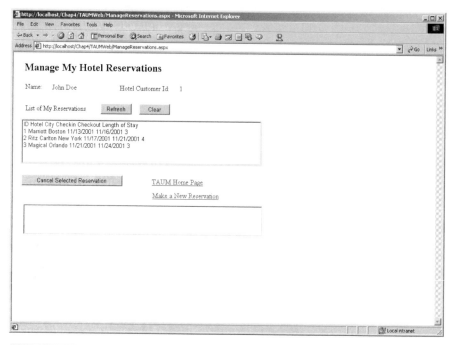

Figure 4-26   *Manage reservations page of TAUM Web site.*

Internally, TAUM maintains a database of user IDs and corresponding hotel customer IDs. The interface **ITAUMUser** encapsulates this database maintained by TAUM. The class library project **TAUMLib** contains a collection-based implementation of such a database. The file **TAUMTravelDefs.cs** contains the definitions of interfaces and of a structure.

```
// TAUMTravelDefs.cs

using System;
using System.Collections;
using TAUMLib;

public interface ITAUMUser
{
  bool Login(string userid);
  bool Register(string userid, string firstName,
          string lastName, string emailAddress);
  bool Unregister(string userid);
  bool ChangeEmailAddress(string userid,
          string emailAddress);
  bool GetUserInfo(string userid, out UserInfo info);
}
```

```
public interface ITAUMAdmin
{
  ArrayList GetUsers();
  decimal CalculateFee(decimal amount);
}

public struct UserInfo
{
  public int HotelCustomerId;
  public string FirstName;
  public string LastName;
  public string EmailAddress;
  public decimal Balance;
}
```

Login will return **true** if **userid** is found. **Register** will register a new user with the Hotel Broker. Methods are also provided to unregister and change the e-mail address. These methods will call the corresponding methods of the **ICustomer** interface. **GetUserInfo** will return a **UserInfo** struct as an **out** parameter. This struct defines a **TAUM** user. The method **GetUsers** of the **ITAUMAdmin** interface returns an array list of **UserInfo** structs.

The class **TAUM** wraps access to the **Customers** class, whose methods get invoked indirectly through methods of **ITAUMUser**. The class **TAUM** also contains a public member **hotelBroker** of type **HotelBroker**. Thus, to gain complete access to the Hotel Broker system, a client program or Web page simply has to instantiate an instance of **TAUM**. Here is the start of the definition of **TAUM**.

```
public class TAUM : ITAUMUser, ITAUMAdmin
{
  public HotelBroker hotelBroker;
  private Customers customers;
  private ArrayList users;
  private UserInfo currentUser;
  public TAUM()
  {
    users = new ArrayList();
    hotelBroker = new HotelBroker();
    customers = new Customers();
    InitializeUsers();
  }
  // Initialize users with data from Customers list
  private void InitializeUsers()
  {
    ArrayList array = customers.GetCustomer(-1);
    foreach (CustomerListItem cust in array)
    {
      string userid = cust.FirstName;
```

```
            int custid = cust.CustomerId;
            User user = new User(userid, custid, 0m);
            users.Add(user);
        }
    }
    ...
```

The class **TAUM** also implements the interface **ITAUMAdmin**.

```
public interface ITAUMAdmin
{
    ArrayList GetUsers();
}
```

The method **GetUsers** returns an array list of **UserInfo**.

4.5.1.5 TAUM WEB SITE VERSION 2

Now we are ready to put the finishing touches on our TAUM Web site for
hotel reservations. We will add another three ASP.NET Web pages to complete the Version 2 functionality: **Login.aspx**, **RegisterNewUser.aspx**, and
Main.aspx. The Version2 subdirectory contains the source code files for
these three Web pages.

1. *Main.aspx*. The home page of the TAUM Web Site is **Main.aspx**.
   Figure 4-27 shows this home page for the user "Mark Doe" who has
   just registered. A link is provided to log in as a different user, if
   desired. There are links for "Make a Hotel Reservation" and "Manage
   Your Hotel Reservations." These pages are the same as shown for
   Version 1.

2. *Login.aspx*. The start page for the Version 2 application is **Main.aspx**.
   If there is no currently logged-in user, the new user will be redirected
   to **Login.aspx**. Let's experiment with registering and logging in. Figure
   4-28 shows the login page. In our implementation we offer John as a
   possible user ID. Later you can quickly log in as "John Doe" by simply
   clicking Login. Now click Register.

3. *RegisterNewUser.aspx*. The "Register New User" page allows the
   user to pick a user ID and to enter some identifying information (first
   name, last name, and e-mail address). Figure 4-29 shows this page
   after "Mark Doe" has entered information for himself. When done
   entering information, the user should click Register, which will directly
   bring up the Travel Agency Union Member home page, bypassing a
   need for a separate login.

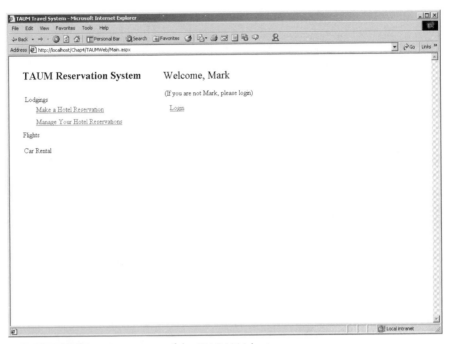

Figure 4-27   *Home page of the TAUM Web site.*

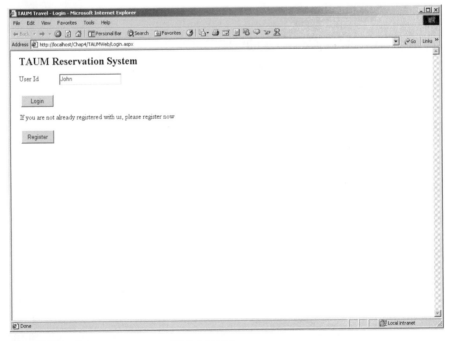

Figure 4-28   *Login page of TAUM Web site.*

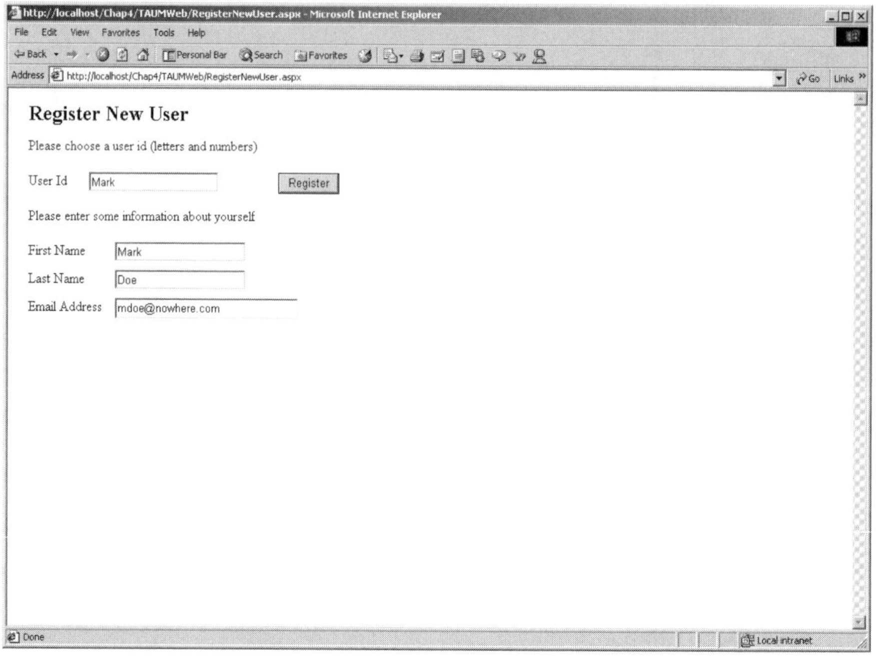

Figure 4-29 *Register New User page of the TAUM Web site.*

4.5.2 ASP.NET State Fundamentals

An ASP.NET application consists of all the Web pages and code files that can be invoked from a virtual directory and its subdirectories on a Web server. In addition to **.aspx** files and code-behind files such as those we have already examined, an application can also have a **global.asax** file and a configuration file **web.config**.

Preserving state across HTTP requests is a major facet of Web programming, and ASP.NET provides several facilities that are convenient to use. There are two main types of state to be preserved:

- *Application State* is global information that is shared across all users of a Web application.
- *Session State* is used to store data for a particular user across multiple requests to a Web application. A Web session is defined as a series of requests and responses between a single HTTP client and a Web server within a specified time span. ASP.NET provides excellent support for session and we discuss it in Section 4.5.2.1.

In this section we examine the features of ASP.NET applications. Then we investigate the mechanisms for working with application state (Section

4.5.2.3), as well as how to configure ASP.NET applications. Throughout the section, our illustration is based on Version 2 of the TAUM Web site.

4.5.2.1 SESSION STATE: ASP.NET VERSUS ASP

Since session state was first introduced in ASP, it has been a key Web application feature that supports e-commerce activities such as shopping carts. However, it has several major limitations:

- *Process Dependent.* ASP session state exists in the process that hosts ASP; therefore, any actions that affect the process also affect the session state. When the process is recycled or fails, the session state is also lost.
- *Machine Dependent.* ASP session state is machine-specific. As users move from server to server in a Web server farm, their session state does not follow them. Each ASP server provides its own session state, and unless the user returns to the same server, a server-specific session state is useless.
- *Cookie Dependent.* Browser clients that turn off HTTP cookies can't take advantage of the session state under ASP.

ASP.NET session state provides a solution to address all of these issues associated with ASP session state:

- *Process Independent.* Besides supporting ASP-style session state, ASP.NET session state can run in a separate process from the ASP.NET host process. This decouples the session-state process from ASP.NET applications that created it.
- *Machine Independent.* With ASP.NET, we can solve the server farm problem by moving to an out-of-process model. This new model allows all servers in the farm to share a session-state process that runs on an administrative server. Therefore, it's no longer machine-specific.
- *Cookie Independent.* ASP.NET now offers a cookieless state, which can be turned on with a single setting in the application configuration file, **web.config**.

Now let's start exploring in detail what ASP.NET can do as far as managing application and session states is concerned.

4.5.2.2 GLOBAL.ASAX

ASP.NET supports an optional global file, **Global.asax**, which contains code for responding to application-level events, as well as global objects and variables. This file resides in the root directory of the application. Visual Studio.NET will by default create a **Global.asax** file for you when you create an ASP.NET Web Application project. The following is the **Global.asax** file for our TAUM Web site Version 2, which follows a similar format of an **.aspx** file:

```csharp
using System;
using System.Collections;
using System.ComponentModel;
using System.Web;
using System.Web.SessionState;
using TAUMLib;

namespace TAUMWeb
{
  /// <summary>
  /// Summary description for Global.
  /// </summary>
  public class Global : System.Web.HttpApplication
  {
    protected void Application_Start(Object sender,
                                EventArgs e)
    {
      HotelState.TAUM = new TAUM();
    }

    protected void Session_Start(Object sender,
                        EventArgs e)
    {
      Session["UserId"] = "";
    }

    protected void Application_BeginRequest(Object sender,
                                      EventArgs e)
    {

    }

    protected void Application_EndRequest(Object sender,
                                    EventArgs e)
    {

    }

    protected void Session_End(Object sender, EventArgs e)
    {

    }
```

```
        protected void Application_End(Object sender,
                                      EventArgs e)
        {

        }
    }
}
```

A list of common application-level events is shown in this code, and these events exist in the typical life cycle of an ASP.NET Web application:

- **Application_Start** is raised only once during an application's lifetime, on the first instance of **HttpApplication**. Application-level initialization code can go here. For example, **TAUM** object, the global, static data member of **HotelState**, is instantiated in our code above.
- **Session_Start** is raised at the start of each session. Session variables are usually initialized in this event handler. For example, we initialize a session variable **UserId** to be a blank string in the code above. We discuss session variables later in this section.
- **Application_BeginRequest** is raised at the start of an individual request. Normally you can process HTTP requests in the **Page** class.
- **Application_EndRequest** is raised at the end of an individual request.
- **Session_End** is raised at the end of each session. Normally you do not need to do clean-up for data initialized in **Session_Start**, because garbage collection will take care of normal clean-up. However, if you have opened an expensive resource, such as a database connection, you may wish to call its **Dispose** method here.
- **Application_End** is raised at the very end of an application's lifetime, when the last instance of **HttpApplication** is garbage collected.

In addition to these events, there are other events concerned with security, such as **AuthenticateRequest** and **AuthorizeRequest**. We discuss them in Section 4.5.4.

4.5.2.3 APPLICATION STATE

ASP.NET provides two major mechanisms to manage application states: static member variable and application object. Static members of a class are shared across all instances of a class. Hence static data members can be used to hold application state. In our TAUM Web site the class **HotelState** has a single static member **TAUM** of the class **TAUM**, which holds shared data, such as lists of cities and hotels. The shared data is the same for all users of the application.

```
class HotelState
{
  static public TAUM TAUM;
}
```

If you like, you may perform a small experiment at this stage by adding a Web page named **HotelAdmin.aspx** and its supporting C# file to the TAUM Web site (Version 2). These files are located under C:\OI\Web\ TAUMWebsite\HotelAdmin, assuming the book examples are installed under C:\OI\Web. The following modification to **Main.aspx** makes the hotel administration interface **IHotelAdmin** available to the special user with the user ID "admin":

```
private void Page_Load(object sender,
                       System.EventArgs e)
{
  // Put user code to initialize the page here
  string userid = (string)Session["UserId"];
    if (userid == "")
    Response.Redirect("Login.aspx");
  if (userid == "admin")
  {
    lblAdmin.Visible = true;
    linkHotelAdmin.Visible = true;
  }
  else
  {
    lblAdmin.Visible = false;
    linkHotelAdmin.Visible = false;
  }
  ...
```

When this privileged user logs in, a special home page is displayed that provides a link to "Administer Hotels," as illustrated in Figure 4-30.

If you follow the link to "Administer Hotels," you will be brought to a page showing a list of all the hotels. Select the first hotel (Marriott) on the list and click the Delete Selected Hotel button and then the Refresh button. You will now see an updated list of hotels, as shown in Figure 4-31.

Alternatively, you can store global application information in the built-in **Application** object, which is an instance of the class **HttpApplicationState** and can be referenced through the **Application** property of the **Page** class. The **HttpApplicationState** class provides a **Hashtable** that you can use for storing both objects and scalar values at the application level. Similar to static member variables, **Application** does not preserve data outside of the ASP.NET process, which means the data will be cleared when the ASP.NET process is garbage collected.

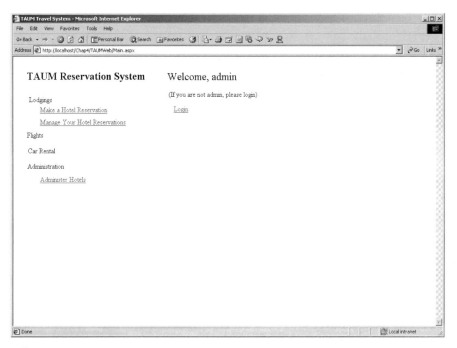

Figure 4-30   *Home page of the TAUM Web site tailored for administrators.*

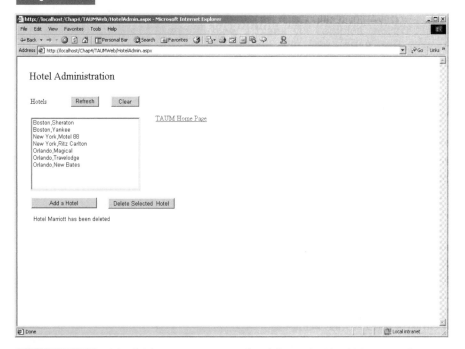

Figure 4-31   *Hotel Administration page after deleting the Hotel Marriott in Boston.*

As an alternative to using the class **HotelState** with the static member **TAUM** that we previously used, we could use the **Application** object. In **Global.asax** we can then instantiate a **TAUM** object and store it in the **Application** object using HotelState as the index or key.

```
protected void Application_Start(Object sender,
    EventArgs e)
{
    Application["HotelState"] = new TAUM();
}
```

Conversely, you can retrieve the **TAUM** object associated with the made-up index HotelState and cast it to a **TAUM** object, as illustrated in the following code segment:

```
TAUM TAUM = (TAUM)Application["HotelState"];
string name = TAUM.CurrentUser.FirstName;
```

Using this technique, you can completely replace the static data member, **HotelState.TAUM**, with the **Application** object.

4.5.2.4 SESSION STATE

You can store session information for individual users in a built-in **Session** object, which is an instance of the class **HttpSessionState** and can be referenced through the **Session** property of the **Page** class. The **HttpSessionState** class provides a key-value dictionary that you can use for storing both objects and scalar values, in exactly the same manner employed by **HttpApplicationState**.

Our TAUM Web site uses a session variable UserId for storing a string representing the user ID. As discussed before, this session variable is created and initialized in **Global.asax**.

```
protected void Session_Start(Object sender, EventArgs e)
{
    Session["UserId"] = "";
}
```

We use this session variable in the **Page_Load** event of our home page **Main.aspx** to detect whether we have a returning (having a valid session) user or a new user. A new user is redirected to the login page, while a returning user whose session is still valid may proceed.

```
private void Page_Load(object sender, System.EventArgs e)
{
    // Put user code to initialize the page here
    string userid = (string)Session["UserId"];
    if (userid == "")
      Response.Redirect("Login.aspx");
    ...
}
```

There are a few concepts and relationships in the ASP.NET session management worth noting here:

- *Session State and Cookies*. Although by default ASP.NET uses cookies to identify which requests belong to a particular session, it is easy to configure ASP.NET to run cookieless. In this mode the session ID, normally stored within a cookie, is instead embedded within the URL. We discuss cookieless configuration in Section 4.5.3.
- *Session State Timeout*. By default the session state times out after 20 minutes. This means that if a given user is idle for that period of time, the session is torn down, and a request from the client will now be treated as a request from a new user, creating a new session. Again, it is easy to configure the timeout period, as we will discuss in the section on configuration.
- *Session State Store*. ASP.NET cleanly solves the session-sharing issue for the Web server farm (multiple Web servers grouped together) and many other issues through a session-state model that separates storage from the application's use of the stored information. By default, the session-state store is an in-memory cache. It can be configured to be memory on a specific machine or to be stored in a SQL Server database. In those cases, the session data is not tied to a specific server and can be safely used within a Web farm.

4.5.3 Configuration Under ASP.NET

In the previous section, we have seen a number of cases where it is desirable to be able to configure ASP.NET application for session and state. At a high level, there are two types of configurations:

- *Server configuration* specifies default settings that apply to all ASP.NET applications.
- *Application configuration* specifies settings specific to a particular ASP.NET application.

ASP.NET provides simple yet flexible configuration mechanisms that are based on XML. In this section, we look at some simple examples to see how configurations are done under ASP.NET.

4.5.3.1 CONFIGURATION FILES

There are two types of XML-based configuration files under ASP.NET:

- *Server Configuration File (**machine.config**)*. This file is located within a version-specific folder under \WINNT\ Microsoft.NET\Framework. Because there are separate files for each version of .NET, it is perfectly possible to run different versions of ASP.NET side by side. Thus if you have working Web applications running under one version of .NET, you can continue to run them while you develop new applications using a later version.

• *Application Configuration Files (**web.config**)*. This optional file is located at the root of the virtual directory on a per-application basis, and VS.NET creates it for each ASP.NET application by default. If the file is present, any settings in **web.config** will override the default server settings in **machine.config**. Otherwise, the default configuration settings will be used.

Both **machine.config** and **web.config** files have the same XML format, and the root element of the configuration file is always **<configuration>**. The **web.config** file that is automatically created by Visual Studio provides a lot of useful hints on what settings are available and how to set them:

```xml
<?xml version="1.0" encoding="utf-8" ?>
<configuration>

  <system.web>

    <!-- DYNAMIC DEBUG COMPILATION
         Set compilation debug="true" to enable ASPX
         debugging.  Otherwise, setting this value to
         false will improve run time performance of this
         application.
         ...
    -->
    <compilation
        defaultLanguage="c#"
        debug="true"
    />

    <!-- CUSTOM ERROR MESSAGES
         Set mode="on" or "remoteonly" to enable custom
         error messages, "off" to disable. Add
         <error> tags for each of the errors you want to
         handle.
    -->
    <customErrors
    mode="Off"
    />

    <!-- AUTHENTICATION
         This section sets the authentication policies of
         the application. Possible modes are "Windows",
         "Forms", "Passport" and "None"
    -->
    <authentication mode="None" />
```

. . .

```
</system.web>
</configuration>
```

4.5.3.2 APPLICATION TRACING

Earlier in the chapter we examined page-level tracing, which can be done by enabling the **Trace="true"** attribute in the **@Page** directive. Page-level tracing is quite useful during development but is rather intrusive during deployment and production, where the page trace is sent back to the browser along with the regular response. In addition, when you have a large Web application that consists of hundreds of ASP.NET Web pages, it becomes rather difficult to do.

Application tracing, which is specified in **web.config**, writes the trace information to a log file, which can be viewed via a separate URL. As a demonstration of the use of **web.config**, let's switch on application tracing for our TAUM Web site (Version 2). Actually, it is amazingly easy to do since we just have to change the **web.config** as follows:

```
<!-- APPLICATION-LEVEL TRACE LOGGING
 Application-level tracing enables trace log output for
every page within an application.
 Set trace enabled="true" to enable application trace
logging.  If pageOutput="true", the trace information will
be displayed at the bottom of each page.  Otherwise, you can
view the application trace log by browsing the "trace.axd"
page from your web application root.
-->
<trace enabled="true"
    requestLimit="10"
    pageOutput="false"
    traceMode="SortByTime"
    localOnly="true"
/>
```

The difference between application tracing and page-level tracing is that no tracing information would be included in the normal page returned to the browser during application tracing. Now we can just run the TAUM Web site application as if nothing has happened.

After some user interactions, we can enter the URL *localhost/ Chap4/TAUMWeb/trace.axd*, where *localhost/Chap4/TAUMWeb* is the root of our application and trace.axd is a special HTTP handler to view tracing information. You will see top-level trace information with a line for each trip to the server, as shown in Figure 4-32. If you click on the "View Details" link, you will see a detailed page trace, similar to what we saw earlier in the chapter.

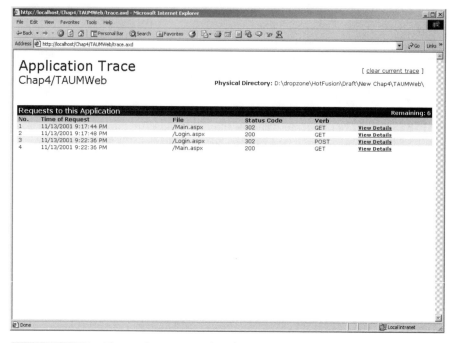

| **Figure 4-32** | *The application trace log shown in the browser.* |

4.5.3.3 SESSION CONFIGURATION

As another example of configuration, modify the **web.config** file for Version 2 of the TAUM Web site to change the timeout value to be one minute.

```
<?xml version="1.0" encoding="utf-8" ?>
<configuration>
  <system.web>
...
    <!--   SESSION STATE SETTINGS
    By default ASP.NET uses cookies to identify
    which requests belong to a particular session.
    If cookies are not available, a session can be
    tracked by adding a session identifier to the
    URL. To disable cookies, set sessionState
    cookieless="true".
    -->
    <sessionState
     mode="InProc"
     stateConnectionString="tcpip=127.0.0.1:42424"
```

```
    sqlConnectionString=
        "data source=127.0.0.1;user id=sa;password="
    cookieless="false"
    timeout="1"
    />
...
  </system.web>
</configuration>
```

Now run the application, log in, do some work, and return to the home page. You should be greeted by your login name without having to log in again. Then you can do some more work, wait more than a minute or two, and return to the home page. Because the session will have timed out, you will be redirected to log in again.

4.5.4 Application Security Under ASP.NET

Ensuring the safety of Web-based applications has long been a major concern for companies doing business on the Internet. Within each Web application, there are at least five basic security characteristics that need to be addressed:

- *Authentication.* The process of identifying each individual, which means assuring that the user is, in fact, who the user claims to be
- *Authorization.* Determination of the appropriate access to resources for the authorized individual
- *Impersonation.* The process in which a server application executes with the identity of the entity, usually an authorized remote user
- *Data Integrity.* Receipt of the data that was sent
- *Nonrepudiation.* The inability to deny that a transaction has been completed

Data integrity and nonrepudiation are mostly accomplished by hardware configuration, solid server software, and encryption with digital certificates. Improved over its predecessor ASP, ASP.NET addresses the first three issues with an array of built-in facilities and by leveraging the power of .NET Framework. In this section, we go over these topics as well as basic IIS security at a high level, and you can refer to Microsoft .NET documentation for details.

4.5.4.1 IIS SECURITY

IIS is the first line of defense because its security may still be present when ASP.NET security measures are not available. Since ASP.NET uses IIS, your IIS settings do affect the security of Web applications based on ASP.NET.

You may be aware of the anonymous access that is supported by IIS by default, as shown in Figure 4-33. Anonymous access does not require a user

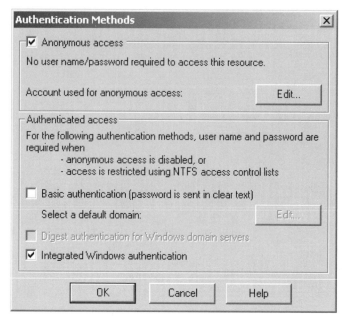

Figure 4-33 *Anonymous access that is supported by IIS.*

name or password to access an account, and the visitor runs under some default user account. Anonymous access is useful for public Web sites and services that do their own authentication by asking for a user name or password or by some other means. In such a scenario you could use ASP.NET forms-based authentication. You can build forms to get the user name and password and then validate them against a configuration file or database.

IIS supports the major HTTP authentication schemes. These schemes, which require you to configure IIS appropriately, are listed in Table 4-3. In each of these scenarios IIS authenticates the user if the credentials match an existing user account. Secure Sockets Layer (SSL) is used whenever you need to encrypt the HTTP communication channel. SSL can degrade performance. We do not discuss SSL in this chapter.

You will also have to adjust access to the necessary files (graphics, data store files, etc.) and other resources (e.g., databases) to those user accounts (authorization). For public Web sites and Web services this approach is not useful because users will not have user accounts.

Table 4-3	*IIS Authentication Schemes*
Scheme	**Type of Authentication**
Basic	User and password information is effectively sent as plain text. This is standard HTTP authentication and is not secure.
Basic over SSL	Basic authentication, but the communication channel is encoded, so that the user name and password are protected.
Digest	Uses secure hashing to transmit user name and password. This is not a completely secure method because the hash codes stored on the server are reversible.[2] It was introduced in HTTP 1.1 to replace basic authentication.
Windows Integrated Security	Traditional Windows security using NTLM or Kerberos protocols. IIS authenticates if the credentials match a user account. Cannot be used across proxies and firewalls. NTLM is the legacy Windows security protocol.
Certificates over SSL	Client obtains a certificate that is mapped to a user account.

Microsoft has introduced the Passport authentication scheme. While ASP.NET does have support for Passport (**System.Web.Security. PassportIdentity** class) on the server side, as of this writing developer tools to handle the client side for Passport authentication do not exist. Passport avoids the problem of requiring specific accounts on specific machines.

4.5.4.2 AUTHENTICATION IN ASP.NET

ASP.NET supports three types of authentication schemes based on the concept of authentication provider. Authentication providers refer to code modules that contain the code necessary to authenticate the requestor's credentials, and there are three types of them available under ASP.NET: Windows built-in, Passport-based, and Forms-based. To activate an ASP.NET authentication service, you must configure the **<mode>** attribute of the **<authentication>** element in of the application's configuration file **web.config**. This attribute could have one of the following values:

- *Windows*. This is a two-step process. Authentication is first performed by IIS in one of three ways: basic, digest, or Integrated Windows Authentication. When IIS authentication is done, ASP.NET uses the authenticated identity to authorize access.

---

[2] A message digest is another name for the result of applying a hash code to a message.

- *Forms.* By default, unauthenticated requests are redirected to an HTML form using HTTP client-side redirection. The user provides credentials and submits the form. If the application authenticates the request, the system issues a cookie that contains the credentials or a key for reacquiring the identity. Subsequent requests are issued with the cookie in the request headers; they are authenticated and authorized by an ASP.NET handler using whatever validation method the application developer specifies. We discuss this in detail in Section 4.5.4.3.
- *Passport.* ASP.NET authentication services provide a convenient wrapper around the services provided by Microsoft Passport SDK. This option enables single sign-on at a centralized location.
- *None.* None of ASP.NET authentication services are active. Note that IIS authentication services may still be present.

The following section of **web.config** enables forms-based (cookie) authentication for an application.

```
<configuration>
      <security>
            <authentication mode="Forms"/>
      </security>
</configuration>
```

4.5.4.3 FORMS-BASED AUTHENTICATION AND AUTHORIZATION

Forms-based authentication allows Web applications to provide their own login user identification and do their own credential verification. ASP.NET handles authenticating users, all the necessary cookie management, and redirecting unauthenticated users to the login page. Forms-based authentication is a very popular technique that has been successfully implemented at many public Web sites.

ASP.NET forms-based authentication uses **web.config**, a login form, and a cookie to authenticate the user.[3] Typically in this scenario you set up the Web site for anonymous access so that no users will be screened out by IIS. In order to illustrate how forms-based authentication works under ASP.NET, we add forms-based authentication to our TAUM Web site example (currently there is no authentication in Version 2).

All source code files that we use here are under Chap4\ FormsBasedAuthentication. We only modify a few files here to incorporate the new authentication scheme, and all changes will be explained in detail. Actually, it could be a good hands-on exercise for you to start from Version 2 and go through all the changes yourself.

In order to use forms-based authentication and authorization, an application has to be configured to use its scheme. Here is the updated version of

---

[3] You do not have to use a cookie, but it is used for automatic authentication.

the **web.config** file for our example, with the corresponding section for authentication and authorization shown:

```
...
<authentication mode="Forms">
 <forms name="HotelBrokerCookie" path="/"
    loginUrl="Login.aspx" protection="All" timeout="10">
    <credentials passwordFormat="Clear">
        <user name="John" password="John" />
        <user name="Jane" password="Jane" />
        <user name="admin" password="" />
    </credentials>
 </forms>
</authentication>
<authorization>
 <allow users="John" />
 <deny users="*" />
</authorization>
...
```

The authentication mode is set to Forms. The forms element has several attributes that define how the authentication is set up. The name attribute is the name of the cookie. The path attribute indicates where on the site the cookie is valid; the slash (/) indicates the entire site. The loginUrl indicates where the login form resides. The protection attribute indicates how the cookie should be encrypted. "All" indicates that the cookie should be validated and encrypted. Other options are None, Encryption, and Validation. Timeout indicates the number of minutes before the cookie becomes invalid (expires).

The credential elements indicate how the password should be stored in the configuration file. For simplicity we have used clear text. You could also specify SHA1 or MD5 to encrypt the passwords.[4] If passwords are stored in **web.config**, it should be secured against download (which is the default). Passwords for the configuration file can be encrypted with the static **FormsAuthentication** method **HashPasswordForStoringInConfigFile**.[5] The user elements indicate the user names and passwords.

The authorization section determines which authenticated users are authorized to access the Web site. ASP.NET allows you to specify groups and users who are allowed to access the Web site. Inside the **<authorization>** section of **web.config** you can use the **<allow>** and **<deny>** elements with user accounts or groups. To specify groups you use the **roles** attribute; to specify users you use the **users** attribute. The asterisk (*) symbol used with

---

[4] These encryption (cryptographic) services are implemented under System.Security. Cryptography namespace.
[5] Storing passwords in a configuration file is convenient for development and testing work. If you do your own validation, as we do with the database example, you do not need to use the web.config file.

one of those elements means all. A question mark (?) used with a user attribute means "anonymous access."

A reference to a specific user overrides his or her membership in a group or a wildcard. Deny references take precedence over allow references. These settings do not help you assign users to particular roles or prevent access to different areas of the Web site, and only access to the entire Web site is controlled.

We plan to use redirection and cookie validation to update our TAUM Web site, and we need to change **Login.aspx**, **Main.aspx**, and their corresponding C# code. First, we need to update the login page to allow users to enter their passwords; you can use VS.NET Forms Designer to make this GUI change. The new password text box (**txtPassword**) hides the password with asterisks (*). The only other change is in the **Login_Click** method:

```
private void Login_Click(object sender, EventArgs e)
    {
        bool ok = TAUM.Login(txtUserId.Text);
        if (FormsAuthentication.Authenticate(txtUserId.Text,
                                   txtPassword.Text))
        {
            FormsAuthentication.SetAuthCookie
                               (txtUserId.Text, true);
            Session["UserId"] = txtUserId.Text;
            Response.Redirect("Main.aspx");
        }
        else
        {
            lblErrorMessage.Text =
                    "Could not authenticate user.";
        }
    }
```

The **FormsAuthentication** class's **Authenticate** method validates the user name and password from the **web.config** file. If a valid cookie is on the system, the user is not redirected to the login page. **SetAuthCookie** creates a cookie, and the **Response.Redirect** method redirects the user to the **Main.aspx** page. If the second argument is true, a persistent cookie is placed on the user's system. (Once it has been created, you can inspect the cookie using "Internet Option…" under IE or go to C:\WINNT\Profiles\ YourLoginName\Local Settings\Temporary Internet Files.) Persistent cookies are a security risk, because the cookie can be stolen as it is transmitted (hijacked). You should use SSL to protect the cookie. You can remove the session or persistent cookie with the **SignOut** method of **FormsAuthentication**. The check of the authorization section of **web.config** to see if the user has the rights to access the page is done on each request.

Now you are ready to change **Main.aspx** to take advantage of the cookie that we just created:

```
private void Page_Load(object sender,
                       System.EventArgs e)
{
    // Put user code to initialize the page here
    string userid = User.Identity.Name;
        if (userid == "")
        Response.Redirect("Login.aspx");
    if (userid == "admin")
    {
        lblAdmin.Visible = true;
        linkHotelAdmin.Visible = true;
    }
    else
    {
        lblAdmin.Visible = false;
        linkHotelAdmin.Visible = false;
    }
    if (!IsPostBack)
    {
        // added a statement to deal with login issues
        bool ok =
            HotelState.TAUM.Login(User.Identity.Name);
        string name =
            HotelState.TAUM.CurrentUser.FirstName;
        lblUserName.Text = "Welcome, " + name;
        lblLogin.Text = "(If you are not " + name +
            ", please log in)";
    }
}
```

Main.aspx can refer to the name of the user through the **Page.User** object (this user does not map to the Windows 2000 account, and it implements the **System.Security.Principal.Iprincipal** interface). The type of identity object is **FormsIdentity**, and it provides a way for an application to access the cookie authentication.

Now you can try the newly implemented authentication and authorization scheme by accessing *localhost/Chap4/FormsBasedAuthentication /Main.aspx*. At the first try, you will be redirected to the new **Login.aspx**, as shown in Figure 4-34. After you log in as user John Doe ("John" as user name and password), you will be redirected to **Main.aspx**.

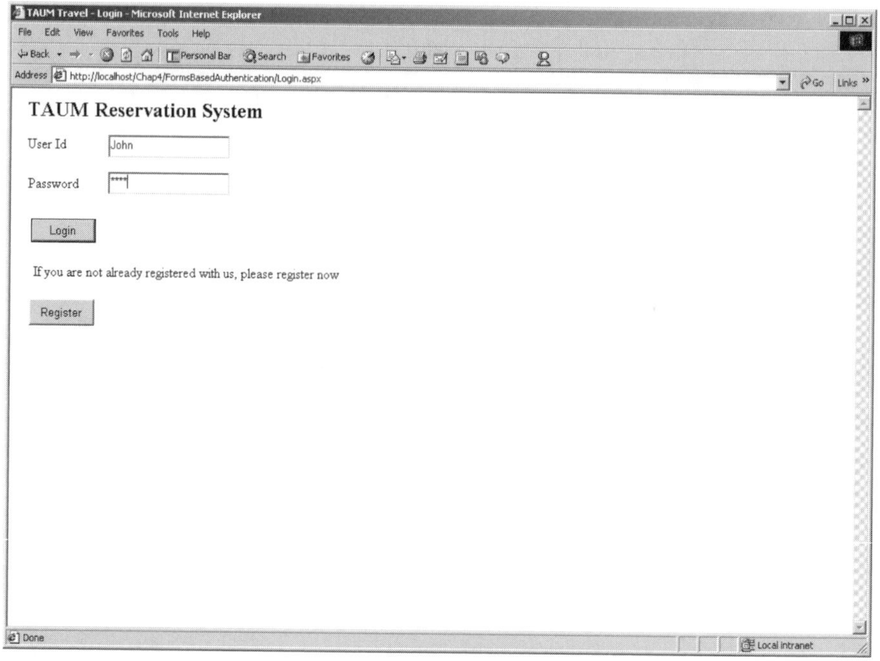

Figure 4-34   *The new login page **Login.aspx** with password entry box.*

If you succeed and log in as John Doe once, subsequent tries will succeed without the login page even from a new IE browser window, because we have created a persistent cookie. To avoid persistent cookies, set the second argument of **SetAuthCookie** to **false**. Now if you launch another IE browser and attempt to hit the **Main.aspx** page, you will be redirected to log in again because the cookie is not saved across browser sessions.

If you try to log in as Jane Doe ("Jane" as user name and password), you seem to get stuck at **Login.aspx** even if you type them in as shown in **web.config**. This is due to authorization failure because Jane Doe is not in the "**allow users**" list of **authorization** configuration in **web.config**, even when authentication succeeds. The remedy is to add this name in the "**allow users**" list. When you do, Jane's login works like a charm.

4.5.4.4 IMPERSONATION

An important feature for any server application is the ability to control the identity under which server application code is executed. Impersonation refers to a process where a server application executes with the identity of the client who is making the request. This feature could be handy when you want to test a Web application using a different identity from the one you logged in as.

Unlike ASP, ASP.NET does not provide per-request impersonation. ASP.NET applications can optionally choose to fulfill impersonating requests. If desired, an application can be easily configured to impersonate on every request with the following configuration directive:

```
<configuration>
   <security>
    <identity>
      <impersonation enable="true"/>
    </identity>
   </security>
</configuration>
```

If impersonation is enabled for a given application, ASP.NET always impersonates the access token that could be either an authenticated user token or the token for the anonymous user (such as IUSR_MACHINENAME). When anonymous access is not enabled in IIS, the user request will be impersonated as the authenticated user.

Since ASP.NET does on-the-fly compilation, enabling impersonation requires that all accounts have read/write access to the application's codegen directory (where dynamically compiled objects are stored by the ASP.NET run time) as well as the global assembly cache (%windir%\assembly). This may need some permission setup for files and directories under Windows 2000, when impersonation is done through restrictive accounts such as IUSR_MACHINENAME of IIS.

4.6 Migrating from ASP to ASP.NET

By now, we hope that you fully appreciate the benefits of developing Web applications using ASP.NET instead of ASP. Throughout the chapter, we have explored new features of ASP.NET and how it can help us write more efficient, more powerful, cleaner, and faster Web applications. In this section we look at existing ASP applications and evaluate options for moving forward. Then we briefly compare the two programming paradigms at a relatively low level by discussing compatibility issues, API changes, and major semantic differences. Finally, we go over some basic rules for your ASP coding today to prepare for the upcoming .NET migration.

4.6.1 To Migrate or Not to Migrate

So this is the sixty-four-thousand-dollar question: Should you migrate from ASP to ASP.NET? This sounds like a no-brainer, especially if you are a hard-core Microsoft Web developer who is working in the trenches and wants to adopt the coolest technologies. However, in the real business world, it is not a black-and-white issue. Since most corporate Information Technology (IT) departments have to answer a fundamental return-of-investment (ROI) question, it helps to point out that migration will incur cost (time, material, and labor), either apparent or hidden. Here are several viable options and you can decide which to choose, based on what kind of business you are in and where in the technology adoption curve you want to position yourself.

4.6.1.1 OPTION 1: DO NOT MIGRATE

Microsoft ASP.NET is a brand new technology and there is a certain degree of risk associated with adopting new technology early. You may recall that Microsoft Visual Basic did not go blazing hot until Version 3.

From a technology standpoint, ASP and ASP.NET can run side by side on an IIS Web server without interference; there is no chance of corrupting an existing ASP application simply by installing ASP.NET. The ASP.NET run time will process only those files with an **.aspx** file name extension; files with the extension **.asp** will continue to be processed by the existing, unchanged ASP engine. Therefore, keeping old ASP code in production should not limit your company's ability to move forward.

Furthermore, even if you just want to keep your large-scale and mission-critical ASP Web applications around without developing any new ASP.NET code, as long as it performs to your expectation, there are few reasons to go through a complete development cycle and incur various costs just to adopt a cool technology today.

4.6.1.2 OPTION 2: START FROM SCRATCH NOW

Starting from scratch may be the optimal long-term solution, because ASP.NET does provide a brand new programming model and .NET Framework introduces a major architectural change. In order to take full advantage of the new ASP.NET, especially the power of .NET Framework, you probably should redesign and rewrite ASP Web applications from the ground up. It is especially relevant if there are major issues with the current applications that are beyond simple tuning or minor migration.

Obviously, this "early adopter" approach could come with a hefty price tag and steep learning curve.

4.6.1.3 OPTION 3: MIGRATE

For ASP.NET, significant improvements have been made in the areas of performance, state management, scalability, deployment, security, Web farm support, and Web services infrastructure. Either phased-in or as a whole, a lot of the ASP Web applications will be migrated to ASP.NET over time, hopefully with minor changes. According to the Microsoft ASP.NET development team, they did an excellent job in preserving backward compatibility with ASP applications. Therefore, in a lot of cases, migration from ASP to ASP.NET does not appear to demand a very large and hard-to-recover investment.

4.6.2 Areas of Change

Besides what we discussed earlier in this chapter, such as server controls and new event-based Web Forms architecture, there are a few major ways in which ASP and ASP.NET differ:

- Changes in intrinsic objects
- Changes in layout and coding styles
- Changes in application configurations
- Changes in session and state management
- Changes in security model and practice
- Changes in languages (VB.NET)

Most ASP applications seem to be based on Microsoft Visual Basic Scripting Edition (VBScript). Microsoft Visual Basic.NET would probably be the language of choice for most of the developers who are performing the migration. In short, major changes made to VB.NET almost guarantee that existing ASP pages containing VBScript will not port directly to ASP.NET. In most cases, though, the necessary changes will involve only a few lines of code. New features of VB.NET are discussed in detail in Appendix B.

JScript has been used mostly for client-side programming, and the new-and-improved JScript.NET is covered in depth in Appendix D. In this section, we cover neither the syntax changes of VB.NET nor those of JScript.NET.

4.6.2.1 CHANGES IN INTRINSIC OBJECTS

ASP API consists of a few intrinsic objects, including **Request**, **Response**, **Page**, and a few others, which we covered in Section 4.3. The most significant change in ASP.NET is the use of **NameValueCollection** type, instead of the ASP array of strings, to store and retrieve **Request.Form**, **Request.Cookies**, and **Request.QueryString**, just to name a few.

Let's look at an example that shows the implications of this. Recall example VB.aspx in Section 4.2, which retrieves and displays the travel destination for the user. It is a little restrictive because the user can only choose to go one place at a time. Suppose you want to make the destination drop-down list as a multiselect, meanwhile showing multiple destinations that the user chooses to go at the same time. Here is a way to make the code changes to create a new Web page, **exampleMultiVB.aspx**:

```
<!-- exampleMultiVB.aspx -->
<%@ Page Language="VB" %>
<html>
<head>
    <link rel="stylesheet"href="example.css">
</head>
<body>
<form action="exampleMultiVB.aspx">
    <h3> Name: <input name="Name"
    type=text
    value="<%=Request.QueryString("Name")%>">
    Destination:
    <select name="Destination"
    multiple="multiple" size=2>
     ...
        <%
            Dim J As Integer
            For J = 0 To Request.QueryString.GetValues( _
            "Destination").length - 1
        %>
            <%=Request.QueryString("Name") %>,
            you chose to travel to
            <%=Request.QueryString.GetValues( _
            "Destination")(J) %> <br/>
        <% Next %>
    <% Else If (Request.QueryString("Name") = _
    Nothing) %>
        Please try again!
    <% Else If (Request.QueryString("Destination") = _
    Nothing) %>
        Please try again!
    <% End If %>
</form>
</body>
</html>
```

Notice that we use **Request.QueryString.GetValues ("Destination")(J)** to traverse the collection of **QueryString** content, instead of using **Request.QueryString("Destination")(J)**, as we would in ASP.

Another key change you need to be aware of is the **Page** object. Functions have to be declared inside a **<script>** block, instead of **<% %>**, plus render functions that mix HTML with function code are no longer supported. Therefore the following ASP code has to migrate.

```
<!-- RenderFunc.asp -->
<html>
<body>
<% Sub RenderedByASP() %>
<H3> I am rendered by ASP. </H3>
<% End Sub %>
<%
   Call RenderedByASP()
%>
</body>
</html>
```

The corresponding ASP.NET code becomes the following:

```
<!-- RenderFunc.aspx -->
<html>
<body>
<script language="VB" runat="server">
Sub ResponseByASPDotNet()
   Response.Write("<H3> Now, I am streamed from " & _
             "ASP.NET. </H3>")
End Sub
</script>
<%
   Call ResponseByASPDotNet()
%>
</body>
</html>
```

4.6.2.2 CHANGES IN LAYOUT AND CODING STYLE

There are three language choices in ASP.NET for developing Web pages: C#, Visual Basic .NET, and JScript. However, you cannot mix the supported languages together in a single page, which is different from ASP.

Under ASP.NET, there are no limitations on number of lines of directives and their placements, while ASP restricts directives to the first line of the Web page.

There are quite a few layout and coding style changes in ASP.NET. Refer to the latest Microsoft ASP.NET documentation for details.

4.6.2.3 CHANGES IN APPLICATION CONFIGURATIONS

Instead of using system registry and the IIS Metabase, as in ASP, ASP.NET introduces a brand new, XML-based, centralized configuration model that uses application- and server-specific configuration files. Each ASP.NET application has its own **web.config** file that lives in its application root directory.

This strategy fits well with the WYSIWYG programming model for VS.NET and is easily extensible.

For detailed configuration options and available settings, please refer to Section 4.5.3 and ASP.NET documentation.

4.6.2.4 CHANGES IN SESSION AND STATE MANAGEMENT

As illustrated in Section 4.5.2, ASP.NET provides more than one way to persist the session states of a Web application. Table 4-4 lists all four options for setting the **mode** attribute for **sessionState** in **web.config**.

Table 4-4	*Session State Mode Settings in ASP.NET*
Option	**Description**
Inproc	Session state is stored locally (ASP style).
StateServer	Session state is stored in a state service process located remotely or locally (if the local server runs the state service).
SqlServer	Session state is stored in a SQL Server database.
Off	Session state is disabled.

One important thing to keep in mind regarding migration: Even when ASP and ASP.NET applications coexist on the same physical server and use the same model to preserve the session state, state variables stored in the intrinsic **Session** or **Application** objects cannot be shared between ASP and ASP.NET Web pages.

4.6.2.5 CHANGES IN SECURITY MODEL AND PRACTICE

As mentioned in Section 4.5.4, ASP.NET cooperates with IIS to provide a centralized security model based on the application configuration file **web.config**. More extensible options such as Passport are provided, whereas in ASP you either have to use pure Windows/IIS-based authentication and authorization or roll your own.

4.6.3 Best Practices to Prepare for Migration

Based on the changes we have seen so far in ASP.NET, here is a list of best practices that can help future migration efforts even when we program in ASP today:

- *Avoid Mixing Languages.* Since ASP.NET requires only one inline <% %>, interleaving VBScript and JScript is definitely not recommended.
- *Declare Functions Inside <Script> Blocks.* Declaring functions inside <% %> is not supported.

- *Avoid Render Functions.* We explained such changes in Section 4.6.2.1.
- *Explicitly Free Resources.* Freeing resources is a good practice to help the Common Language Runtime garbage collector.
- *Use Option Explicit.* This cleanly organizes how variables are declared and initialized.

In summary, development skills gained through developing ASP Web applications are in no way obsolete. With careful preparation and in-depth research, changing from ASP to ASP.NET may not be as daunting as it first seems to be.

Summary

ASP.NET is a unified Web development platform that greatly simplifies the implementation of sophisticated Web applications. In this chapter we introduced the fundamentals of ASP.NET and covered Web Forms, which make it easy to develop interactive Web sites. Server controls present the programmer with an event model similar to what is provided by controls in ordinary Windows programming. This high-level programming model rests on a lower-level request/response programming model, which is common to earlier approaches to Web programming and is still accessible to the ASP.NET programmer.

It is fairly easy to manage sessions and states under ASP.NET. Configuration is based on XML files and is very flexible. There are a great variety of server controls, including wrappers around HTML controls, validation controls, and rich controls. Data binding makes it easy to display data from a variety of data sources. The VB.NET development environment includes a Form Designer, which makes it very easy to lay out Web Forms visually and add event handlers.

ASP.NET can provide the easiest and most scalable way to build, deploy, and run distributed Web applications that can target any browser or device for building powerful Web applications and services.

In Chapter 5 we cover ADO.NET, which is a standards-based programming model for creating distributed, data-sharing applications. We further explore how various kinds of data binding are done under .NET.

ADO.NET

*A*ccessing data has become a major task for software development, for both stand-alone and Web-based applications. ADO.NET,
the Active Data Objects for the .NET Framework, offers a consistent and scalable solution for access to various data sources.

ADO.NET is an evolutionary improvement to ActiveX Data
Objects (ADO). It is a standards-based programming model for
creating distributed, data-sharing applications. ADO.NET offers
several advantages over previous versions of ADO and over other
data-access components. These benefits fall into the following categories: interoperability, maintainability, programmability, and
performance.

5.1 Overview

ADO.NET is a set of classes that expose data access services to the .NET programmer. ADO.NET provides a rich set of components for creating distributed, data-sharing applications. It is an integral part of the .NET Framework,
providing access to relational data, XML, and application data. ADO.NET
supports a variety of development needs, including the creation of front-end
clients and middle-tier business objects that access various data sources.
Using ADO.NET, applications may connect to these data sources and
retrieve, manipulate, and update data.

ADO.NET includes .NET data providers for connecting to a database,
executing commands, and retrieving results. Those results are either

processed directly or placed in an ADO.NET **DataSet** object in order to be exposed to the user in an ad hoc manner. The ADO.NET **DataSet** object can also be used independently of a .NET data provider to manage data local to the application or it can be sourced from XML.

5.1.1 ADO.NET Design Goal

As application development has evolved, new applications have become loosely coupled based on the Web application model. Nowadays, more and more applications use XML as transfer syntax for information exchange over network connections. Web applications use HTTP as the vehicle for communication between tiers, and states have to be explicitly maintained between requests. This new model is very different from the connected data architecture and tightly coupled style of programming that characterized the client/server era, where a connection was held open for the duration of the program's lifetime. In addition, the scope of an application may be expanded to allow access to data sources of various kinds, including different relational databases, data files, and XML streams.

Today's developer needs an entirely new programming model for data access, one in which the data access mechanism is uniform, that is, the components for data access share a common type system, design pattern, and naming conventions.

ADO.NET was designed to meet the needs of this new programming model: disconnected data architecture; tight integration with XML-based, common data representation with the ability to combine data from multiple and varied data sources; and optimized facilities for interacting with a database, all native to the .NET Framework.

First, ADO.NET is designed to leverage current ADO knowledge. Microsoft's design for ADO.NET addresses many of the requirements of today's application development model. At the same time, the programming model stays as similar as possible to ADO, so current ADO developers do not have to learn a brand new data access technology. Moreover, ADO.NET coexists with ADO. While most new .NET applications will be written using ADO.NET, ADO remains available to the .NET programmer through an interoperability mechanism. We compare ADO.NET and ADO at the end of this chapter.

Second, ADO.NET is designed to support the *n*-tier programming model. ADO.NET provides first-class support for the disconnected, *n*-tier programming environment in which Web-based applications are written. The concept of working with a disconnected set of data has become a focal point in the programming model. The ADO.NET solution for *n*-tier programming is the **DataSet** object.

Finally, ADO.NET is designed to provide XML support. XML and data access are intimately tied together. XML is all about encoding data, and data access is increasingly becoming all about XML. The .NET Framework does not just support Web standards—it is built entirely on top of them. XML support is built into ADO.NET at a fundamental level. The XML class framework in .NET and ADO.NET are part of the same architecture—they integrate at many different levels. You no longer have to choose between the data access set of services and their XML counterparts; the ability to cross over from one to the other is inherent in the design of both.

5.1.2 ADO.NET Architecture

Data processing has traditionally relied primarily on a connection-based, two-tier model. As data processing increasingly uses multitiered architectures, programmers are switching to a disconnected approach to provide better scalability for their applications.

ADO.NET leverages the power of XML to provide disconnected access to data. ADO.NET was designed hand-in-hand with the .NET XML framework—both are components of a single architecture.

ADO.NET and the .NET XML framework converge in the **DataSet** object. The **DataSet** can be populated with data from an XML source, whether it is a file or an XML stream. The **DataSet** can be written as W3C-compliant XML, XML Schema Definition language (XSD) schema, regardless of the source of the data in the **DataSet**. Because the native serialization format of the **DataSet** is XML, it is an excellent medium for moving data between tiers, making the **DataSet** an optimal choice for information exchange over the Internet and in Web-based applications.

The **DataSet** can also be synchronized with an **XmlDataDocument** object to provide relational and hierarchical access to data in real time.

The ADO.NET components have been designed to factor data access from data manipulation. Two central components of ADO.NET accomplish this: the class **DataSet** and the .NET data provider, which is a set of components including the classes **Connection**, **Command**, **DataReader**, and **DataAdapter** objects.

The **DataSet** is the core component of the disconnected architecture of ADO.NET. The **DataSet** is explicitly designed for data access independent of any data source. As a result it can be used with multiple and differing data sources and XML data, or used to manage data local to the application. The **DataSet** contains a collection of one or more **DataTable** objects made up of rows and columns of data, as well as primary key, foreign key, constraint, and relation information about the data in the **DataTable** objects.

The other core element of the ADO.NET architecture is the .NET data provider, whose components are explicitly designed for data manipulation and fast, forward-only, read-only access to data. The **Connection** object provides connectivity to a data source. The **Command** object enables access to database commands that return data, modify data, run stored procedures, and send or retrieve parameter information. The **DataReader** provides a high-performance stream of data from the data source. Finally, the **DataAdapter** provides the bridge between the **DataSet** object and the data source. The **DataAdapter** uses **Command** objects to execute SQL commands at the data source to both load the **DataSet** object with data and to reconcile changes made to the data in the **DataSet** object with the data source.

You can write .NET data providers for any data source. The .NET Framework ships with two .NET data providers: the SQL Server .NET Data Provider and the OLE DB .NET Data Provider.

Figure 5-1 illustrates the components of the ADO.NET architecture.

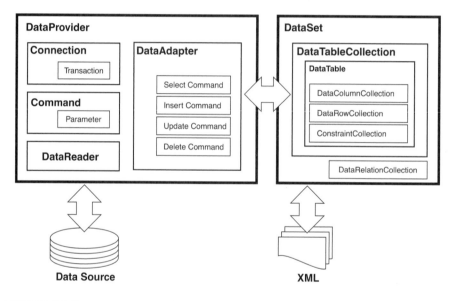

Data Source   **XML**

| Figure 5-1 | *Components of ADO.NET architecture.* |

5.2 Simple Example

Before we get into the details of ADO.NET, let us take a look at a few simple examples that will give a general idea of how ADO.NET can work for you.

To use ADO.NET, you need to include the **System.Data** namespace in your applications. In Visual Basic, the following statement is used to include the namespace **System.Data**.

```
Imports System.Data
```

In C#, the following statement is used to include the **System.Data** namespace.

```
using System.Data;
```

Now let us create simple ADO.NET applications that return results from a data source and write the output to the console. The sample programs are pretty straightforward because ADO.NET supplies a rich set of components to support access to data sources. These components are discussed in the following sections.

Programs **SimpleSample1.vb** and **SimpleSample1.cs** are Visual Basic and C# programs that connect to the **MyDatabase** database on Microsoft SQL Server 2000 and return a list of Categories using a **DataReader**. In order to access SQL Server database, the **System.Data.sqlClient** namespace also needs to be included. Program **SimpleSample1.vb** is as follows:

```
' SimpleSample1.vb
Imports System
Imports System.Data
Imports System.Data.SqlClient

Public Class Sample

    Public Shared Sub Main()
        ' create an object for connection to SQL
        ' server database
        Dim MySqlConn As SqlConnection = New SqlConnection(_
            "server=(local)\NetSDK; " & _
            "uid=QSUser; " & _
            "pwd=QSPassword; " & _
            "database=Northwind" _
        )
        ' obtain the SqlCommand object for the connection
        Dim Cmd As SqlCommand = MySqlConn.CreateCommand()
        ' Set the SQL statement that is to be executed
        ' at the data source.
        Cmd.CommandText = _
            "select CategoryID, CategoryName from " &_
                "Categories"
        ' open database
        MySqlConn.Open()
        ' send CommandText to the SqlConnection
        ' so as to build an SqlReader
        Dim MyReader As SqlDataReader = Cmd.ExecuteReader()
        ' keep reading data as long as it is available
        Do While MyReader.Read()
            ' present the data retrieved
            Console.WriteLine(
```

```
                                    vbTab + " {0} " + vbTab + " {1} ", _
                                    MyReader.GetInt32(0), _
                                    MyReader.GetString(1)
                          )
                  Loop

                  ' close the DataReader and connection
                  MyReader.Close()
                  MySqlConn.Close()

          End Sub
      End Class
```

This program may be compiled with the following command:

```
vbc SimpleSample1.vb /r:System.Data.dll
```

The same functionality may be implemented in C#, with the program
SimpleSample1.cs:

```
// SimpleSample1.cs
using System;
using System.Data;
using System.Data.SqlClient;

class Sample {

    public static void Main(string[] args) {
            // Create an object for connection
            // to SQL Server database.
            SqlConnection Conn = new SqlConnection(
                    "server=(local)\\NetSDK; " +
                    "uid=QSUser; " +
                    "pwd=QSPassword; " +
                    "database=Northwind"
            );
            // obtain the SqlCommand object for the connection
            SqlCommand Cmd = Conn.CreateCommand();
            // set the SQL statement that is to be executed
            // at the data source
            Cmd.CommandText =
                    "select CategoryID, CategoryName from ⇓
                            Categories";
            // open database
            Conn.Open();
            // send CommandText to the SqlConnection
            // so as to build an SqlReader.
            SqlDataReader MyReader = Cmd.ExecuteReader();
            // Keep reading data as long as it is available.
            while (MyReader.Read()) {
                    // present the data retrieved
```

```
                    Console.WriteLine(
                        "\t{0}\t{1}",
                        MyReader.GetInt32(0),
                        MyReader.GetString(1)
                    );
                }
                Close the DataReader and Connection
                MyReader.Close();
                Conn.Close();
        }
}
```

This program may be compiled with the following command:

```
csc SimpleSample.csc /r:System.Data.dll
```

Alternatively, a data source may also be accessed via OLE DB Data Provider, using the programs **SimpleSample2.vb** and **SimpleSample2.cs**:

```
' SimpleSample2.vb
Imports System
Imports System.Data
Imports System.Data.OleDb
Imports Microsoft.VisualBasic

Public Class Sample

Sub Main()
    ' Create an object for connection
      ' to database via OLEDB.
    Dim MyOleDbConn As OleDbConnection = _
          New OleDbConnection( _
                "server=(local)\NetSDK; " & _
                "uid=QSUser; " & _
                "pwd=QSPassword; " & _
                "database=Northwind; " & _
                "Provider=SQLOLEDB" _
          )

        ' Obtain the SqlCommand object for the connection.
        Dim Cmd As OleDbCommand = _
              MyOleDbConn.CreateCommand()

        ' Set the SQL statement that is to be executed
        ' at the data source.
        Cmd.CommandText =
              "select CategoryID, CategoryName from ⇓
                    Categories"

        ' Open database.
        MyOleDbConn.Open()
```

```
                ' Send CommandText to the OleDbConnection
                ' so as to build an SqlReader.
                Dim MyReader As OleDbDataReader = ⇓
                       Cmd.ExecuteReader()

                ' Keep reading data as long as it is available.
                Do While MyReader.Read()
                       ' Present the data retrieved.
                       Console.WriteLine(
                               vbTab + " {0} " + vbTab + " {1} ", _
                               MyReader.GetInt32(0),
                               MyReader.GetString(1)
                       )
                Loop

                ' Close the DataReader and connection.
                MyReader.Close()
                MyOleDbConn.Close()

        End Sub
End Class

// SimpleSample2.cs
using System;
using System.Data;
using System.Data.OleDb;

class Sample {

  static void Main(string[] args)
  {
     // create an object for connection to database viaOLE DB
     OleDbConnection Conn = new OleDbConnection(
            "server=(local)\\NetSDK;" +
            "uid=QSUser;pwd=QSPassword;" +
            "database=Northwind;" +
            "provider=sqloledb"
     );

     // obtain the OleDbCommand object for the connection
     OleDbCommand Cmd = Conn.CreateCommand();

     // set the SQL statement that is to be executed
     // at the data source
     Cmd.CommandText =
            "select CategoryID, CategoryName from Categories";

     // open database
     Conn.Open();
```

```
// send CommandText to the OleDbConnection
// so as to build an SqlReader
OleDbDataReader  MyReader = Cmd.ExecuteReader();

// keep reading data as long as it is available
while (MyReader.Read())
{
      // present the data retrieved
      Console.WriteLine(
            "\t{0}\t{1}",
            MyReader.GetInt32(0),
            MyReader.GetString(1)
      );
}

// close the DataReader and connection
MyReader.Close();
Conn.Close();
}
}
```

We will come back to these examples when we discuss .NET data providers and ADO.NET **DataSet**.

5.3 ADO.NET Data Providers

A .NET data provider is used to connect to a database, execute commands, and retrieve results. Those results are either processed directly or placed in an ADO.NET **DataSet** in order to be exposed to the user in an ad hoc manner, combined with data from multiple sources, or transferred between tiers. The .NET data provider is designed to be lightweight, creating a minimal layer between the data source and your code, which increases performance without sacrificing functionality.

There are four core objects that make up a .NET data provider:

- **Connection**, which establishes a connection to a specific data source
- **Command**, which executes a command at a data source, exposes parameters, and can enlist a transaction from a connection
- **DataReader**, which reads a forward-only, read-only stream of data from a data source
- **DataAdapter**, which populates a **DataSet** and resolves updates with the data source

The .NET Framework includes the SQL Server .NET Data Provider (for Microsoft SQL Server 7.0 or later) and the OLE DB .NET Data Provider. Each data provider has its own set of core objects. The programs in Section 5.2 use the objects corresponding to the data provider actually used.

5.3.1 The SQL Server .NET Data Provider

The SQL Server .NET Data Provider uses its own protocol to communicate with SQL Server. The SQL Server .NET Data Provider is lightweight and performs well, accessesing a SQL Server data source directly without adding an OLE DB or Open Database Connectivity (ODBC) layer.

To use the SQL Server .NET Data Provider, you must have access to Microsoft SQL Server 7.0 or later. In the class library, SQL Server .NET Data Provider classes are located in the **System.Data.SqlClient** namespace. For earlier versions of Microsoft SQL Server, use the OLE DB .NET Data Provider with the SQL Server OLE DB Data Provider (SQLOLEDB).

To use the SQL Server .NET Data Provider, you will want to include namespace **System.Data.SqlClient** in your applications.

In a Visual Basic program, the following statement is used to include namespace **System.Data.SqlClient**.

```
Import System.Data.SqlClient
```

In C#, the following statement is used to include the **System. Data.SqlClient** namespace.

```
using System.Data.SqlClient;
```

In Section 5.2, programs **SimpleSample1.vb** and **SimpleSample1.cs** use SQL Server .NET Data Provider. They use the objects corresponding to SQL Server .NET Data Provider. That is

- **SqlConnection** objects are used to establish a connection to the data sources.
- **SqlCommand** objects are used to execute SQL statements on the data sources.
- **SqlDataReader** objects are used to read the data records from the data sources.

5.3.2 The OLE DB .NET Data Provider

The OLE DB .NET Data Provider uses native OLE DB through COM interop to enable data access. The OLE DB .NET Data Provider supports both manual and automatic transactions. For automatic transactions, the OLE DB .NET Data Provider automatically enlists in a transaction and obtains transaction details from Windows 2000 component services.

To use the OLE DB .NET Data Provider, you must also use an OLE DB provider. The following providers are compatible with ADO.NET.

* Microsoft OLE DB Provider SQL Server that uses Driver SQLOLEDB
* Microsoft OLE DB Provider for Oracle that uses Driver MSDAORA
* OLE DB Provider for Microsoft Jet that uses Driver Microsoft.Jet.OLEDB.4.0

The OLE DB .NET Data Provider does not support OLE DB 2.5 interfaces. OLE DB data providers that require support for OLE DB 2.5 interfaces will not function properly with the OLE DB .NET Data Provider. This includes the Microsoft OLE DB Provider for Exchange and the Microsoft OLE DB Provider for Internet Publishing. The OLE DB .NET Data Provider also does not work with the OLE DB Provider for ODBC (MSDASQL).

OLE DB .NET Data Provider classes are located in the **System.Data.OleDb** namespace. To use the OLE DB .NET Data Provider, you will want to include the namespace **System.Data.OleDb** in your applications.

In Visual Basic, the following statement is used to include the namespace **System.Data.OleDB.**

```
Import System.Data.OleDb
```

In C#, the following statement is used to include the **System.Data.OleDb** namespace.

```
using System.Data.OleDb;
```

The OLE DB .NET Data Provider requires the installation of MDAC 2.6 or later.

In Section 5.2, programs **SimpleSample2.vb** and **SimpleSample2.cs** use OLE DB .NET Data Provider. They use the objects corresponding to OLE DB .NET Data Provider:

* **OleDbConnection** objects are used to establish a connection to the data sources.
* **OleDbCommand** objects are used to execute OLEDB statements on the data sources.
* **OleDbDataReader** objects are used to read the data records from the data sources

5.3.3 Choosing a .NET Data Provider

Depending on the design and data source of your application, your choice of .NET data provider can improve the performance, capability, and integrity of your application.

In general SQL Server .NET Data Provider is recommended for

- Middle-tier applications using Microsoft SQL Server 7.0 or later
- Single-tier applications using Microsoft Data Engine (MSDE) or Microsoft SQL Server 7.0 or later

OLE DB .NET Data Provider is recommended for

- Middle-tier applications using Microsoft SQL Server 6.5 or earlier
- Middle-tier applications using other relational database management systems, such as Oracle

Please also note that

- Use of the OLE DB .NET Data Provider with a Microsoft Access database for a middle-tier application is not recommended.
- Support for the OLE DB Provider for ODBC (MSDASQL) is disabled.

5.3.4 Common Model

In Section 5.2, programs that use SQL Server Data Provider and OLE DB Data Provider are not identical. In other words, accesses to various data sources are not consistent on this level.

ADO.NET exposes a common model for .NET data provider objects so that a single set of code can be written to work regardless of the .NET data provider. This scheme is realized based on the fact that classes in the data providers of both kinds implement the same set of interfaces:

- Both **SqlConnection** and **OleDbConnection** classes implement interface **IDbConnection**.
- Both **SqlCommand** and **OleDbCommand** classes implement interface **IDbCommand**.
- Both **SqlDataReader** and **OleDbDataReader** classes implement implement interface **IDbDataReader**.

Method **AccessDatabase** in **CommonSample.vb** and **CommonSample.cs** programs works with both the SQL Server .NET Data Provider and the OLE DB .NET Data Provider. This method uses interfaces rather than the class that implement them, so that the discrepancy between data providers or data sources can be hidden. The **CommonSample.vb** program is as follows:

```
' CommonSample.vb
Imports System
Imports System.Data
Imports System.Data.SqlClient
Imports System.Data.OleDb
Imports Microsoft.VisualBasic
```

```
Public Class Common

    Sub AccessDatabase(ByVal Conn As IDbConnection)
        ' obtain the Command object for the connection
        Dim Cmd As IDbCommand = Conn.CreateCommand()

        ' set the SQL statement that is to be executed
        ' at the data source
        Cmd.CommandText =
            "select CategoryID, CategoryName from ⇓
                Categories"

        ' open database
        Conn.Open()

        ' send Command to the connection
        ' so as to build a DataReader
        Dim MyReader As IDataReader = Cmd.ExecuteReader()

        ' keep reading data as long as it is available
        Do While MyReader.Read()
            ' Present the data retrieved.
            Console.WriteLine(
                vbTab + " {0} " + vbTab + " {1} ", _
                MyReader.GetInt32(0),
                MyReader.GetString(1)
            )
        Loop

        ' close the DataReader and the connection
        MyReader.Close()
        Conn.Close()
    End Sub

    Sub Main()
        AccessDatabase(
            New SqlConnection( _
                "server=(local)\NetSDK; " & _
                "uid=QSUser; " & _
                pwd=QSPassword; " & _
                "database=Northwind" _
            )
        )
        AccessDatabase(
            New OleDbConnection( _
                "server=(local)\NetSDK; " & _
                "uid=QSUser; " &_
                pwd=QSPassword; " & _
                "database=Northwind; " & _
                "Provider=SQLOLEDB" _
```

```
            )
          )
    End Sub
End Class
```

The **CommonSample.cs** program is as follows:

```csharp
// CommonSample.cs
using System;
using System.Data;
using System.Data.SqlClient;
using System.Data.OleDb;
class Sample {
    public static void AccessDatabase(IDbConnection Conn) {
        // obtain the Command object for the connection
        IDbCommand Cmd = Conn.CreateCommand();
        // set the SQL statement that is to be executed
        // at the data source
        Cmd.CommandText =
            "select CategoryID, CategoryName from ⇓
                Categories";

        // open database
        Conn.Open();
        // send CommandText to the connection so as to build
        // a IDataReader
        IDataReader MyReader = Cmd.ExecuteReader();
        // keep reading data as long as it is available
        while (MyReader.Read()) {
            // Present the data retrieved.
            Console.WriteLine(
                "\t{0}\t{1}",
                MyReader.GetInt32(0),
                MyReader.GetString(1)
            );
        }

        // close the DataReader and the connection
        MyReader.Close();
        Conn.Close();
    }

    public static void Main() {
        AccessDatabase(
            new  SqlConnection(
                "server=(local)\\NetSDK; " +
                "uid=QSUser; " +
                pwd=QSPassword;" +
                "database=Northwind"
```

```
                    )
            );
            AccessDatabase(
                    new OleDbConnection(
                            "server=(local)\\NetSDK; " +
                            "uid=QSUser; " +
                            pwd=QSPassword; " +
                            "database=Northwind; " +
                            "provider=sqloledb"
                    )
            );
    }
}
```

5.4 Using .NET Data Provider to Access Data

A data provider in the .NET Framework serves as a bridge between an application and a data source. In this section, we look at how its classes work in order to access data.

5.4.1 Connection

Each data provider supplies a connection class, and its instance represents an open connection to a specific data source. When a connection instance is constructed, a connection string is given as an argument to the constructor that specifies the parameters of the connection.

Using SQL Server .NET Data Provider, an **SqlConnection** object may be created to establish a connection to an SQL Server database. In a Visual Basic program, the following statements perform this task:

```
Dim Conn As SqlConnection = New SqlConnection( _
    "server=(local)\NetSDK; " & _
    "uid=QSUser; " & _
    "pwd=QSPassword; " & _
    "database=Northwind" _
)
```

In a C# program, the following statements perform this task:

```
SqlConnection Conn = new  SqlConnection(
    "server=(local)\\NetSDK; " +
    "uid=QSUser; " +
    "pwd=QSPassword; " +
    "database=Northwind"
);
```

Using OLE DB .NET Data Provider, an **OleDbConnection** object may be created to establish a connection to a specific data source via an OLE DB object. In a Visual Basic program, the following statements perform this task:

```
Dim MySqlConn As OleDbConnection = New OleDbConnection ( _
    "Provider = SQLOLEDB; " &_
    "Data Source = localhost; " &_
    "Integrated Security = SSPI; " &_
    "Initial Catalog = MyDatabase"
)
```

In a C# program, the following statements perform this task:

```
OleDbConnection MyOleDbConn = New OleDbConnection (
    "Provider = SQLOLEDB; " +
    "Data Source = localhost; " +
    "Integrated Security = SSPI; " +
    "Initial Catalog = MyDatabase"
);
```

After a **Connection** object is created, its **Open** method is called to open it for use and the **Close** method is called after use.

5.4.2 Command

When a connection is established to a data source, a **Command** object is created whereby actions are taken against the data source. First, an instance of command class is created. This can be done in various ways. In Sections 5.2 and 5.3.4, for example, the method **CreateCommand** of the **Connection** object can be used to create a **Command** object. Then an SQL statement is associated with the **Command** object in various ways. In Sections 5.2 and 5.3.4, for example, the SQL statement is directly assigned to the property **CommandText**. Finally, **DataReader** object, **DataSet** object, **DataAdapter** object, and the **Command** object may be used to query or update the data source. In this section, we concentrate on creating the **Command** object; the other objects are discussed in the following subsections.

There are several ways in which a **Command** object may be created and be associated with an SQL statement and a **Connection** object. For example, a **Command** object may also be created with a constructor that takes a string of SQL statements and a **Connection** object as arguments.

With SQL Server .NET Data Provider, a constructor for class **SqlCommand** is used. In a Visual Basic program, the following statement performs this task:

```
Dim MySqlCmd As SqlCommand = New SqlCommand( _
    "select CategoryID, CategoryName from Categories", _
    MySqlConn _
)
```

In a C# program, the following statement performs this task:

```
SqlCommand MySqlCmd = New SqlCommand(
    "select CategoryID, CategoryName from Categories",
    MySqlConn
);
```

In this case, **MySqlConn** is the **SqlConnection** object that we created in Section 5.4.1.

With OLE DB .NET Data Provider, a constructor for class **OleDb-Command** is used. In a Visual Basic program, the following statement performs this task:

```
Dim MyOleDbCmd As OleDbCommand = New OldDbCommand( _
    "select CategoryID, CategoryName from Categories", _
    MyOleDbConn _
)
```

In a C# program, the following statement performs this task:

```
OleDbCommand MyOleDbCmd = New OldDbCommand(
    "select CategoryID, CategoryName from Categories",
    MyOleDbConn
);
```

In this case, **MyOleDbConn** is the **OleDbConnection** object that we created in Section 5.4.1.

5.4.3 DataReader

DataReader provides a nonbuffered stream of data that allows procedural logic to efficiently process results from a data source sequentially. Using the **DataReader** can increase application performance and reduce system overhead because only one row at a time is ever in memory. This is a good choice when large amounts of data are to be retrieved because the data is not cached.

A **DataReader** is created when the **ExecuteReader** method of the **Command** object is invoked. This method creates a **DataReader** object and executes the SQL statement that is associated with the **Command** object, against the data source. Using SQL Server .NET Data Provider, you may call the **ExecuteReader** method of the **SqlCommand** object to create an **SqlDataReader** object. In a Visual Basic program, the following statement performs this task:

```
Dim MySqlReader As SqlDataReader = MySqlCmd.ExecuteReader()
```

In a C# program, the following statement performs this task:

```
SqlDataReader MySqlReader = MySqlCmd.ExecuteReader();
```

In this case, **MySqlCmd** is the **SqlCommand** object that we created in Section 5.4.2.

Using OLE DB .NET Data Provider, you may call the **ExecuteReader** method of the **OleDbCommand** object to create an **OleDbDataReader** object. In a Visual Basic program, the following statement performs this task:

```
Dim MyOleDbReader As OleDbDataReader = _
  MyOleDbCmd.ExecuteReader()
```

In a C# program, the following statement performs this task:

```
OleDbDataReader MyOleDbReader = MyOleDbCmd.ExecuteReader();
```

In this case, **MyOleDbCmd** is the **OleDbCommand** object that we created in Section 5.4.2.

Once a **DataReader** object is created and the related SQL statement is executed, we are ready to retrieve the query result. For this purpose, method **Read** of the **DataReader** object is called in order to get a single record from the data source or a single row from the database. This method returns **TRUE** if a record is successfully fetched, and returns **FALSE** otherwise. As shown in Section 5.2, this method is used to construct a loop whereby the designated records in a data source can be retrieved one after another. In a Visual Basic program, a loop may look like this:

```
Do While myReader.Read()
    ' Present the data retrieved.
    Console.WriteLine(
        vbTab & " {0} " & vbTab & " {1} ",
        MyReader.GetInt32(0),
        MyReader.Getstring(1)
    )
Loop
```

In a C# program, a loop may look like this:

```
While (myReader.Read()) {
    // Present the data retrieved.
    Console.WriteLine(
        "\t{0}\t{1}",
        MyReader.GetInt32(0),
        MyReader.Getstring(1)
    );
}
```

Here, **GetInt32** and **GetString** are methods of **DataReader** that return the specified fields of a data record in their native types. There are a series of such methods, including **GetDateTime**, **GetDouble**, and **GetDecimal**, one for each data type available in the .NET Framework.

5.4.4 Single Value Retrieval

Method **ExecuteScalar** of a **Command** object allows a single value to be retrieved from the data source. It provides a shortcut whereby the query result can be fetched without the need to create a **DataReader** object.

Here is a Visual Basic program that fetches a single value from a query with SQL Server Data Provider:

```
Dim MyCmd As SqlCommand = New SqlCommand( _
    "select count(*) from employee",
    MySqlConn
)
Dim Count As Int32 Cint(MyCmd.ExecuteScalar())
```

The following C# program does the same thing.

```
SqlCommand MyCmd = new SqlCommand(
    "select count(*) from employee",
    MySqlConn
);
Int32 Count = (Int32)MyCmd.ExecuteScalar();
```

The return type of method **ExecuteScalar** is an **Object**; you need to convert the return value to its actual type.

5.4.5 Multiple Result Sets

When a **Command** object contains a number of SQL statements, multiple result sets are generated when the Command is executed. In this case, method **NextResult** may be used to iterate through the data set in order. Once invoked, this method moves to the next result set; it returns **TRUE** if the next result exists and **FALSE** if it does not.

Here is a Visual Basic program that retrieves multiple result sets with SQL Server Data Provider:

```
' Command with multiple queries;
' the SQL statements are separated by ';'.
Dim MyCmd As SqlCommand = New SqlCommand( _
    "select CustomerID, CustomerLastName " &_
        "from Customer; " &_
    "select EmployeeID, EmployeeLastName " &_
        "from Employee", _
    MySqlConn
)
MyCmd.Open()
Dim MyReader As SqlDataReader = MyCmd.ExecuteReader()

Do
    ' write the column name for the current result set
    Console.WriteLine( _
```

```
            vbTab & MyReaderGetName(0) &_
            vbTab & MyReaderGetName(1)   _
        )

        Do While MyReader.Read()
            Console.WriteLine( _
                vbTab & MyReader.GetInt32(0) &_
                vbTab & MyReader.GetString(1) _
            )
        Loop

Loop Until Not MyReader.NextResult()

MyReader.Close()
MySqlConn.Close()
```

The following C# program does the same thing.

```
// command with multiple queries;
// the SQL statements are separated by ';'
SqlCommand MyCmd = new SqlCommand(
    "select CustomerID, CustomerLastName from Customer; " +
    "select EmployeeID, EmployeeLastName from Employee",
    MySqlConn
);
MyCmd.Open();
SqlDataReader MyReader = MyCmd.ExecuteReader();

do {
    // write the column name for the current result set
    Console.WriteLine( _
        vbTab & MyReaderGetName(0) &_
        vbTab & MyReaderGetName(1)
    );

    while (MyReader.Read()) {
        Console.WriteLine( _
            vbTab & MyReader.GetInt32(0) &_
            vbTab & MyReader.GetString(1)
        );
} while (MyReader.NextResult())

MyReader.Close();
MySqlConn.Close();
```

5.4.6 Non-Query SQL Statements

The command class can also deal with SQL statements that do not generate results: **INSERT**, **UPDATE**, and **DELETE**. When a command is associated with one of these SQL statements, it can be executed with method **ExecuteNonQuery**, which returns the number of rows that have been affected.

Here is a Visual Basic program that inserts a row in a table in the source database with SQL Server Data Provider:

```
Dim MyCmd As SqlCommand = New SqlCommand( _
    "insert into Customer " &_
        (CustomerID, CustomerLastName) " &_
        "values (12345, 'Smith')", _
    MySqlConn
)
MySqlConn.Open()
Console.WriteLine( _
    "{0} row has been inserted. ", _
    MyCmd.ExecuteNonQuery()
)
MySqlConn.Close()
```

The following C# program does the same thing.

```
SqlCommand MyCmd = new SqlCommand(
    "insert into Customer " +
        (CustomerID, CustomerLastName) " +
        "values (12345, 'Smith') ",
    MySqlConn
);
MySqlConn.Open();
Console.WriteLine(
    "{0} row has been inserted. ",
    MyCmd.ExecuteNonQuery()
);
MySqlConn.Close();
```

5.4.7 Stored Procedures and Functions

A stored procedure or function encapsulates database operations in a single command whereby performance may be optimized and security enhanced in a distributed processing environment. Let us consider an example in which a stored procedure is first created and then invoked with SQL Server Data Provider. Here is such a program in Visual Basic.

```
' command that creates a stored procedure
Dim CreateCmd As SqlCommand = New SqlCommand( _
    "create procedure GetEmpNames " &_
    "  @EmpID nchar(8), " &_
```

```
        "   @EmpFirstName nchar(32) out, " &_
        "   @EmpLastName nchar(32) out " &_
        "as select @EmpFirstName = EmployeeFirstName, " &_
        "           @EmpLastName = EmployeeLastName " &_
        "     from Employee ", _
        "     where EmployeeID = @EmpID", _
        MySqlConn _
    )
    ' command that drops a stored procedure if it exists
    Dim DropCmd As SqlCommand = New SqlCommand( _
        "if exists ( " &_
        "       select name from sysobjects " &_
        "         where name = 'GetEmpNames' " &_
        "           and type = 'P'" &_
        "drop procedure GetEmpNames", _
        MySqlConn _
    )

    ' open the connection
    MySqlConn.Open()
    ' Drop the procedure if it exists.
    DropCmd.ExecuteNonQuery()
    ' Create the procedure.
    CreateCmd.ExecuteNonQuery()

    ' command that invokes the stored procedure
    Dim InvokeCommand As SqlCommand = New SqlCommand( _
        "GetEmpNames", _
        MySqlConn _
    )
    ' set the command type.
    InvokeCmd.CommandType = CommandType.StoredProcedure

    ' Fill the parameters collection for communication with the
    procedure.
    ' Input parameter and query criteria.
    Dim InvokeParam As SqlParameter
    InvokeParam = InvokeCmd.Parameters.Add( _
        "@EmpID", _
        SqlType.Nchar, _
        8 _
    )
    ' No need to set direction because default is Input.

    ' Output parameters and query results.
    ' First name
    InvokeParam = InvokeCmd.Parameters.Add( _
        "@EmpFirstName", _
        SqlType.Nchar, _
        32 _
```

```
)
' Set direction.
InvokeParam.Direction = ParameterDirection.Output
' Last name
InvokeParam = InvokeCmd.Parameters.Add( _
    "@EmpLastName", _
    SqlType.Nchar, _
    32 _
)
' Set direction.
InvokeParam.Direction = ParameterDirection.Output

' Provide the value for query criteria.
InvokeCmd.Parameters("@EmpID").Value = "12345"

' Invoke the stored procedure.
InvokeCmd.ExecuteNonQuery()

' Present the query results.
Console.WriteLine( _
    "Employee ID is {0} and name is {1} {2}.", _
    InvokeCmd.Parameter("@EmpID").Value, _
    InvokeCmd.Parameter("@EmpFirstName").Value, _
    InvokeCmd.Parameter("@EmpLastName").Value _
)
```

In this program, three **Command** objects are created for creating the stored procedure, dropping the stored procedure if it exists, and invoking the stored procedure. This stored procedure retrieves the first and last names of an employee with a given ID. It has one input parameter and two output parameters.

When the **Command** object that invokes the stored procedure is created, the procedure name is given as the **CommandText**. Having created this object, you have to set its property **CommandType** as **StoredProcedure**. We did not set **CommandType** before for our SQL statement–related **Command** objects because the default for **CommandText** is **Text**.

Your program communicates with the stored procedure in the database via its parameters. For this purpose, the parameters have to be populated into the parameter collection of the **Command** object that invokes the procedure. The query criteria are supplied to the input parameter and query results are fetched from the output parameter.

Property **Direction** for the output parameters needs to be set explicitly. It is not necessary to set the input parameter because the default for this property is **Input**.

The following C# program does the same thing.

```
// command that creates a stored procedure
SqlCommand CreateCmd = New SqlCommand(
    "create procedure GetEmpNames " +
```

```
    "   @EmpID nchar(8), " +
    "   @EmpFirstName nchar(32) out, " +
    "   @EmpLastName nchar(32) out " +
    "as select @EmpFirstName = EmployeeFirstName, " +
    "          @EmpLastName = EmployeeLastName " +
    "     from Employee " +
    "     where EmployeeID = @EmpID",
    MySqlConn
);
// command that drops a stored procedure if it exists
Dim DropCmd As SqlCommand = New SqlCommand(
    "if exists (" +
    "      select name from sysobjects " +
    "        where name = 'GetEmpNames' " +
    "          and type = 'P'" +
    "drop procedure GetEmpNames",
    MySqlConn
);

// open the connection
MySqlConn.Open();
// drop the procedure if it exists
DropCmd.ExecuteNonQuery();
// create the procedure
CreateCmd.ExecuteNonQuery();

// command that invokes the stored procedure
Dim InvokeCommand As SqlCommand = New SqlCommand(_
    "GetEmpNames",
    MySqlConn
);
// set the command type
InvokeCmd.CommandType = CommandType.StoredProcedure;

// fill the parameters collection for communication with the
procedure.
// input parameter and query criteria
SqlParameter InvokeParam;
InvokeParam = InvokeCmd.Parameters.Add(
    "@EmpID",
    SqlType.Nchar,
    8
);
// no need to set direction—default is Input

// Output parameters and query results.
// First name
InvokeParam = InvokeCmd.Parameters.Add(
    "@EmpFirstName",
    SqlType.Nchar,
```

```
    32
);
// set direction.
InvokeParam.Direction = ParameterDirection.Output
// Last name
InvokeParam = InvokeCmd.Parameters.Add(
    "@EmpLastName",
    SqlType.Nchar,
    32
);
// set direction
InvokeParam.Direction = ParameterDirection.Output;

// Provide the value for query criteria.
InvokeCmd.Parameters["@EmpID"].Value = "12345";

// Invoke the stored procedure.
InvokeCmd.ExecuteNonQuery();

// present the query results
Console.WriteLine(
    "Employee ID is {0} and name is {1} {2}.",
    InvokeCmd.Parameter["@EmpID"].Value,
    InvokeCmd.Parameter["@EmpFirstName"].Vaue
    InvokeCmd.Parameter["@EmpLastName"].Value
);
```

5.4.8 Transactions

Transactions are used to control data commitment in databases. For example, a fund-transfer transaction may credit one account and debit another. Either both actions are completed successfully (commit) or both are cancelled (rollback).

ADO.NET data providers supply transaction classes whereby database transactions are controlled. A transaction starts when method **BeginTransaction** of the object **Connection** is called. It ends when either method **Commit** or method **Rollback** of the **Transaction** object is invoked; the former is called when all the actions since the start of the transaction are done successfully and the latter is called otherwise.

Here is a Visual Basic program in which a transaction is carried out with SQL Server Data Provider:

```
' command and transaction object
Dim MySqlCmd As SqlCommand = New SqlCommand
Dim MySqlTrn As SqlTransaction

' open the Connection
MySqlConn.Open()
```

```vb
' assign the connection to the command.
MySqlCmd.Connection = MySqlConn

' begin the transaction
MySqlTrn = MySqlConn.BeginTransaction()
' assign the transaction to the command
MySqlCmd.Transaction = MySqlTrn

' use the error-handling construct to carry out
' the transaction
Try
    ' Credit one account.
    MySqlCmd.CommandText = _
        "update account set balance = " &_
               "balance + 100 where id = 12345"
    MySqlCmd.ExecuteNonQuery()

    ' Debit another account.
    MySqlCmd.CommandText = _
        "update account set balance = " &_
        "balance - 100 where id = 67890"
    MySqlCmd.ExecuteNonQuery()

    ' Everything is OK if you reach here.
    MySqlTrn.Commit()
Catch e as Exception
    ' Something is wrong and an exception is caught.
    MySqlTrn.RollBack()
Finally
    MySqlConn.Close()
End Try
```

Here is a C# program.

```csharp
// command and transaction object
SqlCommand MySqlCmd = New SqlCommand;
SqlTransaction MySqlTrn;

// open the connection
MySqlConn.Open();
// assign the connection to the command
MySqlCmd.Connection = MySqlConn;

// begin the transaction
MySqlTrn = MySqlConn.BeginTransaction();
// assign the transaction to the command
MySqlCmd.Transaction = MySqlTrn;

// use the error-handling construct
// to carry out the transaction
Try
```

```
    // credit one account
    MySqlCmd.CommandText =
        "update account set balance = " +
            "balance + 100 where id = 12345";
    MySqlCmd.ExecuteNonQuery();

    // debit another account
    MySqlCmd.CommandText =
        "update account set balance = " +
            "balance - 100 where id = 67890";
    MySqlCmd.ExecuteNonQuery();

    // everything is OK if you reach here
    MySqlTrn.Commit();
Catch e as Exception
    // something is wrong and an exception is caught
    MySqlTrn.RollBack();
Finally
    MySqlConn.Close();
End Try
```

5.5 DataSet and DataAdapter

ADO.NET supplies the **DataSet** class whereby disconnected and distributed data processing can be supported. A **DataSet** object is a memory-resident representation of data that provides a consistent relational programming model regardless of the data source. It represents a complete set of data, including tables, constraints, and relations between tables. Methods and member objects are consistent with those in the relational database model.

Because the **DataSet** has no knowledge of the database behind it, it is the **DataAdapter** that bridges the **DataSet** to the source of its data. Logically, a **DataAdapter** class belongs to a specific data provider and is used to populate the **DataSet** from the database and to update the database from the **DataSet**.

5.5.1 Building Blocks of DataSet

A **DataSet** contains a **DataTableCollection** object that is a collection of zero or more tables represented by **DataTable** objects. **DataTable** class is defined in the **System.Data** namespace and an instance of the class represents the memory-resident data of a single table. The **DataTable** object contains a collection of columns represented by the object **DataColumnCollection**, which defines the schema of a **DataTable**. Each column of the **DataTable** object is defined in a **DataColumn** object in the collection. The **DataTable** object also has a collection of rows that are represented by the object **DataRowCollection**, which contains the data in the table. Each row of the **DataTable** object is represented in a **DataRow** object in the collection. Along with the current state, a **DataRow** retains its original state and tracks changes that occur to the data.

In the **DataSet**, the relationship between its tables is defined in a member object **DataRelationCollection**. It is analogous to a join path that might exist between the primary key and foreign key in relational database. Each **DataRelation** object in the collection defines the matching columns of two **DataTables** in the **DataSet**. We consider the relationship between **DataTables** in Section 5.5.5.

In addition, a **DataSet** may have a collection of constraints represented by the object **ConstraintColletion**. A constraint is a rule used to maintain the integrity of the data in the table. For example, when a value is deleted and the value is also used in one or more related tables, a **ForeignKeyConstraint** determines whether the values in the related tables are also deleted, set to null values, set to default values, or no action occurs. An exception will be raised if a constraint is violated when data is changed.

5.5.2 Populate DataSet from Database

In Section 5.4, we used **DataReader** to perform a read-only and forward-only data retrieval from a database. Alternatively, you may use **DataAdapter** to populate the data into a **DataSet** that allows you to manipulate the data in disconnected and interactive mode.

Here is a Visual Basic program that uses **DataAdapter** to retrieve a table from a database, filling the query result to a **DataSet**. When this happens, all the rows of the table are listed on the screen.

```
Sub Test1(ByRef MySqlConn As SqlConnection)
   Try
      Dim MySqlDataAdapter As SqlDataAdapter = New _
         SqlDataAdapter( _
            "select emp_id, FirstName, LastName " &_
              "from employee", _
            MySqlConn _
         )
         ' create a DataSet using constructor
         Dim MyDataSet As DataSet = New DataSet()
         MySqlDataAdapter.Fill(MyDataSet)
         Dim NumRows As Int32
         ' populate the DataSet using the DataAdapter
         ' with the Fill method
         ' fill method returns number of rows inserted
         ' in the DataTable
           NumRows = MySqlDataAdapter.Fill( _
             MyDataSet,
```

```
            "AllEmployees"
        )
        Dim MyDataRow As DataRow
        ' loop over all the rows-
        For Each MyDataRow In _
            MyDataSet.Tables("AllEmployees").Rows
            ' note that DataRow is a collection of fields
            Console.WriteLine( _
                MyDataRow("emp_id").ToString() & _
                " : " & _
                MyDataRow("FirstName") & _
                " " & _
                MyDataRow("LastName") _
            )
        Next
    Catch ex As Exception
        Console.WriteLine(ex.ToString)
    End Try
End Sub
```

As shown, it is easy to populate a **DataSet** from a table in a database, as long as you have enough memory to hold the data you want to retrieve.

The creation of a **DataAdapter** object is very much like creating a command. You need to specify an SQL statement and a connection as the arguments of its constructor. Then invoke method **Fill** of the **DataAdapter** object to populate the **DataSet** or, more accurately, a **DataTable** of the **DataSet**. Note that a name, "**AllEmployees**", is also supplied and is assigned to the **DataTable** as an index for retrieval purposes.

Having been populated to the **DataSet**, the rows of the table are organized in the **DataRowCollection** object that is a property of the corresponding **DataTable**, namely **Rows**. Using a **For Each ... Next** construct, you may easily fetch them. Moreover, each row, in turn, is a collection of data fields and can be retrieved by its index.

The following C# program does this:

```
public void Test1(SqlConnection MySqlConn) {
    try {
        SqlDataAdapter  MySqlDataAdapter = new SqlDataAdapter(
            "select emp_id, FirstName, LastName from employee",
            MySqlConn
        );
        // create a DataSet using constructor
        DataSet MyDataSet = new DataSet();
        MySqlDataAdapter.Fill(MyDataSet);
        Int32 NumRows ;
        // Populate the DataSet using the DataAdapter
        // with the Fill method
        // fill method returns number of rows
```

```
    / inserted in the DataTable
    NumRows = MySqlDataAdapter.Fill(
       MyDataSet,
       "AllEmployees"
    );
    // loop over all the rows
    foreach(DataRow MyDataRow in
       MyDataSet.Tables["AllEmployees"].Rows) {
       // Note that DataRow is a collection of fields.
       Console.WriteLine(
          MyDataRow["emp_id"].ToString() +
          ": " +
          MyDataRow["FirstName"] + " " +
          MyDataRow["LastName"]
       );
    }
 }
 catch (Exception ex) {
    Console.WriteLine(ex.ToString());
 }
}
```

Using OLE DB Data Provider, you may populate a **DataSet** with an **OleDbDataAdapter** object in the same way.

In the sample shown here, the **DataAdapter** is created when the corresponding constructor is invoked with the **SELECT** statement and connection as arguments. Alternatively, an instance of **DataAdapter** may also be created with a constructor that has no arguments. Then the **SELECT** statement and connection can be set to the corresponding properties. In Visual Basic, this looks like this:

```
Dim MyDataAdapter As New SqlDataAdapter()
MyDataAdapter.SelectCommand = New SqlCommand()
MyDataAdapter.SelectCommand.CommandText = _
   "select ID, FirstName, LastName from employee"
MDataAdapter.SelectCommand.Connection = MySqlConn
```

In C# it looks like this:

```
SqlDataAdapter MyDataAdapter = new SqlDataAdapter();
MyDataAdapter.SelectCommand = New SqlCommand();
MyDataAdapter.SelectCommand.CommandText =
   "select ID, FirstName, LastName from employee";
MDataAdapter.SelectCommand.Connection = MySqlConn;
```

Here, the **SelectCommand** object represents the **SELECT** command for the **Fill** method. It has two major properties: the **Connection** and the **CommandText** for the **SELECT** statement.

5.5.3 Define a New DataTable

Sometimes you may want to create a **DataTable** object from scratch, manipulate it, and save it to a database. This is especially useful when you need a staging table to consolidate data elements from multiple sources.

In the following Visual Basic program note that a name is assigned to the **DataTable** as an index for retrieval purposes.

```
Dim StagingTable As DataTable = _
   New DataTable("StagingTable")
```

In C#, this is done as follows:

```
DataTable StagingTable = new DataTable("StagingTable");
```

Alternatively, you may want to create a **DataSet** and then create a **DataTable** that is associated with the **DataSet**.

```
Dim StagingTable As DataTable = New DataTable()
Dim DataConsolidation As DataSet = New DataSet()
StagingTable = DataConsolidation.Tables.Add("StagingTable")
```

In C#, this is done as follows:

```
DataTable StagingTable = new DataTable();
DataSet DataConsolidation = new DataSet();
StagingTable =
   DataConsolidation.Tables.Add("StagingTable");
```

So far, there is no structure defined in the **DataTable** that we have just created. Suppose that the staging table is to hold the employee data from two companies after they merge. The columns that are added to the **DataTable** might include the following:

- *FirstName* of type **String**. This is the first name of the employee.
- *LastName* of type **String**. This is the last name of the employee.
- *Salary* of type **Double**. This is the salary of the employee.
- *IncomeTaxWithhold* of type **Double**. This is calculated at 25% of the employee's salary.
- *ID* of type **Int32**. This is unique and not null.

Here is a Visual Basic program that adds these columns, together with designated calculations and constraints, to the **DataTable**.

```
Dim Col As DataColumn = StagingTable.Columns.Add( _
   "ID", _
   Type.GetType("System.Int32") _
)
' constraints for ID
Col.AllowDBNull = False
Col.Unique = True
```

```vb
StagingTable.Columns.Add(
    "FirstName",
    Type.GetType("System.String")
)
StagingTable.Columns.Add(
    "LastName",
    Type.GetType("System.String")
)
StagingTable.Columns.Add(
    "Salary",
    Type.GetType("System.Double")
)
' calculation for IncomeTaxWithhold
StagingTable.Columns.Add( _
    "IncomeTaxWithhold", _
    Type.GetType("System.Double"), _
    "Salary * 0.25" _
)
```

In C#, the program would be as follows:

```csharp
DataColumn Col = StagingTable.Columns.Add(
    "ID",
    Type.GetType("System.Int32")
);
// constraints for ID
Col.AllowDBNull = false;
Col.Unique = true;

StagingTable.Columns.Add(
    "FirstName",
    Type.GetType("System.String")
);
StagingTable.Columns.Add(
    "LastName",
    Type.GetType("System.String")
);
StagingTable.Columns.Add(
    "Salary",
    Type.GetType("System.Double")
);
// calculation for IncomeTaxWithhold
StagingTable.Columns.Add(
    "IncomeTaxWithhold",
    Type.GetType("System.Double"),
    "Salary * 0.25"
);
```

You may want to generate IDs automatically instead of populating them. This can be done in Visual Basic as follows.

```
Dim Col As DataColumn = StagingTable.Columns.Add( _
    "ID", _
    Type.GetType("System.Int32") _
)
Col.AutoIncrement = True
Col.AutoIncrementSeed = 200 ' Starting from 200
Col.AutoIncrementStep = 3
```

Or in C#, as follows.

```
DataColumn Col = StagingTable.Columns.Add (
    "ID",
    Type.GetType("System.Int32")
);
Col.AutoIncrement = true;
Col.AutoIncrementSeed = 200;    // Starting from 200
Col.AutoIncrementStep = 3;
```

5.5.4 Manipulate a DataTable

After creating a **DataTable** in a **DataSet**, you can perform the same activities that you would when using a table in a database, such as select, insert, update, and delete. In addition, you may also monitor the errors and events. When modifying data in a **DataTable**, you can also verify whether the changes are accurate and determine whether to accept or reject the changes programmatically.

5.5.4.1 INSERT DATA

After a **DataTable** object is created and its structure defined, the method **NewRow** can be called to add a new row to the **DataTable**. The new row, an instance of class **DataRow**, is created based on the structure of the table, as defined by the **DataColumnCollection**. Alternatively, a new row may also be added with method **DataTable.Rows.Add()**.Then the data fields of the new row may be populated. Both string or integer index may be used to reference a data field in the row.

Here is a Visual Basic program that creates a new row for **StagingTable** and populates it.

```
Dim MyNewRow As DataRow = StagingTable.NewRow()
' suppose AutoIncrement is used and ID needs not to
' be populated
' alternatively, a new row can be added
' in the following way:
'    Dim MyRow As DataRow = New DataRow
'    StagingTable.Rows.Add(MyRow)
```

```
MyNewRow("FirstName") = "John"
' alternatively, an integer index may be used, such as
' MyRow(1) = "John".
MyNewRow("LastName") = "Smith"
MyNewRow("Salary") = 123456
' Note that the IncomeTaxWithhold is calculated and
' populated as well.
StagingTable.Rows.Add(MyNewRow)

' note that the IncomeTaxWithhold is calculated and
' populated as well
```

5.5.4.2 SELECT DATA

Using its rows and columns Collections, you may access the contents of a **DataTable**. The **DataTable.Select** method is used to return an array of rows that meet certain criteria, including search criteria and row state. This method takes optional arguments of filter expression, sort expression, and **DataViewRowState**. The filter expression identifies which rows to return based on DataColumn values, such as "LastName = 'Smith'". The sort expression follows standard SQL conventions for ordering columns, such as "LastName ASC".

The **Select** method determines which version of the rows to view or manipulate based on a **DataViewRowState**. **DataViewRowState** has the following set of enumeration values:

- *Unchanged.* An unchanged row.
- *Deleted.* A deleted row.
- *OriginalRows.* Original rows, including unchanged and deleted rows.
- *Added.* A new row.
- *ModifiedCurrent.* A current version, which is a modified version of original data.
- *ModifiedOriginal.* The original version of a modified row.
- *CurrentRows.* Current rows, including unchanged, added, and modified rows; that is, all rows with the deleted ones removed.

Here is a Visual Basic program that selects all the employees with a salary above $100K and returns the result in a descendant order of salary.

```
Dim MyCol As DataColumn
Dim MyRow As DataRow

' Fetch an array of result rows using method Select.
Dim ResultRows() As DataRow = StagingTable.Select( _
    "Salary > 100000", _
    "Salary DESC", _
```

```
        DataViewRowState.CurrentRows _
)

' test to see whether we got anything.
If (ResultRows.Length < 1) Then ' No luck.
    Console.WriteLine("No records found")
Else ' yes.  present the result
    ' column names as headers
    For Each MyCol In StagingTable.Columns
        Console.Write(vbTab & MyCol.ColumnName)
    Next
    ' header for RowStat
    Console.WriteLine(vbTab + "Status")

    ' loop over all the rows in the result set
    For Each MyRow In ResultRows
        ' using column as index, fetch the data field
        For Each MyCol In StagingTable.Columns
            Console.Write( _
                vbTab & _
                MyRow(MyCol).ToString() _
            )
        Next
        ' RowStat
        Console.WriteLine( _
            vbTab + _
            System.Enum.GetName( _
            MyRow.RowState.GetType(), _
            MyRow.RowState _
        ) _
    )

    Next
End If
```

The following C# program does the same thing.

```
DataRow[] ResultRows = StagingTable.Select(
    "Salary > 100000",
    "Salary DESC",
    DataViewRowState.CurrentRows
);

// test to see whether we got anything
if(ResultRows.Length < 1)
{ // no luck.
    Console.WriteLine("No records found");
}
else { // yes.  present the result
    // Column names as headers
    foreach(DataColumn MyResCol
```

```
        in StagingTable.Columns) {
        Console.Write("\t" + MyResCol.ColumnName);
    }
    // header for RowStat
    Console.WriteLine("\t" + "Status");

    // loop over all the rows in the result set
    foreach(DataRow MyResRow in ResultRows) {
        // using column as index, fetch the data field
        foreach(DataColumn MyResCol
            in StagingTable.Columns) {
            Console.Write(
                "\t" +
                MyResRow[MyResCol].ToString()
            );
        }
        // RowStat
        Console.WriteLine(
            "\t" +
            System.Enum.GetName(
                MyResRow.RowState.GetType(),
                MyResRow.RowState
            )
        );
    }
}
```

The **DataTable.Select** method provides a mechanism for filtering data and is similar to view in a relational database.

5.5.4.3 EDIT OR UPDATE DATA

Updating or editing the data in a **DataTable** is straightforward. You simply assign a new value to a data field. For example, in Visual Basic this would be

```
MyRow("LastName") = "Jones"
```

and in C# this would be

```
MyRow["LastName"] = "Jones";
```

When a column value is updated in a **DataRow**, the state of the **DataRow** is set to **Modified**. Later, the changes may be either committed or rolled back using either the **AcceptChanges** or **RejectChanges** method.

AcceptChanges and **RejectChanges** methods are available at both **DataTable** level and **DataRow** level. In the following example, each row is checked to make sure that the last name field is not empty. Any row that violates this rule is then rejected at the row level. Finally, the valid changes are accepted at the table level.

```
Dim MyDataRow As DataRow
For Each MyDataRow In _
    DataConsolidation.Tables("StagingTable").Rows
    ' The field LastName cannot be empty.
    If MyDataRow("LastName") = "" Then
            ' Reject the changes on the row
            ' if the rule is violated.
            MyDataRow.RejectChanges()
    End If
Next
' Accept all the changes that can be accepted.
DataConsolidation.Tables("StagingTable").AcceptChanges()
```

The following C# program does the same thing.

```
// Loop over all the rows in the DataTable StagingTable.
foreach(DataRow MyDataRow in
    DataConsolidation.Tables["StagingTable"].Rows) {
    // The field LastName cannot be empty.
    if( MyDataRow["LastName"].Equals("")) {
    // Reject the changes on the row
    // if the rule is violated.
      MyDataRow.RejectChanges();
    }
}
// Accept all the changes that can be accepted.
DataConsolidation.Tables["StagingTable"].AcceptChanges();
```

In the C# example, it is supposed that there is no constraint defined on the row **LastName**. As you can see, you may program a constraint based on whether the changes can be either accepted or rejected. With the help event processing (discussed in Section 5.5.4.5), a mechanism is supported as programmable constraints whereby a rule can be applied automatically.

When its column value is directly modified, the **DataRow** manages column values using the following row versions:

- *Current*. It holds any changes that have been made to the row. If you make a change to a value in a row, the new value is the **Current** value.
- *Original*. If the **DataTable** was filled using a **DataAdapter**, the **Original** version is the version of the row as it was first added to the table. Added rows do not have an **Original** row version.
- *Default*. The row contains its default values.
- *Proposed*. This version represents the changes being made in edit mode. **Current** values are propagated to the **Original** row version when **AcceptChanges** is called. **Original** values are propagated to the **Current** row version when **RejectChanges** is called.

DataRow has three methods for suspending the state of the row while editing. These are **BeginEdit**, **EndEdit**, and **CancelEdit**. Calling the **BeginEdit** method puts a **DataRow** into edit mode. In this mode, events are temporarily suspended, allowing the user to make changes to more than one row without triggering validation rules. The following example shows how this mechanism works.

```
Dim t As New DataTable("table1")
Dim c As New DataColumn(
    "col1",
    Type.GetType("System.Int32")
)
t.Columns.Add(c)
' Add a UniqueConstraint to the table.
t.Constraints.Add(New UniqueConstraint(c))
' Add two rows into the table.
Dim r As DataRow
r = t.NewRow()
r(0) = 1
t.Rows.Add(r)   ' This row can be accessed as t.Rows(0).
r = t.NewRow()
r(0) = 2
t.Rows.Add(r)   ' This row can be accessed as t.Rows(1).
' So far so good,  but we are now going to violate
' the constraint.

' Enter the edit mode.
r.BeginEdit()
' Change the value; the rule of the constraint is violated.
t.Rows(0)(0) = 3
t.Rows(1)(0) = 3
' the constraint is not enforced as in the edit mode
' now we are ready to leave the edit mode
Try
' now the constraint is enforced and the exception raised
    t.Rows(0).EndEdit()
    t.Rows(1).EndEdit()
    ' So you will not reach here.
    t.AcceptChanges()
Catch e As Exception
    ' print the UniqueConstraint exception
    Console.WriteLine(e.Message)
End Try
```

The following C# program does the same thing.

```csharp
DataTable  t = new DataTable("table1");
DataColumn c = new DataColumn(
    "col1",
    Type.GetType("System.Int32")
);

t.Columns.Add(c);
// Add a UniqueConstraint to the table.
t.Constraints.Add(new UniqueConstraint(c));
// Add two rows into the table.
DataRow r;
r = t.NewRow();
r[0] = 1;
t.Rows.Add(r);   // This row can be accessed as t.Rows(0).
r = t.NewRow();
r[0] = 2;
t.Rows.Add(r);   // This row can be accessed as t.Rows(1).
// so far so good; but we are now going
// to violate the constraint
// enter the edit mode
r.BeginEdit();
// Change the value;
// the rule of the constraint is violated.
t.Rows[0][0] = 3;
t.Rows[1][0] = 3;
// The constraint is not enforced
// because we are in the edit mode.
// Now we are ready to leave the edit mode.
try {
    // Now the constraint is enforced and
    // the exception raised.
    t.Rows[0].EndEdit();
    t.Rows[1].EndEdit();
    // so you will not reach here
    t.AcceptChanges();
}
catch (Exception e) {
    // Print the UniqueConstraint exception.
    Console.WriteLine(e.Message);
}
```

5.5.4.4 DELETE OR REMOVE DATA

There are two methods you can use to delete a **DataRow** object from a **DataTable** object. The **Remove** method of the **DataRowCollection** object deletes a **DataRow** from the **DataRowCollection**. The method **Remove** of the object **DataRowCollection** takes a **DataRow** as an argument and removes it from the collection. In Visual Basic this looks like

```
StagingTable.Rows.Remove(MyRow)
```

In C# it would be

```
StagingTable.Rows.Remove(MyRow);
```

The **Delete** method of the **DataRow** object only marks the row for deletion; the actual removal occurs when the application calls the **AcceptChanges** method. By using **Delete**, you can programmatically check which rows are marked for deletion before actually removing them. When a row is marked for deletion, its **RowState** property is set to **Deleted**. A **DataRow** object may mark itself for deletion. For example, in Visual Basic this might be

```
MyRow.Delete()
```

And in C# this would be

```
MyRow.Delete();
```

If the application calls the **AcceptChanges** method of the **DataTable** object, the row is removed from the **DataTable**. In contrast, if the application calls **RejectChanges**, the **RowState** of the row reverts to what it was before being marked as **Deleted**.

5.5.4.5 HANDLE EVENTS

The **DataTable** object provides a series of events that can be processed by an application:

- *ColumnChanged*. This event occurs after a specified **DataColumn** has been changed in a **DataRow**.
- *ColumnChanging*. This event occurs when a specified **DataColumn** is being changed in a **DataRow**.
- *RowChanged*. This event occurs after a **DataRow** has been changed.
- *RowChanging*. This event occurs when a **DataRow** is being changed.
- *RowDeleted*. This event occurs after a **DataRow** has been deleted.
- *RowChanging*. This event occurs when a **DataRow** is being deleted.

You may write a piece of code that handles each event, following a specific syntax. In Visual Basic a routine that handles **ColumnChanged** event should look like this:

```
Private Sub OnColumnChanged( _
    sender As Object, _
    args As DataColumnChangeEventArgs _
)
    ...
End Sub
```

In C# it should look like this:

```
protected void OnColumnChanged(
    Object sender,
    DataColumnChangeEventArgs args
){
    ...
}
```

Here, the argument sender is the object that raises this event. Argument "args" is of a special type. For example, **DataColumnChangeEventArgs** has the following property:

- *Column*. This property is used to get the **DataColumn** with a changing value.
- *ProposedValue*. This property is used to get and set the proposed value.
- *Row*. This property is used to get the **DataRow** with a changing value.

Then this routine has to be associated with the event that it handles. In Visual Basic this would be

```
AddHandler MyDataTable.ColumnChanged, _
    New DataColumnChangeEventHandler( _
        AddressOf OnColumnChanged _
    )
```

or in C#,

```
MyDataTable.ColumnChanged  +=
    new DataColumnChangeEventHandler(OnColumnChanged);
```

The following program in Visual Basic enforces a business rule that the column **LastName** in table **StatingTable** may not be empty.

```
Sub Test3(ByRef MySqlConn As SqlConnection)
    Dim MySqlDataAdapter As SqlDataAdapter = New _
        SqlDataAdapter( _
            "select emp_id, firstname, lastname " &_
            "from employee", _
```

```
                    MySqlConn _
            )
    ' create a DataSet using Constructor
    Dim MyDataSet As DataSet = New DataSet()
    MySqlDataAdapter.Fill(MyDataSet, "AllEmployees")
    Dim MyDataTable As DataTable = _
            MyDataSet.Tables("AllEmployees")
    ' associate the routine to the event
    AddHandler MyDataTable.ColumnChanged, _
            New DataColumnChangeEventHandler( _
                AddressOf OnColumnChanged _
            )
    ' make changes
    Dim MyCol As DataColumn
    Dim MyRow As DataRow
    If MyDataTable.Rows.Count > 0 Then
            MyRow = MyDataTable.Rows(0)
            ' event triggered and change accepted
            MyRow("firstname") = "SAM"
            ' event triggered and change rejected
            MyRow("LastName") = ""
    End If
    ' now it is safe to accept changes
    MyDataTable.AcceptChanges()
End Sub

'Event Handler
Private Sub OnColumnChanged( _
    ByVal sender As Object, _
    ByVal args As DataColumnChangeEventArgs _
)
    If args.Column.ColumnName = "LastName" Then
            If args.ProposedValue.ToString = "" Then
                args.Row.RejectChanges()
            End If
    End If
End Sub
```

In this program, subroutine **OnColumnChanged** is invoked each time a change is made to a row. It checks the value of column **LastName** and rejects the changes on this row if the value is empty.

The following C# program does the same thing.

```
public void Test3(SqlConnection MySqlConn ) {
    SqlDataAdapter MySqlDataAdapter= new SqlDataAdapter(
            "select emp_id, firstname, lastname " +
                "from employee",
                MySqlConn
    );
    // create a DataSet using Constructor
```

```csharp
DataSet MyDataSet  = new DataSet();
MySqlDataAdapter.Fill(MyDataSet, "AllEmployees");
DataTable MyDataTable  =
     MyDataSet.Tables["AllEmployees"];
// associate the routine to the event
DataTable  MyEmpDataTable =
     MyDataSet.Tables["AllEmployees"];
// associate the routine to the event
MyEmpDataTable.ColumnChanged +=
  new DataColumnChangeEventHandler(OnColumnChanged);
// make changes
DataRow MyRow;
if(MyEmpDataTable.Rows.Count > 0 ) {
     MyRow = MyEmpDataTable.Rows[0];
     // event triggered and change accepted
     MyRow["firstname"] = "SAM";
     // event triggered and change rejected
     MyRow["LastName"] = "";
}
// now, it is safe to accept changes
     MyEmpDataTable.AcceptChanges();
}

protected  void OnColumnChanged(
    object sender,
    DataColumnChangeEventArgs args
) {
    if(args.Column.ColumnName.Equals("LastName")) {
        if(args.ProposedValue.ToString().Equals("")) {
            args.Row.RejectChanges();
        }
    }
}
```

In this example, the argument sender is not used. However, the following Visual Basic statement allows you to access the actual sender of the event, which is a **DataTable**.

```vb
Dim t As DataTable = CType(sender, DataTable)
```

In C# this would be

```csharp
DataTable t = (DataTable)sender;
```

5.5.5 Relation Between DataTables

A **DataRelation** object is used to relate two **DataTable** objects to each other through their **DataColumn** objects. This facility allows you to deal with the master/detail, or parent/child data in relational models For example, in a Department/Employee relationship, the De table is the parent and the Orders table is the child of the relationship. These two tables are often joined together via the column **DepartmentID**, which is the primary key in the parent table and foreign key in the child table.

A **DataSet** object has a collection of **DataRelation** objects, each of which define a relation between **DataTables** in the **DataSet**. When a **DataRelation** is defined, joins between the related tables can be supported. From a row in the parent table, a collection of related rows in the child table can be retrieved using method **GetChildRows** of **DataRow** class. On the other hand, related row or rows in the parent **DataTable** may also be retrieved using the **GetParentRow** or **GetParentRows** methods of a **DataRow** object in the child **DataTable**.

The following Visual Basic program iterates the department and employee data and displays the records hierarchically.

```vb
Dim MyDataSet As New DataSet()

Dim ParentDataAdapter As SqlDataAdapter
Dim ChildDataAdapter As SqlDataAdapter
ParentDataAdapter = New SqlDataAdapter( _
    "select * from Department", _
    mySqlConnection _
)

ChildDataAdapter = New SqlDataAdapter( _
    "select * from employee", _
    mySqlConnection _
)

Try
    ' Populate both parent and child tables.
    ParentDataAdapter.Fill(MyDataSet, "Department")
    ChildDataAdapter.Fill(MyDataSet, "Employee")

    ' add Relation that joins the parent and child.
    ' the name of the relation is "DepartmentEmployee"
    ' both tables are joined via column DepartmentID
    MyDataSet.Relations.Add( _
        "PublishersEmployee", _
        MyDataSet.Tables("Department").Columns("DEP_ID"), _
        MyDataSet.Tables("Employee").Columns("DEP_ID") _
    )

    ' iterate over the data
    Dim ParentDataRow As DataRow
    Dim ChildDataRow As DataRow
    For Each ParentDataRow In _
        MyDataSet.Tables("Department").Rows
        Console.WriteLine( _
            "Department: " + _
```

```
                    ParentDataRow("NAME").ToString() _
            )
    ' fetch the child rows through the join
    For Each ChildDataRow In _
            ParentDataRow.GetChildRows( _
                MyDataSet.Relations("DepartmentEmployee") _
            )
            Console.WriteLine( _
                "    Employee: " &_
                ChildDataRow("FirstName").ToString() &_
                " " &_
                ChildDataRow("LastName").ToString() _
                )
        Next
    Next
    Catch e As Exception
        Console.WriteLine(e.ToString())
End Try
```

A C# version of this program is as follows.

```csharp
DataSet MyDataSet = new DataSet();

SqlDataAdapter ParentDataAdapter;
SqlDataAdapter ChildDataAdapter;
ParentDataAdapter = new SqlDataAdapter(
    "select * from Department",
    MySqlConn
);

ChildDataAdapter = new SqlDataAdapter(
    "select * from employee",
    MySqlConn
);

try {
    // populate both parent and child tables
    ParentDataAdapter.Fill(MyDataSet, "Department");
    ChildDataAdapter.Fill(MyDataSet, "Employee");

    // add Relation that joins the parent and child
    // the name of the relation is "DepartmentEmployee"
    // both tables are joined via column DepartmentID
    MyDataSet.Relations.Add(
      "PublishersEmployee",
      MyDataSet.Tables["Department"].Columns["DEP_ID"],
      MyDataSet.Tables["Employee"].Columns["DEP_ID"]
    );

    // iterate over the data
    foreach (DataRow ParentDataRow in
```

```
            MyDataSet.Tables["Department"].Rows) {
            Console.WriteLine(
                  "Department: " +
                  ParentDataRow["NAME"].ToString()
            );
            // Fetch the child rows through the join.
            foreach( DataRow ChildDataRow in
                  ParentDataRow.GetChildRows(
                    MyDataSet.Relations["DepartmentEmployee"]
                  )
            ) {
                  Console.WriteLine(
                  "    Employee: " +
                  ChildDataRow["FirstName"].ToString() +
                  " " +
                  ChildDataRow["LastName"].ToString()
                  );
            }
      }
}
catch( Exception e ) {
      Console.WriteLine(e.ToString());
}
```

Relationships are created between matching columns in the parent and child tables. That is, the **DataType** for both columns must be identical.

Relationships can also cascade various changes from the parent **DataRow** to its child rows. To control how values are changed in child rows, add a **ForiegnKeyConstraint** to the **ConstraintCollection** of the **DataTable** object. The **ConstraintCollection** defines what action to take when a value in a parent table is deleted or updated.

When a **DataRelation** is created, it first verifies that the relationship can be established. After it is added to the **DataRelationCollection**, the relationship is maintained by disallowing any changes that would violate it. Between the period when a **DataRelation** is created and when it is added to the **DataRelationCollection**, it is possible for additional changes to be made to the parent or child rows. An exception is generated if this results in a relationship that is no longer valid.

DataRelation objects are contained in a **DataRelationCollection**, which you can access through the **Relation** property of the **DataSet** and the properties **ChildRelations** and **ParentRelations** of the **DataTable**.

5.5.6 Update Database from DataSet

Having manipulated **DataTables** in a **DataSet**, you may want to save the changes that you have made back into the data source or database. The **Update** method of the **DataAdapter** classes is used for this purpose.

5.5.6.1 UPDATE METHOD

When an application calls the **Update** method, the **RowState** property of each row is examined and the required **INSERT**, **UPDATE**, or **DELETE** statements created accordingly. Recall that a **DataAdapter** object has a property **SelectCommand**. It supports the **Fill** method and accommodates the statement and connection. Similarly, a **DataAdapter** also has properties **InsertCommand**, **UpdateCommand**, and **DeleteCommand**. These properties support the **Update** method and accommodate the corresponding **INSERT**, **UPDATE**, and **DELETE** statements and connections.

You may define these command properties by specifying the corresponding SQL statements and connections. However, if your **DataTable** maps to or is generated from a single database table, you can take advantage of the **CommandBuilder** object to generate these command properties of the **DataAdapter** automatically. In this case, the properties **InsertCommand**, **UpdateCommand**, and **DeleteCommand** are created based on the information in the **SelectCommand** property discussed in Section 5.5.2.

In Section 5.5.6.2, we give you an example where a single database table is updated with the corresponding **DataSet**. When multiple tables with relations between them are involved, special care has been taken to maintain the data integrity. Such an example is shown in Section 5.5.6.3. Finally, you may also control the order in which the **DataRows** are processed by method **Update**. Such an example can be found in Section 5.5.6.4.

5.5.6.2 A SCENARIO WITH A SINGLE TABLE

The following example shows how a table is updated with the corresponding **DataSet** with automatically generated command properties.

In Visual Basic, a single table is updated as follows.

```
' define a DataAdapter with the SelectCommand
' specified implicitly
Dim MySqlDataAdapter As SqlDataAdapter = _
  New SqlDataAdapter ( _
    "select ID, FirstName, LastName from employee", _
    MySqlConn _
  )

' InsertCommand, UpdateCommand, and DeleteCommand
' are automatically generated for the DataAdapter
' based on information in SelectCommand
Dim MyCommandBuilder As SqlCommandBuilder = _
  New SqlCommandBulder ( _
    MyDataAdapter _
  )

' populate a DataSet
```

```
Dim MyDataSet As DataSet = New DataSet
MySqlConn.Open()
MyDataAdapter.Fill(MyDataSet)

' modify the data in the DataSet
...

' update the database with the DataSet
' note that without the OleDbCommandBuilder this would fail
MyDataAdapter.Update(MyDataSet)

MySqlConn.Close()
```

In C# a single table is updated as follows.

```
// define a DataAdapter with the SelectCommand
// specified implicitly
SqlDataAdapter MySqlDataAdapter = new SqlDataAdapter(
    "select emp_id, firstname, lastname from employee",
    MySqlConn
);

DataSet MyDataSet = new DataSet();

// InsertCommand, UpdateCommand, and DeleteCommand are
// automatically generated for the DataAdapter based
// on information in SelectCommand
SqlCommandBuilder MyCommandBuilder =
    new SqlCommandBuilder(MySqlDataAdapter);
// populate a DataSet
MySqlConn.Open();
MySqlDataAdapter.Fill(MyDataSet);

//modify the data in the DataSet
DataRow r;
r = MyDataSet.Tables[0].Rows[0];
r.BeginEdit();
r["FirstName"] = "JOE";
r.EndEdit();
// update the database with the DataSet
MySqlDataAdapter.Update(MyDataSet);
```

5.5.6.3 A SCENARIO WITH MULTIPLE TABLES

Committing the changes in a **DataSet** containing multiple related tables requires that the data integrity be maintained. For example, the referential integrity means that the foreign key in any referencing table must always refer to a valid row in the referenced table. Hence, a parent row in the referenced table cannot be deleted if it is being referenced in the referencing table. Similarly, inserts cannot be made to the referencing table if the corresponding rows do not exist in the referenced table.

As far as the INSERT operation is concerned, new rows can be added to the child table if they correspond to valid, or already existing, rows in the parent table. A row should not be added to the child table if it refers to an invalid row in the parent table. First, the new row should be inserted in the parent table, and then only the corresponding child rows should be added to the child table. For the same reason, while reconciling the changes with the database, the **Update** method on the **DataAdapter** object corresponding to the parent table should be called first.

In the following schematic sample in Visual Basic, a new department, as well as the new employees, are added.

```
Dim MyDataSet As DataSet

' DataAdapters for both parent and child
Dim DeptDataAdapter As New SqlDataAdapter( _
    "select *  from Department", _
    mySqlConn _
)
Dim EmpDataAdapter As New SqlDataAdapter( _
    "select *  from Employee", _
    mySqlConn _
)

' automatically build the commands for parent and child
Dim DeptCmdBuilder = New SqlCommandBuilder( _
    DeptDataAdapter _
)
Dim EmpCmdBuilder = New SqlCommandBuilder( _
    EmpDataAdapter _
)
MyDataSet = New DataSet()
' populate the DataSet.
mySqlConn.Open()
DeptDataAdapter.Fill(MyDataSet, "Department")
EmpDataAdapter.Fill(MyDataSet, "Employee")

' set up the relation between parent and child
' based on DeptID
MyDataSet.Relations.Add( _
    "DeptEmp", _
    MyDataSet.Tables("Department").Columns("DEP_ID"), _
    MyDataSet.Tables("Employee").Columns("DEP_ID") _
)

' add a new department with a NewDeptID
' as the primary key
' ...
```

```
Dim newRow As DataRow _
    = MyDataSet.Tables("Department").NewRow()
newRow("DEP_ID") = "1111"
newRow("name") = "RND"

Dim newChildRow As DataRow _
    = MyDataSet.Tables("Employee").NewRow()
' SetParentRow will automatically set
' the foreign key, DEP_ID
newChildRow.SetParentRow(newRow)
' take a look at it
Console.WriteLine(newChildRow("DEP_ID"))

newChildRow("EMP_ID") = "101"
newChildRow("LastName") = "Smith"
newChildRow("FirstName") = "John"

MyDataSet.Tables("Department").Rows.Add(newRow)
MyDataSet.Tables("Employee").Rows.Add(newChildRow)

' the parent table has to be updated first
DeptDataAdapter.Update(MyDataSet, "Department")
EmpDataAdapter.Update(MyDataSet, "Employee")
```

Here, a different overloaded version of the **Update** method is used that allows a single **DataTable** to be processed.

5.5.6.4 PROCESSING ORDERS

In many circumstances, the order in which changes made through the **DataSet** are sent to the data source is important. For example, if a primary key value for an existing row is updated and a new row has been added with the new primary key value, it is important to process the update before the insert.

In the following schematic sample in C#, sets of rows are selected based on their status so that the deleted rows are processed first, then the updated rows, and finally the inserted rows. In this case, another overloaded version of the **Update** method is used that operates on an array of rows.

```
DataTable MyTable = custDS.Tables["Employee"];

// first, process deletes
MyDataAdapter.Update(
    MyTable.Select(
        null,
        null,
        DataViewRowState.Deleted
    )
);
```

```
// next, process updates
MyDataAdapter.Update(
    MyTable.Select(
        null,
        null,
        DataViewRowState.ModifiedCurrent
    )
);

// finally, process inserts
MyDataAdapter.Update(
    MyTable.Select(
        null,
        null,
        DataViewRowState.ModifiedAdded
    )
);
```

Note that both the select expression and the sort expression are null when the **Select** method is invoked.

5.6 XML Integration with ADO.NET

The .NET XML framework and the ADO.NET framework provide a unified programming model for accessing data represented as both XML data, text delimited by tags that structure the data, and relational data, tables consisting of rows, columns, and constraints.

5.6.1 Data Exchange Between XML and DataSet

With ADO.NET you can fill a **DataSet** from an XML stream or document. You can use the XML stream or document to supply to the **DataSet** with data, schema information, or both. The information supplied from the XML stream or document can be combined with existing data or schema information already present in the **DataSet**.

5.6.1.1 WRITING XML FROM A DATASET

An XML document may be created that represents the same data entities in an instance of **DataSet**. Method **WriteXml** of **DataSet** class can be used for this purpose. This method can write the XML document to specified **System.IO.FileStream**, file, or **System.Xml.XmTextlWriter** (see Chapter 7). The following C# program shows how these versions of the method are used.

```
// a file
string FileName1 = "MyXmlDoc1.xml";
// Write current schema and data to the file.
MyDataSet.WriteXml(FileName1);
// a FileStream
string FileName2 = "MyXmlDoc2.xml";
System.IO.FileStream MyFileStream2 =
    new System.IO.FileStream(
    FileName2,
    System.IO.FileMode.Create);
// write to the FileStream.
MyDataSet.WriteXml(MyFileStream2);
// a XmlTextWriter
string FileName3 = "MyXmlDoc3.xml";
System.IO.FileStream MyFileStream3 =
    new System.IO.FileStream(
    FileName3,
    System.IO.FileMode.Create);
System.Xml.XmlTextWriter MyXmlTextWriter3 =
    new System.Xml.XmlTextWriter(
    MyFileStream3,
    System.Text.Encoding.Unicode);
// write to the XmlTextWriter.
MyDataSet.WriteXml(MyXmlTextWriter3);
```

This program creates three XML files—**MyXmlDoc1.xml**, **MyXmlDoc2.xml**, and **MyXmlDoc3.xml**—that are identical.

Method **WriteXml** may also take the second argument with type **XmlWriteMode**. This enumeration has three possible values:

- *WriteSchema*. This is the default **XmlWriteMode** when **WriteXml** is called. In this mode, the current contents of the **DataSet** are written as XML data with the relational structure as inline XSD schema.
- *IgnoreSchema*. In this mode, the current contents of the **DataSet** are written as XML data without an XSD schema.
- *DiffGram*. In this mode, the entire **DataSet** is written as a **DiffGram**, including original and current values.

A **DiffGram** is an XML serialization format that includes the original and current data of an element, as well as a unique identifier that associates the original and current versions to one another. The example of the **DiffGram** format that follows tells you that Employee 12345 is transferred from Department 7890 to 6789. Both the current, or "modified," version and the original, or "before," version are included in this XML document.

```
<diffgr:diffgram
    xmlns:mydata="urn:schemas-my-com:xml-mydata"
    xmlns:diffgr="urn:schemas-my-com:xml-diffgram-v0">
    <MyDataSet>
```

```
<Employee  diffgr:ID="Employee1"
            mydata.RowOrder="0"
            diffgr:HasChanges="Modified">
    <EmployeeID>12345</EmployeeID>
    <DepartmentID>6789</DepartmentID>
</Employee>
<Employee ... >
    ...
</Employee>
...
</MyDataSet>
<diffgr:before>
    <Employee  diffgr:ID="Employee1"
                mydata.RowOrder="0">
        <EmployeeID>12345</EmployeeID>
        <DepartmentID>7890</DepartmentID>
    </Employee>
</diffgr:before>
</diffgr:diffgram>
```

Moreover, you may use method **GetXml** of class **DataSet** to return the XML in a string. If the **DataSet** has changes, calling this method is identical to calling **WriteXml** with **XmlWriteMode** set to **DiffGram**; otherwise it is equivalent to calling **WriteXml** with **XmlWriteMode** set to **IgnoreSchema**. For example, this C# statement prints the XML of **MyDataSet** onscreen.

```
System.Console.Write(MyDataSet.GetXml());
```

5.6.1.2 LOADING A DATASET FROM XML

The contents of a **DataSet** object may be loaded from an XML stream or document. Method **ReadXml** of **DataSet** class can be used to fill a **DataSet** from XML. It reads XML data from a file, a stream, or an **XmlReader**. In addition, this method may take the second argument with type **XmlReadMode**. This enumeration has the following possible values:

- *Auto*. In this, the default mode, the **ReadXML** method examines the XML and chooses the most appropriate option in the following order.
  - If the XML is a DiffGram, DiffGram is used.
  - If the DataSet contains a schema or the XML contains an inline schema, ReadSchema is used.
  - If the DataSet does not contain a schema and the XML does not contain an inline schema, InferSchema is used.

If you know the format of the XML being read, for best performance it is recommended that you set an explicit **XmlReadMode** rather than allowing the Auto default.

- *ReadSchema*. In this mode, the **ReadXml** method reads any inline schema and loads the data and schema. If the **DataSet** already contains a schema, new tables are added from the inline schema to the existing schema in the **DataSet**. If any tables in the inline schema already exist in the **DataSet**, an exception is thrown. If the **DataSet** does not contain a schema and there is no inline schema, no data is read. Inline schema can be in either XML Schema Definition (XSD) language or XML-Data Reduced (XDR) language schema format. XSD is the preferred format.
- *IgnoreSchema*. In this case, the method **ReadXml** ignores any inline schema and loads the data into the existing **DataSet** schema. Any data that does not match the existing schema is discarded. If the data is a **DiffGram**, **IgnoreSchema** has the same functionality as **DiffGram**.
- *InferSchema*. In this mode, the method **ReadXml** ignores any inline schema, inferring schema from the data, and loads the data. If the **DataSet** already contains a schema, the columns are added to existing tables where they exist, or to new tables where existing tables don't exist. An exception is thrown if a column already exists but has an incompatible mapping type property.
- *DiffGram*. In this mode, the method **ReadXml** reads a **DiffGram** and adds the data to the current schema.
- *Fragment*. In this mode, the method **ReadXml** continues reading multiple XML fragments until the end of the file is reached. Fragments that match the **DataSet** schema are appended to the appropriate tables. Fragments that do not match the **DataSet** schema are discarded.

If the **DataSet** already contains data, the new data from the XML is added to the data already present in the **DataSet**. **ReadXml** does not merge from the XML into the **DataSet** any row information with matching primary keys. To overwrite existing row information with new information from XML, use **ReadXml** to create a new **DataSet**, then merge the new **DataSet** into the existing **DataSet**. Note that loading a **DiffGram** using **ReadXML** with an **XmlReadMode** of **DiffGram** will merge rows that have the same unique ID.

5.6.2 Schemas of DataSet and XML

Schema of a **DataSet** contains definitions of its tables, columns, relations, and constraints. You may write the schema as an XML Schema Definition (XSD) language schema that can be transported in an XML document with or without data.

5.6.2.1 WRITING DATASET SCHEMA AS XSD

Similar to the method **WriteXML** discussed previously, method **WriteXMLSchema** of Class **DataSet** writes the Schema of a **DataSet** instance to a file, stream, or **XmlWriter**.

You can write the schema of a **DataSet** (its tables, columns, relations, and constraints) as XSD schema, so that you can transport it, with or without related data, in an XML document. XSD schema, which can be written to a file, a stream, an **XmlWriter**, or a string, is useful for generating a strongly typed **DataSet**.

You can specify how a column of a table is represented in XSD using the property **ColumnMapping** of the **DataColumn** object.

5.6.2.2 LOADING DATASET SCHEMA BY READING XSD

Using method **ReadXmlSchema** of class **DataSet**, you may read the schema defined in an XSD and load it into a **DataSet** object. The **ReadXmlSchema** method also supports XML-Data Reduced (XDR) language schema formats, but XSD is the preferred format.

The **ReadXmlSchema** method takes a single argument of a file name, a stream, or an **XmlReader** containing the XML document to be loaded. The XML document may contain only schema, or it may contain schema inline with XML elements containing data.

If the **DataSet** already contains a schema, the new columns are added to existing tables and new tables are added if they do not already exist. If a column being added already exists in the **DataSet** but has an incompatible type with the column found in the XML, an exception is thrown.

If the XML document passed to **ReadXmlSchema** contains no inline schema information, **ReadXmlSchema** will infer the schema from the elements in the XML document. We discuss this topic in the next section.

5.6.2.3 INFERRING DATASET SCHEMA FROM XML

There are three ways in which schema of a **DataSet** may be inferred from an XML document:

- Using the method **ReadXml** with an **XmlReadMode** of **InferSchema**
- Using the method **ReadXmlSchema** if the document being read contains no inline schema
- Using the method **InferXmlSchema** of class **DataSet**

The **InferXmlSchema** method also allows you to specify that particular XML namespaces are ignored when the schema is inferred. This method takes two required arguments: the location of the XML document, specified by a file name, a stream, or an XmlReader, and a string array of XML namespaces to be ignored by the operation.

The inference process first determines, from the XML document, which elements will be inferred as tables. From the remaining XML, the inference process determines the columns for those tables. For nested tables, the inference process generates nested **DataRelations** and **ForeignKeyConstraints**.

Following is a brief summary of inference rules:

- Elements that have attributes are inferred as tables.
- Elements that have child elements are inferred as tables.
- Elements that repeat are inferred as a single table.
- If the document, or root, element has no attributes and no child elements that would be inferred as columns, it is inferred as a **DataSet**. Otherwise, the document element is inferred as a table.
- Attributes are inferred as columns.
- Elements that have no attributes or child elements and do not repeat are inferred as columns.
- For elements that are inferred as tables that are nested within other elements also inferred as tables, a nested **DataRelation** is created between the two tables. A new, primary key column named "TableNameID" is added to both tables and used by the **DataRelation**. A **ForeignKeyConstraint** is created between the two tables using the "TableNameID" column.
- For elements that are inferred as tables and that contain text but have no child elements, a new column named "TableNameText" is created for the text of each of the elements. If an element is inferred as a table and has text, but also has child elements, the text is ignored.

5.6.3 Typed DataSet

A typed **DataSet** is a class that derives from a **DataSet**. It therefore inherits all of the methods, events, and properties of a **DataSet**. Additionally, a typed **DataSet** provides strongly typed methods, events, and properties. In practice, this means you can access tables and columns by name, instead of using collection-based methods.

A typed **DataSet** can be generated from an XML schema that complies with the XSD standard. A utility **xsd.exe** is available for this purpose and the following command serves as an example of how it works.

```
xsd.exe /d /l:C# MyTypeDataSet.xsd ⇓
    /n:MyTypedDataSetNamespace
```

In this syntax, the **/d** directive tells the tool to generate a **DataSet**. The **/l:** tells the tool what language to use; C# in this case. The optional **/n:** directive tells the tool to generate a namespace for the **DataSet** called **MyTypedDataSetNamespace**. The output of the command is

MyTypedDataSet.cs, which can be compiled and used in an ADO.NET application. The generated code can be compiled as a library or a module.

Following is the syntax for compiling the generated code as a library using the C# compiler.

```
csc.exe /t:library MyTypedDataSet.cs ⇓
    /r:System.dll /r:System.Data.dll
```

The **/t:** directive tells the tool to compile to a library, and the **/r:** directives specify dependent libraries required to compile. The output is **MyTypeDataSet.dll**, which can be passed to the compiler when compiling an ADO.NET application with the **/r:** directive.

Following is the syntax for accessing the namespace passed to **XSD.EXE** in an ADO.NET application.

In addition, the program that defines classes for a typed **DataSet** can be automatically created when you specify your XSD schema using VisualStudio.NET.

Chapter 11 includes an example of how a typed **DataSet** serves as the transfer syntax in a distributed system.

Summary

As an evolutionary improvement of ADO, ADO.NET has the following advantages over the former ADO.

First, ADO uses **RecordSet** object to represent data, which looks like a single table. ADO.NET uses **DataSet** object to represent data, which contains multiple tables. When dealing with multiple tables, therefore, ADO has to form a JOIN query that assembles data from the tables in question and generates a **RecordSet**. On the other hand, a **DataSet** itself may contain multiple tables, and a **DataRelation** object is supported that associates rows in one **DataTable** with that in another.

Second, **RecordSet** of ADO only supports sequential access in its data. **DataSet** in ADO.NET supports much more flexible ways in which its data elements can be accessed.

Third, ADO does not support data manipulation in disconnected mode. Even though it provides a **RecordSet** class, the data manipulation operations have to be performed as calls via database connection. ADO.NET, on the other hand, allows you to manipulate the data element in **DataSet** with the database connection closed. The database connection is only needed when the **DataSet** is filled and the database is updated. This means network traffic and overhead on the database server can be reduced dramatically.

Fourth, ADO maintains database locks and an active connection for a long period of time so that the scalability of applications can be seriously degraded. ADO.NET supports data manipulation in disconnected mode so as to promote the scalability of applications.

Finally, ADO.NET relates the **DataSet** closely to XML, which allows ADO.NET to better fit into a new framework of emerging technologies. In Chapter 11, we show you a clean and simple implementation of a distributed system using type **DataSet** as transfer syntax for data exchange that is automatically generated based on an XSD schema.

Web Services

The Internet is quickly evolving from a vehicle for page delivery into a service provider. .NET Framework supports built-in facilities for creating and exposing Web Services.

Under the .NET programming environment, Web Services can be easily created in various languages and tested interactively. On the client site, proxy to a service may be generated automatically based on downloadable specifications.

In this chapter, we show you how services are built and how they are accessed from clients.

6.1 Defining Web Services

Under .NET Framework, it is very simple to define Web Services. Just follow these four steps.

1. Implement a class with the designated services as its methods in a supported language, such as C#, Visual Basic, or JScript.
2. Mark each method that will be accessible as part of the service with custom attributes: **[WebMethod]** in C#, **<WebMethod()>** in Visual Basic, or **WebMethodAttribute** in JScript.
3. Save the source code of the class as a file with the suffix .asmx.
4. Make this file URI-addressable in Microsoft's Internet Information Server (IIS).

Now let's create a simple Web Service that says "Hello!" This service can be implemented in C#, Visual Basic, and JScript. A directory hierarchy is arranged for this small project:

- The root directory is **WebService** and is configured as a virtual directory of Microsoft's Internet Information Server (IIS), under the same name.
- The services and their clients will be tested in your PC, a single machine environment. Therefore, all the programs that implement the service are under subdirectory **HelloServer**.
- Each program that is written in a different language is located in a separate subdirectory under **HelloServer**, namely CS for C#, VB for Visual Basic, and JS for JScript.

This arrangement can help you understand how the Web Services work even though they are tested on a single PC.

6.1.1 "Hello!" Service in C#

This is our Web Service written in C#.

```
// helloCS.asmx
<%@WebService Language="C#" Class="HelloCS"%>

using System;
using System.Web.Services;

public class HelloCS : WebService {
    [WebMethod] public String Greeting(String name) {
        return String.Concat(
        "Hello, ",
        name,
        "! This is a greeting from Web Service ⇓
          written in C#.");
    }
}
```

In this program, method **Greeting(String name)** of class **HelloCS** is marked with the custom attribute **[WebMethod]** and will be available through the Web.

The program is saved as **…\WebService\HelloServer\CS\ HelloCS.asmx**, because the directory **WebService** has been configured as a virtual directory of IIS. This file is also URI-addressable as *localhost/WebService/HelloServer/CS/HelloCS.asmx*. You may use a browser to access it. In this page, clicking the link **Greeting** brings up a page for testing this method. This page is shown in Figure 6-1.

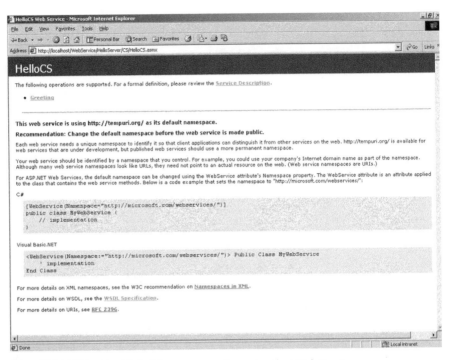

Figure 6-1   *The HelloCS.asmx page for testing the Web Service.*

When you type your name as the requested parameter of method **Greeting** and hit the Invoke button, the Web Service method may return a string method in XML format, as shown in Figure 6-2. By the way, you do not need to be worried about its format or the strange XML tag. The page is for test purposes only; the Web Service will not be used this way.

This is a very nice feature of Web Service because it allows you to test your services without having to write a client of it. Moreover, you reap a rich set of debugging information if your service did not work.

A Web Service description can also be created, generated in Web Service Description Language (WSDL), an XML-based language. This description can also be used to build the proxy at the client site. We discuss this issue in the next section.

Using your browser, you may retrieve the WSDL description of your Web Service by accessing *localhost/WebService/HelloServer/CS/HelloCS. asmx?WSDL*, shown in Figure 6-3. It is important to note that this description tells all the details about *what* the service is, but nothing about *how* it is implemented.

Again, you do not need to be worried if you are not familiar with XML: Only the client-site computer reads this description and creates the proxy programs for the Web Service.

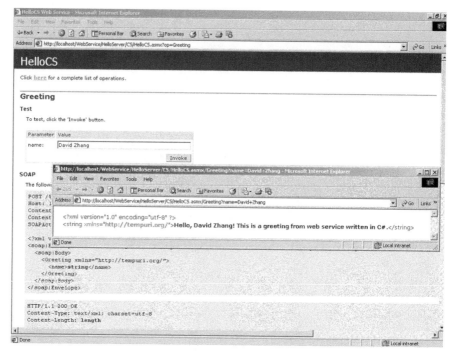

Figure 6-2   *The test result of the Web Service in XML format.*

6.1.2 "Hello!" Service in Visual Basic

The Visual Basic program is as follows.

```
'HelloVB.asmx
<%@ WebService Language="VB" Class="HelloVB" %>

Imports System.Web.Services

Public Class HelloVB : Inherits WebService
    <WebMethod()> Public Function Greeting(Name As String) ⇓
        As String
            Return (String.Concat( _
                "Hello, ", _
                Name, _
                "!! This is a greeting from Web " + _
                "     Service written in VB." _
            ))
    End Function
End Class
```

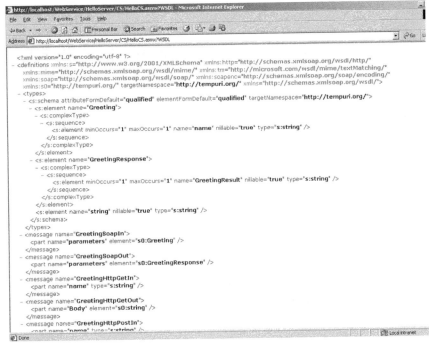

| **Figure 6-3** | *The WSDL description of the Web Service.* |

In this program, method **Greeting(Name As String)** of class **HelloVB** is marked with the custom attribute **<WebMethod()>** and will be available through the Web.

The program is saved as **... \WebService\HelloServer\VB\ HelloVB.asmx**, because the directory **WebService** has been configured as a virtual directory of IIS. This file is also URI-addressable as *localhost/WebService/HelloServer/VB/HelloVB.asmx*. You may use a browser to access it. In this page, clicking **Greeting** brings up a page for testing this method. This page is shown in Figure 6-4.

In this page, when you type your name as the requested parameter of method **Greeting**, then hit the Invoke button, the Web Service method may return a string in XML format, as shown in Figure 6-5.

Using your browser, you may retrieve the WSDL description of your Web Service by accessing *localhost/WebService/HelloServer/VB/HelloVB.asmx?WSDL*, shown in Figure 6-6. As you may have noticed, this description defines a service similar to the service in C#; the only differences are the names and addresses.

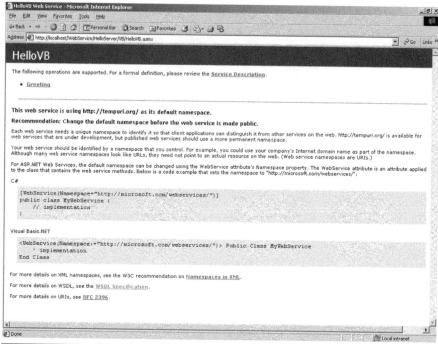

Figure 6-4   The HelloVB.asmx page for testing the Web Service.

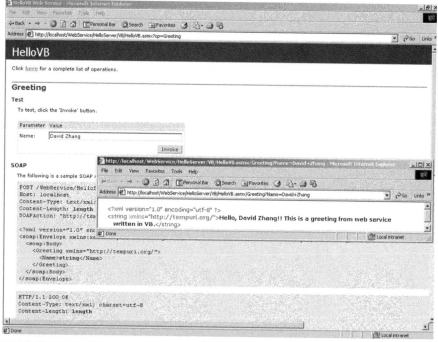

Figure 6-5   The test result of the Web Service in XML format.

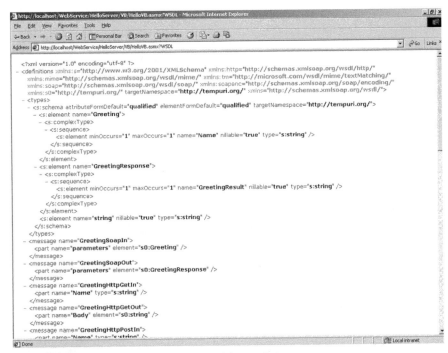

```
<?xml version="1.0" encoding="utf-8" ?>
- <definitions xmlns:s="http://www.w3.org/2001/XMLSchema" xmlns:http="http://schemas.xmlsoap.org/wsdl/http/"
    xmlns:mime="http://schemas.xmlsoap.org/wsdl/mime/" xmlns:tm="http://microsoft.com/wsdl/mime/textMatching/"
    xmlns:soap="http://schemas.xmlsoap.org/wsdl/soap/" xmlns:soapenc="http://schemas.xmlsoap.org/soap/encoding/"
    xmlns:s0="http://tempuri.org/" targetNamespace="http://tempuri.org/" xmlns="http://schemas.xmlsoap.org/wsdl/">
  - <types>
    - <s:schema attributeFormDefault="qualified" elementFormDefault="qualified" targetNamespace="http://tempuri.org/">
      - <s:element name="Greeting">
        - <s:complexType>
          - <s:sequence>
              <s:element minOccurs="1" maxOccurs="1" name="Name" nillable="true" type="s:string" />
            </s:sequence>
          </s:complexType>
        </s:element>
      - <s:element name="GreetingResponse">
        - <s:complexType>
          - <s:sequence>
              <s:element minOccurs="1" maxOccurs="1" name="GreetingResult" nillable="true" type="s:string" />
            </s:sequence>
          </s:complexType>
        </s:element>
        <s:element name="string" nillable="true" type="s:string" />
      </s:schema>
    </types>
  - <message name="GreetingSoapIn">
      <part name="parameters" element="s0:Greeting" />
    </message>
  - <message name="GreetingSoapOut">
      <part name="parameters" element="s0:GreetingResponse" />
    </message>
  - <message name="GreetingHttpGetIn">
      <part name="Name" type="s:string" />
    </message>
  - <message name="GreetingHttpGetOut">
      <part name="Body" element="s0:string" />
    </message>
  - <message name="GreetingHttpPostIn">
      <part name="Name" type="s:string" />
```

Figure 6-6 *The WSDL description of the Web Service.*

6.1.3 "Hello!" Service in JScript

The JScript program is as follows.

```
<!-- HelloJS.asmx -->
<%@ WebService Language="JScript" Class="HelloJS" %>

import System;
import System.Web.Services;

public class HelloJS extends WebService {
    WebMethodAttribute public function ⇓
        Greeting(name : String) : String {
        return String.Concat(
            "Hello, ",
            name,
            "!!! This is a greeting from Web ⇓
                Service written in JScript."
        );
    }
}
```

In this program, method **Greeting(name : String)** of class **HelloJS** is marked with the custom attribute **WebMethodAttribute** and will be available through the Web.

The program is saved as **... \WebService\HelloServer\JS\ HelloJS.asmx**, because the directory **WebService** has been configured as a virtual directory of IIS. This file is also URI-addressable as *localhost/ WebService/HelloServer/JS/HelloJS.asmx*. You may use a browser to access it. This page is shown in Figure 6-7. In this page, clicking **Greeting** brings up a page for testing this method.

When you type your name as the requested parameter of method **Greeting** and hit the Invoke button, the Web Service may return a string method in XML format, as shown in Figure 6-8.

Using your browser, you may retrieve the WSDL description of your Web Service by accessing *localhost/WebService/HelloServer/JS/ HelloJS.asmx?WSDL*, shown in Figure 6-9. As you may have noticed, this description defines a service similar to the services in C# and Visual Basic; the only differences are the names and addresses.

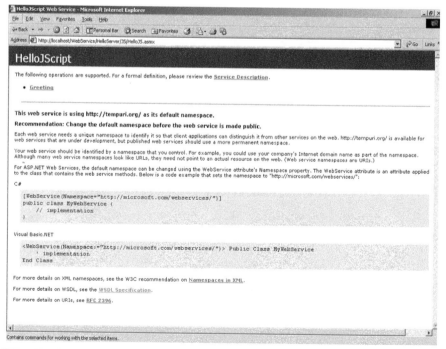

Figure 6-7   *The HelloJS.asmx page for testing the Web Service.*

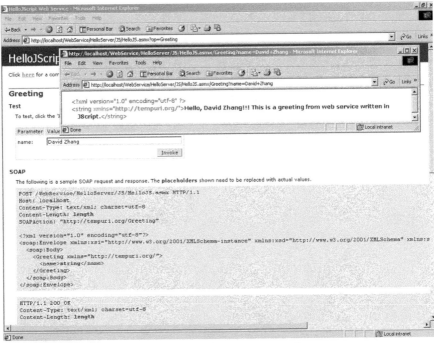

Figure 6-8   The test result of the Web Service in XML format.

Figure 6-9   The WSDL description of the Web Service.

6.2 Clients of Web Services

This section discusses the proxy objects for Web Services, as well as console programs and ASP.NET pages as clients.

6.2.1 Proxy for Web Services

In simple terms, a *proxy* is a local object that serves as a front end for a remote object. For a Web Service, a proxy is an object that was created on the client site. It provides an interface that allows the client programs to access the Web Service on the server site.

In the .NET Framework programming environment, programs for creating a proxy can be automatically generated based on the WSDL description that we discussed in the previous section.

In .NET Framework, a tool called **wsdl** is supplied for this purpose. It retrieves the WSDL description of the designated Web Service from the server site and uses the description as a guideline to create a program for the proxy object. This program is then compiled and a proxy library is created. Finally, the client may access the Web Service through the proxy library.

In the previous section, we created Web Services in C#, Visual Basic, and JScript. Now we are going to generate a proxy class for each Web Service. In the next section, these services will be integrated into client site applications.

In this case, we create all the proxy programs in C#, although proxy programs may be created in other languages, such as Visual Basic and JScript.

The following command creates a proxy program.

```
wsdl http://localhost/webservice/HelloServer⇓
    CS/HelloCS.asmx?WSDL
```

Running this command, a program for the proxy object, namely **HelloCS.cs**, is created. Let's take a look at this program.

```
//----------------------------
// <autogenerated>
//     This code was generated by a tool.
//     Runtime Version: 1.0.2914.16
//
//     Changes to this file may cause incorrect behavior
//     and will be lost if the code is regenerated.
// </autogenerated>
//----------------------------


//
// This source code was auto-generated by wsdl,
// Version=1.0.2914.16.
```

```
//
using System.Diagnostics;
using System.Xml.Serialization;
using System;
using System.Web.Services.Protocols;
using System.Web.Services;


[System.Web.Services.WebServiceBindingAttribute⇓
    (Name="HelloCSSoap", Namespace="http://tempuri.org/")]
public class HelloCS :
System.Web.Services.Protocols.SoapHttpClientProtocol {

    [System.Diagnostics.DebuggerStepThroughAttribute()]
    public HelloCS() {
        this.Url = "http://localhost/ch7/HelloCS.asmx";
    }

    [System.Diagnostics.DebuggerStepThroughAttribute()]
    [System.Web.Services.Protocols. ⇓
        SoapDocumentMethodAttribute(⇓
    "http://tempuri.org/Greeting",
    Use=System.Web.Services.Description. ⇓
        SoapBindingUse.Literal,
    ParameterStyle=System.Web.Services.Protocols. ⇓
        SoapParameterStyle.Wrapped)]
    public string Greeting(string name) {
        object[] results = this.Invoke(⇓
                "Greeting", new object[] {
                    name});
        return ((string)(results[0]));
    }

    [System.Diagnostics.DebuggerStepThroughAttribute()]
    public System.IAsyncResult BeginGreeting(⇓
        string name, ⇓
        System.AsyncCallback callback, ⇓
        object asyncState) {
        return this.BeginInvoke("Greeting", ⇓
                new object[] {name}, callback, asyncState);
    }

    [System.Diagnostics.DebuggerStepThroughAttribute()]
    public string EndGreeting(⇓
        System.IAsyncResult asyncResult) {
        object[] results = this.EndInvoke(asyncResult);
        return ((string)(results[0]));
    }
}
```

It is very important to note that this is an automatically created program. As the comment says, "changes to this file may cause incorrect behavior and will be lost if the code is regenerated." If you want to add any new features to the service locally, you *must not* put your code into this program.

In this program, we can see the **Greeting** method of our service. However, no implementation of the method is found. In addition, another two methods are created, **BeginGreeting** and **EndGreeting**, for asynchronous invocation of the method. We address this issue in Section 6.3.3.

Now this program can be complied with the following command so that the corresponding library, **HelloCS.dll**, can be created.

```
csc /t:library HelloCS.cs
```

Similarly, the programs of the proxy objects for Web Services in Visual Basic and JScript may be created in the following way.

```
wsdl http://localhost/webservice/HelloServer⇓
    VB/HelloVB.asmx?WSDL

csc /t:library HelloVB.cs

wsdl http://localhost/webservice/HelloServer⇓
    JS/HelloJS.asmx?WSDL

csc /t:library HelloJS.cs
```

Now we are ready to access the Web Services defined in the previous section.

In the previous example, the client and server of the Web Services both reside on your PC. If you have multiple PCs connected to a LAN, you may want to put the client and server on different machines. In this case, the argument for the **wsdl** commands should reflect the URI of the Web Services.

6.2.2 Console Program as a Client of Web Services

The following console program accesses our Web Services. Its file name is HelloClient.cs.

```
//HelloClient.cs:
using System;
using System.Web.Services;

class MainApp {
    public static void Main() {
        Console.Write("Your name, please: ");
        String name = Console.ReadLine();
        Console.WriteLine();
        HelloCS myHello0 = new HelloCS();
        Console.WriteLine(myHello0.Greeting(name));
        Console.WriteLine();
```

```
        HelloVB myHello1 = new HelloVB();
        Console.WriteLine(myHello1.Greeting(name));
        Console.WriteLine();
        HelloJS myHello2 = new HelloJS();
        Console.WriteLine(myHello2.Greeting(name));
    }
}
```

The following command compiles this program:

```
csc /r:HelloCS.dll /r:HelloVB.dll ⇓
/r:HelloJS.dll HelloClient.cs
```

In this case, all the proxy libraries, namely **HelloCS.dll**, **HelloVB.dll**, and **HelloJS.dll**, have to be placed in the directory where the client program is created and compiled.

Running the client program generates the following.

```
>HelloClient
```
Your name, please: David Zhang

Hello, David Zhang! This is a greeting from Web Service written in C#.

Hello, David Zhang!! This is a greeting from Web Service written in VB.

Hello, David Zhang!!! This is a greeting from Web Service written in JScript.

```
>
```

As you can see, the number of exclamation points in the greetings indicates the **Greeting()** method of the desirable Web Service objects has been called.

6.2.3 ASP.NET Page as a Client of Web Services

An ASP.NET page that accesses our Web Services is listed here:

```
<%@ Page Language="C#" %>

<html>

<script language="C#" runat="server">
public void Submit_Click(Object sender, EventArgs E) {
    HelloCS myHello1 = new HelloCS();
    Result1.Text = myHello1.Greeting(Name.Text);
    HelloVB myHello2 = new HelloVB();
    Result2.Text = myHello2.Greeting(Name.Text);
    HelloJS myHello3 = new HelloJS();
```

```
        Result3.Text = myHello3.Greeting(Name.Text);
}
</script>

<body>
<h4>Hello.aspx</h4>
<form runat="server">
<asp:TextBox id="Name" Text="" runat="server"/>
<input type="submit" id="Submit" value="Hello"
OnServerClick="Submit_Click" runat="server">
<p><asp:Label id="Result1" runat="server"/>
<p><asp:Label id="Result2" runat="server"/>
<p><asp:Label id="Result3" runat="server"/>
</form>

</body>
</html>
```

This file is saved as **Hello.aspx** in a subdirectory **HelloClient/CS** under the root directory for the IIS virtual directory *localhost/webservice*. In addition, all the proxy libraries must be placed in the subdirectory bin under the root directory for the IIS virtual directory *localhost/webservice*. Using a browser, you may access this client page and get the result shown in Figure 6-10. The number of exclamation points in the greetings indicates that **Greeting()** methods of the desired Web Service objects have been called.

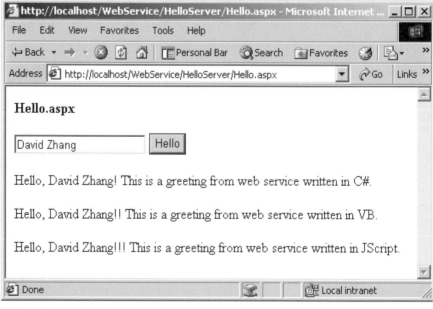

| **Figure 6-10** | *ASP.NET page as client of Web Services.* |

If your client site is a PC other than the server, you should define an IIS virtual directory and arrange the files, including the library and the page itself, in the way previously described.

6.3 Asynchronous Invocation of Web Services

In this section, we first compare synchronous mode and asynchronous mode for Web Service invocation. Then, a standard approach to asynchronous invocation is discussed. The proxy class supplies methods that simplify asynchronous invocation. This alternative approach is described finally.

6.3.1 Synchronous Mode versus Asynchronous Mode

In Section 6.2, we looked at the way Web Services are typically invoked at remote sites:

```
HelloService myHello = new HelloService();
Result = myHello.Greeting(name);
```

In the first statement, an instance of the proxy is created, **myHello**. Communication between the client and server starts when the second statement is executed. First, a request for the specified method of the service, together with the arguments, is sent as a message from the client site to the server site. When the request message is received, the method is invoked at the server site and the designated computational work is done there. Finally, the result is sent as a message back to the client site. During this entire process, the client process is put on hold until the result is returned. That is, the invocation of the Web Services is in *synchronous* mode.

Sometimes, it is more desirable to invoke the Web Services in an *asynchronous* mode, meaning that, once the request for Web Services has been sent, the client thread continues to run until it wants to receive, or wants to wait for, the result from the Web Services. *Asynchronous* invocation requires more programming effort, but it may dramatically improve the overall performance of distributed systems.

6.3.2 Standard Approach to Asynchronous Invocation

.NET Framework provides a standard approach to asynchronous invocation of the remote services, including Web Services and Object Remoting (see Chapter 8).

In synchronous mode, invocation of a remote service is carried out in a single action that covers the entire communication process between client and server. This process includes sending the request, waiting for the result, and finally receiving the result. The client thread is suspended during this process.

In asynchronous mode, however, the process for the invocation of a remote service has to be split into two steps. In the first step, the request is made and the control is returned to the client thread immediately. At this point, the client thread may continue to run, doing something useful, until it is ready to receive the result from the remote service. On the other hand, another thread is spawned behind the scenes that sends the request, waits for the result, and receives the result. On receipt of the result, this thread signals the original client thread, which wakes up if it was waiting.

The following C# program invokes our "Hello!" Web Service asynchronously. Its file name is **HelloClientAsync.cs**.

```
// HelloClientAsync.cs.
   using System;
   using System.Threading;
   using System.Web.Services;
   using System.Runtime.Remoting.Messaging;
   public class HelloClient {
         // event that controls the flow
         public static ManualResetEvent evt;
         // create an instance of the proxy object
         public static HelloCS WebHello = new HelloCS();
         public static string Result;

         // entry point of the program
         public static void Main() {
               // not ready
               evt = new ManualResetEvent(false);

               // create an instance of the client
               // instance in order to use its method
               HelloClient hc = new HelloClient();

               Console.Write("Your name, please: ");
               String name = Console.ReadLine();

               // start calling the web service;
               // it returns immediately without
               // waiting for the result
               hc.RemoteCall(name);

               // the client process continues to run,
               // doing something useful
               Console.WriteLine("Local Client: ⇓
                     Request sent, but hold on.... ⇓
                     I am doing something ...done!");
```

```
        // ready to receive the result from the web
        // service; wait until it is ready
        evt.WaitOne();

        // result is delivered; present it
        Console.WriteLine("Web Service:  {0}", ⇓
            Result);
}

// delegate for the remote method
public delegate String HelloDelegate(⇓
        String name);

// starting part of remote method invocation
public void RemoteCall(String name) {
        // set up the callback method that will be
        // called by the system when the result is
        //ready
        AsyncCallback ac = new
            AsyncCallback(this.RemoteCallBack);

        // an instance of the delegate for the
        // remote method
        HelloDelegate hd = new
                HelloDelegate(WebHello.Greeting);

        // call the remote method - send the
        // request without waiting for the
        // result coming back
        IAsyncResult ar = hd.BeginInvoke(⇓
            name, ac, null);
}

// ending part of remote method invocation
public void RemoteCallBack(IAsyncResult ar) {
        // get the delegate from the result
        // interface
        AsyncResult AR = (AsyncResult) ar;
        HelloDelegate hd = ⇓
                (HelloDelegate)  AR.AsyncDelegate;

        // get the result
        Result = hd.EndInvoke(ar);

        // wake up the client if it is waiting for
        // the result
        evt.Set();
    }
}
```

This program implements a class **HelloClient** that accommodates a set of methods for asynchronous invocation.

The entry point of this program is **Main()**. In **Main()**, an event is first created that will control the asynchronous program flow. As a **ManualResetEvent** object, this event is initially set to "Not Ready" because the constructor was called with an argument "false." Then an instance of **HelloClient** class is created and **RemoteCall** method is called in order to make the request, as the first step of the asynchronous invocation.

Before discussing the program in detail, let's consider a few important building blocks in the standard approach to asynchronous invocation of remote services.

- *Delegates*. A delegate in .NET Framework is similar to a function pointer in C/C++. It is used to encapsulate a reference to a method inside a delegate object. The delegate object can then be passed over to another object, which may invoke the referenced method without having to know at compile time which method will be called. With this feature, a delegate may serve as a vehicle to carry the proxy method from the client thread to the thread that actually communicates with the server site. That thread is a general-purpose service provider and its program has no knowledge of proxy methods at its compile time. In our context, two methods of the delegate object are used, **BeginInvoke** and **EndInvoke**. While the former starts another thread that communicates with the server site and requests its service, the latter delivers the result of the remote service.

- *AsyncCallback*. Having processed the client request, the server object creates the designated result and sends it back to the client. On receipt of the result, the thread that communicates with the server needs to notify the client thread that the result is ready and to deliver the result to the client thread. **AsyncCallback** delegate specifies a callback method for this purpose. This callback method belongs to the **HelloClient** class but will be invoked by another thread.

- *IAsyncResult*. When the callback method is called, an object that implements **IAsyncResult** interface is passed as an argument for the method. It delivers the initial delegate back to the client thread. By invoking the **EndInvoke** method of the delegate, the result can be obtained.

- *ManualResultEvent*. An instance of **ManualResultEvent** is created to control the flow of asynchronous programs. Initially, its status is set to "Not Ready." The thread that is in charge of client/server communication and running the callback method of **HelloClient** invokes the **Set** method of the event object and turns its status into "Ready" when the result from the remote server has been delivered.

On the other hand, the client thread running method **Main()** invokes the **WaitOne** method when it is ready to receive the result from the remove service. At this point, if the status of the event object is still "Not Ready" or the result is not yet available, the client thread is suspended. Otherwise, it may continue.

Now let's go back to our program. Having called **RemoteCall** method, the **Main()** method of the client thread continues to run and prints some messages on the console. Then it is ready to receive the result from the "Hello!" Web Service and, therefore, **evt.WaitOne()** is invoked. If the result is delivered, it is presented. Otherwise, the client thread has to wait.

In class **HelloClient**, delegation **HelloDelegate** has been defined for method **Greeting** of our remote class. This definition specifies the types of the parameter and return value. We may say, in this sense, that a delegation is a signature of the method to which it forwards its calls.

Method **RemoteCall** handles the starting part for the remote method invocation. It first sets up an **AsyncCallback** delegate for our callback method **RemoteCallback**. The thread that communicates with the server site will invoke this method as soon as the result is ready. Then an instance of delegate **HelloDelegate** is created as a vehicle for request of the remove service. Finally, the delegate method **BeginInvoke** is called to put forward the request; both the remote method and the callback delegates are supplied as its arguments.

When the server object generates the result and sends it back to the server, the thread that communicates with the server site invokes method **RemoteCallback** via the corresponding delegate. An object that implements interface **IAsyncResult** is passed as an argument of the callback method. The original delegate is carried by the **AsyncObject** property of the object. By calling the delegate method **EndInvoke**, the result is obtained. After delivering the result, this method invokes **evt.Set** to signal the client thread.

The following program compiles the program.

```
csc /r:HelloCS.dll HelloClientAsync.cs
```

You may run the program and have the following dialogue with it.

```
>HelloClientAsync
Your name, please: David Zhang
Local Client: Request sent, but hold on.... ⇓
    I am doing something ... done!
Web Service:  Hello, David Zhang! This is a ⇓
    greeting from Web Service written in C#.

>
```

6.3.3 Shortcut for Web Services

Recall that the proxy class for the remote server object is automatically generated by **wsdl**. In addition to the method for the service, **Greeting**, another two methods are also created. These are **BeginGreeting** and **EndGreeting**. These two methods provide a shortcut for asynchronous invocation of the Web Services. They simplify the client program by eliminating the explicit use of delegates.

Here is the program using the shortcut.

```
//ShortCut.cs
    using System;
    using System.Threading;
    using System.Web.Services;
    public class HelloClient {
            public static ManualResetEvent evt;
            public static HelloCS WebHello = new HelloCS();
            public static String Result;
            public static void Main() {
                    evt = new ManualResetEvent(false);
                    HelloClient hc = new HelloClient();
                    Console.Write("Your name, please: ");
                    String name = Console.ReadLine();
                    hc.RemoteCall(name);
                    Console.WriteLine(
                            "Local Client: Request sent, " +
                            " but hold on.... I am doing " +
                            "something ... done!");
                    evt.WaitOne();
                    Console.WriteLine("Web Service:  {0}",
                            Result);
            }

            public void RemoteCall(String name) {
                AsyncCallback ac = new
                        AsyncCallback(this.RemoteCallBack);
                IAsyncResult ar = WebHello.BeginGreeting(
                        name,
                        ac,
                        null
                );
            }
```

```
        public void RemoteCallBack(IAsyncResult ar) {
            Result = WebHello.EndGreeting(ar);
            evt.Set();
        }
    }   public void RemoteCallBack(IAsyncResult ar) {
        Result = WebHello.EndGreeting(ar);
        evt.Set();
    }
}
```

As you can see, methods **BeginGreeting** and **EndGreeting** play the same roles as their counterpart methods **BeginInvoke** and **EndInvoke**, without the need to explicitly handle delegates.

Summary

In this chapter, we have seen that the Web Services of .NET Framework have dramatically changed the process of client/server programming. As soon as a service is built, it may be tested interactively. The developer could quickly see by its response whether the service works or get a rich set of debugging information if it does not.

Access to the Web Service at the client is also made easy. Proxy to a Web Service is created in accordance with a specification that is downloaded from the server site. Then various applications, including console programs or ASP.NET pages, may invoke the methods of the server objects through the proxy.

Therefore, .NET Web Services represent a new paradigm of client/server programming. By removing the burdens of dealing with most of the details, Web Services allow the developers to concentrate on their business problems.

Programming XML
with .NET Framework

This chapter discusses System.Xml namespace in .NET Framework, which is also known as XML Framework .NET. The classes in this namespace provide a convenient environment for XML programming. In this chapter, we discuss

- *XML DOM, which works with an XML tree*
- *XML Reader and Writer, which support a forward-only cursor mode for sequential access on an XML stream*
- *XML validation on reading*
- *XML Data Document, which works with relational data*
- *XML Transformation, which allows an XML document to be transformed into another format, using XSLT*

All the source codes in this chapter are written in C#. The following batch command may be used to compile them.

```
csc %1 /r:System.dll /r:System.Data.dll /r:System.XML.dll ⇓
/debug+
```

7.1 Accessing XML

XML.NET provides several foundation classes for accessing an XML document. They fall into two categories, each of which represents an XML.NET technique.

- **XmlDocument** and **XmlNode** support W3C DOM Level 1 and Core Level 2 for tree random access.

- **XmlReader** and **XmlWriter** support sequential forward-only cursor.

There are two methods of processing inbound XML data: **Load** and **Read**.

The **Load** method loads an XML tree into an instance of class **XmlDocument**. It is used to load an XML document from a specified URL or a specified stream reader. Another method, **LoadXml**, loads an XML document from the specified string, which contains XML data.

The **Read** method of class **XmlReader** and **XmlTextReader** supports the forward-only cursor model to read the nodes from a specified stream. Search criteria may also apply so you can get the desirable nodes without having to read the entire document.

Table 7-1 shows the comparison of the two techniques.

Table 7-1	*Comparison of XML Techniques in .NET*	
Technique	**Pros**	**Cons**
XmlDocument/XmlNode Represents an entire XML document.	W3C (DOM) standard. Get node list by tag name or Select node list by XPath criteria.	Have to load whole document into memory, which may consume system resources too much.
XmlReader/XmlWriter Represents a reader/writer that provides fast, non-cached forward-only stream access to XML data.	Better performance with low memory cost. Good for validation with line number tracking.	Sequentially, forward only. Reader is read-only and writer is write-only.

7.1.1 Tree—XML DOM—Random Hierarchy Access Model

The XML DOM model is supported by XmlDocument and XmlNode. The model conforms to W3C DOM Level 1 and Core Level 2 for tree random access.

A sample XML document for purchase orders, **po.xml**, is used in this chapter. The code is as follows:

```
<?xml version="1.0" ?>
<orders >
   <Order sn='13579' status="pending">
      <OrderDate>05/27/2001</OrderDate>
      <BillTo>
         <name>Anew Technologies Inc.</name>
         <street>99 South Bedford Street</street>
         <city>Burlington</city>
         <state>MA</state>
```

```
        <postalcode>01803</postalcode>
    </BillTo>
    <ShipTo>
        <name>Object Innovations Inc.</name>
        <street>420 Boston Turnpike</street>
        <city>Shrewsbury</city>
        <state>MA</state>
        <postalcode>01545</postalcode>
        <via>UPS</via>
        <ShipDate>06/27/2001</ShipDate>
    </ShipTo>
    <Items>
     <Item>
        <skuNumber>123456789</skuNumber>
        <name>Inkjet Printer</name>
        <description>HP DeskJet 932C</description>
        <quantity>1</quantity>
        <unit>PC</unit>
        <unitPrice>199.99</unitPrice>
    </Item>
    <Item>
        <skuNumber>24680</skuNumber>
        <name>CD-R</name>
        <description>Memorex</description>
        <quantity>2</quantity>
        <unit>BOX</unit>
        <unitPrice>100.99</unitPrice>
    </Item>
    </Items>
</Order>
<Order sn='24680'>
    <OrderDate>05/30/2001</OrderDate>
    <BillTo>
        <name>Object Innovations Inc.</name>
        <street>420 Boston Turnpike</street>
        <city>Shrewsbury</city>
        <state>MA</state>
        <postalcode>01545</postalcode>
    </BillTo>
    <ShipTo>
        <name>Anew Technologies Inc.</name>
        <street>99 South Bedford Street</street>
        <city>Burlington</city>
        <state>MA</state>
        <postalcode>01803</postalcode>
        <via>UPS</via>
        <ShipDate>06/27/2001</ShipDate>
    </ShipTo>
    <Items>
    <Item>
```

```xml
      <skuNumber>987654</skuNumber>
      <name>Hard Disk</name>
      <description>Maxtor 40G</description>
      <quantity>1</quantity>
      <unit>PC</unit>
      <unitPrice>299.99</unitPrice>
    </Item>
    <Item>
      <skuNumber>24680</skuNumber>
      <name>ZIP100</name>
      <description>Iomega ZIP100</description>
      <quantity>2</quantity>
      <unit>BOX</unit>
      <unitPrice>120</unitPrice>
    </Item>
    </Items>
</Order>
  <Order sn='987123'>
  <OrderDate>05/31/2001</OrderDate>
  <BillTo>
      <name>Delphi Technology Inc.</name>
      <street>201 Broadway</street>
      <city>Cambridge</city>
      <state>MA</state>
      <postalcode>02139</postalcode>
  </BillTo>
  <ShipTo>
      <name>Delphi Technology Inc.</name>
      <street>303 George Street</street>
      <city>New Brunswick</city>
      <state>NJ</state>
      <postalcode>08901</postalcode>
      <via>UPS</via>
      <ShipDate>06/27/2001</ShipDate>
  </ShipTo>
  <Items>
  <Item>
      <skuNumber>8831456</skuNumber>
      <name>PowerBuilder</name>
      <description>PowerBuilder
        Enterprise Edition</description>
      <quantity>3</quantity>
      <unit>PC</unit>
      <unitPrice>1999.99</unitPrice>
  </Item>
  <Item>
      <skuNumber>991456</skuNumber>
      <name>Oracle 8i</name>
      <description>Oracle Enterprise
       Server</description>
```

```
         <quantity>1</quantity>
         <unit>PC</unit>
         <unitPrice>1100</unitPrice>
      </Item>
      </Items>
   </Order>
</orders>
```

7.1.1.1 TREE TRAVERSE

First, let's consider a program that traverses the entire XML tree in order to understand how the **XmlNode/XmlDocument** works. The program is a **DomTree** class in file **DomTree.cs** as follows.

The **DomTree** class has a public method, WalkTree, which uses method **Load** to load XML from a given file, then calls method WalkThrough recursively to go through the tree from the root node. At each node, the program shows **NodeType**, **Name**, and **Value** of the node, displays **Name** and **Value** of the **Attributes** if it has **Attributes**, then goes deeper to **FirstChild** if its property **HasChildNodes** is true; or goes to **NextSibling** if it has **NextSibling**.

```
//DomTree.cs
using System;
using System.IO;
using System.Xml;

public class DomTree
{
 public static void Main(String[] args) {
   String XmlFileName="po.xml";
   if(args.Length>0) {
     XmlFileName=args[0];
   }
   DomTree aDomTree = new DomTree();
   aDomTree.WalkTree(XmlFileName);
 }
 public  void WalkTree(String XmlFileName){
   try {
    // Load the XML from file.
    Console.WriteLine ();
    Console.WriteLine ("Loading file {0} ...",
                   XmlFileName);
    XmlDocument xmldocument = new XmlDocument();
    xmldocument.Load (XmlFileName);
    // Display contents.
    Console.WriteLine(
      "Display contents of the file {0}",
      XmlFileName);
    XmlNode node= xmldocument;
    // Display all the nodes.
```

```
        WalkThrough(node, Console.Out);
      }
      catch (Exception e){
        Console.WriteLine ("Exception: {0}", e.ToString());
      }
  }
  public  void WalkThrough(XmlNode node,
                             TextWriter twOut){
    try {
        ShowNodeInfo(node, twOut);
        if (node.HasChildNodes)
        {
            WalkThrough(node.FirstChild, twOut);
        }
        if(node.NextSibling!=null) {
            WalkThrough(node.NextSibling, twOut);
        }
    }
    catch (Exception e) {
      Console.WriteLine ("Exception: {0}", e.ToString());
    }
  }
  public static void ShowNodeInfo(XmlNode node,
                                    TextWriter twOut){
    twOut.Write ("{0} [{1}] = {2} " ,
        node.NodeType, node.Name, node.Value);
    int AttrCount=0;
     if(node.Attributes!=null)
     {
        AttrCount = node.Attributes.Count;
     }
    for (int i = 0; i <AttrCount ; i++){
      twOut.Write ("{0} [{1}] = {2} " ,
            "Attribute", node.Attributes[i].Name,
               node.Attributes[i].Value);
    }
    twOut.WriteLine();
  }
} // End class DomTree
```

7.1.1.2 QUERY BY TAG NAME

Then, let's use method **GetElementsByTagName** of class **XmlDocument** to get a list of nodes with a specified tag name. The sample program that follows is composed of four steps.

1. Create an instance of class **XmlDocument**.
2. Load the XML data file, po.xml.

3. Get a node list with tag name Order.

4. For each node in the list, get its Item properties **OrderDate**, **BillTo**, and **ShipTo**. For **BillTo** and **ShipTo**, we need to drill down for their **Name** and **ShipDate**, respectively. Property **InnerXml** of class **XmlNode** contains the markup for the children of the node.

```
// QueryByTagName.cs
using System;
using System.IO;
using System.Xml;

public class SampleCode
{
 public static void Main() {
  SampleCode test = new SampleCode();
 }
 public SampleCode() {
  try  {
   XmlDocument doc = new XmlDocument();
   doc.Load("po.xml");
   Console.WriteLine("------------------");
   // Get each Order.
   XmlNodeList orderList =
doc.GetElementsByTagName("Order");
    foreach(XmlNode order in orderList){
       Console.WriteLine("Order Date  = {0}",
                  order["OrderDate"].InnerXml);
       Console.WriteLine("Bill To Name= {0}",
                  order["BillTo"]["name"].InnerXml);
       Console.WriteLine("Ship To Name= {0}",
                  order["ShipTo"]["name"].InnerXml);
       Console.WriteLine("Ship Date   = {0}",
                  order["ShipTo"]["ShipDate"].InnerXml);
       Console.WriteLine("------------------");
    }
  }
  catch (Exception e) {
    Console.WriteLine ("Exception: {0}", e.ToString());
  }
 } // End Constructor
}// End Class
```

This sample program generates the following output:

```
------------------
Order Date  = 05/27/2001
Bill To Name = Anew Technologies Inc.
Ship To Name = Object Innovations Inc.
Ship Date   = 06/27/2001
```

```
------------------
Order Date    = 05/30/2001
Bill To Name = Object Innovations Inc.
Ship To Name = Anew Technologies Inc.
Ship Date    = 06/27/2001
------------------
Order Date    = 05/31/2001
Bill To Name = Delphi Technology Inc.
Ship To Name = Delphi Technology Inc.
Ship Date    = 06/27/2001
```

7.1.1.3 USING THE PROPERTIES OF AN XMLNODE

In the next sample program, we get **Item** first, then drill up to its parent to find the relevant information. This program takes the following steps.

1. Calls **GetElementsByTagName("Item")** to get the designated node list.

2. Gets **Order** node by the property **ParentNode** of each **Item**.

3. Gets information from the **Order** node.

```
//ParentNode.cs
using System;
using System.IO;
using System.Xml;

public class SampleCode
{
public static void Main() {
  SampleCode test = new SampleCode();
}
public SampleCode() {
 try  {
   XmlDocument doc = new XmlDocument();
   doc.Load("po.xml");
   Console.WriteLine("Get item first, then get its ⇓
parent node");
   Console.WriteLine("------------------");
   // Get each Item.
   XmlNodeList ItemList = doc.GetElementsByTagName("Item");
   foreach(XmlNode Item in ItemList){
      Console.WriteLine("This Item: ");
      Console.WriteLine("{");
      Console.WriteLine("skuNumber  = {0}",
                 Item["skuNumber"].InnerXml);
      Console.WriteLine("Item name = {0}",
                 Item["name"].InnerXml);
      Console.WriteLine("Item description = {0}",
               Item["description"].InnerXml);
```

```
        Console.WriteLine("Quantity   = {0}",
                Item["quantity"].InnerXml);
        Console.WriteLine("Unit    = {0}",
                Item["unit"].InnerXml);
        Console.WriteLine("}");
        //Get grandparent node - Order / Items.
        XmlNode order = Item.ParentNode.ParentNode;
        Console.WriteLine("Was ordered by {0}  On {1}",
                    order["BillTo"]["name"].InnerXml,
                    order["OrderDate"].InnerXml);
        Console.WriteLine("Will be shipped to {0} by {1}",
                    order["ShipTo"]["name"].InnerXml,
                    order["ShipTo"]["ShipDate"].InnerXml);
        Console.WriteLine("------------------");
    }
 }
 catch (Exception e) {
    Console.WriteLine ("Exception: {0}", e.ToString());
 }
}
}
```

This program generates following output:

```
Get Item first and then get its parent node.
------------------
This Item:
{
skuNumber  = 123456789
Item name = Inkjet Printer
Item description = HP DeskJet 932C
Quantity   = 1
Unit   = PC
}
Was ordered by Anew Technologies Inc.  on 05/27/2001
Will be shipped to Object Innovations Inc. by 06/27/2001
------------------
This Item:
{
skuNumber  = 24680
Item name = CD-R
Item description = Memorex
Quantity   = 2
Unit   = BOX
}
Was ordered by Anew Technologies Inc.  on 05/27/2001
Will be shipped to Object Innovations Inc. by 06/27/2001
------------------
This Item:
{
```

```
skuNumber  = 987654
Item name = Hard Disk
Item description= Maxtor 40G
Quantity   = 1
Unit   = PC
}
Was ordered by Object Innovations Inc.  on 05/30/2001
Will be shipped to Anew Technologies Inc. by 06/27/2001
------------------
This Item:
{
skuNumber  = 24680
Item name = ZIP100
Item description = Iomega ZIP100
Quantity   = 2
Unit   = BOX
}
Was ordered by Object Innovations Inc. on 05/30/2001
Will be shipped to Anew Technologies Inc. by 06/27/2001
------------------
This Item:
{
skuNumber  = 8831456
Item name = PowerBuilder
Item description = PowerBuilder EE
Quantity   = 3
Unit   = PC
}
Was ordered by Delphi Technology Inc. on 05/31/2001
Will be shipped to Delphi Technology Inc. by 06/27/2001
------------------
This Item:
{
skuNumber  = 991456
Item name = Oracle 8i
Item description = Oracle Enterprise Server
Quantity   = 1
Unit   = PC
}
Was ordered by Delphi Technology Inc. on 05/31/2001
Will be shipped to Delphi Technology Inc. by 06/27/2001
------------------
```

7.1.1.4 QUERY BY XPATH AND INSERT NEW NODE

Now, let's examine the methods **SelectNodeList**, **InsertAfter**, and **CreateDocumentFragment** of class **XmlDocument**. In the following program, **SelectNodeList** is called with a specified criteria **XPath** so as to get a list of nodes, **XmlNodeList**, that meet the criteria. Then each node in the list is in turn accessed to calculate price and an element node, **Price**, is inserted.

```
//
//DomSum.cs
using System;
using System.IO;
using System.Xml;

public class DomSum
{
public static void Main() {
  DomSum test = new DomSum();
}
public DomSum() {
 try  {
   XmlDocument xmldocument = new XmlDocument();
   xmldocument.Load("po.xml");
   // Select all "Item".
   XmlNodeList ItemList =
     xmldocument.SelectNodes("descendant::Item");
   foreach(XmlNode ItemNode in  ItemList){
   // Handle each "Item".
       double quantity =0;
       double unitPrice =0;
       double price =0;
       quantity =
Double.Parse(ItemNode["quantity"].InnerText);
       unitPrice =
Double.Parse(ItemNode["unitPrice"].InnerText);
       price=quantity*unitPrice;
   // Add price element.
       XmlDocumentFragment nodePrice =
           xmldocument.CreateDocumentFragment();
       nodePrice.InnerXml="<price>"+price+"</price>";
       ItemNode.InsertAfter(
 nodePrice,ItemNode["unitPrice"]);
   }
   xmldocument.Save("po_p.xml" );

 }
 catch (Exception e) {
    Console.WriteLine ("Exception: {0}", e.ToString());
 }
}
} // End Class DomSum.
```

7.1.2 Cursor—Reader/Writer—Sequential Access Mode, Forward Only

Classes **XmlReader** and **XmlWriter** are key players of XML.NET. They support an XML processing technique that is equivalent to the well-known SAX (Simple API of XML).

7.1.2.1 READ THROUGH THE ENTIRE TREE

The following sample program shows how class **XmlTextReader** works. It walks through all the nodes in a tree by calling **XmlTextReader.Read**. Note that method **HasAttributes** indicates whether or not a node has attributes. If it has, method **MoveToNextAttribute** is invoked to get them.

```csharp
//ReadTree.cs
using System;
using System.IO;
using System.Xml;

public class ReadTree
{
 public static void ReadThrough(XmlTextReader reader)
 {
  try {
   int ReadCount=0;
   while ( reader.Read() )
   {
    ReadCount++;
    Console.Write("Read[{0,3}]:",ReadCount);
    ShowNodeInfo(reader, Console.Out);
   }
  }
  catch (Exception e) {
   Console.WriteLine ("Exception: {0}", e.ToString());
  }
 }
 public static void ShowNodeInfo(XmlReader prtreader,
                                 TextWriter twOut){
  if (prtreader.HasValue) {
    twOut.Write ("{0} [{1}] = {2} " ,
      prtreader.NodeType, prtreader.Name,
      prtreader.Value);
  }
  else {
    twOut.Write("{0} [{1}] " ,
      prtreader.NodeType, prtreader.Name);
  }
  if(prtreader.HasAttributes){
   while(prtreader.MoveToNextAttribute()){
    twOut.Write ("{0} [{1}]={2} " ,
```

```
          prtreader.NodeType, prtreader.Name,
          prtreader.Value);
    }
   }
 twOut.WriteLine();
 }
 public static void Main() {
 StringReader stream = null;
 try {
 /* The string containing the XML document with the
most of node types to read
 */
  String sXmlDoc= "<?xml version=\"1.0\"?>" +
 "<!-- This is an example XML document. -->" +
 "<!DOCTYPE doc [" +
 "<!ENTITY foo \"123\">" +
 "]>" +
 "<Items>" +
 "<Item x1='y' x2='z'>Test with an entity: &foo;</Item>" +
 "<Item>test with a child element <more/> stuff</Item>" +
"<Item>test with a CDATA section <![CDATA[<456>]]>def"+
"</Item>" +
 "<Item>Test with an char entity: &#65;</Item>" +
 "<!-- Fourteen chars in this element.-->" +
 "<Item>1234567890ABCD</Item>" +
 "</Items>";

  Console.WriteLine("Reading  XML String ...");
  stream = new StringReader(sXmlDoc);
  XmlTextReader reader= new XmlTextReader(stream);
   reader.WhitespaceHandling=WhitespaceHandling.None;
   ReadXML.ReadThrough(reader);

  Console.WriteLine("=====================");
  Console.WriteLine("Reading XML file ...");
  XmlTextReader reader2 =
      new XmlTextReader("po.xml");
   reader2.WhitespaceHandling
     = WhitespaceHandling.Significant;
 ReadTree.ReadThrough(reader2);
 }
 catch (Exception e){
   Console.WriteLine ("Exception: {0}", e.ToString());
 }
 finally {
  if (stream!=null)
    stream.Close();
 }
 }
} //End class ReadTree.
```

The output of the program is as follows.

```
Reading  XML String ...
Read[  1]:XmlDeclaration [xml] = version="1.0" Attribute [ver-
sion]=1.0
Read[  2]:Comment [] =  This is an example XML document.
Read[  3]:DocumentType [doc] = <!ENTITY foo "123">
Read[  4]:Element [Items]
Read[  5]:Element [Item] Attribute [x1]=y Attribute [x2]=z
Read[  6]:Text [] = Test with an entity:
Read[  7]:EntityReference [foo]
Read[  8]:EndElement [Item]
Read[  9]:Element [Item]
Read[ 10]:Text [] = test with a child element
Read[ 11]:Element [more]
Read[ 12]:Text [] =  stuff
Read[ 13]:EndElement [Item]
Read[ 14]:Element [Item]
Read[ 15]:Text [] = test with a CDATA section
Read[ 16]:CDATA [] = <456>
Read[ 17]:Text [] =  def
Read[ 18]:EndElement [Item]
Read[ 19]:Element [Item]
Read[ 20]:Text [] = Test with an char entity: A
Read[ 21]:EndElement [Item]
Read[ 22]:Comment [] =  Fourteen chars in this element.
Read[ 23]:Element [Item]
Read[ 24]:Text [] = 1234567890ABCD
Read[ 25]:EndElement [Item]
Read[ 26]:EndElement [Items]
====================
Reading XML file ...
Read[  1]:XmlDeclaration [xml] = version="1.0" Attribute [ver-
sion]=1.0
Read[  2]:Element [orders]
Read[  3]:Element [Order] Attribute [sn]=13579 Attribute [sta-
tus]=pending
Read[  4]:Element [OrderDate]
Read[  5]:Text [] = 05/27/2001
Read[  6]:EndElement [OrderDate]
Read[  7]:Element [BillTo]
Read[  8]:Element [name]
Read[  9]:Text [] = Anew Technologies Inc.
Read[ 10]:EndElement [name]
Read[ 11]:Element [street]
Read[ 12]:Text [] = 99 South Bedford Street
Read[ 13]:EndElement [street]
Read[ 14]:Element [city]
Read[ 15]:Text [] = Burlington
Read[ 16]:EndElement [city]
Read[ 17]:Element [state]
```

```
Read[ 18]:Text [] = MA
Read[ 19]:EndElement [state]
Read[ 20]:Element [postalcode]
Read[ 21]:Text [] = 01803
Read[ 22]:EndElement [postalcode]
Read[ 23]:EndElement [BillTo]
Read[ 24]:Element [ShipTo]
Read[ 25]:Element [name]
Read[ 26]:Text [] = Object Innovations Inc.
Read[ 27]:EndElement [name]
Read[ 28]:Element [street]
Read[ 29]:Text [] = 420 Boston Turnpike
Read[ 30]:EndElement [street]
Read[ 31]:Element [city]
Read[ 32]:Text [] = Shrewsbury
Read[ 33]:EndElement [city]
Read[ 34]:Element [state]
Read[ 35]:Text [] = MA
Read[ 36]:EndElement [state]
Read[ 37]:Element [postalcode]
Read[ 38]:Text [] = 01545
Read[ 39]:EndElement [postalcode]
Read[ 40]:Element [via]
Read[ 41]:Text [] = UPS
Read[ 42]:EndElement [via]
Read[ 43]:Element [ShipDate]
Read[ 44]:Text [] = 06/27/2001
Read[ 45]:EndElement [ShipDate]
Read[ 46]:EndElement [ShipTo]
Read[ 47]:Element [Items]
Read[ 48]:Element [Item]
Read[ 49]:Element [skuNumber]
Read[ 50]:Text [] = 123456789
Read[ 51]:EndElement [skuNumber]
Read[ 52]:Element [name]
Read[ 53]:Text [] = Inkjet Printer
Read[ 54]:EndElement [name]
Read[ 55]:Element [description]
Read[ 56]:Text [] = HP DeskJet 932C
Read[ 57]:EndElement [description]
Read[ 58]:Element [quantity]
Read[ 59]:Text [] = 1
Read[ 60]:EndElement [quantity]
Read[ 61]:Element [unit]
Read[ 62]:Text [] = PC
Read[ 63]:EndElement [unit]
Read[ 64]:Element [unitPrice]
Read[ 65]:Text [] = 199.99
Read[ 66]:EndElement [unitPrice]
Read[ 67]:EndElement [Item]
```

```
Read[ 68]:Element [Item]
Read[ 69]:Element [skuNumber]
Read[ 70]:Text [] = 24680
Read[ 71]:EndElement [skuNumber]
Read[ 72]:Element [name]
Read[ 73]:Text [] = CD-R
Read[ 74]:EndElement [name]
Read[ 75]:Element [description]
Read[ 76]:Text [] = Memorex
Read[ 77]:EndElement [description]
Read[ 78]:Element [quantity]
Read[ 79]:Text [] = 2
Read[ 80]:EndElement [quantity]
Read[ 81]:Element [unit]
Read[ 82]:Text [] = BOX
Read[ 83]:EndElement [unit]
Read[ 84]:Element [unitPrice]
Read[ 85]:Text [] = 100.99
Read[ 86]:EndElement [unitPrice]
Read[ 87]:EndElement [Item]
Read[ 88]:EndElement [Items]
Read[ 89]:EndElement [Order]
Read[ 90]:Element [Order] Attribute [sn]=24680
Read[ 91]:Element [OrderDate]
Read[ 92]:Text [] = 05/30/2001
Read[ 93]:EndElement [OrderDate]
Read[ 94]:Element [BillTo]
Read[ 95]:Element [name]
Read[ 96]:Text [] = Object Innovations Inc.
Read[ 97]:EndElement [name]
Read[ 98]:Element [street]
Read[ 99]:Text [] = 420 Boston Turnpike
Read[100]:EndElement [street]
Read[101]:Element [city]
Read[102]:Text [] = Shrewsbury
Read[103]:EndElement [city]
Read[104]:Element [state]
Read[105]:Text [] = MA
Read[106]:EndElement [state]
Read[107]:Element [postalcode]
Read[108]:Text [] = 01545
Read[109]:EndElement [postalcode]
Read[110]:EndElement [BillTo]
Read[111]:Element [ShipTo]
Read[112]:Element [name]
Read[113]:Text [] = Anew Technologies Inc.
Read[114]:EndElement [name]
Read[115]:Element [street]
Read[116]:Text [] = 99 South Bedford Street
Read[117]:EndElement [street]
```

```
Read[118]:Element [city]
Read[119]:Text [] = Burlington
Read[120]:EndElement [city]
Read[121]:Element [state]
Read[122]:Text [] = MA
Read[123]:EndElement [state]
Read[124]:Element [postalcode]
Read[125]:Text [] = 01803
Read[126]:EndElement [postalcode]
Read[127]:Element [via]
Read[128]:Text [] = UPS
Read[129]:EndElement [via]
Read[130]:Element [ShipDate]
Read[131]:Text [] = 06/27/2001
Read[132]:EndElement [ShipDate]
Read[133]:EndElement [ShipTo]
Read[134]:Element [Items]
Read[135]:Element [Item]
Read[136]:Element [skuNumber]
Read[137]:Text [] = 987654
Read[138]:EndElement [skuNumber]
Read[139]:Element [name]
Read[140]:Text [] = Hard Disk
Read[141]:EndElement [name]
Read[142]:Element [description]
Read[143]:Text [] = Maxtor 40G
Read[144]:EndElement [description]
Read[145]:Element [quantity]
Read[146]:Text [] = 1
Read[147]:EndElement [quantity]
Read[148]:Element [unit]
Read[149]:Text [] = PC
Read[150]:EndElement [unit]
Read[151]:Element [unitPrice]
Read[152]:Text [] = 299.99
Read[153]:EndElement [unitPrice]
Read[154]:EndElement [Item]
Read[155]:Element [Item]
Read[156]:Element [skuNumber]
Read[157]:Text [] = 24680
Read[158]:EndElement [skuNumber]
Read[159]:Element [name]
Read[160]:Text [] = ZIP100
Read[161]:EndElement [name]
Read[162]:Element [description]
Read[163]:Text [] = Iomega ZIP100
Read[164]:EndElement [description]
Read[165]:Element [quantity]
Read[166]:Text [] = 2
Read[167]:EndElement [quantity]
```

```
Read[168]:Element [unit]
Read[169]:Text [] = BOX
Read[170]:EndElement [unit]
Read[171]:Element [unitPrice]
Read[172]:Text [] = 120
Read[173]:EndElement [unitPrice]
Read[174]:EndElement [Item]
Read[175]:EndElement [Items]
Read[176]:EndElement [Order]
Read[177]:Element [Order] Attribute [sn]=987123
Read[178]:Element [OrderDate]
Read[179]:Text [] = 05/31/2001
Read[180]:EndElement [OrderDate]
Read[181]:Element [BillTo]
Read[182]:Element [name]
Read[183]:Text [] = Delphi Technology Inc.
Read[184]:EndElement [name]
Read[185]:Element [street]
Read[186]:Text [] = 201 Broadway
Read[187]:EndElement [street]
Read[188]:Element [city]
Read[189]:Text [] = Cambridge
Read[190]:EndElement [city]
Read[191]:Element [state]
Read[192]:Text [] = MA
Read[193]:EndElement [state]
Read[194]:Element [postalcode]
Read[195]:Text [] = 02139
Read[196]:EndElement [postalcode]
Read[197]:EndElement [BillTo]
Read[198]:Element [ShipTo]
Read[199]:Element [name]
Read[200]:Text [] = Delphi Technology Inc.
Read[201]:EndElement [name]
Read[202]:Element [street]
Read[203]:Text [] = 303 George Street
Read[204]:EndElement [street]
Read[205]:Element [city]
Read[206]:Text [] = New Brunswick
Read[207]:EndElement [city]
Read[208]:Element [state]
Read[209]:Text [] = NJ
Read[210]:EndElement [state]
Read[211]:Element [postalcode]
Read[212]:Text [] = 08901
Read[213]:EndElement [postalcode]
Read[214]:Element [via]
Read[215]:Text [] = UPS
Read[216]:EndElement [via]
```

```
Read[217]:Element [ShipDate]
Read[218]:Text [] = 06/27/2001
Read[219]:EndElement [ShipDate]
Read[220]:EndElement [ShipTo]
Read[221]:Element [Items]
Read[222]:Element [Item]
Read[223]:Element [skuNumber]
Read[224]:Text [] = 8831456
Read[225]:EndElement [skuNumber]
Read[226]:Element [name]
Read[227]:Text [] = PowerBuilder
Read[228]:EndElement [name]
Read[229]:Element [description]
Read[230]:Text [] = PowerBuilder EE
Read[231]:EndElement [description]
Read[232]:Element [quantity]
Read[233]:Text [] = 3
Read[234]:EndElement [quantity]
Read[235]:Element [unit]
Read[236]:Text [] = PC
Read[237]:EndElement [unit]
Read[238]:Element [unitPrice]
Read[239]:Text [] = 1999.99
Read[240]:EndElement [unitPrice]
Read[241]:EndElement [Item]
Read[242]:Element [Item]
Read[243]:Element [skuNumber]
Read[244]:Text [] = 991456
Read[245]:EndElement [skuNumber]
Read[246]:Element [name]
Read[247]:Text [] = Oracle 8i
Read[248]:EndElement [name]
Read[249]:Element [description]
Read[250]:Text [] = Oracle Enterprise Server
Read[251]:EndElement [description]
Read[252]:Element [quantity]
Read[253]:Text [] = 1
Read[254]:EndElement [quantity]
Read[255]:Element [unit]
Read[256]:Text [] = PC
Read[257]:EndElement [unit]
Read[258]:Element [unitPrice]
Read[259]:Text [] = 1100
Read[260]:EndElement [unitPrice]
Read[261]:EndElement [Item]
Read[262]:EndElement [Items]
Read[263]:EndElement [Order]
Read[264]:EndElement [orders]
```

The basic building blocks in the XML document can be found in the preceding output.

- XmlDeclaration
- Element
- Text
- EndElement
- Attribute
- Character Data (CDATA)
- Processing Instructions (PI)
- Comment
- Entity Reference (DocumentType)

7.1.2.2 READ THE REQUIRED NODES ONLY

Knowing how the reader works, we may now select the nodes that meet the specified conditions. For example, we may want to figure out the total dollar amount of all orders in the document **po.xml** and subtotal on each order. Only nodes **quantity**, **unit**, and **unitPrice** are needed in order to calculate the amount. Therefore, we don't have to load unnecessary information into the memory, saving precious resources on the computer. In this case, we can use **XmlTextReader** to scan the document and pick up the information we need, skipping the rest:

```csharp
//ReadSum.cs
using System;
using System.IO;
using System.Xml;

public class ReadSum
{
 public static void Main() {
  ReadSum test = new ReadSum();
 }
 public ReadSum() {
  XmlTextReader reader =null;
  try  {
   reader = new XmlTextReader ("po.xml");
   double TotalPrice =0;
   double quantity =0;
   double unitPrice =0;
   double ItemPrice =0;
   double subtotal =0;

   while (reader.Read()){
    if(reader.Name.Equals("Order")
      && reader.NodeType==XmlNodeType.Element) {
      Console.WriteLine ();
      subtotal=0;
```

```
    }
    if(reader.Name.Equals("Item")
        && reader.NodeType==XmlNodeType.Element) {
      ItemPrice=0;
      quantity=0;
      unitPrice=0;
    }
    if(reader.Name.Equals("quantity")
        && reader.NodeType==XmlNodeType.Element){
      quantity=Double.Parse(reader.ReadString());
    }
    if(reader.Name.Equals("unitPrice")
        && reader.NodeType==XmlNodeType.Element){
      unitPrice=Double.Parse(reader.ReadString());
    }
    if(reader.Name.Equals("Item")
        && reader.NodeType==XmlNodeType.EndElement) {
      ItemPrice=quantity*unitPrice;
      subtotal+=ItemPrice;
      Console.WriteLine ("ItemPrice={0}", ItemPrice);


    }
    if(reader.Name.Equals("Order")
        && reader.NodeType==XmlNodeType.EndElement) {
      TotalPrice+=subtotal;
      Console.WriteLine ("----------------");
      Console.WriteLine ("Subtotal={0}", subtotal);
    }
  }
  Console.WriteLine ("================");
  Console.WriteLine ("Total={0}", TotalPrice);
}
catch (Exception e) {
    Console.WriteLine ("Exception: {0}", e.ToString());
}
finally
{
  if(reader!=null)
    reader.Close();
}
}
} // end class ReadSum
```

The program generates the following output.

```
ItemPrice=199.99
ItemPrice=201.98
----------------
Subtotal=401.97
```

```
ItemPrice=299.99
ItemPrice=240
----------------
Subtotal=539.99

ItemPrice=5999.97
ItemPrice=1100
----------------
Subtotal=7099.97
================
Total=8041.93
```

You may have noticed that this technique is similar to that of SAX. SAX is an event-based XML parsing technique that provides the event-handling interfaces **StartDocument**, **StartElement**, **Characters**, **EndElement**, and **EndDocument**. In the preceding program, an instance of the class **XmlTextReader** deals with event handling; the class **XmlTextReader** consolidates the functions that were individually implemented in SAX.

By using delegates, the SAX event-handling interfaces may also be implemented based on class **XmlTextReader**.

7.1.3 Validation

So far, we have been dealing with well-formatted XML documents. In real life, the XML data could be ill-formatted; a document would contain errors such as mismatched starting and ending tags. Therefore, validation has to be an integral part of XML data processing. Usually, **XmlException** will be raised when a parsing error.

In addition, it is also necessary to check the elements as well as their types and values against some specification so that they make sense from a business perspective. Currently, there are two standards for XML specifications, Document Type Definition (DTD) and Schema, an XML-based definition of XML data.

XmlValidatingReader is generated from **XmlReader** to support validation on reading.

7.1.3.1 VALIDATIONTYPE PROPERTY AND VALIDATIONEVENTHANDLER EVENT

Property **ValidationType** of class **XmlValidatingReader** indicates how an XML document should be validated.

Table 7-2	*Value of Validation Property*

Value	Description
Auto	1. No validation if non-DTD or schema declared.
	2. DTD validation if there is DTD defined in <!DOCTYPE ...>.
	3. Schema validation if there is no <!DOCTYPE ...> declaration for DTD and there IS XSD schema location declared.
	4. MSXML x-schema validation if there is no DTD declaration and no XSD declaration but there is some namespace with MSXML "x-schema :" URN prefix.
DTD	DTD validation.
Schema	Schema validation: either XSD or XDR but not both.
None	No validation.

Method **ValidationEventHandler** is a callback function that serves as an event handler when DTD or schema validation fails.

Let's see how DTD and schema validation should be carried out. First, we need DTD and schema files for our XML document, **po.xml**. The DTD file for **po.xml** is **po.dtd**.

```
Po.dtd:
<!ELEMENT orders (Order)*>
<!ATTLIST orders xmlns CDATA #IMPLIED>
<!ELEMENT Order (OrderDate,
                 BillTo,
                 ShipTo,
                 Items) >
<!ATTLIST Order sn CDATA #REQUIRED >
<!ATTLIST Order status CDATA #IMPLIED >
<!ELEMENT BillTo (name,
                  street,
                  city,
                  state,
                  postalcode) >
<!ELEMENT ShipTo (name,
                  street,
                  city,
                  state,
                  postalcode,
                  via,
                  ShipDate) >
<!ELEMENT Items (Item)* >
<!ELEMENT Item ( skuNumber,
                 name,
                 description,
                 quantity,
                 unit,
                 unitPrice) >
```

```
<!ELEMENT OrderDate (#PCDATA)>
<!ELEMENT name (#PCDATA)>
<!ELEMENT street (#PCDATA)>
<!ELEMENT city (#PCDATA)>
<!ELEMENT state (#PCDATA)>
<!ELEMENT postalcode (#PCDATA)
<!ELEMENT via (#PCDATA)>
<!ELEMENT ShipDate (#PCDATA)>
<!ELEMENT skuNumber (#PCDATA)>
<!ELEMENT description (#PCDATA)>
<!ELEMENT quantity (#PCDATA)>
<!ELEMENT unit (#PCDATA)>
<!ELEMENT unitPrice (#PCDATA)>
```

The schema file for **po.xml** is **pov.xsd**.

```
<?xml version="1.0" ?>
<xsd:schema xmlns:xsd="http://www.w3.org/2001/XMLSchema"
    xmlns="pov.xsd"
    elementFormDefault="qualified"
    targetNamespace="pov.xsd" >

  <xsd:element name="orders" type="ordersType"/>

  <xsd:complexType name="ordersType">
   <xsd:sequence maxOccurs="unbounded">
     <xsd:element name="Order"  type="OrderType"/>
   </xsd:sequence>
  </xsd:complexType>

  <xsd:complexType name="OrderType">
   <xsd:sequence>
     <xsd:element name="OrderDate" type="xsd:string"  />
     <xsd:element name="BillTo" type="BillToType" />
     <xsd:element name="ShipTo" type="ShipToType"/>
     <xsd:element name="Items" type="ItemsType" />
   </xsd:sequence>
   <xsd:attribute name="sn" type="xsd:string" />
   <xsd:attribute name="status" type="xsd:string" />
  </xsd:complexType>

  <xsd:complexType name="BillToType">
   <xsd:sequence>
     <xsd:element name="name" type="xsd:string"
     minOccurs="1"  />
     <xsd:element name="street" type="xsd:string"
     minOccurs="1"  />
     <xsd:element name="city" type="xsd:string"
     minOccurs="1"  />
     <xsd:element name="state" type="xsd:string"
     minOccurs="1"  />
```

```
      <xsd:element name="postalcode" type="xsd:string"
      minOccurs="1"  />
    </xsd:sequence>
  </xsd:complexType>

  <xsd:complexType name="ShipToType">
    <xsd:sequence>
      <xsd:element name="name" type="xsd:string"
      minOccurs="1"  />
      <xsd:element name="street" type="xsd:string"
      minOccurs="1"  />
      <xsd:element name="city" type="xsd:string"
      minOccurs="1"  />
      <xsd:element name="state" type="xsd:string"
      minOccurs="1" />
      <xsd:element name="postalcode" type="xsd:string"
      minOccurs="1"  />
      <xsd:element name="via" type="xsd:string"
      minOccurs="1"  />
      <xsd:element name="ShipDate" type="xsd:string"
      minOccurs="1"  />
    </xsd:sequence>
  </xsd:complexType>

  <xsd:complexType name="ItemsType">
    <xsd:sequence maxOccurs="unbounded">
      <xsd:element name="Item" type="ItemType" />
    </xsd:sequence>
  </xsd:complexType>

  <xsd:complexType name="ItemType">
    <xsd:sequence>
      <xsd:element name="skuNumber" type="xsd:string"
minOccurs="1"  />
      <xsd:element name="name" type="xsd:string"
minOccurs="1" />
      <xsd:element name="description" type="xsd:string"
 minOccurs="1"  />
      <xsd:element name="quantity" type="xsd:string"
minOccurs="1"  />
      <xsd:element name="unit" type="xsd:string"
minOccurs="1"  />
      <xsd:element name="unitPrice" type="xsd:string"
minOccurs="1"  />
    </xsd:sequence>
  </xsd:complexType>
</xsd:schema>
```

For DTD validation, we need to add **DocumentType** into the XML file.

```
<!DOCTYPE orders SYSTEM "po.dtd">
```

For Schema validation, we need to add the xmlns attribute on the root node:

```
<orders xmlns="pov.xsd">
```

A sample program is as follows.

```
//ReadAndValidate.cs
using System;
using System.IO;
using System.Xml;
using System.Xml.Schema;

public class XmlReadAndValidate
{
  private XmlValidatingReader m_reader = null;
  private Boolean m_success = true;
  public void ReadValidate(String xmlFileName,
      ValidationType validationMethod)
  {
  try
    {
    m_success=true;
    // Validate the XML file with the DTD
    Console.WriteLine();
    Console.WriteLine(
     "Validating XML file, {0},with {1}...",
       xmlFileName, validationMethod );
     m_reader = new XmlValidatingReader(
       new XmlTextReader (xmlFileName));
     m_reader.ValidationType=validationMethod;
     if(validationMethod==ValidationType.Schema)
     {
     XmlSchemaCollection myXmlSchemaCollection
     = new XmlSchemaCollection();
     myXmlSchemaCollection.Add("po.xsd" ,
       new XmlTextReader("po.xsd"));
     m_reader.Schemas.Add(myXmlSchemaCollection);
     }
     // apply the new validation event handler
     m_reader.ValidationEventHandler
     += new ValidationEventHandler(
      this.ValidationEventHandle);
     Console.WriteLine("Validating  with {0}...",
         m_reader.ValidationType );
     XmlDataDocument doc = new XmlDataDocument();
     doc.Load(m_reader);
  // alternatively,
  // Read the XML data directly from reader.
  //   while (m_reader.Read()){}
     Console.WriteLine(
       "Validation finished. Validation {0}",
```

```
            (m_success==true ? "successful" : "failed"));
    }
    catch (XmlException e)
    {
      Console.WriteLine("XmlException: "+e.ToString());
    }
    catch (Exception e)
    {
      Console.WriteLine ("Exception: " + e.ToString());
    }
    finally
    {
      // Finished with XmlTextReader
      if (m_reader != null)
      m_reader.Close();
    }
  }
  public static void Main()
  {
    XmlReadAndValidate RnV = new XmlReadAndValidate();
    RnV.ReadValidate("po_d.xml",ValidationType.DTD);
    RnV.ReadValidate("po_s.xml",ValidationType.Schema);
    RnV.ReadValidate("po_ds.xml",ValidationType.Auto);
    RnV.ReadValidate("po_ds.xml",ValidationType.DTD);
    RnV.ReadValidate("po_ds.xml",ValidationType.Schema);
  }
  public void ValidationEventHandle (object sender,
        ValidationEventArgs args)
  {
    m_success = false;
    Console.Write("\r\n\tValidation error: " +
        args.Message);
    XmlTextReader xtr=(XmlTextReader)m_reader.Reader;
    if (xtr.LineNumber > 0)
    {
      Console.WriteLine("Line #: "+ xtr.LineNumber
        + " Position: " + xtr.LinePosition);
    }
  }
} // End class XmlReadAndValidate
```

7.1.3.2 XMLSCHEMACOLLECTION

In the preceding program, the name of the DTD file was hard-coded into the
XML document. Class **XmlSchemaCollection** provides a way to apply the
specification for validation into a specified URN. In the following program,
for example, we apply the schema **povx.xsd** to **pov.xsd**.

```csharp
//ValidationReadingXMLSchema.cs
using System;
using System.IO;
using System.Xml;
using System.Xml.Schema;

public class ValidationReadingXMLSample
{
  private const String document0 = "po.xml";
  private const String document1 = "po_s.xml";
  private const String document2 = "povx.xsd";

  private XmlValidatingReader
                   myXmlValidatingReader=null;
  private XmlTextReader myXmlTextReader = null;
  private Boolean Success = true;

  public static void Main()
  {
    String[] args = { document0, document1, document2};
    ValidationReadingXMLSample
myValidationReadingXMLSample =
    new ValidationReadingXMLSample();
    myValidationReadingXMLSample.Run(args);
  }

  public void Run(String[] args)
  {
    try
    {
      XmlSchemaCollection myXmlSchemaCollection =
     new XmlSchemaCollection();
      myXmlSchemaCollection.Add("pov.xsd",
    new XmlTextReader(args[2]));
      // Validate the XML file with the schema
      Success = true;
      Console.WriteLine();
      Console.WriteLine(
    "Validation XML file {0} with schema file {1} ...",
       args[0],args[2]);
      myXmlTextReader = new XmlTextReader (args[0]);
      myXmlValidatingReader =
    new XmlValidatingReader(myXmlTextReader);
      myXmlValidatingReader.Schemas.Add(
          myXmlSchemaCollection);
      myXmlValidatingReader.ValidationType
        = ValidationType.Schema;
      Validate();
      // Schema Validation failure
      Success = true;
```

```
      Console.WriteLine();
      Console.WriteLine(
"Validation XML file {0} with schema file {1} ...",
    args[1],args[2]);
      myXmlTextReader = new XmlTextReader (args[1]);
      myXmlValidatingReader =
    new XmlValidatingReader(myXmlTextReader);
      myXmlValidatingReader.Schemas.Add(
          myXmlSchemaCollection);
      myXmlValidatingReader.ValidationType =
          ValidationType.Schema;
      Validate();
    }
    catch (Exception e)
    {
      Console.WriteLine("Exception: " + e.ToString());
    }
    finally
    {
      // Finished with XmlTextReader
      if (myXmlValidatingReader != null)
      myXmlValidatingReader.Close();
    }
  }
private void Validate()
{
    try
    {
      // Set the validation event handler
      myXmlValidatingReader.ValidationEventHandler
    += new ValidationEventHandler(
        this.ValidationEventHandle);

      // Read XML data
      while (myXmlValidatingReader.Read()){}
      Console.WriteLine (
  "Validation finished. Validation {0}",
  (Success==true ? "successful" : "failed"));
    }
    catch (XmlException e)
    {
      Console.WriteLine("XmlException: "+e.ToString());
    }
    catch (Exception e)
    {
      Console.WriteLine ("Exception: " + e.ToString());
    }
}
public void ValidationEventHandle (object sender,
      ValidationEventArgs args)
```

```
  {
    Success = false;
    Console.WriteLine("\tValidation error: "
        + args.Message);
    if (args.Severity == XmlSeverityType.Warning)
    {
      Console.WriteLine(
    "No schema found to enforce validation.");
    } else
      if (args.Severity == XmlSeverityType.Error)
      {
      Console.WriteLine(
    "validation error occurred " +
    " when validating the instance document.");
      }
// XSD schema validation error
    if (args.Exception != null)
    {
      Console.WriteLine(args.Exception.SourceUri + ","
  +   args.Exception.LinePosition + ","
  +   args.Exception.LineNumber);
    }
  }

}// End class ValidationReadingXMLSample
```

7.1.4 Write XML Data

XmlWriter is an abstract class for writing XML data to a specified stream. Class **XmlTextWriter** is derived from **XmlWriter**.

Like **XmlTextReader**, **XmlTextWriter** has a set of methods to support the XML basic building blocks. These are

- **WriteStartDocument** and **WriteEndDocument** for starting and ending a document
- **WriteStartElement** and **WriteEndElement** for starting and ending an element

There is a group of methods for writing data of various types into the element, such as **WriteBoolean**, **WriteDecimal**, and **WriteDouble**. Another group of methods is available for writing various types, such as **WriteAttrBoolean**, **WriteAttrDecimal**, and **WriteAttrDouble**. Furthermore, the other group of methods is used to write simple elements, such as **WriteElementBoolean**, **WriteElementDecimal**, and **WriteElementDouble**.

7.2 Working with Relational Data: XmlDataDocument and DataSet

In .NET Framework, a data entity may be represented in both XML and relational format.

7.2.1 DataSet and Schema: DataSet.ReadSchema

Class **XmlDataDocument** extends **XmlDocument** with an additional property for relational data, **DataSet**, which is the basic building block of the ADO.NET architecture. While **XmlDataDocument** has a **DataSet** property, **DataSet** also has XML-related properties: **Xml**, **XmlData**, and **XmlSchema**.

With the **DataSet** property, its method **ReadXmlSchema** is used in order to get the relational schema from a file. Unlike the XML schema discussed earlier in this chapter, relational schema defines a relational view of data in XML format.

The schema file may be generated by the .NET SDK tool, **xsd.exe**. For example, the following command creates the schema file **po.xsd** for the sample XML file **po.xml**.

```
xsd po.xml
```

The schema file **po.xsd** is listed here.

```
<?xml version="1.0" encoding="utf-8"?>
<xsd:schema id="orders"
 targetNamespace="pov.xsd"
 xmlns="pov.xsd"
 xmlns:xsd="http://www.w3.org/2001/XMLSchema"
 xmlns:msdata="urn:schemas-microsoft-com:xml-msdata"
 attributeFormDefault="qualified"
 elementFormDefault="qualified">
  <xsd:element name="orders" msdata:IsDataSet="true">
    <xsd:complexType>
      <xsd:choice maxOccurs="unbounded">
        <xsd:element name="Order">
          <xsd:complexType>
            <xsd:sequence>
              <xsd:element name="OrderDate"
                           type="xsd:string"
                           minOccurs="0"
                           msdata:Ordinal="0" />
              <xsd:element name="BillTo"
                           minOccurs="0"
                           maxOccurs="unbounded">
```

```xml
        <xsd:complexType>
          <xsd:sequence>
            <xsd:element name="name"
                          type="xsd:string"
                          minOccurs="0"
                          msdata:Ordinal="0" />
            <xsd:element name="street"
                          type="xsd:string"
                          minOccurs="0"
                          msdata:Ordinal="1" />
            <xsd:element name="city"
                          type="xsd:string"
                          minOccurs="0"
                          msdata:Ordinal="2" />
            <xsd:element name="state"
                          type="xsd:string"
                          minOccurs="0"
                          msdata:Ordinal="3" />
            <xsd:element name="postalcode"
                          type="xsd:string"
                          minOccurs="0"
                          msdata:Ordinal="4" />
          </xsd:sequence>
          <xsd:attribute name="Order_Id"
                          type="xsd:int"
                          use="prohibited" />
        </xsd:complexType>
      </xsd:element>
      <xsd:element name="ShipTo"
                    minOccurs="0"
                    maxOccurs="unbounded">
        <xsd:complexType>
          <xsd:sequence>
            <xsd:element name="name"
                          type="xsd:string"
                          minOccurs="0"
                          msdata:Ordinal="0" />
            <xsd:element name="street"
                          type="xsd:string"
                          minOccurs="0"
                          msdata:Ordinal="1" />
            <xsd:element name="city"
                          type="xsd:string"
                          minOccurs="0"
                          msdata:Ordinal="2" />
            <xsd:element name="state"
                          type="xsd:string"
                          minOccurs="0"
                          msdata:Ordinal="3" />
            <xsd:element name="postalcode"
```

```
                        type="xsd:string"
                        minOccurs="0"
                        msdata:Ordinal="4" />
        <xsd:element name="via"
                        type="xsd:string"
                        minOccurs="0"
                        msdata:Ordinal="5" />
        <xsd:element name="ShipDate"
                        type="xsd:string"
                        minOccurs="0"
                        msdata:Ordinal="6" />
      </xsd:sequence>
      <xsd:attribute name="Order_Id"
                        type="xsd:int"
                        use="prohibited" />
    </xsd:complexType>
  </xsd:element>
  <xsd:element name="Items"
                minOccurs="0"
                maxOccurs="unbounded">
    <xsd:complexType>
      <xsd:sequence>
        <xsd:element name="Item"
                        minOccurs="0"
                        maxOccurs="unbounded">
          <xsd:complexType>
            <xsd:sequence>
              <xsd:element name="skuNumber"
                        type="xsd:string"
                        minOccurs="0"
                        msdata:Ordinal="0" />
              <xsd:element name="name"
                        type="xsd:string"
                        minOccurs="0"
                        msdata:Ordinal="1" />
              <xsd:element name="description"
                        type="xsd:string"
                        minOccurs="0"
                        msdata:Ordinal="2" />
              <xsd:element name="quantity"
                        type="xsd:string"
                        minOccurs="0"
                        msdata:Ordinal="3" />
              <xsd:element name="unit"
                        type="xsd:string"
                        minOccurs="0"
                        msdata:Ordinal="4" />
              <xsd:element name="unitPrice"
                        type="xsd:string"
                        minOccurs="0"
```

```
                                 msdata:Ordinal="5" />
                    </xsd:sequence>
                    <xsd:attribute name="Items_Id"
                                   type="xsd:int"
                                   use="prohibited" />
                </xsd:complexType>
              </xsd:element>
            </xsd:sequence>
            <xsd:attribute name="Items_Id"
                     msdata:AutoIncrement="true"
                     type="xsd:int"
                   msdata:AllowDBNull="false"
                   use="prohibited" />
            <xsd:attribute name="Order_Id"
                     type="xsd:int"
                     use="prohibited" />
        </xsd:complexType>
      </xsd:element>
    </xsd:sequence>
    <xsd:attribute name="Order_Id"
             msdata:AutoIncrement="true"
             type="xsd:int"
             msdata:AllowDBNull="false"
             use="prohibited" />
    <xsd:attribute name="sn" form="unqualified"
             type="xsd:string" />
    <xsd:attribute name="status"
             form="unqualified" type="xsd:string" />
  </xsd:complexType>
 </xsd:element>
 </xsd:choice>
</xsd:complexType>
<xsd:unique name="Items_Constraint1"
      msdata:ConstraintName="Constraint1"
      msdata:PrimaryKey="true">
 <xsd:selector xpath=".//Items" />
 <xsd:field xpath="@Items_Id" />
</xsd:unique>
<xsd:unique name="Constraint1"
         msdata:PrimaryKey="true">
 <xsd:selector xpath=".//Order" />
 <xsd:field xpath="@Order_Id" />
</xsd:unique>
<xsd:keyref name="Order_Items" refer="Constraint1"
        msdata:IsNested="true">
 <xsd:selector xpath=".//Items" />
 <xsd:field xpath="@Order_Id" />
</xsd:keyref>
<xsd:keyref name="Items_Item"
        refer="Items_Constraint1"
```

```
                    msdata:IsNested="true">
        <xsd:selector xpath=".//Item" />
        <xsd:field xpath="@Items_Id" />
      </xsd:keyref>
      <xsd:keyref name="Order_ShipTo" refer="Constraint1"
              msdata:IsNested="true">
        <xsd:selector xpath=".//ShipTo" />
        <xsd:field xpath="@Order_Id" />
      </xsd:keyref>
      <xsd:keyref name="Order_BillTo" refer="Constraint1"
              msdata:IsNested="true">
        <xsd:selector xpath=".//BillTo" />
        <xsd:field xpath="@Order_Id" />
      </xsd:keyref>
    </xsd:element>
</xsd:schema>
```

7.2.2 Mapping XML to Tables: DataSet.Tables

By calling **DataSet.ReadXmlSchema**, you establish a master-detail data
model with information on the related tables, columns, and even foreign
keys for the given relational schema.

```
//ShowTableSchema.cs
//The sample code to show the table structure
using System;
using System.IO;
using System.Data;
using System.Xml;

public class ShowTableStructure
{

private void DisplayTableStructure(String FileSchema)   {
  XmlDataDocument doc = new XmlDataDocument();

    //load the schema
  doc.DataSet.ReadXmlSchema(FileSchema);
  Console.WriteLine("\r\nTable structure \r\n");
  Console.WriteLine("Tables count=" +
  doc.DataSet.Tables.Count.ToString());
  for (int i = 0; i < doc.DataSet.Tables.Count; i++)
  {
    Console.WriteLine("\tTableName='" +
            doc.DataSet.Tables[i].TableName + "'.");
    Console.WriteLine("\tColumns count=" +
  doc.DataSet.Tables[i].Columns.Count.ToString());

    for (int j = 0;
```

```
        j < doc.DataSet.Tables[i].Columns.Count; j++)
   {
     Console.WriteLine("\t\tColumnName='" +
       doc.DataSet.Tables[i].Columns[j].ColumnName +
      "',type = " +
doc.DataSet.Tables[i].Columns[j].DataType.ToString());
   }
 }
}
public static void Main(String[] args)  {
 String SchemaFileName=null;
 ShowTableStructure test = new ShowTableStructure();
 if(args.Length>0) {
    SchemaFileName=args[0];
 }
 else {
    Console.Write("Schema File Name: ");
    SchemaFileName=Console.ReadLine();
 }
 test.DisplayTableStructure(SchemaFileName);
}
} // end of class ShowTableStructure
```

Run the program with the command line:

```
>ShowTableSchema po.xsd
```

And the following output is generated.

```
Table structure
Tables count=4
    TableName='Order'.
    Columns count=4
        ColumnName='OrderDate',type = System.String
        ColumnName='sn',type = System.String
        ColumnName='status',type = System.String
        ColumnName='Order_Id',type = Int32
    TableName='BillTo'.
    Columns count=6
        ColumnName='name',type = System.String
        ColumnName='street',type = System.String
        ColumnName='city',type = System.String
        ColumnName='state',type = System.String
        ColumnName='postalcode',type = System.String
        ColumnName='Order_Id',type = Int32
    TableName='ShipTo'.
    Columns count=8
        ColumnName='name',type = System.String
        ColumnName='street',type = System.String
        ColumnName='city',type = System.String
        ColumnName='state',type = System.String
```

```
        ColumnName='postalcode',type = System.String
        ColumnName='via',type = System.String
        ColumnName='ShipDate',type = System.String
        ColumnName='Order_Id',type = Int32
TableName='Item'.
Columns count=7
        ColumnName='skuNumber',type = System.String
        ColumnName='name',type = System.String
        ColumnName='description',type = System.String
        ColumnName='quantity',type = System.String
        ColumnName='unit',type = System.String
        ColumnName='unitPrice',type = System.String
        ColumnName='Order_Id',type = Int32
```

7.2.3 Data Record in Rows: DataSet.Tables[].Rows

In .NET Framework, a data entity may be represented in both XML and Relational format. Therefore, business data may be dealt with either as database records or as XML nodes. On the one hand, ADO.NET technology allows for retrieving of data from a database and presenting it in XML format. On the other hand, an XML document may be loaded into the database.

The following sample program uses a series of SQL **Insert** statements to load XML data based on its relational schema.

```
//Xml2SqlInsert.cs
using System;
using System.IO;
using System.Data;
using System.Xml;

public class Xml2SqlInsert
{
    private const String m_Document = "po.xml";
    private const String m_Schema = "po.xsd";

    public Xml2SqlInsert()
    {
        try
        {
         XmlDataDocument m_datadoc =
              new XmlDataDocument();
          m_datadoc.DataSet.ReadXmlSchema(
              new StreamReader(m_Schema));
         m_datadoc.Load(m_Document);
         BuildSQLInsert(m_datadoc.DataSet);
        }
        catch (Exception e)
        {
```

```
            Console.WriteLine ("Exception: {0}",
                e.ToString());
        }
    }

    public static void Main()
    {
        Xml2SqlInsert X2Sql =
                new Xml2SqlInsert ();
    }

    private void BuildSQLInsert(DataSet dataset)
    {
        // Navigate Dataset
        foreach(DataTable table in dataset.Tables) {

            foreach(DataRow row in table.Rows)  {
            Console.WriteLine("INSERT INTO " +
                table.TableName);
            Console.Write ("{0}", "( ");
            for(int i=0; i<table.Columns.Count; i++){
                DataColumn column=table.Columns[i];
                if(i==0)
                    Console.Write("{0}",column.ColumnName);
                else
                    Console.Write(", {0}",column.ColumnName);
            }
            Console.WriteLine(")");
            Console.WriteLine(" VALUES (");
            for(int i=0; i<row.ItemArray.Length; i++){
                Object value=row.ItemArray[i];
                if(i==0)
                    Console.Write("'{0}'",value.ToString());
                else
                    Console.Write(",'{0}' ",
                        value.ToString());
            }
            Console.WriteLine(") ;");
            }
            Console.WriteLine();
        }
    }
} // End class Xml2SqlInsert
```

7.3 Transform XML

In namespace **System.Xml.Xsl**, **XslTransform** class supports transformation of XML data by using an XSL style sheet.

7.3.1 Working with XML Style Sheet: Xml.Xsl.XslTransform

Method **XslTransform.Transform** is used to transform XML data. In order to do that, an instance of class **XslTransform** needs to be created first. Then its method **Load** is invoked so as to load a specified style sheet. Next, method **Transform** is called with an instance of **XPathDocument** as input, which is constructed with an XML file name. On the other hand, the method takes an instance of **Writer** or **Stream** as output. Alternatively, it may also return an **XmlReader**.

The following sample program transforms a given XML file with a given XSL file and generates a new XML file.

```
//TransXml.cs
using System;
using System.IO;
using System.Xml;
using System.Xml.XPath;
using System.Xml.Xsl;

public class TransXml
{
 public static void Main(String[] args)
 {
   String xmlFileName = null;
   String xslFileName = null;
   String outFileName = null;
   if(args.Length<3){
    Console.WriteLine("Usage: xmlFile xslFile outFile");
    Console.Write("XML FileName:");
    xmlFileName = Console.ReadLine();
    Console.Write("XSL FileName:");
    xslFileName = Console.ReadLine();
    Console.Write("Output FileName:");
    outFileName = Console.ReadLine();
   }
   else {
    xmlFileName = args[0];
    xslFileName = args[1];
    outFileName = args[2];
   }
   try
   {
```

```
      XslTransform xslt = new XslTransform();
      xslt.Load(xslFileName);
      XPathDocument myXPathDocument   =
        new XPathDocument(xmlFileName);
      XmlTextWriter outWriter =
         new XmlTextWriter(outFileName, null);
      outWriter.Formatting=Formatting.Indented;
      xslt.Transform(myXPathDocument, null, outWriter);
      outWriter.Close();
     }
    catch (Exception e)
    {
       Console.WriteLine ("Exception: {0}", e.ToString());
    }
   }
 }
}
```

7.3.2 Transform to XHTML or Another XML

By using the previous program, **TransXML.exe**, you can generate an HTML
page based on the XML document **po.xml** and the XSL file **po.xsl**. The style
sheet for the transformation of the XSL file **po.xsl** is as follows.

```
<?xml version="1.0"?>
<xsl:stylesheet version="1.0"
xmlns:xsl="http://www.w3.org/1999/XSL/Transform">
  <xsl:output method="html" omit-xml-declaration="yes" />
<xsl:template match="/">
<html>
<head>
  <title>Order List</title>
  </head>
<body>
  <xsl:apply-templates select="/orders/Order" />
  </body>
  </html>
  </xsl:template>
<xsl:template match="Order">
<table summary="" border="0">
<tr>
<td>
  <b>Order#:</b>
  <xsl:value-of select="@sn" />
  </td>
<td>
  <b>Date:</b>
  <xsl:value-of select="OrderDate" />
  </td>
  </tr>
```

```
<tr>
<td valign="top">
  <xsl:apply-templates select="BillTo" />
  </td>
<td>
  <xsl:apply-templates select="ShipTo" />
  </td>
  </tr>
<tr>
<td colspan="2">
  <xsl:apply-templates select="Items" />
  </td>
  </tr>
  </table>
  <hr />
  </xsl:template>
<xsl:template match="BillTo">
<table summary="" border="0">
<tr>
  <th colspan="2">Bill To:</th>
  </tr>
<tr>
<td colspan="2">
  <xsl:value-of select="name" />
  </td>
  </tr>
<tr>
<td colspan="2">
  <xsl:value-of select="street" />
  </td>
  </tr>
<tr>
<td colspan="2">
  <xsl:value-of select="city" />
  ,
  <xsl:value-of select="state" />
  <xsl:value-of select="postalcode" />
  </td>
  </tr>
  </table>
  </xsl:template>
<xsl:template match="ShipTo">
<table summary="" border="0">
<tr>
  <th colspan="2">Ship To:</th>
  </tr>
<tr>
<td colspan="2">
  <xsl:value-of select="name" />
  </td>
```

```
      </tr>
   <tr>
   <td colspan="2">
      <xsl:value-of select="street" />
      </td>
      </tr>
   <tr>
   <td colspan="2">
      <xsl:value-of select="city" />
      ,
      <xsl:value-of select="state" />
      <xsl:value-of select="postalcode" />
      </td>
      </tr>
   <tr>
      <th>via:</th>
   <td>
      <xsl:value-of select="via" />
      </td>
      </tr>
   <tr>
      <th>date:</th>
   <td>
      <xsl:value-of select="ShipDate" />
      </td>
      </tr>
      </table>
      </xsl:template>
   <xsl:template match="Items">
   <table summary="" border="1">
   <tr>
      <th>sku#</th>
      <th>name</th>
      <th>description</th>
      <th>quantity</th>
      <th>unit</th>
      <th>@</th>
      </tr>
      <xsl:apply-templates select="Item" />
      </table>
      </xsl:template>
   <xsl:template match="Item">
   <tr>
   <td>
      <xsl:value-of select="skuNumber" />
      </td>
   <td>
      <xsl:value-of select="name" />
      </td>
   <td>
```

```
<xsl:value-of select="description" />
</td>
<td>
<xsl:value-of select="quantity" />
</td>
<td>
<xsl:value-of select="unit" />
</td>
<td>
$
<xsl:value-of select="unitPrice" />
</td>
</tr>
</xsl:template>
</xsl:stylesheet>
```

The following command carries out the transformation and creates file **po.html** as an output.

```
TransXml po.xml po.xsl po.html
```

The output file **po.html** may be viewed by using a browser, as shown in Figure 7-1.

7.4 Serve XML

XML plays an important role in the architecture of .NET Framework. Not only does XML.NET support data presentation and data exchange, it also allows data processing services over the Web, including Web Services and Object Remoting.

7.4.1 Serve XML from Web Servers

Using ASP.NET with **System.Xml**, it is easy to generate XML documents as messages that are exchanged between Web Servers and their clients, such as Internet browsers. Upon receipt of a request from a client, a Web Server may respond in the following ways.

- The server may use ADO.NET technology to retrieve a database and get the result as an instance of **DataSet**. An XML document is then generated as a response by invoking method **DataSet.Xml** or **DataSet.XmlData**.
- The server may use **XmlTextWriter** or **DocumentNavigator** to create XML data as a response to the client.

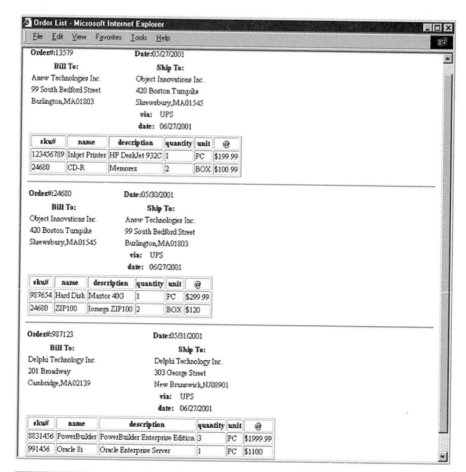

Figure 7-1   *po.html*, transformed from *po.xml* with *po.xsl*.

- The server may also generate a simple text file as a response that contains a simple XML data block in the following format:

```
<starting tag><value><ending tag>
```

- The server may use the XML Web Server control **<asp:Xml>** in ASP.NET to serve XML data to the Internet browser. The ASP.NET code segment **XmlTransform.aspx** is designed to behave like **TransXml.cs**, mentioned before. It captures XML and XSL file names from a Web Form, then shows the transformed data on the Web Server control, **xml1**.

```
<%@ Page Language="C#" %>
<%@ Import Namespace="System.Xml" %>
<%@ Import Namespace="System.Xml.Xsl" %>
    <html>
    <script language="C#" runat="server">
    public void Submit_Click(Object sender, EventArgs E) {
            XmlDocument doc = new XmlDocument();
            doc.Load(Server.MapPath(XmlFile.Text));

            XslTransform trans = new XslTransform();
            trans.Load(Server.MapPath(XslFile.Text));

            xml1.Document = doc;
            xml1.Transform = trans;
    }
    </script>
    <body>
    <form runat="server">
    <h5>XML TransForm
    <asp:TextBox   id="XmlFile"   runat="server" />
    <asp:TextBox   id="XslFile"   runat="server" />
    <input type="submit" id="Submit" value="Transform"
     OnServerClick="Submit_Click" runat="server" />
    </h5>
  <asp:Xml id="xml1" runat="server" />
    </form>
    </body>
    </html>
```

7.4.2 Data Presentation

XML technology supports flexible, page-based data presentation. It separates the content of data from its presentation style. While the XML document contains the data itself, the style sheet, or XSL file, specifies how the data should be presented.

The Web Server may associate an XSL file with the XML document. Using a browser with XSL-rendering capability, such as Microsoft's Internet Explorer 5.0 or later, it presents the data in the designated style. In addition, the downloaded XSL may also be ignored when the data is presented with an XSL file supplied locally at the client site.

7.4.3 Data Exchange

Through the lower-level XML-access primitives of .NET Framework, data may be exchanged over the network between business partners, departments, and suppliers and consumers. XML-based data exchange makes data processing and validation easy.

7.4.4 Web Services and Object Remoting

The Web Service is another application based on XML; Simple Object Access Protocol (SOAP) allows encapsulation of request and response messages in XML format that are easy to manipulate and yet human-readable. XML-based service descriptions may be used to automatically generate the proxy objects at the client sites. See Chapter 6 for the details about Web Services. Furthermore, XML-based SOAP messages may be exchanged over an HTTP channel such that methods of server objects may be invoked from the client sites. See Chapter 8 for more about Object Remoting.

SOAP is becoming a popular model for a new generation of Web applications that deliver services over the Internet, and XML documents are the new wave of Internet traffic.

Summary

This chapter explained XML programming with .NET Framework. Using XML.NET technology, XML-based Web applications can be developed effectively and efficiently.

The useful features of XML.NET include the following

- **XMLDocument**
- **XmlReader**
- **XmlWriter**
- **Validation**
- **XmlDataDocument**
- **Xml.Xsl.Transform**

However, this chapter does not cover all the attractive features of XML.NET, such as **XML.Serialization**. They should be topics of further study.

Object Remoting

*O*bject Remoting is the distributed object system that is built into .NET Framework. You may think of Object Remoting as a built-in facility that allows you to interact with objects that are actually running under the Common Language Runtime on a remote host of the network. With Object Remoting, you may get a proxy to a remote server object and invoke its methods as if it were a local object running under the same Common Language Runtime as your client code.

8.1 Concept

This section discusses the concept of Object Remoting, including communication between applications, building blocks for Object Remoting, server object, channel, formatter, well-known objects and their registration, configuration for Object Remoting, and activation.

8.1.1 Communication Between Applications

In .NET Framework, an application runs in an Application Domain, or an App Domain. This mechanism allows you to isolate one application from another. App Domains are hard boundaries. That is, applications running in different App Domains share no information, such as global variables, between them.

However, applications may communicate with each other at two levels. At one level messages are sent and received between applications. Network programming that was discussed earlier realizes inter-application communication at this level.

At another level, objects in one application can communicate with objects in other applications. Web Services, discussed in Chapter 6, serve as an example of communication at this level. Object Remoting that is being discussed in this chapter, also falls into this category. It allows an object at the client site to remotely invoke a method of an object at the server site.

8.1.2 Building Blocks for Object Remoting

In order to realize Object Remoting, .NET Framework provides the following building blocks:

- *Server Object*. At the sever site, objects are built that will provide the remote clients with their services.
- *Channel*. Messages are exchanged via the channel between the server object and the client object, carrying the request from the client and the response from the server.
- *Formatter*. Messages that are exchanged between server and client are encoded before being sent and decoded after being received. The formatters on both sites are responsible for encoding and decoding.
- *Registration of Well-Known Objects*. The server object needs to be registered so that it is made well known to the network.
- *Configuration of Remoting*. The Remoting service may also be made known to the network through configuration. On the other hand, configuration at the client site allows for client activation of the object.
- *Activation*. Activation mechanisms allow the server objects to be activated for service upon request from the client.

Now let's discuss these building blocks in further detail.

8.1.3 Server Object

A server object may be derived from **System.MarshalByRefObject** and will be marshalled by reference during its remoting. That is, a reference to the object will be made and passed from the server site to the client site, so as to remote access to the object. If the type for server object encapsulates operating system resources, marshalling by reference is preferable. In C#, such a server object can be defined as

```
public class Foo : MarshalByRefObject {
    ...
}
```

Alternatively, a server object may also implement interface **Iserializable** and will be marshalled by value during its remoting. That is, a complete copy of the object will be made and passed from the server site to the client site. If the type for the server object holds a state only, such as **DataSet**, marshalling by value should be used.

If it is not derived from **MarshalByRefObject**, the object will be marshalled by value. In C#, such a server object is simply defined as

```
public class Foo {
    ...
}
```

8.1.4 Channel

Applications communicate using messages over HTTP or TCP channels that are supported by the following classes:

```
System.Runtime.Remoting.Channels.Http
System.Runtime.Remoting.Channels.Tcp
```

In order to use a channel, an object first should be created as an instance of the channel object, such as **System.Runtime.Remoting.Channels.TCP. TCPChannel** for a TCP channel. This object will support communication between the server and client using a TCP socket. Channel objects need to be registered before being used. The **RegisterChannel** method of **System.Runtime.Remoting.ChannelServices** class is used to register the channel.

8.1.5 Formatter

The formatter encodes and decodes the messages that are exchanged between server and client over a channel. By default, an HTTP channel uses a SOAP formatter to transport XML messages between applications. In addition, an HTTP channel may also use another formatter, such as the .NET Framework Binary Formatter. When MIME type is specified on the channel, third-party formatters will also be plugged in.

The TCP channel by default uses plain sockets to transport the binary messages, and it encodes and decodes the messages using the .NET Framework Binary Formatter. Just like an HTTP channel, a TCP channel may also use other formatters, including that for SOAP or third-party plug-ins.

8.1.6 Registration of a Well-Known Object

The server object needs to be registered so that it can be made well known to the network. In .NET Framework, the **RegisterWellKnownType** method of **System.Runtime.Remoting.RemotingConfiguration** is used for this purpose. When this method is invoked, the information about the server object is provided as parameters:

```
. . . .
RemotingConfiguration.RegisterWellKnownType (
   AssemblyName,    // the assembly that the object
                    // belongs to.
   TypeName,        // the object type.
   URI,             // the identifier of the object;
   Mode             // activation mode, see 8.1.8.
);
```

Having called this method, the host program of the server object should be waiting for an incoming request.

8.1.7 Configuration of Remoting

Configuration of Remoting is as an alternative way to make the server object well known to the network. In this case, the information for configuration is supplied in a flat file with the following structure:

```
Name#<application_name>
WellKnownObject#<full_type_name>#<assembly_name> ⇓
#<full_type>#<activation_mode>
Channel#<channel_assembly_name>#<channel_full_type_name>#⇓
  [port=<port_number>]
```

.NET Framework provides the **ConfigureRemoting** method of the **System.Runtime.Remoting.RemotingServices** class for this purpose. This method takes the name of the configuration file as an argument. As can be seen, channel configuration is also included in this activity. Having called this method, the host program of the server object should be waiting for an incoming request.

The client program may also use this method for configuration. The format of the configuration file at the client site is different from that at the server site:

```
Name#<application_name>
Assembly#<AssemblyName>#<RemoteApplicationName># ⇓
<FullTypeName>=<ObjectURI>
RemoteApplication#<RemoteApplicationName># ⇓
<RemoteApplicationURI>
Channel#<channel_assembly_name>#<channel_full_type_name>#⇓
  [port=<port_number>]
```

Having called this method, the client program is ready to access the server object at the remote site.

8.1.8 Activation

There are two ways in which a remoting object may serve its client.

- *SingleCall Mode.* In this mode, whenever a request message arrives, a new instance of the server object is created to serve the request. **SingleCall** mode is advantageous in applications where load balancing is critical. Multiple servers may have the same service, and load balancing can be achieved by using simple techniques, such as DNS round-robin.

- *Singleton Mode.* In this mode, all the requests are served by a single instance of the server object. Singleton mode is useful when both information and resources need to be shared among the requesting clients.

For both **SingleCall** and **Singleton** modes, the client program receives only a proxy when it instances a new remote object. No communication occurs until the client calls on the proxy in order to request the remoting service. When the proxy is called, a request message is generated that is sent to the server site.

In this case, method **System.Activator.GetObject** is used to obtain the proxy:

```
System.Activator.GetObject (
    Type,         // type of the remoting object
    URL           // locator of the remoting object
);
```

Another popular practice is for the object to be activated on request from the user. In this case, the client site has to be configured first and the remoting object, Foo, can be activated in one of the following ways:

```
MyObject = System.Activator.GetInstance(typeof(Foo));
```

Or

```
Foo MyObject = new Foo();
```

8.2 Object Remoting over an HTTP Channel

Now, let's build an application with Object Remoting over an HTTP channel.

8.2.1 Server with Registration of Well-Known Object

First, we build our server object with registration of a well-known object using the following program in C#. Its file name is **HelloServer1.cs**.

```
//HelloServer1.cs
using System;
using System.Runtime.Remoting;
using System.Runtime.Remoting.Channels;
using System.Runtime.Remoting.Channels.Http;

public class HelloServer : MarshalByRefObject {
    public static int Main() {
        // allocate a channel with port specified
        HttpChannel c = new HttpChannel(8765);
        // register the channel
        ChannelServices.RegisterChannel(c);
        // register to make the object well-known
        // to the network - start service
        RemotingConfiguration. ⇓
          RegisterWellKnownServiceType(
            Type.GetType("HelloServer"),   // type name
            "SayHello",            // URI; can be different
                                   // from the object name.
            WellKnownObjectMode.SingleCall
                                   // SingleCall mode
        );
        Console.WriteLine("Press [Enter] to quit ...");
        // ready to server my clients
        Console.ReadLine();
        // stop the service
        return 0;
    }

    // Constructor - logging activation
    public HelloServer() {
        Console.WriteLine("HelloServer: Activated.");
    }

    // Actual service
    public String Greeting(String name) {
        Console.WriteLine(
            // logging the activity
            "HelloServer: Method Greeting called ⇓
              with {0}.",
            name
        );
        // service delivered
        return String.Concat(
```

```
            "Hello, ",
            name
        );
    }
}
```

Object **HelloServer** provides a simple service. It will be marshalled by reference because it is derived from **MarshalByRefObject**. In this program, the activities are to be logged when an instance of **HelloServer** is created or its **Greeting** method is called.

The entry point of this program is **Main()**. In this routine, a channel is first allocated and registered. It is important to note that you have to specify the port when you allocate a channel because the port will become a part of the URI for the client to locate this service.

Then the object is registered as a well-known object so as to start its service. In this example, we use **SingleCall** mode, and the logging capability allows us to monitor the behavior of the object in this mode. Please also note that, for the URI, you may use a name that is different from that of the object, for example, **SayHello** in this case.

Finally, the program starts waiting for the request from its clients. You may press [**Enter**] to stop your service.

The following command compiles this program:

```
csc HelloServer1.cs
```

Now you may run the program to start your service.

```
>HelloServer1
HelloServer: Activated.
Press [Enter] to quit ...
```

As you can see, object **HelloServer** is activated and waiting for the client request.

8.2.2 Client Using Activator.GetObject

Now we can build a client program to access the service. Here is the program in C#. Its file name is **HelloClient1.cs**.

```
//HelloClient1.cs
using System;
using System.Runtime.Remoting;
using System.Runtime.Remoting.Channels;
using System.Runtime.Remoting.Channels.Http;

public class HelloClient {
    public static int Main() {
        ChannelServices.RegisterChannel(
            new HttpChannel());
```

```
// The Activator.MarshalByRefObject methods
// provide the ability to obtain a "proxy" to
// a well-known object.
HelloServer MyHello =
        (HelloServer)Activator.GetObject(
            typeof(HelloServer), // Type
            "http://localhost:8765/SayHello"
                                    // URI
        );
// check if activation is successful
if (MyHello == null) {     // no, so quit
    Console.WriteLine(
      "Fail to locate the server.");
    return -1;
}
else {        // yes, so access the remote service
    Console.Write("Your name, please: ");
    String name = Console.ReadLine();
    Console.WriteLine(MyHello.Greeting(name));
    return 0;
}
}
}
```

Routine **Main()** is the entry point of this program. A channel is first allocated and registered through which it will communicate with the server. Note that there is no need to specify the port. Then, **Activator.GetObject** method is called to get a proxy to the server object. Here, the type and URI of the server object are given as the arguments of the method. Recall that the URI name **SayHello** should be used, rather the Class name **HelloServer**. Here, we assume that both client and server reside in the same machine. If you test them on different machines, the name or IP address of the server machine needs to be supplied, instead of **localhost**.

This action may fail and null would be returned. If the proxy is received successfully, the return value should be a reference to the proxy. Please note that an explicit cast needs to apply to this reference. Now we can call the remote method and enjoy the service.

In order to compile this program, we must have the definition of the server object. A simple solution would be using the executable of the server program as a reference. The following command compiles the client program this way:

```
csc /r:HelloServer1.exe HelloClient1.cs
```

Recall that our server program is waiting for the request on a command window. Therefore, you should run the client program in another command window. Even though the HTTP protocol is employed, you do not need any Web server to run the remoting programs.

```
>HelloClient1
```
Your name, please:

After you start the program, you get a prompt, meaning that a proxy to the remote object has been successfully received. At this time, however, nothing happens at the server site on another command window. That is because no call has been made to the proxy and, thus, no request has been sent.

If you type your name and then hit [**Enter**], you will get a greeting from the server site. Meanwhile, logging text at the server site shows that an instance of the server object is created and its method is called with the argument that you provided. Run the client program and you will see that a new instance is created for each request from the client site.

Here is what was going on at the client site:

```
>HelloClient1
```
Your name, please: David Zhang
Hello, David Zhang

```
>HelloClient1
```
Your name, please: Sam Zhu
Hello, Sam Zhu

And here is what happens at the server site:

```
>HelloServer1
```
HelloServer: Activated.
Press [Enter] to quit ...
HelloServer: Activated.
HelloServer: Method Greeting called with David Zhang.
HelloServer: Activated.
HelloServer: Method Greeting called with Sam Zhu.

8.2.3 Server with Registration of Remoting

Here is the server program in C#. Its file name is **HelloServer2.cs**.

```
// HelloServer2.cs.
using System;
using System.Runtime.Remoting;

public class HelloServer : MarshalByRefObject {
    public HelloServer() {
        Console.WriteLine("HelloServer: Activated.");
    }
    public String Greeting(String name) {
        Console.WriteLine(
            "HelloServer: Method Greeting called ⇓
              with {0}.",
            name
```

```
        );
        return String.Concat(
            "Hello, ",
            name
        );
    }
}
```

This program defines the server object **HelloServer** and the service is started in another program **HelloHost.cs**. This time, marshalling by value is used.

```
//HelloHost.cs
using System;
using System.Runtime.Remoting;

class MainApp {
    public static int Main(String[] args) {
        if (args.Length == 0) {
            Console.WriteLine(
                "Usage: HelloHost ⇓
                    <configuration_file>"
            );
            return -1;
        }
        RemotingConfiguration.Configure(args[0]);
        Console.WriteLine("Press [Enter] to quit ...");
        Console.ReadLine();
        return 0;
    }
}
```

This program takes the name of the configuration file as a command-line argument and then loads the file for configuration to start the service. The configuration file is **HelloServer2.cfg** and it looks like this:

```
Name#HelloServer
WellKnownObject#HelloServer#HelloServer#SayHello#Singleton
Channel#⇓
    System.Runtime.Remoting#⇓
    System.Runtime.Remoting.Channels.HTTP.HTTPChannel#⇓
    port=8765
```

This time we define the server object as in **Singleton** mode.

The following command compiles **HelloServer2.cs** and **HelloHost.cs**:

```
csc /out:HelloServer.dll /target:library HelloServer2.cs
csc HelloHost.cs
```

In this case, a library is created for the server object and executable for the host program. Now you may run the program to start your service:

```
>HelloHost HelloServer2.cfg
HelloServer: Activated.
Press [Enter] to quit ...
```

As you can see, the object **HelloServer** is activated and waiting for the client request.

8.2.4 Client with Registration of Remoting

Now let's create a C# program with remoting registration. Its file name is **HelloClient2.cs**.

```
//HelloClient2.cs
using System;
using System.Runtime.Remoting;

public class HelloClient {
    public static int Main(String[] args) {
        if (args.Length == 0) {
            Console.WriteLine(
                "Usage: HelloClient ⇓
                    <configuration_file>"
            );
            return -1;
        }
        RemotingConfiguration.Configure(args[0]);
        Console.Write("Your name, please: ");
        String name = Console.ReadLine();
        HelloServer MyHello1 = (HelloServer)
            Activator.CreateInstance⇓
                (typeof(HelloServer));
        Console.WriteLine(MyHello1.Greeting(name));
        HelloServer MyHello2 = new HelloServer();
        Console.WriteLine(MyHello2.Greeting(name));
        return 0;
    }
}
```

The configuration file **HelloClientHTTP.cfg** looks like this:

```
Name#HelloServer
Assembly#HelloServer#HelloServer# ⇓
    HelloServer=http://localhost:8765/SayHello
RemoteApplication#HelloServer# ⇓
    http://localhost:8765/SayHello
Channel#System.Runtime.Remoting# ⇓
    System.Runtime.Remoting.Channels.HTTP.HTTPChannel
```

This time the library for the server object can be used as the reference for compilation of the client program:

```
csc /r:HelloServer.dll HelloClient2.cs
```

Now let's run the client program:

```
>HelloClient2 HelloClientHTTP.cfg
Your name, please: David Zhang
Hello, David Zhang

>HelloClient2 HelloClientHTTP.cfg
Your name, please: Sam Zhu
Hello, Sam Zhu
```

Here's what happens at the server site:

```
>HelloServer2
HelloServer: Activated.
Press [Enter] to quit ...
HelloServer: Method Greeting called with David Zhang.
HelloServer: Method Greeting called with David Zhang.
HelloServer: Method Greeting called with Sam Zhu.
HelloServer: Method Greeting called with Sam Zhu.
```

Each time you run the client program, two greeting messages are received because two requests have been made; they are from the following statements:

```
HelloServer MyHello1 = (HelloServer)
    Activator.CreateInstance(typeof(HelloServer));
Console.WriteLine(MyHello1.Greeting(name));
and
HelloServer MyHello2 = new HelloServer();
    Console.WriteLine(MyHello2.Greeting(name));
```

However, the same server is shared for all the requests because **HelloServer2** is configured in **Singleton** mode.

8.2.5 ASP.NET Page as Client

The ASP.NET page can be created to serve as a client of the remote server object. Here is such a page; its file name is **HelloClient.aspx**.

```
<%@ Page Language="VB" Debug="true" %>
<%@ Import Namespace="System.Runtime.Remoting" %>
<html>
<head>
```

```
<script language="VB" runat="server">
Dim Reply As String
Sub Name_Change(Source As Object, E As EventArgs)
    Dim MyHello As HelloServer
    MyHello = new HelloServer()
    reply = MyHello.Greeting(Name.Value)
End Sub
</script>
</head>
<body>
<h3>HelloClient</h3>
<form runat="server">
    <input id="Name" type="text" value="" runat="server" ⇓
        OnServerChange = "Name_Change">
</form>
<p><h3><%=Reply%></h3>
```

In this page, an instance of the **HelloServer** class is created to access the remoting service. You may have noticed that no configuration is found in this page. This function, which is mandatory, is taken care of at the Web application level. In other words, it is implemented in a **global.asax** file or ASP.NET application file.

```
<%@ Import Namespace="System.Runtime.Remoting" %>
<script language="VB" runat="server">
Dim Reply As String
Sub Application_OnStart()
    RemotingServices.ConfigureRemoting(⇓
        HttpContext.Current.Server.MapPath(⇓
            "HelloClientHTTP.cfg")
    )
End Sub
</script>
```

The configuration function is carried out in **Application_OnStart** method. That is, the configuration file is loaded when the page is started.

In this case, your PC is the client of the remoting service, as well as the Web server for the ASP.NET page. Therefore, **HelloClient.aspx**, **HelloClientHTTP.cfg**, and **Global.asax** should reside in a directory that is configured as an IIS virtual directory. Moreover, the library file **HelloServer.dll**, which provides the definition of the server object, has to be in its subdirectory bin. In this case, the virtual directory is "remoting" and our client page can be found at address *localhost/remoting/HelloClient.aspx* (see Figure 8-1).

Figure 8-1   *ASP.NET page as the client of a remoting service.*

8.3 Object Remoting over a TCP Channel

Now, let's build an application with Object Remoting over a TCP channel. As you will see, it is pretty easy to convert the programs for an HTTP channel into programs for a TCP channel.

8.3.1 Server with Registration of Well-Known Object

Here is the program in C#. Its file name is **HelloServer3.cs**.

```
// HelloServer3.cs
using System;
using System.Runtime.Remoting;
using System.Runtime.Remoting.Channels;
using System.Runtime.Remoting.Channels.Tcp;

public class HelloServer : MarshalByRefObject {
    public static int Main() {
        // allocate a channel with the port specified
        TcpChannel c = new TcpChannel(8765);
        // register the channel
        ChannelServices.RegisterChannel(c);
        // register to make the object well-known
        // to the network - start service
```

```
        RemotingConfiguration. ⇓
          RegisterWellKnownServiceType(
              Type.GetType("HelloServer"),  // type name
              "SayHello",          // URI; can be different
                                   // from object name
              WellKnownObjectMode.SingleCall
                                   // SingleCall mode
          );
          Console.WriteLine("Press [Enter] to quit ...");
          // ready to server my clients
          Console.ReadLine();
          // stop the service
          return 0;
    }

    // Constructor - logging activation
    public HelloServer() {
          Console.WriteLine("HelloServer: Activated.");
    }

    // actual service
    public String Greeting(String name) {
          Console.WriteLine(
              // logging the activity
              "HelloServer: Method Greeting ⇓
                    called with {0}.",
              name
          );
          // service delivered
          return String.Concat(
              "Hello, ",
              name
          );
    }
}
```

The boldface statements in this program are different from those in the program for an HTTP channel. There are only two of them and both are concerned with channel allocation.

You may compile and run this program as described in Section 8.2.1.

8.3.2 Client Using Activator.GetObject

Here is the program in C#. Its file name is **HelloClient3.cs**.

```
// HelloClient3.cs
using System;
using System.Runtime.Remoting;
using System.Runtime.Remoting.Channels;
using System.Runtime.Remoting.Channels.Tcp;
```

```
public class HelloServer : MarshalByRefObject {
    public static int Main() {
        // allocate a channel with the port specified
        TcpChannel  c  =  new TcpChannel(8765);
        // register the channel
        ChannelServices.RegisterChannel(c);
        // register to make the object well known
        // to the network - start service
        RemotingConfiguration. ⇓
          RegisterWellKnownServiceType(
            Type.GetType("HelloServer"),  // type name
            "SayHello",         // URI; can be different
                                // from object name
            WellKnownObjectMode.SingleCall
                                // SingleCall mode
        );
        Console.WriteLine("Press [Enter] to quit ...");
        // ready to server my clients
        Console.ReadLine();
        // stop the service
        return 0;
    }

    // Constructor - logging activation
    public HelloServer() {
        Console.WriteLine("HelloServer: Activated.");
    }

    // Actual service
    public String Greeting(String name) {
        Console.WriteLine(
            // logging the activity
            "HelloServer: Method Greeting called ⇓
              with {0}.",
            name
        );
        // service delivered
        return String.Concat(
            "Hello, ",
            name
        );
    }
}
```

The boldface statements in this program are different from those in the program for an HTTP channel. There are only two of them and both are concerned with channel allocation. You may compile and run this program as described in Section 8.2.2.

8.3.3 Server with Registration of Remoting

If you revisit Section 8.2.3, you'll see that the programs we developed are actually channel-neutral. That is, they can be used for any channel. More generally, they may be used for any configuration because the configuration information is loaded from a file. Therefore, the only thing we need to do is to provide a file for the TCP channel:

```
Name#HelloServer
WellKnownObject#HelloServer#HelloServer#SayHello#Singleton
Channel#⇓
    System.Runtime.Remoting#⇓
    System.Runtime.Remoting.Channels.TCP.TCPChannel#⇓
    port=8765
```

You may run the program **HelloServer2** as described in Section 8.2.3.

8.3.4 Client with Registration of Remoting

Similarly, the client program in Section 8.2.4 is also channel-neutral. It may be used for a TCP channel so long as the configuration file **HelloClientTCP.cfg** is loaded.

```
Name#HelloServer
Assembly#HelloServer#HelloServer# ⇓
    HelloServer=http://localhost:8765/SayHello
RemoteApplication#HelloServer# ⇓
    http://localhost:8765/SayHello
Channel#System.Runtime.Remoting# ⇓
    System.Runtime.Remoting.Channels.TCP.TCPChannel
```

You run program **HelloClient2** with **HelloClientTCP.cfg** as described in Section 8.2.3.

8.3.5 ASP.NET Page as Client

Again, the ASP.NET page **HelloASP.aspx** that we developed in Section 8.2.5 is channel-neutral. It works with configuration file **HelloClientTCP.cfg** as well.

8.4 Asynchronous Invocation of the Remote Method

In Chapter 6, we discussed how methods of Web Services are invoked asynchronously so as to improve the overall performance of distributed systems. The standard approach of .NET Framework for asynchronous invocation may also apply to Object Remoting. However, the shortcut for Web Services may not.

A program in C# that invokes our "Hello" remote service asynchronously is as follows. Its file name is **HelloClientAsync.cs**.

```
//HelloClientAsync.cs.
using System;
using System.Threading;
using System.Runtime.Remoting;
using System.Runtime.Remoting.Channels.Tcp;
using System.Runtime.Remoting.Messaging;
using System.Runtime.Remoting.Channels;

// Client object that accommodates the methods for
// asynchronous invocation of remote server object
public class HelloClient {
    // event that controls the flow
    public static ManualResetEvent evt;
    public static String Result;

    // entry point of the program
    public static void Main() {
        // not ready
        evt = new ManualResetEvent(false);

        // create an instance of the client instance
        // in order to use its method
        HelloClient hc = new HelloClient();

        Console.Write("Your name, please: ");
        String name = Console.ReadLine();

        // start calling the web service; it returns
        // immediately without waiting for the result.
        hc.RemoteCall(name);

        // the client process continues to run, doing
        // something useful - get a local greeting
        HelloServer LocalHello = new HelloServer();
        Console.WriteLine(
            "Local: {0}",
            LocalHello.Greeting(name)
        );

        // ready to receive the result from the Web
        // service; wait until it is ready
        evt.WaitOne();

        // result is delivered; present it
        Console.WriteLine("Remote: {0}", Result);
```

```
        }

        // delegate for the remote method
        public delegate String HelloDelegate(String name);

        // starting part of remote method invocation
        public void RemoteCall(String name) {
                // initialize a TCP channel
                ChannelServices.RegisterChannel(
                        new TcpChannel()
                );
                // get the proxy
                HelloServer RemoteHello =
                  (HelloServer)Activator.GetObject(
                        typeof(HelloServer),
                        "tcp://localhost:8765/SayHello"
                );

                // set up the callback method that will be
                // called by the system when the result is ready
                AsyncCallback ac = new
                        AsyncCallback(this.RemoteCallBack);

                // an instance of the delegate for the remote
                // method
                HelloDelegate hd = new
                        HelloDelegate(RemoteHello.Greeting);

                // call the remote method - send the request
                // without waiting for the result to come back
                IAsyncResult ar = hd.BeginInvoke(name, ac, null);
        }

        // ending part of remote method invocation
        public void RemoteCallBack(IAsyncResult ar) {
                // get the delegate from the result interface
                        AsyncResult AR = (AsyncResult) ar;
                        HelloDelegate hd =
                            (HelloDelegate)  AR.AsyncDelegate;

                // get the result
                Result = hd.EndInvoke(ar);

                // wake up the client if it is waiting for
                // the result.
                evt.Set();
        }
}
```

As you can see, this program is similar to the one we developed in Section 6.4.2. One difference is that this program needs to call **Activator. GetObject** in order to obtain a proxy to the remote server object. Alternatively, it may also register remoting by loading a relevant configuration file. Another difference is that the client thread instantiates the server object locally and the same method is invoked to get the greeting from this local object when it is waiting for the result from the remote object. That is viable because we have deployed the implementation of the remote service to the client site, either **HelloServer.exe** or **HelloServer.dll**. Please refer to Section 6.4.2 for a detailed discussion on how asynchronous invocation is realized.

The following command compiles the program:

```
csc /r:HelloServer.exe HelloClientAsync.cs
```

Now we may run a server program with a remote server object in **SingleCall** mode in one command window and this program in another. At the client site, we see

```
>HelloClientAsync
Your name, please: David Zhang
HelloServer: Activated.
HelloServer: Method Greeting called with David Zhang.
Local: Hello, David Zhang
Remote: Hello, David Zhang

>
```

You may have noticed that the server object **HelloServer** was also activated at the client site. That was done per request of the client program to give a local greeting. On the other hand, the server object was activated only once:

```
>HelloServer
HelloServer: Activated.
Press [Enter] to quit ...
HelloServer: Activated.
HelloServer: Method Greeting called with David Zhang.
```

8.5 Deployment of a Service Without Its Implementation

So far, our services of the remote objects have been deployed with their implementation, such as **HelloServer.exe** or **HelloServer.dll** for the **HelloServer** class. Therefore, the client has the ability to use the server object at its own site. At the end of the last section, we saw such an example. That might not be desirable for the following reasons.

- The server object has been designed for the server environment, not the client environment. It may also require resources that are only available on the server. Therefore, a server object outside the server site may not behave properly. To make things worse, it may cause damage on other sites.
- The executable file or library file with implementation of a server object can be large. On the other hand, the definition of the object is adequate for its clients to use it remotely; they do not need the implementation.
- It is a good practice to limit the interaction between software modules to those that are unlikely to change, that is, to limit them by *what* they are but not by *how* they are implemented.

In this section, two approaches are developed to address these issues. Both of them require that our server and client programs be redesigned.

8.5.1 Using Base Class

In order not to deploy the implementation of the remote server object, we may first create an abstract base class for the remote service. This base contains the definition of the server object but not its implementation. The actual server object is derived from the base class and it implements the remote service by overriding the designated methods. The base class, not the server object itself, is then deployed.

Here is the C# program that defines the base class **HelloBase** for our "Hello" remote service. Its file name is **HelloBase.cs**.

```
//HelloBase.cs.
using System;
using System.Runtime.Remoting;
using System.Runtime.Remoting.Channels.Tcp;

public abstract class HelloBase : MarshalByRefObject {
    public abstract String Greeting(String name);
}
```

In this program both class **HelloBase** and method **Greeting** are abstract. The base class in this case is derived from **MarshalByRefObject**.

The following program in C# defines the actual server object **HelloServer** that is derived from class **HelloBase** and implements the method **Greeting**.

```
// HelloServerB.cs
using System;
using System.Runtime.Remoting;
using System.Runtime.Remoting.Channels.Tcp;

public class HelloServer : HelloBase {
    public static int Main() {
```

```
        TCPChannel c = new TcpChannel(8765);
        ChannelServices.RegisterChannel(c);
        RemotingServices.RegisterWellKnownType(
            "HelloServer",
            "HelloServer",
            "SayHello",
            WellKnownObjectMode.Singleton
    );
        Console.WriteLine("Press [Enter] to quit ...");
        Console.ReadLine();
        return 0;
    }
    public HelloServer() {
        Console.WriteLine("HelloServer: Activated.");
    }
    public override String Greeting(String name) {
        Console.WriteLine(
            "HelloServer: Method Greeting called ⇓
              with {0}.",
            name
        );
        return String.Concat(
            "Hello, ",
            name
        );
    }
}
```

The server class **HelloServer** is derived from the base class **HelloBase** and the method **Greeting** is implemented.

The following commands compile the base class and the server class, respectively.

```
csc /out:HelloBase.dll /target:library HelloBase.cs
csc /r: HelloBase.dll HelloServerB.cs
```

The library **HelloBase.dll** may be deployed to the clients. In this case the client program **HelloClient.cs** is as follows:

```
// HelloClientB.cs
using System;
using System.Runtime.Remoting;
using System.Runtime.Remoting.Channels.Tcp;

public class HelloClient : HelloBase {
    private static HelloBase myHello;
    public static int Main() {
        Console.Write("Your name, please: ");
        String name = Console.ReadLine();
        HelloClient obj = new HelloClient();
        Console.WriteLine(obj.Greeting(name));
```

```
        return 0;
    }
    public HelloClient() {
        ChannelServices.RegisterChannel(
            new TcpChannel()
        );
        myHello = (HelloBase)Activator.GetObject(
            typeof(HelloBase),
    "tcp://localhost:8765/SayHello"
        );
    }
    public override String Greeting(String name) {
        return myHello.Greeting(name);
    }
}
```

In this program, the client object **HelloClient** is also derived from the base class **HelloBase**. The proxy obtained by invoking **Activator.GetObject** is of type **HelloBase** as well. However, it is the polymorphism that allows the overridden method **Greeting** of the actual server class **HelloServer** to be called.

The following command compiles the program:

```
csc /r:HelloBase.dll HelloClient.cs
```

This approach may also apply to ASP.NET, and **HelloClient.aspx** may be written like this:

```
<%@ Page Language="C#" Debug="true" %>
<%@ Import Namespace="System.Runtime.Remoting" %>
<html>
<head>
<script language="C#" runat="server">
String Reply;
public void name_change(Object Source, EventArgs E) {
    HelloBase MyHello = (HelloBase)Activator.GetObject(
        typeof(HelloBase),
        "tcp://localhost:8765/SayHello"
    );
    Reply = MyHello.Greeting(Name.Value);
}
</script>
</head>
<body>
<h3>HelloClient</h3>
<form runat="server">
    <input id="Name" type="text" value="" runat="server" ⇓
OnServerChange = "name_change">
</form>
<p><h3><%=Reply%></h3>
```

The proxy to the base class is created when **Activator.GetObject** is called by the page itself, while the initialization of the TCP channel is performed in **global.asax**:

```
<%@ Import Namespace="System.Runtime.Remoting" %>
<script language="VB" runat="server">
Dim Reply As String
Sub Application_OnStart()
    ChannelServices.RegisterChannel(
        new Channels.Tcp.TcpChannel())
End Sub
</script>
```

8.5.2 Using an Interface

Another approach is to define the Web Service as an interface first. Then the actual server object implements the interface. The interface is deployed to the client site to supply the definition, not the implementation, of the service.

The following C# program implements the interface **IHello**. Its file name is **IHello.cs**. In Appendix A, we implement this interface in Visual Basic.

```
// IHello.cs
using System;
public interface IHello {
    String Greeting(String name);
}
```

A C# program, **HelloServiceI.cs**, defines the actual server class. You can find a Visual Basic version of the server class in Appendix B.

```
// HelloServerI.cs
using System;
using System.Runtime.Remoting;
using System.Runtime.Remoting.Channels.TCP;
public class HelloServer : MarshalByRefObject, IHello {
    public static int Main() {
        TCPChannel c = new TCPChannel(8765);
        ChannelServices.RegisterChannel(c);
        RemotingServices.RegisterWellKnownType(
            "HelloServer",
            "HelloServer",
            "SayHello",
            WellKnownObjectMode.Singleton
        );
        Console.WriteLine("Press [Enter] to quit ...");
        Console.ReadLine();
        return 0;
    }
    public HelloServer() {
```

```
        Console.WriteLine("HelloServer: Activated.");
    }
    String IHello.Greeting(String name) {
        Console.WriteLine(
            "HelloServer: Method Greeting called ⇓
                with {0}.",
            name
        );
        return String.Concat(
            "Hello, ",
            name
        );
    }
}
```

The server class **HelloServer** is derived from **MarshalByRefObject**, and it also implements interface **IHello**.

The following commands compile the interface and the server class, respectively:

```
csc /out:IHello.dll /target:library IHello.cs
csc /r: IHello.dll HelloServerI.cs
```

The library **IHello.dll** may be deployed to the clients. The client program **HelloClientI.cs** is as follows:

```
// HelloClientI.cs
using System;
using System.Runtime.Remoting;
using System.Runtime.Remoting.Channels.Tcp;
public class HelloClient : IHello {
    private static IHello myHello;
    public static int Main() {
        Console.Write("Your name, please: ");
        String name = Console.ReadLine();
        IHello obj = (IHello)(new HelloClient());
        Console.WriteLine(obj.Greeting(name));
        return 0;
    }
    public HelloClient() {
        ChannelServices.RegisterChannel(
            new TcpChannel()
        );
        myHello = (IHello)Activator.GetObject(
            typeof(IHello),
            "tcp://localhost:8765/SayHello"
        );
    }
    String IHello.Greeting(String name) {
        return myHello.Greeting(name);
    }
}
```

In this program, the client object **HelloClient** also implements the **Ibase** interface. The proxy obtained by invoking **Activator.GetObject** is of type **IHello** as well. However, it is the polymorphism that allows the overridden method **Greeting** of the actual server class **HelloServer** to be called.

The following command compiles the program:

```
csc /r:IHello.dll HelloClientI.cs
```

This approach may also apply to an ASP.NET page as client. You may try it yourself if you are interested.

Summary

In this chapter, we discussed how to build client/server applications based on the Object Remoting facility of .NET Framework. While the server object lives in one site in the network, a client at the remote sites may get a proxy that serves as a front end whereby the methods of the server object may be invoked.

Compared to the Web Services discussed in Chapter 6, Object Remoting requires more programming effort. However, it provides programmers with more flexibility.

SOAP Client and XML

*I*n *Chapters 6 and 7, we introduced Web Services and XML, as well as how these new technologies can help us program Web applications more effectively. Under the .NET programming environment, Web Services can be easily created using Visual Studio.NET and most of the supporting code is generated automatically. Therefore, developers do not need to have any knowledge of the underlying XML syntax and protocols, such as SOAP and WSDL, which are the foundation of these Web Services.*

However, for those of you who want more flexibility from customized Web applications, it is beneficial to know the details of SOAP so that you can unleash its power.

In this chapter, we start off by describing the basic concept of SOAP. Then we look at the SOAP Message Exchange Model and its relationship to XML. Next, we demonstrate the benefits of SOAP technology by comparing it to existing ones such as DCOM, CORBA, and RMI over IIOP. Finally, we show you how to create a couple of SOAP-based client applications using the .NET platform.

We defer the detailed discussion of WSDL to Chapter 10, where we also discuss how heterogeneous Web platforms interact with each other using SOAP, XML, and Web Services.

9.1 SOAP Concepts

When using existing remote object protocols such as Distributed Component Object Model (DCOM), CORBA, and Remote Method Invocation (RMI) over Internet Inter-Orb Protocol (IIOP), we not only have to know the interface descriptions of the remote services, we also need to know the specific semantics that describe them, such as Java and IDL. Furthermore, some of the protocols have platform-related concerns for interoperability. As more and more large-scale, transaction-based business applications are converted and deployed to the Web environment, it is apparent that we need a more open intra-application communication protocol that is easier to adopt.

As we discuss in Appendix A, programming techniques that have contributed to the Internet and Web-based software boom are evolving from static HTML pages to dynamically generated Web pages powered by CGI and, more recently, ASP. HTTP has been the foundation of all these technical innovations; it provides a common platform for diverse Web applications to communicate with each other.

When we look at the common technologies that most Web developers are used to, HTTP and XML stand out from the crowd. HTTP is pervasive and well supported by the Web developer community, while XML provides a good basis on which heterogeneous systems can communicate with each other and create common representation of the same data elements.

Microsoft, IBM, Ariba, and a few other organizations led the search for the next-generation intra-application communication protocol. The result is SOAP, which was essentially inspired by HTTP and XML.

All examples and concepts that we go over in this chapter are based on the latest version of the SOAP specification, which is Version 1.1 at the time of this writing. This version of the SOAP specification is published on the Web at *www.w3.org/TR/SOAP/*. .NET Framework is SOAP 1.1 compliant. In April 2001, a group of corporations, including Microsoft, IBM, and Ariba, submitted Version 1.1 of the SOAP specification to the W3C as a proposed standard.

9.1.1 What Is SOAP?

In short, SOAP is a simple yet extensible communication protocol for a distributed and heterogeneous environment, such as the Internet.

The definition of SOAP consists of three major components:

- The SOAP envelope (Section 9.1.3) construct defines an overall framework for expressing message content, the recipients, and whether content and recipients are optional or mandatory.

- The SOAP encoding rules (Section 9.1.4) define a serialization mechanism that can be used to exchange instances of application-defined data types.
- The SOAP RPC representation (Section 9.1.6) defines a convention that can be used to represent Remote Procedure Calls and responses.

The extra sophistication of SOAP lies in its ability to deliver information in a structured way that is highly extensible. We go over these benefits of SOAP in later sections. First, let us take a look at a sample SOAP message embedded in an HTTP request:[1]

```
POST /CruiseSchedule HTTP/1.1
Host: www.travelagencygroup.com
Content-Type: text/xml;
charset="utf-8"
Content-Length: nnnn
SOAPAction: "http://localhost/CruiseSchedule"

<SOAP-ENV:Envelope
    xmlns:SOAP-ENV=http://schemas.xmlsoap.org/soap/envelope/
    SOAP-ENV:encodingStyle=⇓
    "http://schemas.xmlsoap.org/soap/encoding/">
    <SOAP-ENV:Body>
        <m:GetLatestCruiseSchedule⇓
          xmlns:m="http://localhost/CruiseSchedule">
            <company_name>Caribbean's Best</company_name>
            <start_date>07/01/2002</start_date>
            <end_date>09/30/2002</end_date>
        </m:GetLatestCruiseSchedule>
    </SOAP-ENV:Body>
</SOAP-ENV:Envelope>
```

For the most part, the message in this code is a regular HTTP request, which performs an HTTP POST action at a URL on our imaginary company's Web site, *www.travelagencygroup.com/CruiseSchedule*. You probably noticed that the additional HTTP header in this request is called "SOAPAction," which indicates the intent of the SOAP request.

The HTTP message body is what we are more interested in because that is where the body of our SOAP message is. By scanning the message body and the "SOAPAction" header, you have probably figured out that this SOAP request is for querying the latest cruise schedules. It takes three parameters: the name of the cruise company, the start date, and the end date for searching cruise departure dates.

---

[1] This is a sample SOAP message in an HTTP request. In an actual request, the Content-Length field would be the total number of bytes in the HTTP message body.

9.1.2 The SOAP Message Exchange Model and XML

As we can see from the code, this SOAP message body is basically an XML document. By definition, all SOAP messages should be encoded using XML. Besides the XML encoding, there are a few factors essential to deciding how we should use SOAP for messaging:

- Similar to HTTP, SOAP messages are usually used in request-response scenarios, even though each individual SOAP message represents a single, one-way transmission of information from the source to the destination.
- SOAP messages are designed to allow message relaying, which means there could be intermediate processing points in the transmission path. When a SOAP message is received, a SOAP-enabled application should be able to "peel off" the layer that is intended for this application and pass on the rest of the message, if applicable.
- Since SOAP is based on a predefined XML Schema, SOAP messages must not contain a Document Type Definition (DTD).
- SOAP messages must not contain processing instructions. To maintain interoperability, the SOAP Message Exchange Model avoids defining specific implementations.

Namespaces are relatively newer concepts of XML. Like C# namespaces, XML namespaces are created to ensure uniqueness among XML elements. By default, there are two namespaces defined in a SOAP message, the SOAP envelope and the SOAP encoding, and their namespace IDs are *schemas.xmlsoap.org/soap/envelope/* and *schemas.xmlsoap.org/soap/encoding/*, respectively. For example, the code previously listed contains an explicitly defined namespace for the SOAP envelope:

```
<SOAP-ENV:Envelope
    xmlns:SOAP-ENV= ⇓
    "http://schemas.xmlsoap.org/soap/envelope/"
…
</SOAP-ENV:Envelope>
```

In the following discussion, the namespace prefix "**xsi**" is associated with the URI *www.w3.org/1999/XMLSchema-instance*, according to the "1999" version of the XML Schemas specification. Similarly, the namespace prefix "**xsd**" is associated with the URI *www.w3.org/1999/XMLSchema*. In addition, we assume that the XML element defined with no namespace prefix refers to the target namespace of the underlying document.

9.1.3 The SOAP Envelope

Every well-defined SOAP message has a SOAP envelope, which contains an optional SOAP header and a SOAP body. We have seen the mandatory components of a SOAP message in Section 9.1.1. The following is the same SOAP message as the one in the earlier code but with an optional header field:

```
<SOAP-ENV:Envelope
    xmlns:SOAP-ENV= ⇓
        "http://schemas.xmlsoap.org/soap/envelope/"
    SOAP-ENV:encodingStyle= ⇓
        "http://schemas.xmlsoap.org/soap/encoding/">
    <SOAP-ENV:Header>
        <a:Authentication ⇓
            xmlns:a=http://localhost/CruiseSchedule ⇓
            SOAP-ENV:mustUnderstand="1">
            <username>MyTravelAgency</username>
            <password>password1</password>
        </a:Authentication>
    </SOAP-ENV:Header>
    <SOAP-ENV:Body>
        <m:GetLatestCruiseSchedule ⇓
            xmlns:m="http://localhost/CruiseSchedule">
            <company_name>Caribbean's Best</company_name>
            <start_date>07/01/2002</start_date>
            <end_date>09/30/2002</end_date>
        </m:GetLatestCruiseSchedule>
    </SOAP-ENV:Body>
</SOAP-ENV:Envelope>
```

SOAP headers are designed to carry additional information that is not part of the data transmitted. For example, this code listing has a SOAP header that contains the authentication information such as user name and password for the message. We know that this message is designed to query a specific Web server about future cruise schedules and the authentication information would only be useful for the parties who demand it. By using the SOAP header, we have easily extended the message format without a prior agreement between the SOAP message senders and recipients.

The SOAP header has an element ID of "**Authentication**," a pair of user name and password values, and a "**mustUnderstand**" attribute value of 1. The SOAP "**mustUnderstand**" global attribute indicates whether this header XML element is mandatory for the recipient to process according to its semantics. If this value is set to 1, as in this example, the message recipient is required to perform authentication before processing of the message body. No cruise scheduling information will be returned if authentication fails. Thus, the optional header element becomes a mandatory one, and it is equivalent to a regular element in the SOAP body.

You probably spotted another global attribute called "**encodingStyle**" in our sample SOAP message. This attribute is used to indicate how the SOAP message content within its scope would be serialized if necessary. In our case, it would be the whole envelope, and the rules are defined by the URI at *schemas.xmlsoap.org/soap/encoding/*.

9.1.4 SOAP Encoding

SOAP encoding is a generalization of basic type systems that you would find in a programming language, such as C#. The purpose of establishing a SOAP encoding mechanism is to provide a narrow set of rules for transmitting structured data in XML format. There are two categories of data types supported by SOAP encoding:

- Simple types, which we commonly refer to as scalar types. Examples include int, float, and string.
- Composite or compound types, which are aggregates of simple types and/or other defined compound types. A role name, ordinal, or both distinguishes each XML element within a SOAP compound type. Major compound types defined in SOAP are Struct and Array.

Since most data types defined in SOAP are very similar to those in the XML Schema Specification for datatypes, we will not go over every one of these data types; you can refer to the XML Schema Specification for details. However, we do want to highlight some of the unique characteristics of SOAP encoding and show you some examples of these data types.

One thing that we would like to remind you is that the SOAP encoding currently supported by .NET Framework is based on *www.w3.org/2001/ XMLSchema* instead of *www.w3.org/1999/XMLSchema*, which is an earlier version of the XML Schema and the basis for the SOAP 1.1 specification. Even though little has changed as far as basic SOAP concepts are concerned, you need to be aware of the differences in implementation under certain circumstances. For example, you probably need to pay attention to the schema version when validating the XML Schema with the latest third-party tools, such as the Schema Quality Checker developed by IBM.

9.1.4.1 SIMPLE TYPES

The following is an XML Schema example and its corresponding data instance:

```
<element name="cruise_id" type="int"/>
<element name="company_name" type="SOAP-ENC:string"/>
<element name="company_name2" type="SOAP-ENC:string"/>
<element name="cruise_start_date" type="date"/>
<element name="cabin_selection">
    <simpleType base="xsd:string">
        <enumeration value="Upper Deck"/>
        <enumeration value="Lower Deck"/>
        <enumeration value="Main Cabin"/>
```

```
    </simpleType>
</element>
<element name="discount" type="float"/>
<element name="thumbnail" type="SOAP-ENC:base64"/>


<cruise_id>123</cruise_id>
<company_name id="coNameStr">Caribbean's Best ⇓
</company_name>
<company_name2 href="#coNameStr"></company_name2>
<cruise_start_date>2002-01-21</cruise_start_date>
<cabin_selection>Main Cabin</cabin_selection>
<discount>0.2</discount>
<thumbnail xsi:type="SOAP-ENC:base64">
F513fsad49IfD6s7SDJ+e=
</thumbnail>
```

This example captures the data for a cruise package using only simple data types from SOAP encoding. There are a few things that are worth noting in this sample:

- Two types of definition are used for strings: **SOAP-ENC:string** and **xsd:string**. **SOAP-ENC:string** represents strings that are regular XML strings (**xsd:string**) and also allow **id** and **href** attributes. In our example, **company_name** and **company_name2** refer to the same string instance with an id of **coNameStr**, also known as multireference.
- **Cabin_selection** is an enumeration type that refers to a set of unique values, including **Upper Deck**, **Lower Deck**, and **Main Cabin**. The value in the instance data can be one and only one of them.
- **Thumbnail**, which represents an image of the cabin, is an array of bytes that are encoded using the base64 encoding scheme in SOAP. One major difference between the base64 schema from SOAP and regular XML is that SOAP does not have line-length limit on its byte arrays.

9.1.4.2 COMPOUND TYPES

Here is an example that is based on the compound types defined in SOAP, including both XML Schema and its corresponding data instances:

```
<element name="Reservation">
<complexType>
    <element name="last_name" type="xsd:string"/>
    <element name="first_name" type="xsd:string"/>
    <element name="cruise_id" type="int"/>
    <element name="cruise_start_date" type="date"/>
    <element name="contact_info" type="xsd:string"/>
```

```
</complexType>
</element>

<element name="Reservations">
<complexType base="SOAP-ENC:Array"/>
<element name="Rsv" type="Reservation"⇩
    maxOccurs="unbounded"/>
</complexType>
</element>


<cur_list:Reservations
SOAP-ENC:arrayType="cur_list:Reservation[2]">
<e1:Reservation>
    <last_name>Doe</last_name>
    <first_name>John</first_name>
    <cruise_id id="popularID">123</cruise_id>
    <cruise_start_date>2002-01-21</cruise_start_date>
    <contact_info>617-555-2345</contact_info>
</e1:Reservation>
<e2:Reservation>
    <last_name>Doe</last_name>
    <first_name>Jane</first_name>
    <cruise_id href="#popularID"></cruise_id>
    <cruise_start_date>2002-01-21</cruise_start_date>
    <contact_info>617-555-4567</contact_info>
</e2:Reservation>
</cur_list:Reservations>
```

There are two major compound types in SOAP encoding: Struct and Array. Struct is a compound type that distinguishes its member elements by their names, while Array uses an ordered sequence. In our example

- **Reservation** is of the Struct type and **Reservations** is an Array of **Reservation**. Compound types can be nested.
- **Cruise_id** is multireferenced by both Structs. In fact, it is also possible to multireference compound types.
- SOAP also supports Arrays that are multidimensional and/or sparse.

9.1.5 SOAP Fault

Within a SOAP message, an optional SOAP fault element could be included to indicate an erroneous condition or certain status information for both the SOAP client and server. SOAP specification dictates that the SOAP fault element appear as a SOAP body entry and not appear more than once within the body element.

The SOAP fault element consists of four subelements:

- *Faultcode*, which is intended for use by software to provide an algorithmic mechanism for identifying the fault. The default values for faultcode are XML qualified names that indicate the origins of the faults, such as **VersionMismatch**, **mustUnderstand**, **Client**, and **Server**.
- *Faultstring*, which is intended to provide a human-readable explanation of the fault, such as a stack trace of a typical .NET exception.
- *Faultactor*, which is intended to provide information about who caused the fault when the message is relayed through intermediate endpoints. It is only optional when there are only two endpoints (single SOAP client and single SOAP server) involved.
- *Detail*, which is intended for carrying application specific error information related to the body element. The absence of the detail element in the fault element indicates that the fault is not related to processing of the body element.

Here is a sample SOAP response message that includes a SOAP fault element. This fault is caused by a data formatting error for **DateTime** type in the SOAP request. The corresponding SOAP response message includes a detailed error description in the faultstring subelement. The faultcode subelement indicates that the SOAP client did not provide appropriate information in order to succeed.

```
<?xml version="1.0" encoding="utf-8"?>
<soap:Envelope ⇓
    xmlns:soap="http://schemas.xmlsoap.org/soap/envelope/">
  <soap:Body>
    <soap:Fault>
      <faultcode>soap:Client</faultcode>
      <faultstring>
          System.Web.Services.Protocols.SoapException: ⇓
          Server was unable to read request. ---&gt; ⇓
          System.Exception: There is an error in XML ⇓
          document (1, 209). ---&gt; ⇓
          System.FormatException: String was not ⇓
              recognized as a valid DateTime.
          at System.DateTime.ParseExact(String s, ⇓
              String[] formats, IFormatProvider provider, ⇓
              DateTimeStyles style)
          at System.Xml.XmlConvert.ToDateTime(String s, ⇓
              String[] formats)
          at System.Xml.Serialization.XmlCustomFormatter. ⇓
              ToDateTime(String value, String[] formats)
          at System.Xml.Serialization.XmlCustomFormatter. ⇓
              ToDateTime(String value)
          at System.Xml.Serialization. ⇓
              XmlSerializationReader.ToDateTime(String value)
```

```
          at n2499d7d93ffa468fbd8861780677ee41. ⇓
             XmlSerializationReader1. ⇓
             Read11_getNewPackages()
          at System.Xml.Serialization.XmlSerializer. ⇓
             Deserialize(XmlReader xmlReader)
          at System.Web.Services.Protocols. ⇓
             SoapServerProtocol.ReadParameters()
          at System.Web.Services.Protocols. ⇓
             SoapServerProtocol.ReadParameters()
          at System.Web.Services.Protocols. ⇓
             WebServiceHandler.Invoke()
          at System.Web.Services.Protocols. ⇓
             WebServiceHandler.CoreProcessRequest()
       </faultstring>
       <detail />
     </soap:Fault>
   </soap:Body>
</soap:Envelope>
```

9.1.6 Using SOAP in HTTP and for RPC

So far we have gone over the structure of SOAP messages and how data
could be encoded. In this section, we briefly describe how to bind the
generic SOAP message format to more concrete network protocols, such as
HTTP and RPC.

9.1.6.1 USING SOAP IN HTTP

SOAP fits well with HTTP because both use a request/response messaging
model and they follow similar semantics. We have seen examples of SOAP
requests embedded in HTTP. Here is a sample response to the SOAP request:[2]

```
HTTP/1.1 200 OK
Content-Type: text/xml;
charset="utf-8"
Content-Length: nnnn

<SOAP-ENV:Envelope
    xmlns:SOAP-ENV= ⇓
        "http://schemas.xmlsoap.org/soap/envelope/"
    SOAP-ENV:encodingStyle= ⇓
        "http://schemas.xmlsoap.org/soap/encoding/"/>
    <SOAP-ENV:Body>
      <m:LatestCruiseSchedule ⇓
          xmlns:m="http://localhost/CruiseSchedule">
          <cruise_id>123</cruise_id>
```

---

[2] This is a sample SOAP message in an HTTP request. In an actual request, the
Content-Length field would be the total number of bytes in the HTTP message body.

```
                    <company_name id="coNameStr">Caribbean's Best ⇓
                    </company_name>
                    <company_name2 href="#coNameStr"> ⇓
                    </company_name2>
                    <cruise_start_date>2002-01-21 </cruise_start_date>
                    <cabin_selection>Main Cabin</cabin_selection>
                    <discount>0.2</discount>
                    <thumbnail xsi:type="SOAP-ENC:base64">
                        F513fsad49IfD6s7SDJ+e=
                    </thumbnail>
                </m:LatestCruiseSchedule>
            </SOAP-ENV:Body>
        </SOAP-ENV:Envelope>
```

Figure 9-1 illustrates a typical software architecture for handling SOAP requests and responses carried by HTTP. When HTTP is used to transport a SOAP message, the content type must be **text/xml**.

9.1.6.2 USING SOAP FOR RPC

SOAP is not designed just for HTTP. In fact, one of its design goals is to encapsulate and exchange RPCs, based on the flexibility of XML. To call an RPC method, the local process needs to know the URI of the remote object that contains this method, the name and parameters of the method, as well as optional information such as authentication. SOAP supports the encoding of payloads for a method call and its corresponding response in SOAP body elements. For example, invocation of a method is modeled as a SOAP Struct, and parameters of the method are modeled as this Struct's members, with matching names and data types. The response of a method call also fits into a Struct, and the return value is the first member of the Struct.

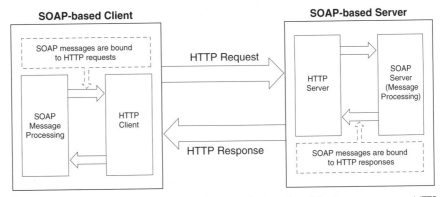

Figure 9-1   *A typical software architecture for handling SOAP messages over HTTP.*

.NET Framework uses SOAP extensively to support its distributed object system, including .NET Object Remoting and ASP.NET Web Services. It supports not only the standard encoding based on *schemas.xmlsoap.org/soap/encoding/*, but also custom encoding, such as XML fidelity.

As discussed in Chapter 8, .NET Object Remoting allows developers to access remote objects or services at a full range of levels, such as delegates, passing objects by value or reference, classes and interfaces, methods and fields, marshalling by value, and marshalling by reference between distributed applications. .NET enables developers to use pluggable transport channels, such as HTTP or TCP channels, and the corresponding SOAP binding to transport XML messages between distributed applications.

The examples in Section 9.3.2 and Section 10.2.1 illustrate in detail how SOAP supports RPC under .NET Framework.

9.2 The Benefits of SOAP

When more and more software is designed with object-oriented methodologies, the distributed object model further extends the object-oriented paradigm. Distributed across a heterogeneous network, each of these distributed object components can interoperate and maximize the overall system performance by using its local resources.

However, achieving interoperability is no easy task as different software vendors have a hard time agreeing on a set of rules for diverse software platforms. Even when APIs are clearly defined, developers still have to spend a tremendous amount of time learning the "dialects" of these software platforms before they can even attempt to think about interoperability.

A number of standards were proposed to solve this problem before SOAP. Three of the most popular distributed object standards are Microsoft's DCOM, OMG's CORBA, and JavaSoft's Java Remote Method Invocation (Java/RMI). Each of these paradigms has sizeable followings to date. So you may well ask why we need another one.

Before we can answer this question, let's briefly go over the differences between SOAP and each of these three standards from a developer's perspective. This will help us better understand the potential benefits that SOAP brings to the table, as well as its limitations. In a sense, when we compare SOAP with these existing standards, we are really comparing the SOAP-based Web Services computing model with its counterparts.

9.2.1 SOAP versus DCOM

You are probably familiar with DCOM, which is also referred to as COM+. DCOM supports remoting objects by running on a protocol called the Object

Remote Procedure Call (ORPC), which interacts with COM's run-time services and facilitates communications between distributed COM objects.

A DCOM server is a body of code that is capable of serving up remote objects at run time. Each DCOM server object can support multiple interfaces that represent different behaviors of the object. A DCOM client calls into the exposed methods of a DCOM server object by acquiring a pointer to its interfaces. The client object then starts calling the server object's exposed methods through the acquired interface pointer as if the server object resided in the client's address space. The actual steps for DCOM RPC are as follows:

1. The client makes a call to the client stub to invoke a remote function.

2. The stub packs the call parameters into a request message and invokes a wire protocol to ship the message to the server.

3. At the server side, the wire protocol delivers the message to the server stub, which then unpacks the request message and calls the actual function on the object.

Since COM is a binary standard, it theoretically allows DCOM server components to be written in diverse programming languages like C++, Java, Visual Basic, and even COBOL. As long as a platform supports COM services, DCOM can be used on that platform. In reality, however, DCOM is primarily used on the Windows platform.

Compared to ORPC, the current base protocol of DCOM, SOAP has a couple of key advantages:

- SOAP builds on the platform-independent, text-based XML, and it makes it especially easy for developers from non-Windows platforms to adopt and communicate with Windows applications. Thus, it has a greater reach than DCOM.

- Firewalls can easily recognize SOAP packets based on their content type (text/xml-SOAP), and can filter based on the interface and method name exposed via HTTP headers. Therefore, SOAP messages can easily go across firewalls, while DCOM cannot, because it relies on dynamically assigned ports for remote method invocations.

9.2.2 SOAP versus CORBA

CORBA relies on IIOP for remoting objects. Everything in the CORBA architecture depends on an Object Request Broker (ORB). The ORB acts as a central object bus over which each CORBA object interacts transparently with other CORBA objects located either locally or remotely.

Similar to DCOM, each CORBA server object has an interface and exposes a set of methods. To request a service, a CORBA client acquires an object reference to a CORBA server object. The client can then make method calls on the object reference as if the CORBA server object resided in the client's address space. The ORB's responsibilities include

- Finding a CORBA object's implementation
- Preparing the CORBA object to receive requests
- Communicating requests to the object implementation
- Carrying the reply (if any) back to the client

IIOP and SOAP are quite close functionally. Both define simple data types and derive complex data types from the simple ones, as shown in the previous section.

Since CORBA is just a specification, it can be used on diverse operating system platforms, including mainframes, UNIX servers, Windows machines, and even handheld devices, as long as there is an ORB implementation for that platform. Major ORB vendors include Inprise and Iona, and the latter has CORBA ORB implementations through its product, called Orbix.

Compared to CORBA over IIOP, SOAP offers a few important benefits:

- CORBA has issues with firewalls or proxy servers similar to those DCOM has, while SOAP is more firewall friendly.
- Many of the high-level services in CORBA, such as security and transactions, are not commonly interoperable. This means that ORB products are somewhat vendor specific and can have a steeper learning curve.
- SOAP offers a low-cost value proposition compared to CORBA. For example, when using HTTP, SOAP servers can be Web servers. Thus, most organizations have extensive Web development experience to support SOAP. On the other hand, CORBA developers are much harder to find and ORB products are usually quite expensive.

9.2.3 SOAP versus RMI-IIOP

Java/RMI, which is based on Java Remote Method Protocol (JRMP), is a mechanism that supports distributed computing in Java. Each Java/RMI server object defines a set of interfaces that can be accessed by a Java client running outside of the server's JVM. These interfaces expose a set of methods that are indicative of the services offered by the server object. For a client to locate a server object for the first time, RMI depends on a naming mechanism called an RMI Registry, which runs on the server machine and holds information about available server objects.

A Java/RMI client acquires an object reference to a Java/RMI server object by performing a lookup for a server object reference. If the lookup is successful, the client invokes methods on the underlying object as if the Java/RMI server object resided in the client's address space. Java/RMI server objects are named using URLs. For a client to acquire a server object reference, it would specify the URL of the server object, just like when you access a Web page over the Internet.

Java/RMI relies heavily on Java Object Serialization, which allows objects to be marshalled (or transmitted) as a stream. Since Java Object Serialization is specific to Java, both the Java/RMI server object and the client object have to be written in Java.

As Java gains popularity among developers, more and more of them are demanding that Java/RMI be expanded to interoperate with legacy applications, including C, C++, and Microsoft Windows applications. Then comes the silver bullet: RMI over IIOP (RMI-IIOP). RMI-IIOP combines the usability of Java/RMI with the interoperability of IIOP into a win-win combination. RMI-IIOP is designed to enable interoperability between Java RMI programs and programs written in languages other than Java.

RMI over IIOP is fundamentally based on IIOP, and it shares some of the same weaknesses of CORBA/IIOP, such as difficulty in crossing firewalls. More importantly, since RMI-IIOP is geared toward experienced Java developers for interoperating with existing non-Java applications, its adoptability for Windows developers who are not familiar with the Java software platform is quite limited.

9.2.4 Limitations of SOAP

SOAP is an evolving communication protocol that is yet to become a standard, and the computing model for Web Services is also evolving. Therefore, it is understandable that SOAP has a few limitations:

- Compared to messages for existing protocols, SOAP messages tend to be larger during wire transfer and can be more resource intensive to parse and generate.
- SOAP does not address higher-level issues such as object activation or lifetime management, including distributed garbage collection and activation. Protocols such as DCOM do offer such additional functionality.
- The current SOAP specification relies on the XML Schema specification to describe interfaces and user-defined types. Unfortunately, XML Schema is also a work in progress. Thus, the SOAP specification appears to be a moving target at times.

As the computing model for Web Services and the SOAP specification mature, especially when more and more vendors fully embrace SOAP as their core distributed communication protocol, some of these limitations could be addressed.

9.2.5 Conclusions

SOAP is a product of evolution and it is a natural step forward from HTTP and XML. Both of these technologies are minimal yet flexible ones that Web developers can agree on. In summary, these are the key benefits of SOAP over other existing protocols:

- SOAP is relatively simple and quick to learn. Most of its features are based on open Internet standards that are widely accepted, such as HTTP and XML.
- SOAP messages can easily go across firewalls. Thus, it can help bring distributed computing out of the confinement of LANs and onto the Internet.
- SOAP is platform-neutral and can be a consensus builder between Microsoft Windows developers and non-Windows developers. We discuss interoperability issues between .NET and other platforms via Web Services in Chapter 10.

The problem space that SOAP is targeting is not exactly the same as that of DCOM, CORBA, or Java/RMI. Developers who adopt SOAP view the whole Internet as the deployment environment instead of the LAN only.

One of the guiding principles for SOAP is not to replace existing distributed application framework, such as DCOM or IIOP, but to augment them, thus providing a better communication platform for Web applications. In a sense, SOAP addresses the platform interoperability issue by bringing its protocol one level higher than what DCOM, CORBA, and Java RMI are using.

Since some of the features of distributed object systems, including distributed garbage collection and activation (objects-by-reference), are left out of the SOAP specification, it is up to the implementers of SOAP to provide actual support and make the whole thing work. Fortunately, .NET CLR provides even stronger support of SOAP than the current specification and offers a more complete solution, at least under the Windows environment.

9.3 Building Simple SOAP Clients Under .NET

9.3.1 Accessing Web Services Using SOAP Clients

To see how SOAP-based clients are created and how SOAP messages are manipulated, we look at a comprehensive example that models a travel agency union's Web Services. The travel agency union, *www.travelagency-group.com*, is a federation of travel agencies in which each member shares some common services. In this example, the union's Web site maintains a list of the latest vacation packages collected from all of its member agencies and allows its members to upload travel packages to share with other members.

The union Web site maintains Web Services written in C#. On the client side, instead of providing ASP.NET pages to serve its members, the union Web site distributes a Win32 client developed using VB.NET. The client communicates to the Web Services using SOAP-encoded messages bound to HTTP.

9.3.1.1 CREATING A WEB SERVICE USING VS.NET

First of all, we need to create a Web Service for the travel agency union using VS.NET. Under the VS.NET Integrated Development Environment (IDE), we select C# Web Service as the type of project and rename the project as **TAUWebService**, from the default name **WebService1**. The VS.NET Wizard should create a few files as a standard Web Services project under C#. There are two files that we need to pay attention to:

- ● ***TAUWebService.asmx***. This is the entry point of .NET Web Services, which receives service requests that are bound to HTTP. The VS.NET project wizard automatically maps our newly created Web Service to the URL of *localhost/TAUWebService/ TAUWebService.asmx*. The default content of **TAUWebService.asmx** looks like this:

```
<%@ WebService Language="c#" ⇓
Codebehind="TAUWebService.asmx.cs" ⇓
Class="TAUWebService.Service1" %>
```

- ● ***TAUWebService.asmx.cs***. This C# file is created to accommodate the business logic code behind the Web Services entry point, **TAUWebService.asmx**. Under VS.NET, this file is not visible from the Solution Explorer, but you can view it by highlighting **TAUWebService.asmx**, clicking the right mouse button, and selecting the View Code option. By default, this file is empty except for a **Hello World!** Web method that has been commented out.

In order to support our functionality, we need to create a new C# class called **TravelPackage**, which represents a vacation package internally on the server side. For simplicity, we create a separate file, **TravelPackage.cs**, in the same namespace as **TAUWebService.asmx.cs**:

```
namespace TAUWebService
{
    using System;

    /// <summary>
    ///     Summary description for TravelPackage.
    /// </summary>
    public class TravelPackage
    {
    public string id;
    public double startingPrice;
    public int numOfDays;
    public DateTime offerStarts;
```

```
public DateTime offerEnds;
public string airline;
public string destination;
public string originCity;
public string agent;

    public TravelPackage()
    {
        //
        // TODO: Add Constructor Logic here
        //
    }
}
}
```

Now that we have laid the foundation of our Web Service application, it is time to develop our business logic. The plan is to develop a few simple functionalities step-by-step:

- Establish the data structure to store and share the travel packages provided by members of the travel agency union
- Allow union members to inquire about travel packages that are loaded on the travel agency union Web site, such as the total packages available and detailed package information
- Allow union members to upload travel packages onto the union Web site

First of all, we create a data structure to store travel packages and initialize it in the constructor of **Service1**, which is the base class of our Web Service, by adding the following code to **TAUWebService.asmx.cs**:

```
//Keep all the travel packages.
private static Hashtable packages = null;

public void initPackages()
{
    if (packages==null)
    {
        packages = new Hashtable();

        //pregenerate a sample package
        TravelPackage p=new TravelPackage();
        p.id = "Sample";
        p.airline="AA";
        p.destination="Orlando, FL";
        p.numOfDays=3;
```

```
                    p.offerStarts=DateTime.Today;
                    p.offerEnds=new DateTime(2002,6,29);
                    p.originCity="Boston, MA";
                    p.startingPrice=800;
                    p.agent="Wonderful";

                    packages.Add(p.id, p);
            }
    }

    public Service1()
    {
            //CODEGEN: This call is required by the ⇓
            //ASP.NET Web Services Designer
            InitializeComponent();
            initPackages();
    }
```

The first real Web method that we create is **getPackageCount**, which retrieves the total number of travel packages loaded into our Web Service:

```
    [WebMethod]
    public int getPackageCount()
    {
      return packages.Count;
    }
```

Before moving forward with further functionality, we need to test our current code to make sure that our code has a solid foundation. You probably have noticed that we have pre-generated a travel package with an ID of Sample; this comes in handy during testing. We can set the default page as **TAUWebService.asmx** and execute our newly created Web Service, which is shown in Figure 9-2.

In Chapter 6, we introduced .NET Web Services and WSDL. When we invoke the only Web method, **getPackageCount**, the result is as shown in Figure 9-3.

We know that one sample package was prepopulated and the total count for travel packages on the union Web site is 1. Our Web Service is working now.

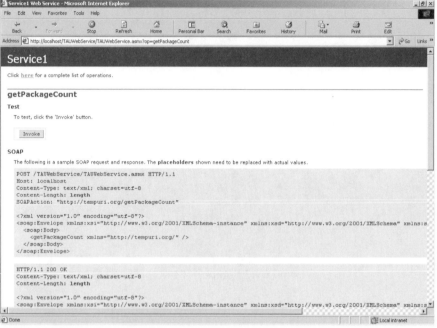

Figure 9-2 *The **TAUWebService.asmx** page executed as a Web Service.*

Figure 9-3 *The **getPackageCount** Web method returns when executed initially.*

The next step is to create more business logic for uploading and retrieving travel packages from our base Web Service. We are adding three new Web methods to **TAUWebService.asmx.cs**:

```
[WebMethod]
public TravelPackage getPackageDetail(string ⇓
                                        packageId)
{
    //Search the package by its id
    TravelPackage p ⇓
                = (TravelPackage)packages[packageId];
    return p;
}


[WebMethod]
public TravelPackage[] getNewPackages(DateTime day)
{
    IDictionaryEnumerator elements ⇓
                        = packages.GetEnumerator();
    Queue theQ = new Queue();
    elements.Reset();
    while(elements.MoveNext())
    {
        TravelPackage p ⇓
                        = (TravelPackage)elements.Value;
        if (day.CompareTo(p.offerStarts)<0)
        {
            theQ.Enqueue(p);
        }
    }
    int count = theQ.Count;
    TravelPackage[] newPacks ⇓
                        = new TravelPackage[count];
    for (int i=0;i<count;i++)
    {
        newPacks[i]=(TravelPackage)theQ.Dequeue();
    }
    return newPacks;
}


[WebMethod]
public TravelPackage uploadPackage2(TravelPackage ⇓
                                        newPackage)
{
    //put the new package into database.
    packages.Add(newPackage.id, newPackage);
    return newPackage;
}
```

The Web method **getPackageDetail** will retrieve one travel package by its ID; **getNewPackages** will search and retrieve a set of travel package offers that start on or after a user-supplied date. Figures 9-4 and 9-5 show the testing results of these two Web methods. We use January 1, 2001, as the parameter for invoking **getNewPackages**. The last Web method, **uploadPackage2**, simply uploads a travel package as an object onto the Web Service.

9.3.1.2 CREATING A VB.NET SOAP CLIENT USING VS.NET

In the previous section, we established a Web Service page **TAUWebService.asmx** on the Web server side. Now we are ready to build a simple client to see how we can utilize SOAP under .NET and how to access .NET Web Services via SOAP. We develop and test the SOAP client using VB.NET under the programming environment of VS.NET.

To create a Windows Forms application using VB.NET in VS.NET IDE, let's create a new project of type Visual Basic Project | Windows Application. We can name this project as **TAUSoapClient** and rename the main form of the application to **TAUSoapClientForm**. Our simple example includes one Windows Form only.

Figure 9-4 *Testing the Web method **getPackageDetail**.*

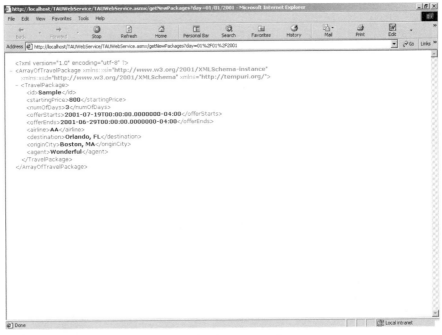

By right-clicking on **TAUSoapClientForm** in the Solution Explorer window, we can inspect the default code generated behind the scene (Windows Form Designer–generated code is omitted).

```
Public Class TAUSoapClientForm
    Inherits System.WinForms.Form

    Public Sub New()
        MyBase.New

        TAUSoapClientForm = Me

        'This call is required by the Win Form Designer.
        InitializeComponent()

        'TODO: Add any initialization after the ⇓
        'InitializeComponent() call
    End Sub

    'Form overrides dispose to clean up the component list.
    Overrides Public Sub Dispose()
        MyBase.Dispose
        components.Dispose
```

```
      End Sub

      'Windows Form Designer generated code is here
      ...
End Class
```

This form gives us a starting point for our application, but it does not look very exciting. We need to add some Windows Forms controls to implement our front-end functionalities. Figures 9-6 and 9-7 show the top half and the bottom half of our forms, with controls.

In Figure 9-6, there are three sets of controls on the form. The first set includes an ActiveX / COM object called **AxInetCtrlsObject.AxInet** and a text box that allows users to enter the URL to our back-end Web Services. The **AxInet** object, Microsoft Internet Transfer ActiveX Control, provides access to the Web using the two most common protocols: HTTP and File Transfer Protocol (FTP). When you use the Internet transfer control with HTTP, you can send HTTP requests and receive HTTP responses from the Internet or from an intranet. In our example, the Web Service URL would be *localhost/TAUWebService/TAUWebService.asmx* by default, where we have installed our Web Service.

The second set of controls in Figure 9-6 is grouped by a **GroupBox** VB.NET control. It contains a couple of **TextBox** and **Button** controls for

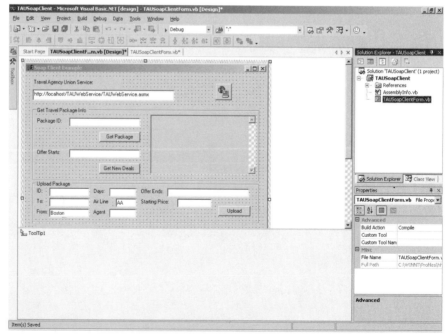

Figure 9-6   *Top half of the **TAUSoapClientForm** shown in VS.NET Designer.*

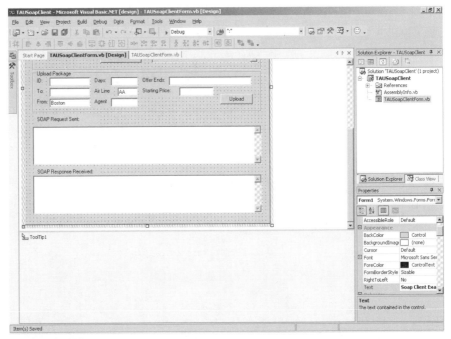

Figure 9-7   *Bottom half of the **TAUSoapClientForm** shown in VS.NET Designer.*

users to enter and execute queries against our Web Service. The query actions, such as searching travel package by ID, map exactly to the back-end business logic we created in Section 9.3.1.1. On the right-hand side, we create a scrollable **TextBox** control to display the query results.

The last set of controls in Figure 9-6 is similar to the second set and is created to support uploading a new travel package by the member agency.

The bottom half of the **TAUSoapClientForm** (Figure 9-7) contains two **TextBox** controls, showing the SOAP messages sent and received between our VB.NET client and the Web Service.

9.3.1.3 PUTTING THE CLIENT AND SERVER TOGETHER

Having laid out the user interface controls on the client side, we are ready to put the complete application together by adding code behind these controls. For example, the following code implements the action behind retrieving a travel package by its ID.

```
Private Sub BtnGetPackage_Click(ByVal sender As _ ⇓
    Object, ByVal e As System.EventArgs) _ ⇓
    Handles BtnGetPackage.Click
    clearTextBox("GetPackage")
    soapRequestXML = "<?xml version=""1.0""?> " & _ ⇓
```

```
        "<Envelope xmlns = " &_ ⇓
        """http://schemas.xmlsoap.org/soap/envelope/"" >" &_ ⇓
        "<Body>" &_ ⇓
            "<getPackageDetail " &_ ⇓
            "xmlns:xsi= ""http://www.w3.org/2001/" &_ ⇓
            "XMLSchema-instance""" &_ ⇓
            "xmlns=""http://tempuri.org/"">" &_ ⇓
            "<packageId> NONE </packageId>" &_ ⇓
            "</getPackageDetail>" &_ ⇓
        "</Body>" &_ ⇓
        "</Envelope>"

If (txtPkgId.Text = "") Then
    MsgBox("Please input a package ID!")
    Return
End If

'Compose the soap message
Dim parser As XmlDocument = New XmlDocument()
parser.LoadXml(soapRequestXML)

'Insert the package ID to the XML
Dim elemList As XmlNodeList = _ ⇓
    parser.GetElementsByTagName("packageId")
elemList(0).InnerText = txtPkgId.Text

'Display the soap message
SOAPReqSent.Text = parser.OuterXml

'Send the soap message
Inet1.Execute(txtURL.Text, "POST", _ ⇓
    parser.OuterXml, "Content-Type: text/xml" _⇓
    & ControlChars.Cr & ControlChars.Lf _ ⇓
    & "SOAPAction: http://tempuri.org/getPackageDetail")
End Sub
```

Since the server-side application is a Web Service, all the SOAP messages that we use in this example are bound to HTTP for transport. In this method, **Inet1** is the instantiated object as a Microsoft Internet Transfer Control, and we use the built-in XML support from .NET (XML.NET) to process the requests and responses. When the user enters the travel package ID and hits the Get Package button, the .NET XML parser replaces the package ID in a preformatted SOAP message with the user's input and composes a new SOAP request. Then the Internet Transfer Control packages the SOAP envelope inside an HTTP POST request and sends it to out to the Web Service. Figure 9-8 shows a successful execution of our Get Package query:

| Figure 9-8 | *Query result of the Get Package action on* **TAUSoapClientForm**. |

To peek under the hood of our SOAP-based client, we can also inspect the actual SOAP messages without the HTTP packaging. The following are the SOAP request and response that support our last query.

```
<?xml version="1.0"?>
<Envelope xmlns="http://schemas.xmlsoap.org/soap/envelope/">
   <Body>
        <getPackageDetail xmlns:xsi="http://www.w3.org/2001/ ⇓
        XMLSchema-instance" xmlns="http://tempuri.org/">
        <packageId>Sample</packageId>
        </getPackageDetail>
```

```
      </Body>
</Envelope>

<?xml version="1.0" encoding="utf-8"?>
<soap:Envelope ⇓
xmlns:soap="http://schemas.xmlsoap.org/soap/envelope/"
xmlns:xsi="http://www.w3.org/2001/XMLSchema-instance"
xmlns:xsd="http://www.w3.org/2001/XMLSchema">
  <soap:Body>
    <getPackageDetailResponse xmlns="http://tempuri.org/">
      <getPackageDetailResult>
        <id>Sample</id>
        <startingPrice>800</startingPrice>
        <numOfDays>3</numOfDays>
        <offerStarts>2001-07-19T00:00:00 ⇓
          .0000000-04:00</offerStarts>
        <offerEnds>2002-06-29T00:00:00 ⇓
          .0000000-04:00</offerEnds>
        <airline>AA</airline>
        <destination>Orlando, FL</destination>
        <originCity>Boston, MA</originCity>
        <agent>Wonderful</agent>
      </getPackageDetailResult>
    </getPackageDetailResponse>
  </soap:Body>
</soap:Envelope>
```

Notice that in the SOAP messages, .NET adopts the 2001 version of the XML schema, which is more recent than the basis for the SOAP 1.1 specification.

Using similar designs, we can implement Get New Deals and Upload functionalities. However, when we hook up the Upload action from the client with the Web Service method **uploadPackage2**, it does not seem to work and we get a SOAP fault message. The SOAP request and response look like this:

```
<?xml version="1.0"?>
<Envelope xmlns="http://schemas.xmlsoap.org/soap/envelope/">
<Body>
      <uploadPackage ⇓
          xmlns:xsi=http://www.w3.org/2001/XMLSchema ⇓
               instance
          xmlns="http://tempuri.org/">

          <id>Orlando1</id>⇓
          <destination>Orlando</destination>⇓
```

```
            <offerEnds>2001-07-31T00:00:00</offerEnds>⇓
            <startingPrice>1200</startingPrice>⇓
            <airline>AA</airline>⇓
            <agent>Wonderful</agent>⇓
            <numOfDays>12</numOfDays>⇓
            <originCity>Boston</originCity>⇓
            <offerStarts>⇓
              2001-06-22T00:00:00⇓
            </offerStarts>⇓
        </uploadPackage>
</Body>
</Envelope>


<?xml version="1.0" encoding="utf-8"?>
<soap:Envelope
xmlns:soap="http://schemas.xmlsoap.org/soap/envelope/">
  <soap:Body>
    <soap:Fault>
      <faultcode>soap:Server</faultcode>
      <faulstring>
          System.Web.Services.Protocols.SoapException: ⇓
              Server was unable to process request. ---&gt; ⇓
          System.NullReferenceException: Value null was found
              where an instance of an object was ⇓
              required. ⇓
          at TAUWebSevice.Service1.uploadPackage2⇓
              (TravelPackage newPackage) in ⇓
              d:\inetpub\wwwroot\tauwebservice\⇓
          tauwebservice.asmx.cs: line 114
      </faultstring>
      <detail />
    </soap:Fault>
  </soap:Body>
</soap:Envelope>
```

We inspect our code for potential errors, but both client and server code appear to be solid. So what is the problem? It turns out that data types depend on which protocol binding is used by the Web Service. Even though these complex data types are supported by SOAP specifications, as we have discussed earlier, SOAP messages that are transmitted via HTTP GET and POST can contain name/value pairs only. Table 9-1 lists the data types supported by .NET Web Services, along with the equivalent data types in C++ and CLR.

Table 9-1	Data Types Supported by .NET Web Services	
XML Schema	**C++**	**CLR**
boolean	bool	Boolean
byte	char, __int8	
double	double	Double
datatype	struct	
decimal		Decimal
enumeration	enum	Enum
float	float	Single
int	int, long, __int32	Int32
long	__int64	Int64
Qname		XmlQualifiedName
short	short, __int16	Int16
string	BSTR	String
timeInstant		DateTime
unsignedByte	unsigned __int8	
unsignedInt	unsigned __int32	UInt32
unsignedLong	unsigned __int64	UInt64
unsignedShort	unsigned __int16	UInt16

We use examples to discuss how to encode data and support complex, custom data types using RPC style SOAP binding in Chapter 10. In order for our example to work with SOAP and HTTP POST, we need to change our upload method in **TAUWebService.asmx** to the following with a new method name of **uploadPackage**. This new method will take a list of simple data types as parameters, instead of using a custom complex type.

```
[WebMethod]
public String uploadPackage(String id,
                String agent,
                String destination,
                String airline,
                int numOfDays,
                DateTime offerStarts,
                DateTime offerEnds,
                String originCity,
                double startingPrice)
    {
        //Check whether the ID has been used
        if (packages.ContainsKey(id))
        {
            return "The ID has been used.";
```

```
        }

        TravelPackage p=new TravelPackage();
        p.id = id;
        p.airline=airline;
        p.destination=destination;
        p.numOfDays=numOfDays;
        p.offerStarts=offerStarts;
        p.offerEnds=offerEnds;
        p.originCity=originCity;
        p.startingPrice=startingPrice;
        p.agent=agent;

        //put the new package into packages.
        packages.Add(p.id, p);
        return "Package "+id+" has been ⇓
            sucessfully loaded";
    }
```

Now we can test our code by invoking the Upload action from the SOAP client. We should be able to upload a new travel package with an ID of Orlando1 and verify the result, as shown in Figure 9-9.

9.3.2 .NET Remoting Using SOAP Clients

As we discussed in Chapter 8, .NET Object Remoting provides a mechanism for developers to create powerful distributed applications across intranets as well as the Internet. When we use HTTP channels to communicate between remote objects, the payload encoding is SOAP by default. We can use the example in Sections 8.2.1 through 8.2.2 of Chapter 8 to take an in-depth look at SOAP clients used in .NET Object Remoting.

Recall that we have created a pair of remoting components in Sections 8.2.1 and 8.2.2: **HelloServer** and **HelloClient**. In order to trace the messages sent between the client and the server, we can monitor the messaging activities on the port where the communication channel resides.

There are quite a few existing tools that can help you trace SOAP messages back and forth, and they can be tremendously helpful when you are debugging SOAP-based applications. One of them is MSSoapT, which is a TCP tracing tool that can be downloaded with Microsoft SOAP Toolkit Version 2.0. This latest version of SOAP Toolkit is a fully supported Microsoft product that provides a set of APIs that implement SOAP and WSDL. Currently, MS SOAP Toolkit supports using SOAP in an environment outside of .NET, such as Visual Basic 6, since .NET has its own implementation of the SOAP specifications. Another tool is a third-party product, proxyTrace, which was developed by Simon Fell and can be downloaded from *www.pocket-soap.com.*

Query result of the Get New Deals action after successful upload of Orlando1 package.

We use MSSoapT to trace our .NET Object Remoting example here. The first thing that we need to do is configure the **HelloClient** to point to a proxy port that the tracing tool can monitor. Figure 9-10 shows how MSSoapT works as a tracing proxy.

Here is the only piece of code in **HelloClient.cs** that needs updating:

```
...
HelloServer MyHello =
    (HelloServer)Activator.GetObject(
        typeof(HelloServer),                    // Type
        "http://localhost:9999/SayHello"        // URI
    );
...
```

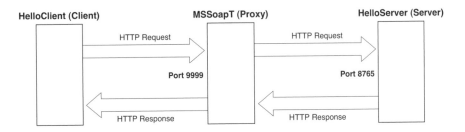

Figure 9-10 *MSSoapT as a tracing proxy for **HelloClient** and **HelloServer**.*

After compiling both **HelloClient.cs** and **HelloServer.cs**, we are ready to trace our remoting applications. First, run the MSSoapT. When you select the File | New | Formatted Trace option from the menu, you will be prompted to set up the trace options. In our example, we want the MSSoapT proxy to listen to port 9999 and forward all requests to port 8765, where **HelloServer** will be listening. After the setup, a new message window will appear inside of MSSoapT. Next, we can run the following command to start the **HelloServer**:

```
>HelloServer
HelloServer: Activated.
Press [Enter] to quit ...
```

Under another command window, we can run the client side, **HelloClient**, type in a name, and hit return. Thus, an RPC request has been sent to the **HelloServer** object through .NET Object Remoting:

```
>HelloClient
Your name, please: Howard
Hello, Howard
```

Not only should you see text messages displayed on the server-side console indicating the successful transmission of the messages, you should also see the "raw" SOAP request and response logged by MSSoapT, as shown in Figure 9-11.

Based on the SOAP request and response shown in Figure 9-11, we can make a few interesting observations:

- The encoding style defined in section 5 of the SOAP 1.1 specification is used:

```
<SOAP-ENV:Envelope
xmlns:xsi="http://www.w3.org/2001/XMLSchema-instance" ⇓
xmlns:xsd="http://www.w3.org/2001/XMLSchema" ⇓
xmlns:SOAP-ENC="http://schemas.xmlsoap.org/soap/encoding/" ⇓
```

Figure 9-11 *The SOAP request and response between **HelloClient** and **HelloServer**.*

```
xmlns:SOAP-ENV="http://schemas.xmlsoap.org/soap/envelope/" ⇓
SOAP-ENV:encodingStyle= ⇓
http://schemas.xmlsoap.org/soap/encoding/
...
```

- Under .NET, the latest version of XML Schema (XSD) is used. Currently, it is based on the 2001 version.
- The SOAP body elements of these messages carry the call to the **Greeting** method defined in **HelloServer**, or the response back from **HelloServer**.

Summary

In this chapter, we have gone over the basics of SOAP and how to build SOAP-based clients in the current release of .NET Framework. SOAP has been playing a very important role in .NET, especially for supporting Web Services and intra-component communication behind the scenes, even though most of the .NET developers are probably not aware of the latter.

Combining with Web Services, another Web programming paradigm that could get broad-based support from various platforms, SOAP provides a simple mechanism for Windows and non-Windows applications to communicate effectively over intranets and the Internet.

The proposed standardization of SOAP and its broad-based acceptance under Microsoft .NET Framework mark a new era of communications of distributed applications under the Windows programming environment and beyond. Finally, we may have found a standard-based "dialect" that even software developers from opposite sides of the tracks can easily understand and adopt.

Interoperating .NET with Other Platforms

.NET Web Services and SOAP are new development concepts and techniques that enable .NET to be a true Web-centric software platform. Under the .NET programming environment, you can easily create Web Services to advertise the functionality of your Web-based applications to your entire company, even over the Internet.

However, Microsoft has not been known for providing the most open and accessible software platforms in the past. Will .NET change that, with the help of CLR, Web Services, and SOAP? In other words, is it now possible to easily interoperate between Web applications and services built on the .NET platform and those on other platforms, such as Sun Microsystems' Java/J2EE?

In this chapter, we will try to answer this question. First, we introduce the basic concepts of WSDL, which is the foundation of interoperations between Web Services built on different platforms. Next, we develop a couple of examples to interoperate .NET with Apache SOAP (which is Java-based) via Web Services. Then we introduce a high-level concept called Universal Description, Discovery, and Integration registry, which provides a common framework for interoperating heterogeneous Web Services. Finally, we discuss the future directions of .NET as a platform to support the new Internet service model.

In Chapter 11, we use a comprehensive case study to put together various new features of the .NET platform, including SOAP and Web Services.

10.1 WSDL and .NET

SOAP is a simple yet powerful communication protocol for a distributed and heterogeneous network environment. It serves as the foundation for Web Services under .NET as well as other software platforms, such as Apache SOAP. Just like TCP/IP or HTTP, the main purpose of SOAP is to describe how components in distributed systems communicate with one another.

Although SOAP provides a generic format to describe the actual messages that are transported by Web Services, it does not provide a way for different Web Services to advertise themselves as services, across intranets and the Internet. WSDL, based on an XML vocabulary, is a high-level mechanism that

- Standardizes the description of Web Services to promote interoperability
- Provides operational information to advertise the usage of these services
- Automates the process of binding between Web Services producers and consumers

Earlier on in the development of Web Services concepts, Microsoft, IBM, and a few other organizations each came up with their own version of description mechanisms for general-purpose Web Services. Microsoft came up with Service Description Language (SDL) and used it to describe Web Services under .NET Beta 1. IBM advocated Network Accessible Service Specification Language (NASSL), which served the same purpose. WSDL is the convergence of these two sets of standards. It has been officially adopted since the Beta 2 version of the .NET platform.

All examples and concepts that we go over in this chapter are based on the latest version of the WSDL specification, Version 1.1 at the time of this writing. This version of the WSDL specification and its XML Schema are published on the Web at *http://www.w3.org/TR/wsdl*. .NET Framework is WSDL 1.1–compliant.

10.1.1 WSDL Defined

WSDL, similar in purpose to the Interface Definition Language (IDL) used in CORBA, is used to produce XML documents that describe network services. Web Services are the broadest types of these network services because the Internet is the computer network scaled to the maximum. To the users of WSDL, these services are collection(s) of communication endpoints that exchange well-formatted messages. XML documents produced under WSDL can provide operational information about these network services, such as

- Service interfaces in abstract form
- Concrete access protocols and format for data transmission

- Implementation details that could help other parties communicate with the service described without sacrificing extensibility

One of the most important benefits of WSDL is its extensibility, which allows communication endpoints and request/response messages to be described regardless of what type of network protocol is used. In fact, WSDL can be used to describe Web Services that are not SOAP-based. WSDL accomplishes its extensibility by using standard-based XML Schema representations, instead of specific semantics of a particular language or a particular type of languages.

There are generally seven major sections in a complete WSDL document, and .NET conforms to this standard:

- *Types*, which contains data types defined based on certain type systems
- *Message*, which defines the messages exchanged in an abstract form
- *Operation*, which describes operations provided by the Web Services in an abstract form, such as the **GetLatestCruiseSchedule** code in Section 9.1
- *Port type*, which aggregates all of the operations supported by endpoints
- *Binding*, which specifies a concrete network protocol such as SOAP and a data format for a port type
- *Port*, which maps a WSDL binding to a network address, such as a URI
- *Service*, which aggregates all of the ports in a WSDL document

In order to better understand how WSDL works, let's take a look at a sample WSDL document generated by .NET in the next few sections. Recall that in Chapter 9, we created a Web Service called **TAUWebService** using VS.NET to support operations such as searching and retrieving vacation packages for the Travel Agency Union (*www.travelagencygroup.com*). We continue to use this example here.

Under .NET, it is extremely easy to inspect specifications for a Web Service after it has been created. Assuming that the URL for **TAUWebService** remains at *localhost/TAUWebService/TAUWebService.asmx*, we can retrieve its corresponding WSDL document simply by using the URL *localhost/TAUWebService/TAUWebService.asmx?WSDL*. Because the complete WSDL document for **TAUWebService** is rather lengthy, we use portions of it to illustrate its structure.

The following is the beginning portion of the **TAUWebService** WSDL definition:

```
<?xml version="1.0" encoding="utf-8"?>
  xmlns:http="http://schemas.xmlsoap.org/wsdl/http/"
  xmlns:mime="http://schemas.xmlsoap.org/wsdl/mime/"
  xmlns:tm="http://microsoft.com/wsdl/mime/textMatching/"
  xmlns:soap="http://schemas.xmlsoap.org/wsdl/soap/"
```

```
xmlns:soapenc="http://schemas.xmlsoap.org/soap/encoding/"
xmlns:s0="http://tempuri.org/"
targetNamespace="http://tempuri.org/"
xmlns="http://schemas.xmlsoap.org/wsdl/">
<types>
  <s:schema attributeFormDefault="qualified"
    elementFormDefault="qualified"
    targetNamespace="http://tempuri.org/">
...
    <s:element name="getPackageDetail">
      <s:complexType>
        <s:sequence>
          <s:element minOccurs="1"
                     maxOccurs="1"
                     name="packageId"
                     nillable="true"
                     type="s:string" />
        </s:sequence>
      </s:complexType>
    </s:element>
    <s:element name="getPackageDetailResponse">
      <s:complexType>
        <s:sequence>
          <s:element minOccurs="1"
                     maxOccurs="1"
                     name="getPackageDetailResult"
                     nillable="true"
                     type="s0:TravelPackage" />
        </s:sequence>
      </s:complexType>
    </s:element>
    <s:complexType name="TravelPackage">
      <s:sequence>
        <s:element minOccurs="1"
                   maxOccurs="1"
                   name="id"
                   nillable="true"
                   type="s:string" />
        <s:element minOccurs="1"
                   maxOccurs="1"
                   name="startingPrice"
                   type="s:double" />
        <s:element minOccurs="1"
                   maxOccurs="1"
                   name="numOfDays"
                   type="s:int" />
        <s:element minOccurs="1"
                   maxOccurs="1"
                   name="offerStarts"
```

```
                              type="s:dateTime" />
            <s:element minOccurs="1"
                       maxOccurs="1"
                       name="offerEnds"
                       type="s:dateTime" />
            <s:element minOccurs="1"
                       maxOccurs="1"
                       name="airline"
                       nillable="true"
                       type="s:string" />
            <s:element minOccurs="1"
                       maxOccurs="1"
                       name="destination"
                       nillable="true"
                       type="s:string" />
            <s:element minOccurs="1"
                       maxOccurs="1"
                       name="originCity"
                       nillable="true"
                       type="s:string" />
            <s:element minOccurs="1"
                       maxOccurs="1"
                       name="agent"
                       nillable="true"
                       type="s:string" />
         </s:sequence>
      </s:complexType>
   ...
```

This code contains the XML header and definitions for namespaces and some of the WSDL types used in **TAUWebService**. For example, by specifying the namespace as "**s**" (*www.w3.org/2001/XMLSchema*), we indicate that the XML Schema (XSD) is used as the default type system. This WSDL document also uses SOAP encoding when necessary (**soapenc** namespace). We discuss other namespaces in the WSDL document in the next few sections.

As shown in the example, the first section of a WSDL document defines the types; there are three elements defined in this fragment of WSDL: **getPackageDetail**, **getPackageDetailResponse**, and **TravelPackage**. As you may recall from Chapter 9, **getPackageDetail** is a Web Service method of **TAUWebService**; **getPackageDetailResponse** represents a message carrying data back from **TAUWebService**. **GetPackageDetailResponse** returns a custom complex data type called **TravelPackage** (**s0** namespace), which is a class that we defined in **TAUWebService**.

The following code segment is the message section of this WSDL document. We selected a couple of messages to go over here and omitted the rest:

```
<message name="getPackageCountSoapIn">
  <part name="parameters" ⇓
      element="s0:getPackageCount" />
</message>
<message name="getPackageCountSoapOut">
  <part name="parameters" ⇓
      element="s0:getPackageCountResponse" />
</message>
...
<message name="uploadPackageSoapIn">
  <part name="parameters" ⇓
      element="s0:uploadPackage" />
</message>
<message name="uploadPackageSoapOut">
  <part name="parameters" ⇓
      element="s0:uploadPackageResponse" />
</message>
<message name="getPackageCountHttpGetIn" />
<message name="getPackageCountHttpGetOut">
  <part name="Body" element="s0:int" />
</message>
...
<message name="uploadPackageHttpGetIn">
  <part name="id" type="s:string" />
  <part name="agent" type="s:string" />
  <part name="destination" type="s:string" />
  <part name="airline" type="s:string" />
  <part name="numOfDays" type="s:string" />
  <part name="offerStarts" type="s:string" />
  <part name="offerEnds" type="s:string" />
  <part name="originCity" type="s:string" />
  <part name="startingPrice" type="s:string" />
</message>
<message name="uploadPackageHttpGetOut">
  <part name="Body" element="s0:string" />
</message>
<message name="getPackageCountHttpPostIn" />
<message name="getPackageCountHttpPostOut">
  <part name="Body" element="s0:int" />
</message>
...
<message name="uploadPackageHttpPostIn">
  <part name="id" type="s:string" />
  <part name="agent" type="s:string" />
  <part name="destination" type="s:string" />
  <part name="airline" type="s:string" />
```

```
<part name="numOfDays" type="s:string" />
<part name="offerStarts" type="s:string" />
<part name="offerEnds" type="s:string" />
<part name="originCity" type="s:string" />
<part name="startingPrice" type="s:string" />
</message>
<message name="uploadPackageHttpPostOut">
<part name="Body" element="s0:string" />
</message>
```
...

You probably noticed that there are multiple part elements in some of these message definitions, such as **uploadPackageHttpPostIn**. Part is an extensible mechanism to describe the content of a message, where multiple parts are used to indicate multiple logical units in the message. For example, the message that uploads a travel package would contain a package ID, travel agent name, and other required information. We can see that some of the types that we defined in the types section, such as **uploadPackage-Response**, are used here as well.

10.1.2 Operation and Port Type

A port type section contains a set of WSDL operations defined in abstract forms. These operations are defined for messages listed in the message section. Here is a section of the WSDL document for **TAUWebService** that contains a single port type:

```
<portType name="Service1Soap">
  <operation name="getPackageCount">
    <input message="s0:getPackageCountSoapIn" />
    <output message="s0:getPackageCountSoapOut" />
  </operation>
  <operation name="getPackageDetail">
    <input message="s0:getPackageDetailSoapIn" />
    <output message="s0:getPackageDetailSoapOut" />
  </operation>
  <operation name="getNewPackages">
    <input message="s0:getNewPackagesSoapIn" />
    <output message="s0:getNewPackagesSoapOut" />
  </operation>
  <operation name="uploadPackage2">
    <input message="s0:uploadPackage2SoapIn" />
    <output message="s0:uploadPackage2SoapOut" />
  </operation>
  <operation name="uploadPackage">
    <input message="s0:uploadPackageSoapIn" />
    <output message="s0:uploadPackageSoapOut" />
  </operation>
</portType>
```

There are four types of transmissions that an endpoint can support:

- *One-way*, where the endpoint receives one input message
- *Request-response*, where one input message is followed by one output message
- *Solicit-response*, where one output message is followed by one input message
- *Notification*, where the endpoint sends one output message

All operations listed in this chapter belong to the request-response type.

10.1.3 Binding

Binding is one of the most important aspects of WSDL because it is the step where actual network protocol, such as SOAP and HTTP, are bound to the abstract definition of the services. Within the binding section, the encoding scheme for the XML messages between the endpoints is also determined.

According to the latest WSDL Version 1.1 specification, only three types of bindings are defined: SOAP 1.1, HTTP GET/POST, and MIME. These are also the only types of binding supported under .NET. We go over them in the following sections using the WSDL description for **TAUWebService**.

10.1.3.1 SOAP BINDING

The following is a sample section of WSDL binding that binds a network service operation **getPackageCount** to a SOAP operation *tempuri.org/getPackageCount*. A set of operations is included in a service called **Service1Soap**, and this name is automatically generated by .NET.

```
<binding name="Service1Soap" type="s0:Service1Soap">
    <soap:binding
        transport="http://schemas.xmlsoap.org/soap/http"
        style="document" />
    <operation name="getPackageCount">
      <soap:operation
         soapAction="http://tempuri.org/getPackageCount"
         style="document" />
      <input>
        <soap:body use="literal" />
      </input>
      <output>
        <soap:body use="literal" />
      </output>
    </operation>
    ...
```

The **soap:binding** element indicates that the message is to be constructed according to the SOAP format with an envelope, header, and body. Some of the WSDL elements map directly to the required elements of SOAP. For example, the **soap:body** element describes how the message parts appear in the SOAP body element.

One thing worth noting here is the **style** attribute for **soap:binding** and **soap:operation**. This attribute indicates whether the operation is RPC-oriented or document-oriented. RPC-oriented SOAP operations send and receive messages that resemble remote method calls, as they have input and output parameters and return values. On the other hand, document-oriented SOAP messages contain one or more documents (in our case, XML documents). All operations of **TAUWebService** are document-oriented, which is the default behavior of Web Service methods (or Web methods for short) under .NET. As far as interoperability is concerned, this is one of the most significant differences between .NET and Web Services from other platforms, such as Apache SOAP. We discuss this in depth in Section 10.2.1.

10.1.3.2 HTTP AND MIME BINDING

By default, all .NET Web Services are generated as executables. These executables can be accessed through a Web browser via HTTP GET and POST, except executables with customized input data types, such as **TravelPackage**, which need serialization during invocation. Therefore, applicable HTTP bindings are included automatically in order to describe the interaction. Here is a sample section from the WSDL document for **TAUWebService**:

```
<binding name="Service1HttpGet"
    type="s0:Service1HttpGet">
  <http:binding verb="GET" />
  <operation name="getPackageCount">
    <http:operation location="/getPackageCount" />
    <input>
      <http:urlEncoded />
    </input>
    <output>
      <mime:mimeXml part="Body" />
    </output>
  </operation>
...
  </binding>
...
```

This WSDL segment provides two pieces of protocol-specific information: that the service supports HTTP GET and that the relative URL to invoke this operation is **"/getPackageCount"**. Combined with the WSDL service description listed in Section 10.1.4, it provides all we would need to access **TAUWebService** via HTTP.

Multipurpose Internet Mail Extensions (MIME) is an official Internet standard that specifies how messages must be formatted so that they can be exchanged between different e-mail systems. In short, MIME defines an extensible set of different formats to accommodate transferring nontextual message bodies over the Internet. MIME is also an evolving standard designed to transfer textual message bodies in character sets other than US-ASCII.

WSDL does not intend to define and extend the whole set of MIME types, only a selected few, such as **multipart/related**, **text/xml**, and **application/x-www-form-urlencoded**. As shown in the sample WSDL segment, a **mime:mineXml** element is used to describe an XML payload that is not SOAP-compliant but does use the same XML Schema for SOAP encoding. The following is a sample response of our **getPackageCount** HTTP GET request:

```
HTTP/1.1 200 OK
Content-Type: text/xml; charset=utf-8
Content-Length: 80

<?xml version="1.0" encoding="utf-8"?>
<int xmlns="http://tempuri.org/">1</int>
```

Even though there is no SOAP envelope in the body of the HTTP response, the message itself is still a well-formatted XML document.

10.1.4 Port and Service

A WSDL port maps one communication endpoint with a single concrete network address. A WSDL service is a set of such ports with no low-level binding information. The following is a sample WSDL service in **TAUWebService** with three different ports:

```
<service name="Service1">
  <port name="Service1Soap" binding="s0:Service1Soap">
    <soap:address⇓
      location="http://localhost/TAUWebService/⇓
      TAUWebService.asmx" />
  </port>
  <port name="Service1HttpGet"⇓
      binding="s0:Service1HttpGet">
    <http:address⇓
      location="http://localhost/TAUWebService/⇓
      TAUWebService.asmx" />
  </port>
  <port name="Service1HttpPost"⇓
      binding="s0:Service1HttpPost">
```

```
<http:address⇓
    location="http://localhost/TAUWebService/⇓
    TAUWebService.asmx" />
  </port>
</service>
```

In this segment, one service provides three different ports. All three ports point to the URL: *localhost/TAUWebService/TAUWebService.asmx*.

10.2 Interoperating with .NET by Examples

One of the most significant benefits of Web Service is its ability to communicate with peers from other organizations via the Internet in a platform-independent manner. In this section, we look into two simple examples of interoperating between Web Services. In the first example, we build an Apache SOAP client written in Java, to access **TAUWebService**, the Web Service that we built in Chapter 9. For the second example, we build a .NET C# client to access a simple Apache SOAP Web Service, **HelloWorld**, thus completing the full circle.

Both of our examples are based on the SOAP format and HTTP transport protocol. They represent one of the mechanisms that Web Services use to communicate with each other, regardless of which software or hardware platforms that they are built on.

Interoperating between Web Services today is not quite as easy as advertised, even though the concepts of SOAP and XML seem quite simple. The main reason is the lack of maturity of the technologies and protocols. Since numerous individuals and organizations, including Microsoft, IBM, and Apache, are involved in creating and implementing these protocols, coordination between independent efforts becomes paramount. Therefore, it is not totally surprising to experience interoperability (interop for short) issues between different implementations. However, as the technologies and standards become more established over time, interoperating should become much easier.

Many in the SOAP and Web Services community are actively working to solve interop issues and are testing different implementations. The "SOAP Builders" on Yahoo! Groups (*groups.yahoo.com/group/soapbuilders*) is such an online community.

10.2.1 Accessing .NET Web Services from an Apache SOAP Client

For simplicity, we will reuse the Web Service that we built in Chapter 9: **TAUWebService**. In order to access our .NET Web Service from a Java client based on Apache SOAP, we need to complete the following steps:

1. Set up the environment to run an Apache SOAP server and client. Even though we do not need the Apache SOAP server in the first example, it is more efficient to configure both sides at the same time.

2. Based on the WSDL document provided by the .NET for **TAUWebService**, build an Apache SOAP client using Java.

3. Test our Apache SOAP client and .NET Web Service by sending and receiving SOAP messages.

10.2.1.1 CUSTOMIZING .NET WEB SERVICES FOR INTEROPERATING

SOAP specification, discussed in Chapter 9, dictates that the contents of the SOAP message sent to and from a Web Service should be in XML. However, it doesn't strictly outline the encoding of the XML. In general, there are two types of encoding that .NET supports: literal/document style (Section 5 of the SOAP specification) and RPC encoded style (Section 7). "Literal style" refers to an encoding scheme based on an XSD schema, such as *www.w3.org/2001/ XMLSchema*; "RPC encoded style" refers to customized encoding based on input and output parameters of remote method calls. The default encoding for ASP.NET Web Services is to use an XSD schema, while Apache SOAP only supports RPC encoded style. Therefore, we need to modify **TAUWebService** to use RPC encoding first.

As a mechanism for working with SOAP Web Services that expect different encoding styles, ASP.NET provides an attribute-based mechanism for controlling the format of the XML inside the SOAP message. Changing the SOAP encoding style under .NET is quite simple. Using VS.NET, we can first create a new Web Service called **TAUWebService1**, which is identical to **TAUWebService**. We only have to add the **SoapRpcService** class modifier to the beginning of the **TAUWebService** class definition and add a **SoapRpcMethod** method modifier to the beginning of every Web method that we want to convert to RPC encoding style. The following is the only code segment of **TAUWebService1.asmx.cs** that is changed from **TAUWebService**:

```
using System;
using System.Collections;
using System.ComponentModel;
using System.Data;
using System.Diagnostics;
```

```
using System.Web;
using System.Web.Services;
//Added for compatibility with Apache SOAP
using System.Web.Services.Protocols;
//Added for compatibility with Apache SOAP
using System.Web.Services.Description;
//Added for compatibility with Apache SOAP
using System.Xml;
//Added for compatibility with Apache SOAP
using System.Xml.Serialization;

namespace TAUWebService1
{
/// <summary>
/// Summary description for Service1.
/// </summary>
[SoapRpcService()]
public class Service1 : System.Web.Services.WebService
{
...

    [WebMethod]
    //Added for compatibility with Apache SOAP
    [SoapRpcMethod]
    public int getPackageCount()
    {
        return packages.Count;
    }


    [WebMethod]
    //Added for compatibility with Apache SOAP
    [SoapRpcMethod]
    public TravelPackage getPackageDetail(string packageId)
    {
        //Search the package by its id
        TravelPackage p = ⇓
            (TravelPackage)packages[packageId];
        return p;
    }
    ...
```

If we compare the two WSDL documents that describe **TAUWebService** and **TAUWebService1**, we should be able to see the subtle differences between interfacing with these two SOAP encoding styles. For example, the following shows a segment of the binding section of **TAUWebService**:

```
<binding name="Service1Soap" type="s0:Service1Soap">
    <soap:binding tranport=⇓
        "http://schemas.xmlsoap.org/soap/http" ⇓
        style="document" />
    <operation name="getPackageCount">
      <soap:operation soapAction=⇓
```

```
      "http://tempuri.org/getPackageCount" ⇓
      style="document" />
   <input>
      <soap:body use="literal" />
   </input>
   <output>
      <soap:body use="literal" />
   </output>
</operation>
   ...
```

We can compare this segment with the corresponding section of the WSDL document for **TAUWebService1**, which is located at *localhost/TAUWebService/TAUWebService1.asmx?WSDL*. We can see the differences easily:

```
<binding name="Service1Soap" type="s0:Service1Soap">
   <soap:binding transport=⇓
   "http://schemas.xmlsoap.org/soap/http" ⇓
   style="document" />
   <operation name="getPackageCount">
      <soap:operation soapAction=⇓
      "http://tempuri.org/getPackageCount" ⇓
      style="rpc" />
      <input>
         <soap:body use="encoded" namespace=⇓
         "http://tempuri.org/" encodingStyle=⇓
         "http://schemas.xmlsoap.org/soap/encoding/" />
      </input>
      <output>
         <soap:body use="encoded" namespace=⇓
         "http://tempuri.org/" encodingStyle=⇓
         "http://schemas.xmlsoap.org/soap/encoding/" />
      </output>
   </operation>
      ...
```

10.2.1.2 CONFIGURING APACHE SOAP SERVER AND CLIENT

Formerly known as the Apache Group, the Apache Software Foundation (*www.apache.org*) is a not-for-profit corporation created to promote open, collaborative software development projects. As one of the key projects, Apache XML Project is designed to provide commercial-quality, standards-based XML solutions that are developed in an open and cooperative environment.

Apache SOAP is an initiative from the Apache XML Project (*xml.apache.org*) and is an implementation of the SOAP submission to the World Wide Web Consortium (W3C, *www.w3c.org*). It is based on, and supersedes, the IBM SOAP4J implementation. As one of the most popular

SOAP implementations, Apache SOAP provides a set of powerful Java APIs that we can use to build Web Services, similar to those provided by .NET.

In order to execute the examples that we develop in this section and in Section 10.2.2, we need to install and configure an Apache SOAP server and a client environment. Apart from the Apache SOAP API libraries, we also need to install another Web server that can execute Java Servlets and Java Server Pages (JSPs). Jakarta Tomcat from Apache, which is a well-implemented Java Servlets engine, is such a Web server.

The following is a suggested sequence of steps to configure Apache SOAP:

1. Make sure that the Java Development Kit (JDK) is installed; the preferred version is 1.2.2 or higher. The JDK can be downloaded from Sun JavaSoft (*www.javasoft.com*) and installed according to the accompanying instructions.

2. Download and install a released version of Jakarta Tomcat from Apache. We recommend that you deploy examples in this book on a Tomcat server that is Version 3.2 or higher. Make sure that you follow the instructions from the Apache Web site to complete the installation. By default, Tomcat runs on port 8080. We want to keep it that way, as this avoids conflicts with existing Web servers. For example, the IIS that .NET requires runs on port 80 by default.

3. Download and install the latest version of Apache SOAP API (Version 2.2 or higher). Make sure that you follow the instructions from the Apache Web site to complete the installation. Then configure the installed Tomcat server to include the Apache SOAP administration URL and make sure that the CLASSPATH for Tomcat includes all required Apache SOAP libraries. Here are some sample changes to the **tomcat-apache.conf** file under **%TOMCAT_HOME%\conf**, assuming that **D:\soap** is where the Apache SOAP is installed:

```
...
Alias /soap "D:/soap/webapps/soap"
<Directory "D:/soap/webapps/soap">
    Options Indexes FollowSymLinks
</Directory>
ApJServMount /soap/servlet /soap
<Location "/soap/WEB-INF/">
    AllowOverride None
    deny from all
</Location>
<Directory "D:/soap/webapps/soap/WEB-INF/">
    AllowOverride None
    deny from all
</Directory>
```

```
<Location "/soap/META-INF/">
    AllowOverride None
    deny from all
</Location>
<Directory "D:/soap/webapps/soap/META-INF/">
    AllowOverride None
    deny from all
</Directory>
...
```

4. At the end of our installation, we should be able to verify the previous installations by pointing a Web browser to the Apache SOAP administration page, shown in Figure 10-1, without causing errors or Java exceptions. We assume that the Tomcat Web server has been started and that its document root can be reached at *localhost:8080/index.html*. We also assume that the root URL of Apache SOAP is at *localhost:8080/soap/*.

Another tool worth looking at is the Web Services Toolkit (WSTK) from IBM alphaWorks (*www.alphaworks.ibm.com/tech/webservicestoolkit*). WSTK is a GUI-based, powerful WSDL-generation tool that supports Apache SOAP API. It is compliant with WSDL 1.1 and SOAP 1.1 specifications.

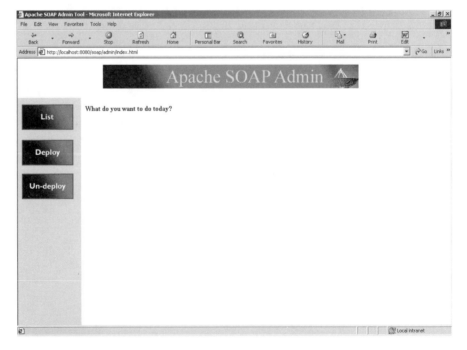

Figure 10-1 *The Apache SOAP administration page.*

The latest version of WSTK, Version 2.3, is based on Apache SOAP API 2.1 and by default, comes with a developer version of the IBM WebSphere Application Server. WSTK can also configure Tomcat with Apache SOAP automatically. For ease of configuration, we use generic Apache SOAP to implement the examples in this book.

10.2.1.3 OUR FIRST APACHE SOAP CLIENT FOR .NET WEB SERVICES

Generic Apache SOAP implementation cannot automatically create the proxy for a Web Service based on its WSDL document. In fact, it is not even WSDL aware. Even though this is somewhat inconvenient, the WSDL document generated for **TAUWebService1** by .NET provides sufficient information for us to figure out its interface manually. Our goal is to develop an Apache SOAP client to access two Web methods from **TAUWebService1**: **getPackageCount** and **getPackageDetail**.

The following Java program accesses the .NET Web Service, **TAUWebService1**, based on Apache SOAP API. The file name for this program is **DotNetTestClient.java**:

```
import java.io.*;
import java.net.*;
import java.util.*;
import org.apache.soap.util.xml.*;
import org.apache.soap.*;
import org.apache.soap.encoding.*;
import org.apache.soap.encoding.soapenc.*;
import org.apache.soap.rpc.*;

public class DotNetTestClient
{
  public static void main (String[] args) ⇓
    throws Exception {
    Response resp = null;
      // Process the arguments; ⇓
     // Only two types of Web methods are supported
    if (args.length > 2 || args.length < 1) {
        System.err.println("Usage:");
        System.err.println("  java " + ⇓
           DotNetTestClient.class.getName() + ⇓
        " WebMethodName");
        System.exit (1);
    }
    else if (args.length == 1 &&⇓
    args[0].equals("getPackageCount")) {
        String encodingStyleURI = ⇓
             Constants.NS_URI_SOAP_ENC;
         URL url = new URL ⇓
           ("http://localhost/TAUWebService1/⇓
           TAUWebService1.asmx");
```

```
        Call call = new Call ();
        call.setTargetObjectURI ("http://tempuri.org/");
        call.setMethodName ("getPackageCount");
        call.setEncodingStyleURI(encodingStyleURI);

         resp = call.invoke(url, ⇓
          "http://tempuri.org/getPackageCount");
    }
    else {
        System.err.println("Web method " + args[0] ⇓
             + " not supported!");
        System.exit (1);
    }

    // Check the response.
    if (resp.generatedFault ()) {
      Fault fault = resp.getFault ();
      System.out.println ("Ouch, the call failed: ");
     System.out.println ("  Fault Code   = " + ⇓
      fault.getFaultCode ());
     System.out.println ("  Fault String = " + ⇓
      fault.getFaultString ());
    } else {
      Parameter result = resp.getReturnValue ();
      System.out.println ("The result of the query is:\n" ⇓
        + result.getValue ());
    }
  }
}
```

This code describes a typical workflow of binding an Apache SOAP client to a Web Service, regardless of the service's implementation:

1. Specify the encoding style for the SOAP message as **NS_URI_SOAP_ ENC**, which is the default.

2. Create the **org.apache.soap.rpc.RPCMessage.Call** object.

3. Set the target URI into the **Call** object using the **setTarget-ObjectURI(...)** method.

4. Set the method name that you wish to invoke into the **Call** object using the **setMethodName(...)** method.

5. Execute the **Call** object's **invoke(...)** method and capture the **Response** object, which is returned from **invoke(...)**.

6. Check the **Response** object to see whether a fault was generated using the **generatedFault()** method. If a fault was returned, retrieve it using the **getFault(...)** method. Otherwise extract any result or returned parameters using the **getReturnValue()** and **getParams()** methods, respectively.

You can use the following command to compile **DotNetTest-Client.java**, where **SOAP_CP** contains the required CLASSPATH to Apache SOAP libraries.

```
>javac -classpath %SOAP_CP% DotNetTestClient.java
```

You may run this program and obtain the following output from the Java client:

```
>java -cp %SOAP_CP% DotNetTestClient getPackageCount
The result of the query is:
1


>
```

10.2.1.4 ENHANCING THE APACHE SOAP CLIENT

Accessing the other Web method, **getPackageDetail**, is more complicated because it returns a user-defined complex data type of **TravelPackage**. When a SOAP request is processed, its input and output parameters must be serialized into or de-serialized from XML before they can be transmitted or received. Under .NET, serialization and de-serialization of XML are handled by ASP.NET (**System.Xml.Serialization**) automatically behind the scenes. However, Apache SOAP only provides a number of predefined serializers and deserializers for common Java data types such as Java arrays or **java.lang.String**. In our case, we need to manually create a deserializer for the **TravelPackage** object type in order to enable Apache SOAP clients to accept this custom data type.

The following code (**TPSerializer.java**) is a sample deserializer for **TravelPackage**, where the **marshall** method implements the serialization and the **unmarshall** method implements the deserialization, respectively. The **unmarshall** method is currently the focus of our discussion.

```
import java.util.Vector;
import org.apache.soap.*;
import org.apache.soap.encoding.SOAPMappingRegistry;
import org.apache.soap.encoding.soapenc.*;
import org.apache.soap.rpc.*;
import org.apache.soap.messaging.*;
import java.net.URL;
import org.apache.soap.util.xml.*;
import java.io.*;
import org.w3c.dom.*;
import org.apache.soap.util.*;
import java.lang.reflect.*;

public class TPSerializer implements Serializer, ⇓
                                    Deserializer
{
```

```java
public void marshall(String inScopeEncStyle, ⇓
                     Class javaType, Object src,
                     Object context, Writer sink,
                     NSStack nsStack,
                     XMLJavaMappingRegistry xjmr,
                     SOAPContext ctx)
  throws IllegalArgumentException, IOException
{
...
}

public Bean unmarshall(String inScopeEncStyle, ⇓
                       QName elementType, Node src,
                       XMLJavaMappingRegistry xjmr,
                       SOAPContext ctx)
  throws IllegalArgumentException
{
  Element root = (Element)src;
  String name = root.getTagName();

  // if SOAP encoding is not provided,
  // a null reference will be returned
  if (SoapEncUtils.isNull(root))
  {
    return new Bean(TravelPackage.class, null);
  }

  TravelPackage ret = new TravelPackage();
  NodeList list = root.getElementsByTagName("id");
  if (list == null || list.getLength() == 0) {
    throw new IllegalArgumentException("No 'id' ⇓
      Element");
  }
  Element el = (Element)list.item(0);
  ret.setId(((Text)el.getFirstChild()).getData());

  list = root.getElementsByTagName("startingPrice");
  if (list == null || list.getLength() == 0) {
    throw new IllegalArgumentException("No ⇓
      'startingPrice' Element");
  }
  el = (Element)list.item(0);
  ret.setStartingPrice(Double.parseDouble ⇓
  (DOMUtils.getChildCharacterData(el)));

  list = root.getElementsByTagName("numOfDays");
  if (list == null || list.getLength() == 0) {
   throw new IllegalArgumentException("No ⇓
     'numOfDays' Element");
  }
```

```
el = (Element)list.item(0);
ret.setNumOfDays(Integer.parseInt ⇓
    (DOMUtils.getChildCharacterData(el)));

list = root.getElementsByTagName("offerStarts");
if (list == null || list.getLength() == 0) {
  throw new IllegalArgumentException("No ⇓
    'offerStarts' Element");
}
el = (Element)list.item(0);
ret.setOfferStarts( ⇓
      ((Text)el.getFirstChild()).getData());

list = root.getElementsByTagName("offerEnds");
if (list == null || list.getLength() == 0) {
  throw new IllegalArgumentException("No ⇓
'offerEnds' Element");
}
el = (Element)list.item(0);
ret.setOfferEnds(((Text)el.getFirstChild()).getData());

list = root.getElementsByTagName("airline");
if (list == null || list.getLength() == 0) {
  throw new IllegalArgumentException("No 'airline' ⇓
    Element");
}
el = (Element)list.item(0);
ret.setAirline(((Text)el.getFirstChild()).getData());

list = root.getElementsByTagName("destination");
if (list == null || list.getLength() == 0) {
  throw new IllegalArgumentException("No 'destination'⇓
      Element");
}
el = (Element)list.item(0);
ret.setDestination ⇓
  (((Text)el.getFirstChild()).getData());

list = root.getElementsByTagName("originCity");
if (list == null || list.getLength() == 0) {
  throw new IllegalArgumentException("No 'originCity' ⇓
      Element");
}
el = (Element)list.item(0);
ret.setOriginCity ⇓
  (((Text)el.getFirstChild()).getData());
```

```
      list = root.getElementsByTagName("agent");
      if (list == null || list.getLength() == 0) {
        throw new IllegalArgumentException("No 'agent' ⇓
          Element");
      }
      el = (Element)list.item(0);
      ret.setAgent(((Text)el.getFirstChild()).getData());
      return new Bean(TravelPackage.class, ret);
    }
}
```

In this code example, the **TPSerializer** class needs to implement both the **org.apache.soap.util.xml.Serializer** and **org.apache.soap.util.xml. Deserializer** interfaces in order to serve as serializer and deserializer for a custom class. In the **unmarshall** method, an XML input document **src** is parsed and instance variables for the **TravelPackage** class are populated according to their counterparts in the XML input.

If you are familiar with Java, the deserialization process here is quite similar to the object deserialization in Java, the key difference being that Java objects are de-serialized from XML documents instead of from binary streams. If you are looking for guidance to write your own serializer or deserializer, reviewing our example or predefined ones that come with Apache SOAP source code should help.

You may compile and run **DotNetTestClient.java** after adding a handler for the Web method of **getPackageDetail**, which is quite similar to that of **getPackageCount**. The handler needs to include some extra code for mapping the newly created serializer or deserializer of the **TravelPackage** object type:

```
SOAPMappingRegistry smr = new SOAPMappingRegistry ⇓
    (Constants.NS_URI_CURRENT_SCHEMA_XSD);
TPSerializer tpSer = new TPSerializer();
smr.mapTypes(Constants.NS_URI_SOAP_ENC, ⇓
    new QName("http://tempuri.org/encodedTypes", ⇓
        "TravelPackage"), ⇓
        TravelPackage.class, tpSer, tpSer);
```

You will get the following output from this updated Java client:

```
>java -cp %SOAP_CP% DotNetTestClient getPackageDetail ⇓
 Sample
The result of the query is:
ID: Sample
Starting price: 800.0
Number of days: 3
Offer starts on: 2001-07-14T00:00:00.0000000-04:00
Offer ends on: 2001-06-29T00:00:00.0000000-04:00
Airline: AA
```

```
Destination city: Orlando, FL
Origin city: Boston, MA
Travel agency: Wonderful

>
```

10.2.2 Accessing Apache Web Services from a .NET SOAP Client

In order to enable a .NET SOAP client to access Apache Web Services, we need to complete the following steps:

1. Build and deploy a Web Service using Apache SOAP. For simplicity, we will build a Web Service that returns a **HelloWorld** string.

2. Create a WSDL document that is .NET compliant, based on the Apache Web Service we deployed earlier.

3. Generate a C# proxy using the **wsdl.exe** utility provided by .NET.

4. Create a simple .NET C# client that references this proxy and test it with the Apache Web Service by sending and receiving SOAP messages.

10.2.2.1 CREATING AND DEPLOYING APACHE SOAP WEB SERVICES

Creating an RPC-based Web Service is a very simple process involving two basic steps. First, develop either a standard Java class or an Enterprise Java Bean (EJB), which includes the methods you want to expose as Web methods. The implementation of the Web Service does not need to know anything about Apache SOAP. Second, create an Apache SOAP deployment descriptor for your service.

Here is a simple Java class called **HelloWorld**. We will use it as the basis for our Apache SOAP Web Service:

```
package chap10;

import java.io.*;

public class HelloWorld
{
    public static void main(String[] args) {
        // Testing the helloWorld method
        if (args.length < 1) {
            System.err.println("Usage:");
            System.err.println("  java " + ⇓
                HelloWorld.class.getName() + ⇓
                " Location/Person");
            System.exit (1);
        }
```

```
        else {
            HelloWorld hw = new HelloWorld();
            System.out.println(hw.helloWorld(args[0]));
        }
    }

    public String helloWorld(String inStr) {
      return("Hello World from " + inStr + "!");
    }
}
```

The only method in this class is **helloWorld** (Java is case-sensitive, like C#), which is also what we want to expose as a Web method. When running as a Web method, it takes a string from the Web Service input and returns a concatenated string with proper greetings. We need to compile this code into a Java class file (byte code) before deploying the Web Service:

```
>javac -classpath %SOAP_CP% HelloWorld.java
```

Once the Java class file for **HelloWorld.java** is generated, we need to add it to the required CLASSPATH for Apache Tomcat and restart the Apache Tomcat/SOAP server.

Now we are ready to deploy this Web Service to the Apache SOAP server with an XML-based deployment descriptor. Documentation for Apache SOAP explains pretty clearly how to write a deployment descriptor by hand. Here is a sample that deploys the **HelloWorld** class with an Apache SOAP service name of **HelloWorld**:

```
<isd:service
    xmlns:isd="http://xml.apache.org/xml-soap/deployment"
            id="urn:HelloWorld">
  <isd:provider type="java"
              scope="Application"
              methods="helloWorld">
    <isd:java class="chap10.HelloWorld" static="false"/>
  </isd:provider>

  <isd:faultListener>
    org.apache.soap.server.DOMFaultListener
  </isd:faultListener>
</isd:service>
```

This deployment descriptor links a service with the ID of **HelloWorld** to a Java class **chap10.HelloWorld** and its exposed method **helloWorld()** (**urn** is an Apache SOAP resource prefix indicating service name). Assuming that the Apache SOAP server URL is located at *localhost:8080/soap/servlet/rpcrouter*, the following command would deploy the **HelloWorld** Web Service using the deployment descriptor stored in a file named **DeploymentDescriptor.xml**:

```
>java -cp %SOAP_CP% ⇓
org.apache.soap.server.ServiceManagerClient ⇓
http://localhost:8080/soap/servlet/rpcrouter deploy ⇓
DeploymentDescriptor.xml

>
```

Figures 10-2 and 10-3 show that the **HelloWorld** Web Service has been successfully deployed according to the updated Apache SOAP administration page.

10.2.2.2 GENERATING WSDL DOCUMENTS BASED ON APACHE SOAP

Since generic Apache SOAP does not use WSDL documents to describe Web Services, we can create the WSDL document by hand using the syntactic rules discussed in Section 10.1. Third-party tools, such as IBM WSTK, provide their utility to generate WSDL documents automatically. However, they are not always useful. For example, IBM WSTK generates WSDL files that are incompatible for .NET, even though they conform to WSDL and SOAP 1.1 specifications. To be more specific, WSTK still uses the 1999 version of XSD,

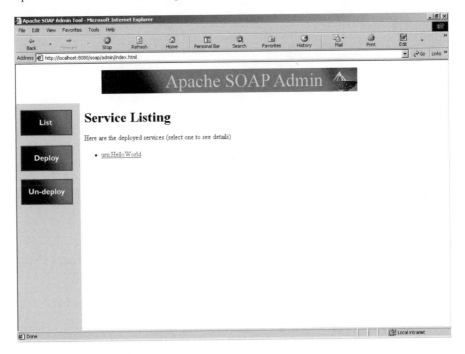

| Figure 10-2 | *The Apache SOAP service listing page after deploying **HelloWorld**.* |

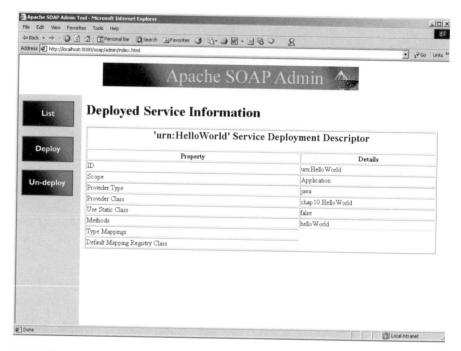

Figure 10-3   *Details of the **HelloWorld** service after deployment.*

while .NET upgrades to the 2001 version of XSD recently; .NET requires that **targetNamespace** be spelled out when new types are declared, while WSTK does not. The list goes on and on. Sometimes, it might be more time-consuming to change WSDL documents of other styles to be .NET-compliant than to write everything from scratch.

Here is a WSDL document for the **HelloWorld** service (the actual service name is HelloWorld_Service) that complies with the WSDL implementation of .NET:

```
<?xml version="1.0" encoding="UTF-8"?>
<definitions name="HelloWorld_Service"
  xmlns:xsd="http://www.w3.org/2001/XMLSchema"
  targetNamespace=
    "http://www.helloworldservice.com/HelloWorld"
  xmlns:soap="http://schemas.xmlsoap.org/wsdl/soap/"
  xmlns:tns="http://www.helloworldservice.com/HelloWorld"
  xmlns="http://schemas.xmlsoap.org/wsdl/">

  <message name="InhelloWorldRequest">
    <part name="meth1_inType1"
        type="xsd:string"/>
  </message>
```

```xml
<message name="OuthelloWorldResponse">
  <part name="meth1_outType"
        type="xsd:string"/>
</message>


<portType name="HelloWorld_Service">
  <operation name="helloWorld">
    <input message="tns:InhelloWorldRequest"/>
    <output message="tns:OuthelloWorldResponse"/>
  </operation>
</portType>


<binding name="HelloWorld_ServiceBinding"
         type="tns:HelloWorld_Service">
  <soap:binding style="rpc"
      transport="http://schemas.xmlsoap.org/soap/http"/>
  <operation name="helloWorld">
    <soap:operation soapAction="urn:HelloWorld"/>
    <input>
      <soap:body encodingStyle=
            "http://schemas.xmlsoap.org/soap/encoding/"
          namespace="urn:HelloWorld"
          use="encoded"/>
    </input>
    <output>
      <soap:body encodingStyle=
            "http://schemas.xmlsoap.org/soap/encoding/"
          namespace="urn:HelloWorld"
          use="encoded"/>
    </output>
  </operation>
</binding>

<service name="HelloWorld_Service">
  <documentation>IBM WSTK 2.0 generated service ⇓
   definition file</documentation>
  <port binding="tns:HelloWorld_ServiceBinding"
        name="HelloWorld_ServicePort">
    <soap:address location=
        "http://localhost:8080/soap/servlet/rpcrouter"/>
  </port>
</service>

</definitions>
```

10.2.2.3 GENERATING PROXY FOR WEB SERVICES UNDER .NET

The .NET platform provides a set of utilities, such as **wsdl.exe**, to generate the interface (proxy) that allows the client programs to access Web Services. The following command generates a proxy program in C#, assuming that the description of the **HelloWorld** service is stored in a file called **HelloWorld_MSStyle.wsdl**:

```
C:\>wsdl /out:helloWorldProxy.cs HelloWorld_MSStyle.wsdl
Microsoft (R) Web Services Description Language Utility
[Microsoft (R) .NET Framework, Version 1.0.2914.16]
Copyright (C) Microsoft Corp. 1998-2001. All rights reserved.

Writing file 'helloWorldProxy.cs'.

>
```

10.2.2.4 RUNNING THE C# CLIENT FOR APACHE SOAP WEB SERVICES

With VS.NET, we are ready to build a simple C# client to access the Apache SOAP Web Service that we built. The detailed process is identical to the one we discussed in Section 6.2. First, convert the C# proxy to a DLL using .NET CLR utilities. Then create a VS.NET project called **ApacheSOAPClient** with the following C# code to access the **HelloWorld** service:

```
using System;
using System.Xml;
using System.Web.Services;

namespace ApacheSoapClient
{
/// <summary>
/// Summary description for Class1.
/// </summary>
class ApacheSoapClient
{
    static void Main(string[] args)
    {
        Console.Write("Your name, please: ");
        String name = Console.ReadLine();
        Console.WriteLine();
        HelloWorld_Service myHello = ⇓
                new HelloWorld_Service();
        Console.WriteLine⇓
                (myHello.helloWorld(name));
        Console.WriteLine();
    }
}
}
```

Executing this code with the Apache Tomcat running at port 8080 will yield the following output:

```
>ApacheSoapClient.exe
Your name, please: Howard

Hello World from Howard!

>
```

Thus, we have successfully completed the full circle of interoperating Web Services: We have created an Apache SOAP client to access .NET Web Services and another .NET client to access an Apache SOAP Web Service. SOAP-based messages have been sent and received successfully in both cases.

10.3 Universal Description, Discovery, and Integration

In the previous few chapters, we have built several Web Services under .NET. Suppose that we are building a Web-facing business that provides functionalities useful to organizations and/or users on the Internet. For example, a travel agency union provides Web services such as **TAUWebService**. If we choose to provide such services to external customers or partners, how do we "advertise" them so that other businesses can easily find our services over the Internet? And how do we discover businesses worldwide that offer the exact products and services that we want to use?

Today's search engines or Web directory services, like Yahoo!, are not sufficient to advertise such sophisticated business-to-business (B2B), technology-oriented services. We need a standard-based, platform-neutral registry for Web Services, similar to a "yellow pages" for businesses on the Internet. Thus, the concept of UDDI was born.

10.3.1 What UDDI Is

UDDI, short for Universal Description, Discovery, and Integration, is a project that aims to create a platform-independent, open framework for describing services, discovering businesses, and integrating business services through the Internet (see *www.uddi.org/*). The UDDI project evolved from prior efforts by Ariba, IBM, and Microsoft. As of late 2001, over two hundred major software and platform vendors, including Oracle and Sun Microsystems, have participated in the UDDI community.

The UDDI project takes advantage of emerging standards and protocols such as XML and SOAP, as well as established protocols such as HTTP and Domain Name System (DNS), to form its communication protocols and provide cross-platform interoperability. To date, both IBM and Microsoft have

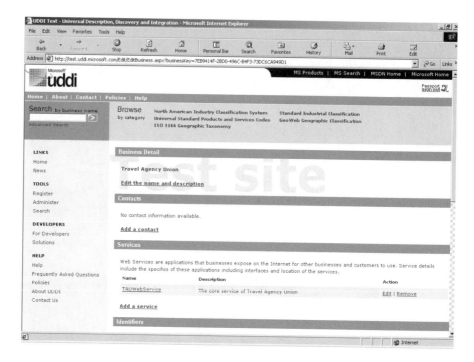

Figure 10-4   *TAUWebService* published to the Microsoft test UDDI registry.

implemented test and production versions of their business registries that are based on the UDDI protocol. Microsoft's test UDDI registry is located at *test.uddi.microsoft.com* and registration is free. To register our fictional business under this registry, our only requirement is to obtain a Microsoft passport. Figure 10-4 shows that the **TAUWebService** has been published to the Microsoft test UDDI registry under the business entry of the travel agency union.

10.3.2 Connecting Enterprises Using SOAP, UDDI, and WSDL

The primary motivation to create UDDI registries is to publish Web Services to the Web (to the world) so that requestors of these services can easily find and use them. We can look at all parties involved to understand UDDI's role in Web Services:

- *Web Service.* The application that is deployed on an accessible network and provides certain functionalities to a qualified group of users or to the general public on the Internet. Usually, its service interface is described through a platform-neutral description language, such as WSDL.

- *Service Provider.* The owner of the Web Services published, which also hosts these services.
- *Service Requestor.* The user of the Web Services, which invokes desired services based on their published descriptions.
- *Service Registry.* The searchable repository, where service providers can publish their Web Services and service requestors can find desired Web Services and corresponding binding information.

Since WSDL is a general-purpose, XML-based language designed to describe various Web Services, it is a perfect companion for UDDI. When a service requestor finds a Web Service that fits his or her needs, he or she could attempt to bind to that particular service using its description and invoke the service to perform a certain task. In order to invoke the service in a platform-neutral fashion, clients and servers of Web Services use SOAP binding as the foundation for communications between network endpoints.

We can use **TAUWebService** as an example. First, the travel agency union (service provider) learns from its members about the need to build a Web Service and works out its members' requirements. Next, the union implements **TAUWebService** (service) using the software and hardware platform it desires, which is .NET. Finally, it publishes its service to the Microsoft UDDI registry and provides its service description externally using WSDL.

As a member of the union that is interested in **TAUWebService**, travel agency A would look for it in the Microsoft UDDI registry and find the service description for **TAUWebService**. Travel agency A may operate on a totally different platform from the union, such as Apache/Linux. Ideally, travel agency A can adopt tools from its own platform to automatically generate a SOAP-based proxy to bind and access **TAUWebService**. If that is not possible, it can easily analyze the standard-based WSDL descriptions and generate the proxy by hand. Travel agency A may also need to incorporate authentication-related issues with SOAP message headers. As a result, travel agency A now has the ability to use the Web Service anytime, as long as it is available.

10.3.3 The State of UDDI Development Today

Microsoft and IBM provide two of the best-known UDDI registries to the Internet public. Some early adopters have advertised their Web Services in these registries. However, the UDDI standard is still evolving as Web Services are gaining more and more tractions in the computer software and service industries. .NET provides tools such as **disco.exe** to find and bind to a particular Web Service based on URI, but currently it does not provide a built-in support for UDDI.

However, Microsoft does provide a separate UDDI SDK (*uddi. microsoft.com/developer*) that provides APIs to perform all UDDI-related operations. The latest version to date is Beta 1.5.

Because Web Services can be used inside large corporations as intranet facilities, enterprise-level UDDI registries could facilitate the use of Web Services between different departments, as well as between the enterprise and its selected group of external partners. Using Web Services and UDDI provides tremendous potential in this arena as corporations can focus more on the performance and reliability of these services than security requirements.

Summary

In this chapter, we discussed how to interoperate Web Services between .NET and other software platforms. We used Apache SOAP as the example for an alternative platform. As in any interoperating endeavor, the key to success here is to establish a set of common standards and protocols. For Web Services, SOAP, XML, and WSDL provide the common ground for communications over the network.

In this chapter, we have gone through a full circle in Web Services interoperations. First, we built a Web Service **TAUWebService1** under .NET and successfully accessed it via Apache SOAP Java API. Then we built and deployed a simple Web Service using Apache SOAP, and successfully accessed it using C# code and .NET tools, which support WSDL. As the underlying technologies and standards mature, this process should become smoother and more straightforward.

Interoperating is extremely important for the future growth of Web Services. As more and more businesses and enterprises join the action, diversity of all the software and hardware platforms involved is a given. As standards like SOAP and XML gradually take center stage in distributed computing, software platforms such as .NET may become the top choice of Web programmers in the future, due to these platforms' strong support for open standards.

A Case Study:
A Distributed Web Application

*I*nternet *technology has been changing people's lifestyles and business practice models. Now, the Internet itself is experiencing a paradigm shift. It is quickly evolving from Web sites that deliver simple user interface pages to a next generation of programmable Web-based applications.*

In previous chapters, we discussed major features of the .NET technology, including ASP.NET, ADO.NET, and Web Services. Not only do these features make development of Web-based applications much easier and simpler, they also allow for more powerful, distributed information-processing systems to be built based on the Internet. In such a system, ADO.NET interfaces the data sources, ASP.NET facilitates browser-based information presentation, and Web Services deliver functional services over the Web. Furthermore, existing applications may also be integrated in this framework.

In the case study presented in this chapter, we build a Web-based distributed application for a group of travel agencies that have formed a loosely coupled consortium called Travel Agency Union, or TAU, in order to share their business opportunities. Information systems of the participant agencies are extended using .NET technology, creating an integrated system over which information can be exchanged. We call this integrated system TAU.NET. TAU.NET unites the participant agencies to form a large entity that can help agencies better serve their customers.

11.1 The TAU Business Model

Each TAU member is a travel agency that runs its business independently, providing its customers with products and services, such as flight reservations, hotel reservations, rental car reservations, and group tours and cruises. Each agency processes its business transactions using the following functions.

- *Inquiry.* Allows the agency and/or its customers to retrieve products and services information
- *Reservations.* Allows the agency and/or its customers to reserve and manipulate the transaction with desired products and services
- *Bill/Payment.* Bills the customers and acquires the payment from the customers as well as receives the invoices and makes the payment to the vendors

By joining TAU, member agencies can expand their functionality into the distributed environment of the Internet. The enhanced functions include

- *Inquiry.* A member agency may allow other member agencies to retrieve its products and services. In addition, a customer may retrieve the products and services via a single entry point, the Web site of his or her own agency.
- *Reservations.* Via the Web site of a single agency, a customer may manipulate his or her transaction with products and services of multiple TAU agencies, including reserve products and/or services, as well as update and cancel reservations.
- *Bill/Payment.* For a transaction involving multiple TAU agencies, the agency that directly interacts with the customer calculates the total cost and bills the customer. Other agencies that are involved in this transaction maintain their own accounts receivable information for the products and services they provide.

TAU.NET is a business network that provides users with a single entry point to accessing all the resources shared by its members. The business concept of TAU.NET is shown in Figure 11-1.

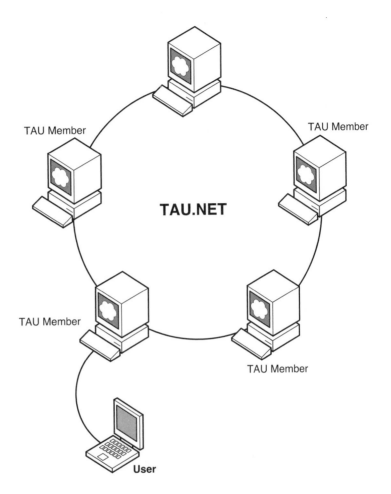

| Figure 11-1 | *Basic business concept of TAU.NET.* |

11.2 The Goals of TAU.NET System Design

11.2.1 Cell Systems

Before joining TAU, each member agency runs its business using a proprietary system of its own. We call these local agency systems the Cell Systems. The Cell Systems are heterogeneous in nature; they may be different in terms of system design, data structure, data storage, and user interface.

Each desired TAU functionality must be implemented as an extension of the Cell Systems. That is, there should be no central server in the TAU system. The Cell Systems, with the support of the TAU extensions, interact over the Internet to fulfill the goal of the distributed system. The TAU extensions are discussed in Section 11.2.4.

11.2.2 Information Exchange

Due to the heterogeneity of the Cell Systems, the distributed functions have to be supported by information exchange between their data storages. A standard data format is needed in order for the Cell Systems to share information. XML serves as an ideal vehicle to carry such information over the Internet.

11.2.3 Remote Services

In a distributed environment without a central server, each Cell System is extended to provide remote services over the Internet. These services allow the Cell System to communicate with its partner Cell Systems in order to exchange information that supports the distributed functions. Web Services are the natural choice for this purpose.

11.2.4 TAU.NET Node

A TAU.NET node is the extension for the Cell System of a participant agency, through which the Cell System joins the network of TAU. The Cell Systems communicate with each other via their TAU.NET nodes.

Communication between the TAU.NET nodes is based on Web Services. On the one hand, the TAU.NET acts as a server supplying Web methods with a standard interface. On the other hand, the TAU.NET node serves as a client supplying proxies whereby the remote Web methods can be called. In other words, the TAU.NET nodes constitute a middle tier that hooks the Cell Systems of the participant agencies so as to form an integral distributed system.

Figure 11-2 illustrates the concepts of TAU.NET Node and TAU.NET members.

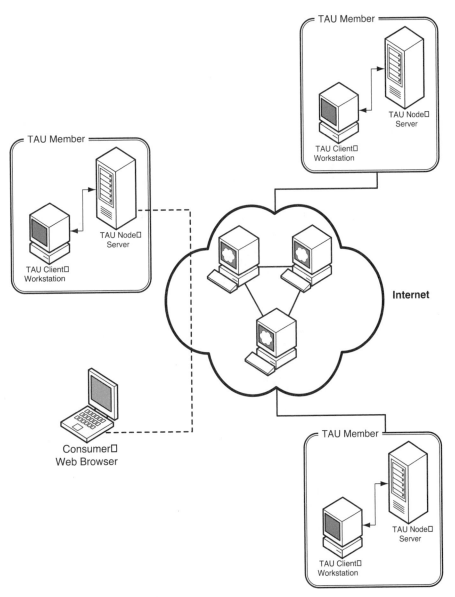

Figure 11-2   *Concept of TAU.NET.*

11.3 Architecture

11.3.1 Overview

As discussed in the previous section, a TAU.NET node is implemented as an extension for the Cell Systems under .NET Framework. It supports the communication between the Cell Systems of the participant agencies.

A TAU.NET member system is composed of a TAU.NET Node and a Cell System. The TAU.NET Node consists of two sets of components, TAU.NET Node Interface and TAU.NET Node Adaptor.

As shown in Figure 11-3, the Cell System contains three major modules, corresponding to the business functions that were discussed in Section 11.1. These are

- Inquiry module
- Reservation module
- Bill/Payment module

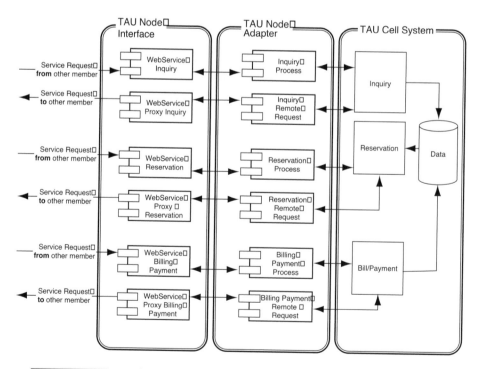

Figure 11-3   *Architecture of TAU.NET Node.*

The modules in the Cell System are linked to the corresponding components in the TAU.NET Node so that their functions can be extended to the distributed environment of TAU.NET. The TAU.NET Node Adaptor components include the Process component and Remote Request component; they talk directly to the Cell System modules. On the other hand, the TAU Node Interface components include the **Server** objects and **Client Proxy** object for the Web Services; they talk to the remote TAU.NET Nodes via the Internet.

When an agency initiates a distributed inquiry transaction, the Inquiry module of its Cell System puts a request to the Inquiry Remote Request component in its TAU.NET Node Adaptor. This component translates the user request into the appropriate request of remote Web Services. Then the Proxy object in the TAU Node Interface is instantiated so that the remote Web Services are invoked.

In order to invoke a remote Web Service, a SOAP request message is sent to the server site, where it is received by the Inquiry Server component. Calling the services or methods of the Inquiry Process component in the TAU.NET Node Adapter on the server site, the Inquiry Server component generates the query result and sends it back to the client's TAU.NET Node. In the TAU.NET Node Adapter on the server site, the Inquiry Process component interacts with the Inquiry module of the Cell System in order to fulfill the requested query.

On the client site, the Inquiry Proxy object receives the query result and passes it to the Inquiry module of the Cell System via the Inquiry Remote Request component.

Distributed Reservation and Bill/Payment transactions can be processed in a similar way. However, databases in the Cell Systems of both client site and server site need to be updated.

Components in TAU.NET Node Adaptor are implemented using ADO.NET, which supports consistent and scalable access to various data sources. Therefore, they need to be customized for different kinds of data sources so that all the discrepancies of the data sources are concealed from the TAU.NET Node Interface. That is, the requests and results are all represented as ADO.NET DataSet objects through which the TAU.NET Node Interface objects interact with the local data.

Furthermore, ADO.NET provides abundant functionality whereby the DataSet objects can be processed in a disconnected fashion. That is, DataSet objects are filled from the database; they are then manipulated in the TAU.NET Node Adaptor, and the database is finally updated if necessary. The Fill and Update operations are carried out in batch mode, but data manipulation can be performed without a database connection. That minimizes the required resource for the interaction between the TAU.NET Node Adaptor and Cell System.

In addition, business rules are also implemented in the components of TAU.NET Node Adapter. The data in DataSet objects is manipulated based on these rules.

The communication between TAU.NET Nodes is based on SOAP, and messages in XML format deliver the requests and results over the HTTP channels. Data of any type can be transferred. More specifically, the query results can be directly delivered as a DataSet object. Consequently, the components in TAU.NET Node Interface are very simple to implement; it simply provides a transparent channel for the TAU.NET Node Adaptors to their exchange DataSets.

11.3.2 Schema for Data Exchange

As we have decided, the DataSet class is used for data exchange. The DataSet can be represented in XSD Schema, which is an XML standard.

11.3.2.1 SCHEMA FOR INQUIRIES ABOUT TAU PRODUCTS AND SERVICES

Generally speaking, there are several fields in the schema that are crucial to a travel product or service:

- Unique Product/Service ID
- Category
- Destination or Location
- Rate and Unit
- Effective and Expiration date

In addition, there may be multiple line items as details and references to original sources.

The schema can be represented as DataSet, XML, and its outline in VS.NET.

See Figure 11-4 for DataSet ERD, and Figure 11-5 for XML outline and XML Schema file **TauServiceDataSet.xsd**.

The schema file is in XML format as follows.

```
<?xml version="1.0" encoding="utf-8" ?>
<xsd:schema id="TauServiceDataSet"
    targetNamespace=
      "http://tempuri.org/TauServiceDataSet.xsd"
    elementFormDefault="qualified"
    xmlns="http://tempuri.org/TauServiceDataSet.xsd"
    xmlns:xsd="http://www.w3.org/2001/XMLSchema"
    xmlns:msdata="urn:schemas-microsoft-com:xml-msdata">
  <xsd:element name="TauServiceDataSet"
      msdata:IsDataSet="true">
    <xsd:complexType>
      <xsd:choice maxOccurs="unbounded">
        <xsd:element name="TAU_SERVICE">
          <xsd:complexType>
            <xsd:sequence>
```

```xml
                <xsd:element name="SERVICEID"
                             type="xsd:string" />
                <xsd:element name="BOOKINFOID"
                             type="xsd:string"
                             minOccurs="0" />
                <xsd:element name="CATEGORYCODE"
                             type="xsd:string"
                             minOccurs="0" />
                <xsd:element name="RATE"
                             type="xsd:decimal"
                             minOccurs="0" />
                <xsd:element name="UNIT"
                             type="xsd:string"
                             minOccurs="0" />
                <xsd:element name="EFFECTIVEDATE"
                             type="xsd:dateTime"
                             minOccurs="0" />
                <xsd:element name="THROUGHDATE"
                             type="xsd:dateTime"
                             minOccurs="0" />
                <xsd:element name="LOCATIONCODE"
                             type="xsd:string"
                             minOccurs="0" />
                <xsd:element name="TAU_SERVICE_DETAIL">
                  <xsd:complexType>
                    <xsd:sequence>
                      <xsd:element name="SERVICEID"
                                   type="xsd:string" />
                      <xsd:element name="LineItemOrder"
                                   type="xsd:int" />
                      <xsd:element name="ItemDesc"
                                   type="xsd:string"
                                   minOccurs="0" />
                      <xsd:element name="ItemUrl"
                                   type="xsd:string"
                                   minOccurs="0" />
                    </xsd:sequence>
                  </xsd:complexType>
                </xsd:element>
              </xsd:sequence>
            </xsd:complexType>
          </xsd:element>
        </xsd:choice>
      </xsd:complexType>
      <xsd:unique name="TauServiceDataSetKey1"
                  msdata:PrimaryKey="true">
        <xsd:selector xpath=".//TAU_SERVICE" />
        <xsd:field xpath="SERVICEID" />
      </xsd:unique>
    </xsd:element>
  </xsd:schema>
```

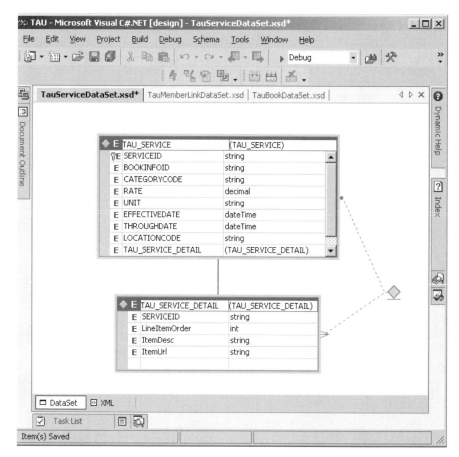

Figure 11-4   *TauServiceDataSet entity relational diagram in VS.NET.*

11.3.2.2 DATA SCHEMA FOR INQUIRIES ABOUT MEMBER SERVICES

There is no central server in TAU.NET, nor is there any central controller in the entire Internet. As far as name resolving is concerned, TAU.NET may use Internet standards. That is, member systems store each other's reference information, and messages are passed between them to synchronize this reference information. To achieve this, the members should share the basic information about their service scope, such as category and destination or location.

The schema should have basic information fields, such as member ID, member name, and service URL. One member may have one or more categories of service to provide and one or more locations or destinations to serve. Figures 11-6 and 11-7 show the schema in two views.

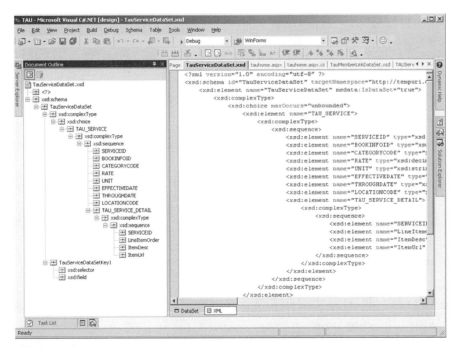

Figure 11-5   *Schema outline for **TauServiceDataSet** in VS.NET.*

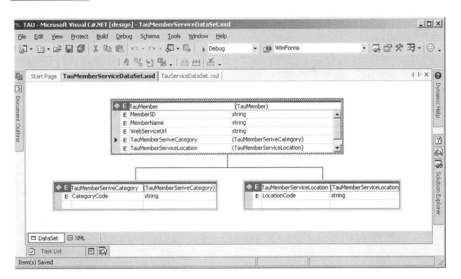

Figure 11-6   *Diagram of a member service information schema.*

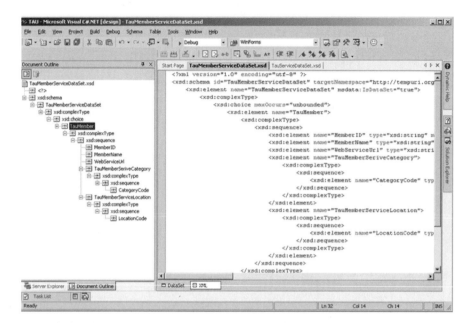

Figure 11-7   *Document outline of a member service information schema.*

In XML format, the schema file of TauMemberServiceDataSet has text as follows.

```
<?xml version="1.0" encoding="utf-8" ?>
<xsd:schema id="TauMemberServiceDataSet"
    targetNamespace=
"http://tempuri.org/TauMemberServiceDataSet.xsd"
    elementFormDefault="qualified"
    xmlns=
 "http://tempuri.org/TauMemberServiceDataSet.xsd"
    xmlns:xsd="http://www.w3.org/2001/XMLSchema"
    xmlns:msdata="urn:schemas-microsoft-com:xml-msdata">
  <xsd:element name="TauMemberServiceDataSet"
        msdata:IsDataSet="true">
    <xsd:complexType>
      <xsd:choice maxOccurs="unbounded">
        <xsd:element name="TauMember">
          <xsd:complexType>
            <xsd:sequence>
              <xsd:element name="MemberID"
                    type="xsd:string"
                    minOccurs="0" />
              <xsd:element name="MemberName"
                    type="xsd:string"
                    minOccurs="0" />
              <xsd:element name="WebServiceUrl"
```

```
            type="xsd:string"
            minOccurs="0" />
        <xsd:element
            name="TauMemberServiceCategory">
          <xsd:complexType>
            <xsd:sequence>
              <xsd:element name="CategoryCode"
                  type="xsd:string"
                  minOccurs="0" />
            </xsd:sequence>
          </xsd:complexType>
        </xsd:element>
        <xsd:element
            name="TauMemberServiceLocation">
          <xsd:complexType>
            <xsd:sequence>
              <xsd:element name="LocationCode"
                  type="xsd:string"
                  minOccurs="0" />
            </xsd:sequence>
          </xsd:complexType>
        </xsd:element>
      </xsd:sequence>
    </xsd:complexType>
  </xsd:element>
</xsd:choice>
    </xsd:complexType>
  </xsd:element>
</xsd:schema>
```

11.3.2.3 OTHER SCHEMA FOR DATA EXCHANGE

The reservation transaction information schema is shown in Figure 11-8. The service may have booking information in diverse forms based on the category or vendor. **BOOKDATA** stores the booking data based on the schema referred by **BOOKINFOID**.

The schemas for data exchange to serve Billing and Payment transactions are beyond the scope of this case study.

11.3.2.4 CLASSES FOR THE SCHEMAS

When VS.NET is used to construct the schema, the corresponding classes are generated by the tool, creating programs **TauServiceDataSet.cs**, **TauMemberService.cs**, and **TauBookDataSet.cs**. Alternatively, the classes of a schema may be created using command xsd.exe. The following commands generate the classes in TAU namespace:

```
xsd TauServiceDataSet.xsd /dataset /n:TAU
xsd TauMemberService.xsd /dataset /n:TAU
xsd TauBookDataSet.xsd /dataset /n:TAU
```

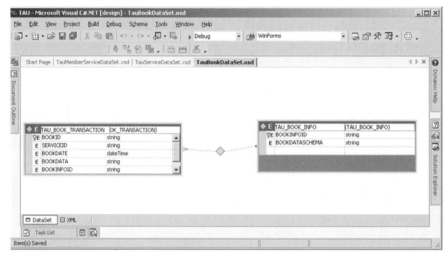

Schema for booking a service.

11.3.3 TAU.NET Node Interface

11.3.3.1 SERVER OBJECTS FOR WEB SERVICES

Having defined the schema for data exchange, we can work on setting the protocol of the Web methods for data exchange. Each member should implement all those Web methods in order to communicate with each other.

First, let's consider the Web Service for inquiries about products and services. Two criteria, category and destination or location, may be commonly used to inquire about travel services; consequently, two Web methods should be provided, as follows:

```
[WebMethod]
public TauServiceDataSet
 GetServiceDataSetByCategory(
                    String categoryCode);
[WebMethod]
public TauServiceDataSet
 GetServiceDataSetByLocation(
                    String locationCode);
```

The **categoryCode** string may be a code for information about lodging, airline tickets, or car rentals. The **locationCode** string is about the destination or location the travel agency serves.

Second, let's consider the Web Service for inquiries about member services. This method is used to get an overview of available services provided by this member. Using this information, other members can build up or refresh their own repositories for member services in TAU.NET.

```
[WebMethod]
public TAU.TauMemberServiceDataSet
 GetMemberServiceInfo ();
```

Finally, let's consider the Web Service for making reservations. Two methods are required here. One is used to get the reservation information for a specific travel service:

```
[WebMethod]
public TauBookDataSet
 GetReservationInfo(string serviceID);
```

The other one is for making a reservation on a particular service specified by a given DataSet:

```
[WebMethod]
public string
 MakeReservation (TauBookDataSet bookData);
```

All these methods can be gathered in one Web Service file, **TauService.asmx**. Figures 11-9 and 11-10 show the Web Service Description screens on Internet Explorer.

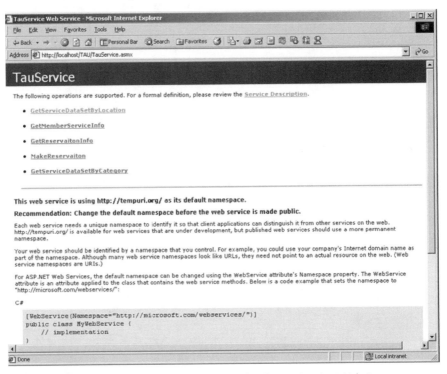

Figure 11-9   *Using a Web browser to display the **TauService** Web Service description.*

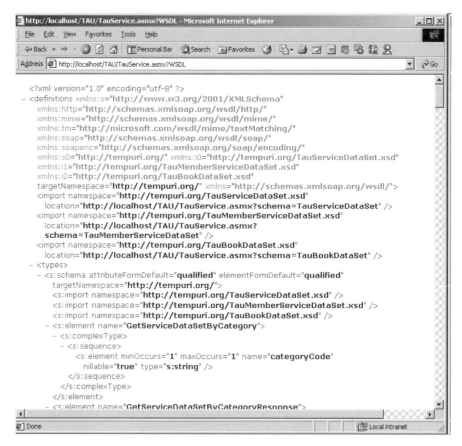

Figure 11-10   *WSDL of the TAU.NET Web Service **TauService**.*

11.3.3.2 PROXY OBJECTS FOR WEB SERVICES

The .NET utility program, wsdl.exe, can generate the Client Proxy for the TAU.NET Web Service.

The following command creates the code TauService.cs, which defines a Client Proxy class, **TauService** in the **TAU.Proxy** namespace. The Client Proxy class serves as an access point at the client site to the remote Web Services.

```
wsdl http://localhost/TAU/TauService.asmx /n:TAU.Proxy
```

Because all the members implement a Web Service with a standard interface, the same service on various member systems may be invoked by using a general-purpose Client Proxy object. In this case, the URL of the target service needs to be specified as a property of the Client Proxy object. For example, if we want to request the Web method **GetServiceDataSetByLocation** in *www.TauMember1.com*, we first need to create a new object:

```
TAU.Proxy.TauService objService;
  objService = new TAU.Proxy.TauService();
```

Second, we set its Url property value:

```
  objService.Url =
 "http://www.TauMember1.com/TAU/TauService.asmx";
```

Third, we instantiate the DataSet to receive the return:

```
  TAU.Proxy.TauServiceDataSet objDataSetTemp;
  objDataSetTemp = new TAU.Proxy.TauServiceDataSet();
```

Finally, we specify the Web method to fill the DataSet:

```
objDataSetTemp =
objService.GetServiceDataSetByLocation(
                                   "BOSTON");
```

11.4 TAU.NET Node Adaptor

Now let's consider the TAU.NET Node Adaptor in which the data is manipulated and the business rule realized.

11.4.1 TAU.NET Node Adaptor to Link Cell System Database

The following code segment is designed to implement the Web method in the Web Service **GetServiceDataSetByLocation**. We need to connect a database in the Cell System to retrieve the travel service records and detail line items according to the criteria on location.

```
[WebMethod]
public TauServiceDataSet
 GetServiceDataSetByLocation(String locationCode)
{
 TAU.TauServiceDataSet returnDataSet
         = new TAU.TauServiceDataSet();
 try
 {
  sqlConnection1.Open();
 sqlDATauServiceLocation.SelectCommand.Parameters
["@LocationCode"].Value
 = locationCode;
sqlDATauServiceDetailLocation.SelectCommand.Parameters
```

```
["@LocationCode"].Value = locationCode;
sqlDATauServiceLocation.Fill (returnDataSet,
              "TAU_SERVICE");
sqlDATauServiceDetailLocation.Fill(returnDataSet,
              "TAU_SERVICE_DETAIL");
}
catch (Exception e)
{
    returnDataSet.Reset();
     throw e;
}
finally
{
 sqlConnection1.Close();
}
 return returnDataSet;
}
```

In this code segment, **sqlConnection1**, an instance of **System. Data.SqlClient.SqlConnection**, is used to support connection to the SQL database.

SqlDATauServiceLocation is an instance of **SqlDataAdapter** that is built on the following SQL statement:

```
SELECT TAU_MEMBER.NAME AS Name,
      TAU_MEMBER.SERVICEURL AS WebServiceUrl,
      TAU_MEMBER_LOCATION.LOCATIONCODE AS Location
FROM TAU_MEMBER INNER JOIN TAU_MEMBER_LOCATION ON
TAU_MEMBER.TAUMEMBERID = TAU_MEMBER_LOCATION.TAUMEMBERID
WHERE (TAU_MEMBER_LOCATION.LOCATIONCODE = @LocationCode)
```

sqlDATauServiceDetailLocation is an instance of **SqlDataAdapter** that is based on this SQL script:

```
SELECT TAU_SERVICE_DETAIL.SERVICEID AS SERVICEID,
 TAU_SERVICE_DETAIL.LineItemOrder
                         AS LineItemOrder,
 TAU_SERVICE_DETAIL.ItemDesc AS ItemDesc,
 TAU_SERVICE_DETAIL.ItemUrl AS ItemUrl
FROM TAU_SERVICE_DETAIL INNER JOIN TAU_SERVICE ON
 TAU_SERVICE_DETAIL.SERVICEID = TAU_SERVICE.SERVICEID
WHERE (TAU_SERVICE.LOCATIONCODE = @LocationCode)
```

In this simple case, the implementation of the TAU.NET Node Adaptor components is embedded in the implementation of the Web method. Should applications become more complex, the TAU.NET Node Adaptor components should be implemented as separated classes and the Web method should access the data via its instances.

11.4.2 TAU.NET Node Adaptor to Serve a Web Page

In the previous section, we built a TAU.NET Node Adaptor to produce a DataSet containing records about travel service items by retrieving a relational database on a Cell System. Here, we implement another TAU.NET Node Adaptor as a client to request the Web method. This adapter is used from an ASP.NET page, which means the DataSet returning the Web Service would be served to a Web server page and Web browser eventually.

The ASP.NET page is designed as shown in Figure 11-11. We have a master DataGrid and a detail DataGrid. When the Search button is clicked, we load the DataSet for those DataGrid via the Web Service.

The following code is for the button click:

```
private void buttonLoad_Click(object sender,
                    System.EventArgs e)
    {
    objTauServiceDataSet = new TAU.TauServiceDataSet();
    this.LoadDataSet(this.locationCode.Text);
    this.masterDataGrid.SelectedIndex = -1;
    this.masterDataGrid.DataBind();
    this.detailDataGrid.Visible = false;
    Application["objTauServiceDataSet"] =
        this.objTauServiceDataSet;
    }
```

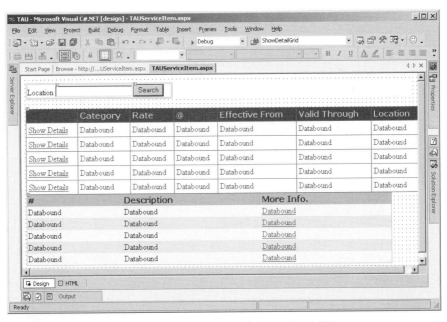

Figure 11-11   *Design of the ASP.NET page showing TAU.NET service item information.*

In this code, **this.LoadDataSet(this.locationCode.Text)** is designed to load the DataSet via the Web Service.

```
public void LoadDataSet(string locationCode)
{
TAU.Proxy.TauService objService;
objService = new TAU.Proxy.TauService();
objService.Url="http://localhost/TAU/TauService.asmx";
TAU.Proxy.TauServiceDataSet objDataSetTemp;
objDataSetTemp = new TAU.Proxy.TauServiceDataSet();
try
{
objDataSetTemp =
objService.GetServiceDataSetByLocation(
                                    locationCode );
}
catch (System.Exception eFillDataSet)
{
// Add exception handling code here.
   throw eFillDataSet;
}
try
{
// Merge the records that were just pulled from the data store
into the main dataset
objTauServiceDataSet.Merge(objDataSetTemp);
}
catch (System.Exception eLoadMerge)
{
    // Add exception handling code here
    throw eLoadMerge;
}
}
```

Once the selection changes on the master DataGrid, we show the corresponding detail by following code logic:

```
private void masterDataGrid_SelectedIndexChanged(
        object sender, System.EventArgs e)
{
    this.ShowDetailGrid();
}
private void ShowDetailGrid()
{
if ((this.masterDataGrid.SelectedIndex != -1))
```

```
{
    System.Data.DataView parentRows;
    System.Data.DataView childRows;
    System.Data.DataRowView currentParentRow;
    this.objTauServiceDataSet =
((TAU.TauServiceDataSet)
  (Application["objTauServiceDataSet"]));
    parentRows = new DataView();
    parentRows.Table =
    this.objTauServiceDataSet.Tables["TAU_SERVICE"];
    currentParentRow=parentRows
[this.masterDataGrid.SelectedIndex];
childRows = currentParentRow.CreateChildView(
        "TAU_SERVICE_TAU_SERVICE_DETAIL");
this.detailDataGrid.DataSource = childRows;
this.detailDataGrid.DataBind();
this.detailDataGrid.Visible = true;
}
else
{
 this.detailDataGrid.Visible = false;
}
}
```

Finally, we get the page shown in Figure 11-12.

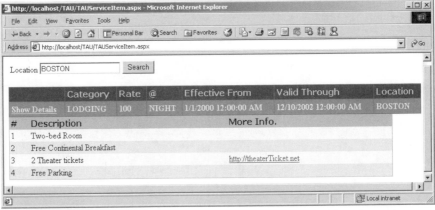

Figure 11-12 *ASP.NET Web page showing the result retrieved from the Web Service.*

Summary

In this chapter, we looked at a Web-based application that uses .NET Framework technology, including ADO.NET, Web Services, and ASP.NET. This application has challenging requirements; it would be a nightmare for developers using the old technology.

As can be seen, our approach is really clean and simple. The distributed functions are implemented by a lightweight extension; no substantial changes are required to each Cell System. .NET Framework and the Internet provide the infrastructure for information exchange. All these characteristics facilitate a new paradigm for development of distributed information processing.

In our discussion, we have just dealt with very basic aspects of systems like this. There are a number of open issues yet to be addressed, including mechanisms for handling distributed transactions, an interesting topic for research and development.

Web Programming Fundamentals

*T*he Web is increasingly important as a means of deploying not only information content but also complete applications. The great advantage of the Web is ease of deployment. All that is needed on the client computer is a Web browser; no large client EXEs and DLLs need to be installed and maintained. Many companies are moving toward this style of application, and in the future doubtless many more will do so.

This appendix surveys the most important technologies for developing Web applications, culminating with the use of COM+ to develop three-tiered distributed applications. The basic architecture is the same. The two main differences are that the presentation tier is a thin client hosted in a Web browser, and the communications protocol between the client and the middle tier is HTTP in place of DCOM.

In keeping with our endeavor to make this book as self-contained as possible, we do not assume a prior background in Web application development. We explain all the basic concepts. Naturally in order to implement real applications you will need to dig deeper, but this appendix should be enough to give you a foundation in Web programming.

A.1 Classical Web Technology

The Internet originated in the early 1970s as an outgrowth of the ARPAnet, created for the U.S. Defense Department and intended as a highly robust network connecting military research establishments. Through funding by the National Science Foundation it was extended to academic institutions, then commercial organizations became connected also.

The explosive growth of the Internet started in 1993 with the appearance of the first Web servers and the creation of the World Wide Web. The Web is a hypertext-based communications system allowing clients to access rich information (text, graphics, audio, etc.) from servers distributed across the Internet using multiple protocols. The Web was developed at CERN, the European Particle Physics Laboratory (*www.cern.ch*), as a new kind of information system enabling researchers to share information during a project. It was largely the work on one man, Tim Berners-Lee, who remains highly active. Hypertext technology was used to link together a web of documents that could be traversed in any manner to find information. The Web was based on open specifications using Internet protocols with free sample implementations.

The role of standards in Web technology cannot be overemphasized. The Web provides the glue that connects diverse servers and clients all over the world. These servers and clients run on many different computer platforms. The only way they can be sure of being able to connect with each other is by adhering to agreed-upon standard protocols. There are three important standards in the classical Web:

- HTML (Hypertext Markup Language) for documents distributed over the Web
- HTTP (Hypertext Transfer Protocol) as the communications protocol for Web clients to talk to Web servers
- CGI (Common Gateway Interface) as the protocol for Web servers to talk to applications programs

A.1.1 Hypertext and HTML

Hypertext is a nonlinear way of arranging information. Information resides on pages. A link leads directly to a different location on the same or on a different page, possibly on another Web site somewhere else in the world. The destination of a link is called an *anchor*. HTML is a language for describing hypertext documents that can be accessed over the Web. HTML was invented by Tim Berners-Lee as part of his creation of the World Wide Web at CERN. It is based on the earlier standard markup language SGML.

HTML documents are plain ASCII text documents that can be created by any text editor. An *element* is a fundamental component of a document.

Examples of elements are heads, paragraphs, and lists. *Tags* are used to denote the various elements in an HTML document. A tag consists of a left angle bracket (<), a tag name, and a right angle bracket (>). Tags are usually paired, with the end tag looking just like the beginning tag but with a slash (/):

```
<H1> Sample first-level heading </H1>
```

Some elements have attributes that include additional information within a start tag:

```
<P ALIGN=CENTER> A centered paragraph </P>
```

HTML is not case-sensitive (except for some escape sequences).

Here is the complete HTML for a hypothetical personal home page, based on an example Microsoft used to distribute with the Personal Web Server for Windows 95:

```
<HTML>
<head>
<title>
   My Home Page
</title>
</head>
<body>

<h2 align=center>
    Bob's Home Page
</h2>
Welcome to my web server running on Windows 2000.
<p>
<hr>
Here are some of my interests:
<ul>
<li> Movies
<li> Reading
<li> Computers
</ul>
<hr>
Here are some links to some other interesting Web sites:
<p>
<a href="http://www.microsoft.com">www.microsoft.com</a>
<p>
<a href="http://www.objectinnovations.com">www.objectinnova-
tions.com</a>

</body>
</html>
```

A.1.1.1 UNIFORM RESOURCE LOCATORS

The Web uses Uniform Resource Locators (URLs) to specify the location of files (or other data) on servers throughout the Internet. The URL specifies the access method, the address of the server, and the address of the file (or other data):

```
scheme://host.domain [:port]/path/filename
```

Common schemes are

file	a file on your local system
ftp	a file on an FTP server
http	a file on a Web server

The port number can be usually omitted (http servers normally use 80, the default).

A.1.1.2 WEB BROWSERS

A Web browser is a client program that can access and display content from the Web. It incorporates communications software for retrieving information using various protocols such as HTTP. It reads and displays HTML pages. If a browser does not know how to interpret a particular tag it usually just ignores it.

The Web browser is what makes HTML come alive. Instead of plain text, the tags enable many kinds of visual and even nonvisual elements, including sound. Currently the most popular Web browsers are from Microsoft and Netscape. Figure A-1 illustrates how the HTML code in our example would be displayed inside Microsoft Internet Explorer. Note that Internet Explorer can display a local file on hard disk as well as one that has been fetched over the Internet.

A.1.1.3 HTML FORMS

The simplest kinds of HTML pages display information. This in itself is tremendously valuable, because of the ease with which a browser can enable you to surf the Web, retrieving information from all over the world. But you can do more. HTML provides a forms capability, allowing the user to enter data, which is sent to the Web server as part of the request. The Web server can then execute a program (by means we discuss later) and send a customized response back to the user.

As an illustration the following simple form has two text controls and one button. The user can enter the name of a server (where the price data is

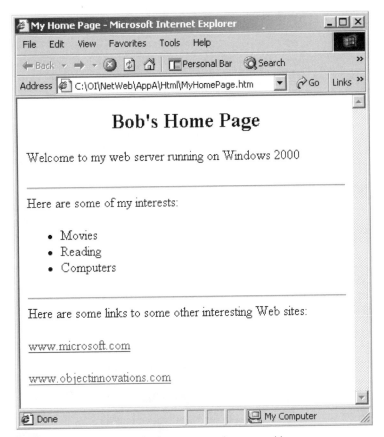

Web browser displaying a simple personal home page.

stored) and an item. Clicking the Get Price button will then send this information to the Web server, which will run a program to look up the price of the item and return a response back to the client. Figure A-2 illustrates how this form would appear in a browser. (You won't be able to run it until later, after we have set up the PriceList.Price COM component that is used in the background.)

Here is the HTML code that will display this form:

```
<!-- price.htm -->
<HTML>
<HEAD>
<TITLE>Price of an Item</TITLE>
</HEAD>
<BODY>
```

```
<FORM METHOD="POST" ACTION="price.asp">
Server
<INPUT TYPE = "text" NAME="txtServer">
<P>
Item
<INPUT TYPE = "text" NAME="txtItem" VALUE = "dog bone">
<P>
<INPUT TYPE = "submit" NAME="btnGetPrice" VALUE = "Get Price">
</FORM>

</BODY>
</HTML>
```

The parameters of the **<FORM>** tag are used to specify how and where to send the form results. **METHOD = "POST"** indicates that the data will be sent in a data block instead of URL parameters. **ACTION="price.asp"** indicates the URL to catch the form results. Because price.asp and price.htm are located on the same server and in the same directory, other URL qualifiers are omitted.

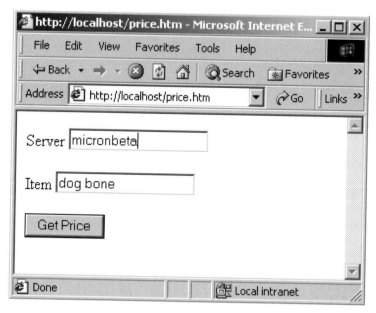

Figure A-2   *An HTML form for looking up price information.*

A.1.2 Internet Servers

An Internet server provides the user with the ability to publish information on the Internet or an intranet. A Web server publishes HTML pages for access over the Web using HTTP. Internet servers can also provide information using other protocols, such as FTP and Gopher. While FTP is still very important as an efficient file transfer protocol, Gopher is fading in importance, and later versions of Microsoft Internet servers do not support it. An Internet server also provides for other services, such as security, logging, and administration. Microsoft's latest product is Internet Information Services (IIS) 5.0, which comes bundled with Windows 2000 and Windows XP.

A Web server responds to requests from Web browsers by delivering an HTML document (or some other document type such as plain text). There are three kinds of HTML response pages:

- A static HTML page is prepared in advance of the request.
- A dynamic HTML page is created dynamically by the server in response to the request. The server may execute a CGI script or an Internet Server API (ISAPI) DLL. Active Server Pages (ASPs) are an important Microsoft technology for generating dynamic HTML pages. We discuss CGI, ISAPI, and ASP later in this appendix.
- A directory listing will be sent back if the server is configured to support directory browsing, so there is no default home page.

A.1.3 HTTP

HTTP is used by Web clients to communicate with Web servers. A simple request will just ask for an HTML page (or other document type). A more complex request can submit form data gathered by an HTML form. HTTP uses plain text. HTTP by default uses port 80. HTTP is a stateless protocol. The connection between client and server is terminated after each response from the server. An HTTP session contains a header, a method, and request data.

The interaction of a Web browser and Web server is elegant in its simplicity. The client makes a request and gets a response. The interaction is over. The next request, perhaps initiated by a link in an HTML page, may be to another Web server. There is a request and a response. And so on. Figure A-3 illustrates this simple architecture.

| Figure A-3 | *Web client talks to Web server using HTTP.* |

A.1.3.1 HTTP HEADERS

A request header sent by the client to the server specifies the method used for the request and the capabilities of the client (e.g., the different kinds of file types that the client supports). A response header sent by the server to the client provides the status of the transaction (e.g., success or failure) and the type of data that is being sent.

Here is an example of a request header where the client requests a static (pre-existing) page from the server using the HTTP GET method.

```
GET /bylaws.htm HTTP/1.0
Accept: text/htm
Accept: text/plain
Accept: image/gif
...
User-Agent: Mozilla/2.0
From: bob@www.smallcompany.com
          --- blank line ---
```

Here is how this request is parsed by the server:

1. Client issues GET request for bylaws.htm via HTTP version 1.0.
2. List of acceptable MIME (Multipurpose Internet Mail Extension) types.
3. User's browser is compatible with the HTTP Mozilla/2.0. (The name was coined by Netscape as a combination of Mosaic and Godzilla. Netscape saw their browser as a "Mosaic killer." Microsoft emulated Netscape, so their requests would not be rejected by a Web server expecting to hear from a Netscape client.)
4. User is identified in the From field.

A.1.3.2 WEB SERVER RESPONSE

Here is a typical response from a Web server:

```
HTTP/1.0 200 OK
Date: Tuesday, 07-Aug-01 20:55:00 EST
Server: IIS/5.0
MIME-version: 1.0
Last-modified: Monday, 02-Aug-01 7:15:00 EST
```

```
Content-type: text/plain
Content-length: 3500
        --- blank line ---
<data goes here>
```

And here is how this response should be parsed:

1. Server agrees to use HTTP 1.0 and sends success code 200.
2. Date is sent, and server is identified as IIS version 5.0.
3. MIME version 1.0 is being used.
4. The MIME type is specified in Content-type. We are using plain text.
5. Byte count of data is given.
6. The data itself follows after a blank line.

A.1.3.3 HTTP METHODS

The HTTP protocol has just four different methods that the client can choose. The most common are GET and POST.

GET   Get an HTML page and send any form results by concatenating onto the URL.

POST   Send form results separately as part of the data body rather than by concatenating onto the URL.

PUT   Concatenate form results to the target URL specified in the ACTION parameter of the **<FORM>** tag. It has a 2K limit.

HEAD   Request transaction status and header information only (used typically for diagnostics).

A.1.4 CGI

CGI is a standard for external gateway programs to interface to Web servers. Gateway programs are often called scripts and can be written in scripting languages such as Perl as well as in ordinary languages like C. A script is a stand-alone program and runs in a separate process. CGI specifies the mechanisms for scripts to receive and send data to the Web server. CGI uses environment variables, such as **QUERY_STRING**. The server can send data to the script through standard input. The script can send data to the server through standard output.

     The fact that CGI programs run in a separate process makes them much less efficient than other mechanisms and raises a major impediment to scalability. We examine other more efficient mechanisms later in this appendix. But CGI is a standard supported by all Web servers and is conceptually easy to understand, so we study it briefly to gain a basic understanding of the principles of Web servers.

A.1.4.1 A DYNAMIC WEB PAGE

In place of requesting a pre-existing Web page, a client may specify a program in a URL. The Web server recognizes from the URL that a program is to be called in place of delivering static data. It calls the program. The program and the Web server work cooperatively to create the Web page, which is returned to the client via HTTP.

In our example the client asks for the program datetime.exe to determine the date and time and to return the values on a Web page. Here is a hypothetical request header:

```
GET /scripts/datetime.exe HTTP/1.0
Accept: text/htm
Accept: text/plain
Accept: image/gif
...
User-Agent: Mozilla/2.0
From: bob@www.smallcompany.com
        --- blank line ---
```

The Web server arranges for the following server-side processing.

1. The Web server receives the HTTP request and calls the program date-time.exe indicated in the URL.

2. The datetime.exe program writes a header giving the content type it will return, a blank line, and then the data.

```
/* datetime.c */

#include <time.h>
#include <stdio.h>

void main()
{
    char dbuffer [9];
    char tbuffer [9];
    printf("content-type: text/plain\n");
    printf("\n");
    _strdate( dbuffer );
    printf( "The current date is %s \n", dbuffer );
    _strtime( tbuffer );
    printf( "The current time is %s \n", tbuffer );
}
```

3. The Web server creates the complete HTTP response.

```
HTTP/1.0 200 OK
...
Content-type: text/plain
...
        --- blank line ---
The current date is 08/04/01
The current time is 14:51:32
```

A.1.4.2 MORE ABOUT HTML FORMS

HTML provides a **<FORM>** tag that can be used to collect information from a client and specify an action to be performed by a server.

```
<FORM ACTION = "url"> ... </FORM>
```

The attributes are:

- **ACTION** gives the URL that can specify a script to be executed on the server.
- **METHOD** is the HTTP method, such as GET or POST.
- **ENCTYPE** specifies the encoding of the form contents, and is only used for **POST**. At present there is only one ENCTYPE defined:

```
application/x-www-form-urlencoded
```

Here is a sample HTML form (getdate.htm) that provides a button that can be used for invoking the datetime.exe program on the server.

```
<!-- getdate.htm -->
<HTML>
<HEAD>
<TITLE>Get Date</TITLE>
</HEAD>
<BODY>

<FORM ACTION="scripts\datetime.exe" METHOD="POST">
<P>
 <INPUT TYPE=SUBMIT VALUE="Get Date and Time">
</FORM>

</BODY>
</HTML>
```

A.2 An Internet Programming Testbed

At this point it would be a good idea to make sure that you have a good test-bed for exercising Web applications. There are a lot of pieces that have to be running for such an application to work! Rather than following a big bang approach and going for broke, we suggest you safeguard your bank account and exercise some simple Internet functionality first. These examples should also help solidify your understanding of the Internet fundamentals that we have been discussing.

A.2.1 Internet Explorer 6.0

Internet Explorer 6.0 comes bundled with all versions of Windows 2000 and is installed automatically when you install the operating system. It is integral to Windows, beginning with Window 98. It will start out as your default browser, and if you double-click on an .htm file on your local hard disk, you should find that Internet Explorer comes up and opens that file. As a test, open the file getdate.htm discussed in the previous section. You can use this form to test a CGI script. (You will not be able to test the script until later, and you will need to access the HTML page using HTTP rather than as a local file.) Figure A-4 illustrates what you should see. You will need to do some configuration of your browser to allow the use of an unsigned ActiveX control. We discuss that later.

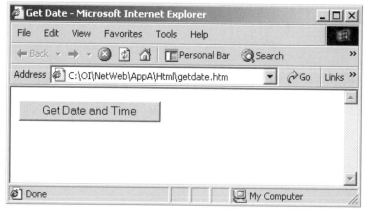

Figure A-4   *An HTML form for testing a CGI script.*

A.2.2 Internet Information Services 5.0

Microsoft's Web server is provided by Internet Information Services 5.0. (The IIS acronym used to stand for Internet Information Server.) IIS is bundled with Windows 2000 Server and above, and is installed by default. IIS is administered by another MMC snap-in. Bring up this administration tool from Start | Programs | Administrative Tools | Internet Services Manager. The first thing to check is that the Web Service is running. In the administration tool click on the name of your server under Internet Information Services. You should see a list of four services, all running, including Default Web Site, which has port 80, as you would expect. You can start, stop, and pause from toolbar buttons or by right-clicking the service you are interested in. (You can also start and stop the services from the Computer Management snap-in in Windows 2000. Click on Administrative Tools | Computer Management | Services and Applications | Internet Information Services.) Figure A-5 illustrates the running services.

A.2.2.1 PUBLISHING TO YOUR WEB SITE

You publish to your Web site by copying files to the folder Inetpub\wwwroot, which should be in the partition on which Windows 2000 is installed. By default the Web server will look in the wwwroot directory for files to send back to the requesting browser. As a first example, copy MyHomePage.htm to wwwroot. You should now be able to access this file from anyplace on your LAN by using the URL

```
http://yourservername/myhomepage.htm
```

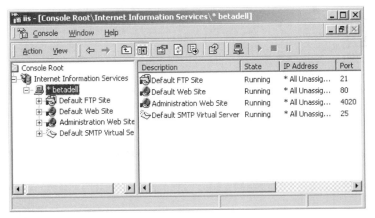

Figure A-5　　*You administer IIS from Internet Services Manager snap-in.*

where you put in the actual name of your server computer. If you are running Internet Explorer on the same machine as your server, you could use the following URL:

```
http://localhost/myhomepage.htm
```

where **localhost** is used as the name of the server.

Rather than risk disrupting any files in wwwroot, we will do all our work from now on in subfolders. Create a folder called **club**, then put **getdate.htm** under it. Copy the folders **club** and **Html** to **wwwroot**. From the browser you could give a complete path down to the particular file, such as

```
http://localhost/html/myhomepage.htm
```

But it will be more convenient to change the home directory in the IIS administration program. We will change the home directory to **club**. Right-click on Default Web Site and choose Properties from the context menu. Select the Home Directory tab. Specify **club** as a subdirectory in the local path. See Figure A-6. Note the Directory Browsing checkbox. Don't check it now, but we will try that option shortly.

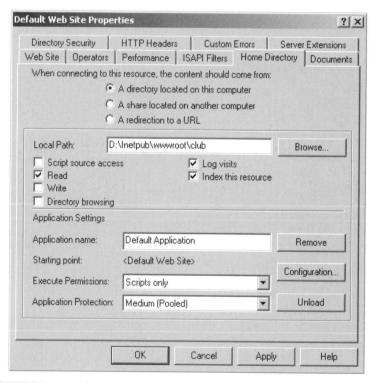

Figure A-6   *Specifying a different home directory.*

Now go back to your browser, and this time just type in the name of your computer, without any specific file:

```
http://localhost/
```

You are brought to the home page of the Von Neumann Computer Club. See Figure A-7.

How did that happen? This happens all the time. You often just type in the name of a site, not a specific file (e.g., http://www.microsoft.com). All you need to do is name a page in the home directory default.htm. That is exactly what we did in the club directory, as you can easily verify.

A.2.2.2 DIRECTORY BROWSING

When we were talking about the responses a Web server can make to a request, we said there are three different types. The first is a static content

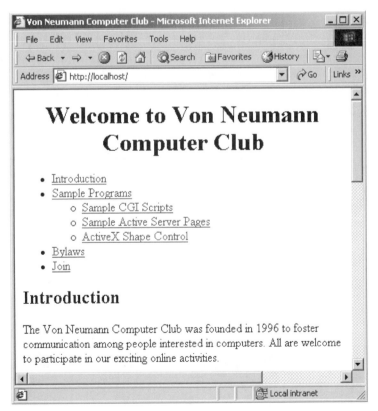

Figure A-7 *Navigating to a default home page.*

page, typically in HTML. The second is a dynamic page generated by a program, such as a CGI script. The third possibility is a directory listing. This can be enabled in the administration program, as was illustrated in Figure A-6. Go back to the home directory properties, change the home directory to be the html subdirectory, and enable directory browsing. Now visit the following URL:

```
http://localhost/
```

There is no default.htm file, but directory browsing is enabled, so you get back a directory browsing with links to files (and subdirectories, if any). See Figure A-8.

This option will be convenient for navigating among the various test pages—you can just click the link. Normally you would not want to enable directory browsing in a commercial site.

A.2.2.3 RUNNING CGI SCRIPTS

Now let's run some CGI scripts. Copy the EXE files datetime.exe and home-page.exe to Inetpubs\Scripts. First open getdate.htm in the browser and click the button. You should now have the datetime.exe script executed, and the result returned to your browser, as shown in Figure A-9. Note that you could get the same result by directly entering the URL:

```
http://localhost/scripts/datetime.exe
```

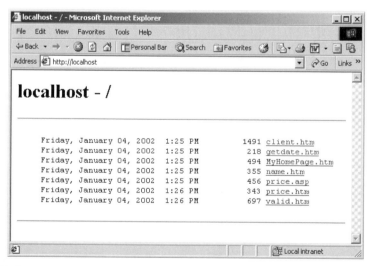

Figure A-8   *Directory browsing has been enabled.*

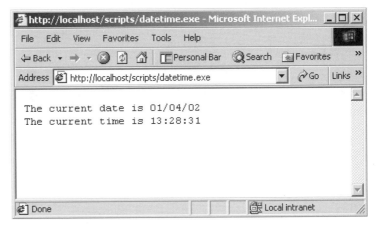

Results from running a CGI script.

Next we will run the other script by opening the page name.htm. This example is a little more interesting. A simple form is displayed where you can enter a name. Try entering the name "John" and click the Submit button. You will now see a customized home page come up, with John's name in it, as shown in Figure A-10.

The CGI program wrote the HTML text to standard output, so that the Web server could compose a complete HTTP response header to send to the browser. You can inspect the course code in AppA\homepage\ homepage.cpp. The code is a little involved. It has to retrieve the information

Figure A-10   *A customized home page created by a CGI script.*

from the form sent by the browser. The CGI protocol calls for this information to be passed via environment variables. We won't go through the details, because soon we will be using ASP, which is *much* easier.

Our purpose in presenting these examples is to show the basic mechanism of a Web server in its simplest guise (simple from the Web server perspective, not for the poor Web programmer). The architecture is illustrated in Figure A-11. The Web client issues a request via HTTP to a Web server, possibly passing information from a form. The Web server passes this information on to a Web program, using the CGI protocol. The Web program creates part of the response, which it passes back to the Web server. The Web server completes the response header and sends the complete response to the client.

If you try entering a complete name, like John Smith, you will see something funny displayed in the page that comes back: "John+Smith's home page." This is part of special encoding that HTTP does. If you are writing at the raw CGI level, you have to deal with it. Since we are not, we won't go into the details.

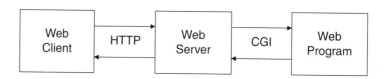

| **Figure A-11** | *Architecture of a dynamic page being created by a Web program.* |

A.3 Microsoft Web Technologies

Microsoft emerged from nowhere on the Internet a few years ago to become one of the major players. They really turned the company on a dime and embraced the new computing model. Microsoft introduced many new technologies of its own for developing Internet-based applications. If you plan to develop your own Internet applications using Microsoft tools you need to be familiar with their core Internet technologies, which we survey in this section. There are many specialized products, such as Site Server and Commerce Server, which we do not cover. Our focus is on the fundamentals, laying the groundwork for a discussion of applying COM+ to Web application development in the last section.

A.3.1 Microsoft Client-Side Web Technologies

Microsoft's original focus was on the client, as was the initial focus of Java. In both cases the objective was to enhance the client-side environment in various ways and to offload some processing from the server. Both initiatives have proved much more difficult to carry out in practice than was anticipated. The problem comes from the greatest strength of the Web—its universality. There are many different Web browsers, and an effective client-side technology should work in all of them, in order to attain universal reach. But that is impossible, because some users still use old browsers. The only common denominator is plain vanilla HTML.

An important distinction in the design of a Web-based application is whether it is to be deployed on the Internet or on an intranet. The latter is a network within a company based on Internet protocols, but with all the clients within the company, so the company has control over both what is deployed on the server and what is deployed on the client. In contrast, on the Internet there are outside clients over which the company has no control. For example, a company may choose to use an Internet application because it wants external users to be able to access its Web site, learn about its products, and hopefully become customers. It would be self-defeating to employ some specialized client-side technology that only some clients would be able to use. On the other hand, an application to support its salespeople in the field could rely on client-side technology, because all its salespeople could be equipped with laptops that have the proper software installed.

Although an application may be intended for an intranet, putting in dependencies on its always being an intranet application limits its flexibility. If the application is an Internet application from the start, new users can be easily accommodated. There is much more flexibility. We use the phrase "Web application" to mean both Internet and intranet applications.

Although the server side is emerging as more important, we begin with a discussion of client-side technologies. This order matches the historical development, and certain client technologies such as scripting apply also to the server.

We are starting to see renewed interest on client-side technologies such as DHTML (Dynamic HTML), because there are significant intrinsic benefits from doing some work on the client and presenting a richer user interface, and there will be pressure in the industry to converge on some universal standards.

A.3.1.1 SCRIPTING

In some cases it is extremely useful to do some processing on the client, for example in validating input fields in an HTML form. How many times have you filled out a form on the Web and made a mistake, which you did not discover until after the form was submitted to the server and then bounced back to you? Wouldn't it be better to do simple validation on the client before submitting it to the server? Client-side scripting is ideal for this kind of job.

The basic idea is very simple. Events like clicking a button invoke a handler function. An object model gives you access to data that is entered in the form. Your script code in the handler function can do necessary validation, and then, if valid, submit the request under program control. The following file valid.htm provides an example. Access this file in Internet Explorer from the Web site on your local host, enter an invalid date, and click Submit. You should get an error message. See Figure A-12. If you submit a valid date, your request should be submitted to the server. (The response is the current date and time—it has nothing to do with the date you entered—this program is only a demo.)

Here is the code. It should be largely self-explanatory. Note that the code is placed inside HTML comments, so that a browser that does not understand VBScript will simply ignore it and not display something funny to the user.

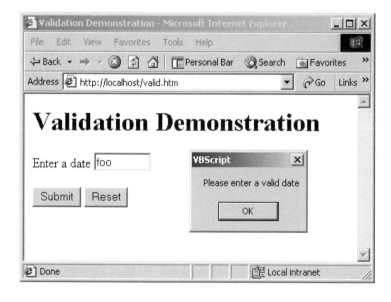

Figure A-12   *Validating a form on the client side.*

```
<!-- valid.htm -->
<HTML>
<HEAD>
<TITLE>Validation Demonstration</TITLE>

<SCRIPT LANGUAGE="VBScript">
<!--
Sub btnSubmit_OnClick
  Dim form
  Set form = Document.Form1
  If IsDate(form.txtName.Value) Then
      MsgBox "Date is valid"
      form.Submit
  Else
      MsgBox "Please enter a valid date"
  End If
End Sub
-->
</SCRIPT>
</HEAD>
<BODY>

<H1>Validation Demonstration</H1>
<FORM NAME = "Form1" ACTION="scripts\datetime.exe"
METHOD="POST"
    ENCTYPE="application/x-www-form-urlencoded">
<P>
Enter a date <INPUT NAME="txtName" VALUE="" SIZE=8>
<P>
 <INPUT NAME="btnSubmit" TYPE=BUTTON VALUE="Submit">
 <INPUT TYPE=RESET VALUE="Reset">
</FORM>

</BODY>
</HTML>
```

A.3.1.2 VBSCRIPT AND JAVASCRIPT

For convenience, all of our scripting examples are in VBScript. Since VBScript is a subset of Visual Basic, the syntax is widely known. We use Visual Basic extensively in this book, so examples in VBScript should be readily understood.

In real life you should seriously consider using JavaScript on the client, because it is more standard. In particular JavaScript will run in both Microsoft and Netscape Web browsers. You should stay away from advanced features, which are supported differently.

A.3.1.3 ACTIVEX CONTROLS

ActiveX controls are an especially rich kind of COM component. They plug into a client development environment. A Web browser ActiveX control can very easily create a Web browser application using Visual Basic. It is almost as easy using Visual C++. Like all COM components an ActiveX control is language neutral and can be used in many languages.

The great thing about ActiveX controls is that they plug right into your development environment and can be used by an application programmer just like built-in controls. No knowledge of COM is required. Thousands of ActiveX controls are available from third-party vendors.

The way they play in Web applications is through a special **<OBJECT>** tag in HTML. Using this tag, you can place an ActiveX control (indeed any COM object) in an HTML page. The CLSID (Class ID) is used to identify the control. You can call methods and set properties using scripting language. Here is a sample HTML page with a Shape Preview control inserted.

```
<!-- client.htm -->
<HTML>
<HEAD>
<TITLE>ActiveX Control Demo</TITLE>
</HEAD>
<BODY>

<H2>ActiveX Control Demo<BR>
</H2>
<script language = "vbscript">
<!--
sub NewShape
    if btnShape.Item(0).Checked then
        txtShape.Value = "Rectangle"
        Shape1.ShapeType = 0
    elseif btnShape.Item(1).Checked then
        txtShape.Value = "Ellipse"
        Shape1.ShapeType = 1
    else
        txtShape.Value = "No selection"
    end if
end sub

sub cmbColor_onChange
    if cmbColor.selectedIndex = 0 then
        txtColor.Value = "Red"
        Shape1.ForeColor = &H0000FF
    elseif cmbColor.selectedIndex = 1 then
        txtColor.Value = "Blue"
        Shape1.ForeColor = &HFF0000
```

```
        else
            txtColor.Value = "No selection"
        end if
    end sub

-->
</script>
<P>
Select a shape and a color<BR>
<P>
Shape: <INPUT TYPE="RADIO" NAME="btnShape"
    VALUE="Rectangle" OnClick="NewShape">Rectangle
<INPUT TYPE="RADIO" NAME="btnShape"
    VALUE="Ellipse" OnClick="NewShape">Ellipse
<P>
Color: <SELECT NAME="cmbColor" >
<OPTION SELECTED VALUE="Red">Red
<OPTION VALUE="Blue">Blue</SELECT>        <BR>

<P>
Your selection is shown via text boxes<BR>
<P>
Shape: <INPUT NAME="txtShape" VALUE="" MAXLENGTH="25" SIZE=25>
<P>
Color: <INPUT NAME="txtColor" VALUE="" MAXLENGTH="25" SIZE=25>

<P>
Your selection is shown via an ActiveX Control<BR>
<P>

<object id ="Shape1" width=100 height=50
    classid="clsid:B1028D2C-35A7-11D1-A01B-00A024D06632"
    codebase="http://localhost/shape.dll"
>
</object>

</BODY>
</HTML>
```

To run this demo, first build the Shape Preview control, which will register it. Then you can open up client.htm in Internet Explorer (either locally or through the Web site on your local host). Through radio buttons and a drop-down list box you can set the shape and color of the control, which will be shown in both text boxes and live by the control itself.

A.3.1.4 SAFETY CONFIGURATION IN INTERNET EXPLORER

If you have the default settings in Internet Explorer, you will get an error message when you try to set any of the control properties, such as when you click the Rectangle radio button. Figure A-13 shows an error message announcing that your security settings prohibit running an "unsafe" ActiveX control.

To change the settings in Internet Explorer 6.0 so that you can run the control, go to the menu Tools | Internet Options. Select the Security tab. Click the Custom Level button, and in the dialog that comes up choose the Prompt radio button for the first three settings on ActiveX controls:

- Download signed ActiveX controls
- Download unsigned ActiveX controls
- Initialize and script ActiveX controls not marked as safe.

See Figure A-14.

Now go back to the demo. When you try to set one of the properties, you will receive a warning message box, not a fatal error. You can choose to let the scripts run. Do so. You should now be able to set the shape and color, and the shape and color chosen will be reflected visually in the control, as illustrated in Figure A-15.

The approach Microsoft took to safety with respect to ActiveX controls is different from Sun's original approach in Java. Sun did not allow Java applets to run outside a so-called sandbox, which prevented them from touching any system resources where they might do damage. Although this approach was safe, it restricted the utility of Java applets. ActiveX controls have configurable security, as we have seen. Marking a control safe for scripting is something that the control developer does, placing a setting in the Registry that indicates the control is safe. The developer should do extensive testing before so marking a control. A user has no real way of knowing how safe a control really is just because it has been marked as safe.

A.3.1.5 DOWNLOADING AN ACTIVEX CONTROL

Once we configured the safety setting for scripting, our control just ran, because it was already installed and registered on our system. But to require a user of an ActiveX control to separately obtain and install it defeats the advantage of a thin client. The user is back in the business of having to install and maintain software on the client. What we want is the ability to download and automatically install an ActiveX control on demand. That capability is provided by the codebase attribute in the **<OBJECT>** tag. Look again at how the Shape Preview control was specified.

An ActiveX control on this page is not safe.
Your current security settings prohibit running unsafe controls on this page.
As a result, this page may not display as intended.

OK

Figure A-13   *Safety message from Internet Explorer.*

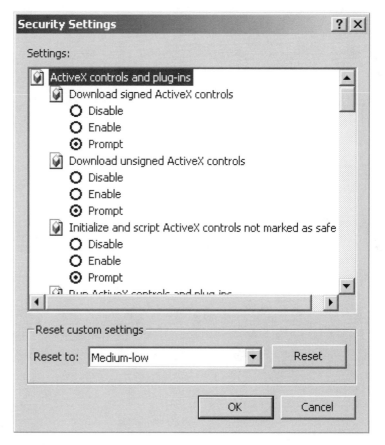

Figure A-14   *Setting safety options in Internet Explorer 6.0.*

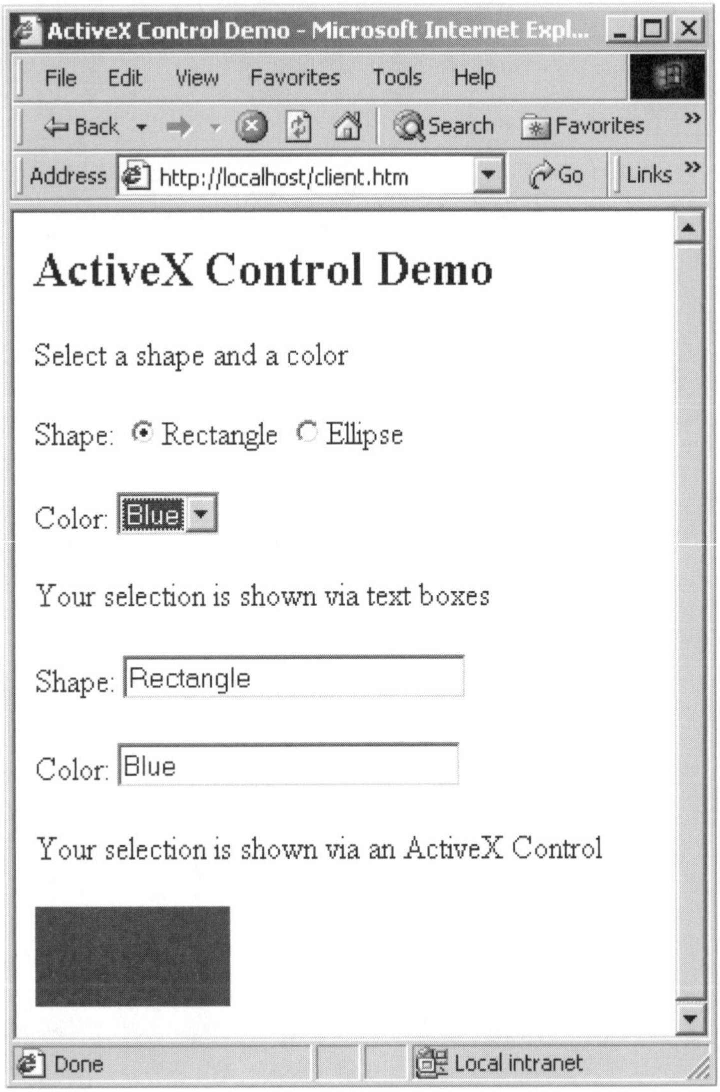

Figure A-15   *Exercising an ActiveX control on a Web page.*

```
<object id ="Shape1" width=100 height=50
   classid="clsid:B1028D2C-35A7-11D1-A01B-00A024D06632"
   codebase="http://localhost/shape.dll"
>
</object>
```

The codebase specifies a URL where the control can be found and downloaded, if it is not currently installed on the local system. (This example is somewhat artificial. For convenience we specify localhost as the name of the server. We are going through the HTTP protocol, even though in this example we do not go to a remote machine.) To see how this works, unregister the control (you can run the unreg_shape.bat file in Shape). Next copy shape.dll to the home directory on the Web server, which is currently Inetpub\wwwroot\Html. Now again visit client.htm using the URL *localhost/client.htm*. Refresh to make sure you are going to the Web server for the page. You should get a security warning. See Figure A-16.

Click Yes. The control shape.dll will now be downloaded to your system and installed (i.e., registered). You should then be able to set the properties as before, and see the shape and color displayed by the control.

The Microsoft Authenticode technology uses a digital signature to sign controls. The digital signature is obtained from a signature authority, an independent company such as Verisign, which takes applications from individuals and companies for a digital signature. The digital signature can be used in various ways, such as providing robust identification of yourself in e-mail and electronic commerce. In the case of companies, the signature authority does some validation that the company is a legitimate business entity and then issues a certificate, which can be used for signing the ActiveX control. When the user brings up a Web page having a signed ActiveX control, the certificate will appear, identifying the company. If the company is well

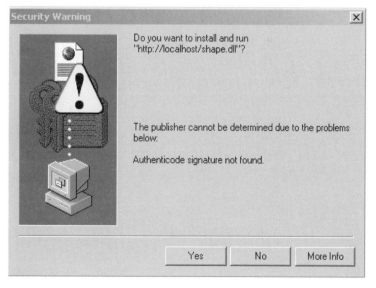

Figure A-16   *Security warning for an unsigned ActiveX control.*

known, the user may choose to go ahead and download it. If the company is not known to the user, the user may choose not to download it for safety's sake—the choice is the user's.

A.3.2 Microsoft Server-Side Web Technologies

As we have discussed, client-side technologies are not universal. ActiveX controls, for example, require that the user be running Microsoft's Internet Explorer as the Web browser. The great advantage of server-side technology is that you can choose your own platform and tools for your servers, and if you stick to plain vanilla HTML (and possibly the core part of JavaScript), a very wide variety of clients will be able to run your applications.

A.3.2.1 INTERNET SERVER API (ISAPI)

CGI is standard and straightforward, but it suffers an enormous disadvantage. Every Web program that is launched by a Web server using CGI runs as a separate process. This both incurs significant overhead and severely limits scalability. Microsoft's solution is the Internet Server API (ISAPI), which defines an interface to server extensions implemented as DLLs. These DLLs run in the same address space as the Web server. Figure A-17 shows the basic architecture.

Conceptually ISAPI works the same way as CGI. The Web server passes on a request from the Web client. In place of using environment variables the Web server communicates with the ISAPI DLL through an extension control block or ECB. The Web server provides callback functions **ReadClient** and **WriteClient** to read and write data from the Web server (which is done through **stdin** and **stdout** with CGI). The extension DLL parses the data received from the server and composes its response, which it passes back to the server. The server then adds the header information and sends a complete response back to the Web client.

Visual C++ makes it easy to create ISAPI extension DLLs through ISAPI Extension Wizard. Several MFC classes are provided to wrap the ISAPI server functionality. You might enjoy doing a small demo. Create a new Visual C++ project called Hello. The project type should be ISAPI Extension Wizard. See Figure A-18.

Figure A-17   *Basic ISAPI architecture.*

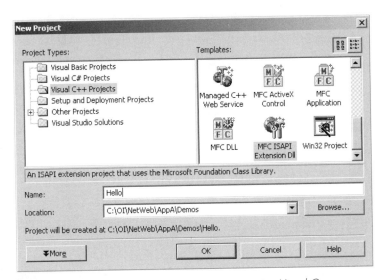

Figure A-18 *Creating a new ISAPI extension project using Visual C++.*

In the next screen accept the default to generate a Server Extension object. Click Finish. In the generated project edit the **Default** method of the **CHelloExtension** class to simply return the message "Hello from ISAPI."

```
void CHelloExtension::Default(CHttpServerContext* pCtxt)
{
    StartContent(pCtxt);
    WriteTitle(pCtxt);

    *pCtxt << _T("Hello from ISAPI\r\n");

    EndContent(pCtxt);
}
```

Build the DLL, then copy hello.dll to the Inetpub\Scipts directory. You can then invoke your extension DLL through the URL

```
http://localhost/scripts/hello.dll
```

Figure A-19 shows the result.

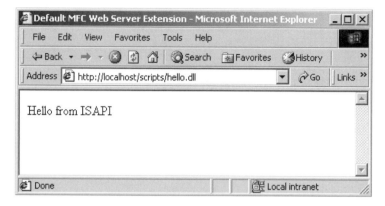

Figure A-19   *Invoking an ISAPI extension DLL through Internet Explorer.*

A slightly more interesting example is provided by join.htm in the Von Neumann Computer Club Web site. To get ready for this example, first build the ISAPI project in the directory AppA\clubisap and copy clubisap.dll to Inetpub\Scripts.

Next go back to Internet Services Manager and change the home directory to wwwroot\club. Also turn off directory browsing. See Figure A-6. Since there is a default.htm file in the club directory, you can now bring up the Club's home page from the URL *localhost/*. Click the Join link. You will then be brought to the simple form shown in Figure A-20.

Figure A-20   *Enrollment form.*

Type in your name and click Join Now. You will see a debugging message referring to a file open succeeding and adding a string to the file. The clubisap.dll extension DLL writes data to a flat file. The file is created the first time the server writes to it. You may try adding some more members to the club, then clicking List Members. You should get back a list of the members in the club, as recorded in the flat file.

Naturally in real life you would probably use a database rather than a flat file. We will in fact call database code from the Web server in the last section, when we make use of COM+ applications on the Web server.

ISAPI is the technology of choice when you are looking for absolutely the best performance in a Web application. Programming with ISAPI is somewhat low level, and for everyday use Microsoft has provided a higher-level technology, ASP, the subject of the next section.

A.3.2.2 ASP

ASP is the most popular Microsoft technology for implementing Web applications. ASPs run on the server, thus avoiding the various problems we have discussed concerning client-side technology. They are efficient and they are easy to program. In this section we give a bare introduction to get you up and running; we discuss ASP in more detail in the next main section.

ASP differs from CGI and ISAPI in the way it gets invoked. An ASP file is actually an extended HTML file with additional script content, not a separate file that gets executed by the server. Thus a browser may point directly to an ASP file. In fact, any HTML file can be made into an ASP file simply by renaming its extension. This makes it possible to easily migrate static HTML files to dynamic ASP files.

To get started let's look at an example. Our ASP examples are in the folder AppA\ASP. Copy the folder ASP to Inetpub\wwwroot. Bring up Internet Services Manager to make ASP your home directory. While you are there check to make sure that the Execute Permissions include Scripts. Also, you may wish to enable Directory Browsing for your convenience. Figure A-21 illustrates the proper settings.

Now view the file datetime.asp. Be sure to go through HTTP to the Web server, using the URL http://localhost/datetime.asp. You should see the date and time displayed. They are in a slightly different format, because the script code ran VBScript functions rather than C library functions, as was the case with our previous CGI example. Figure A-22 illustrates what the browser will display for this page.

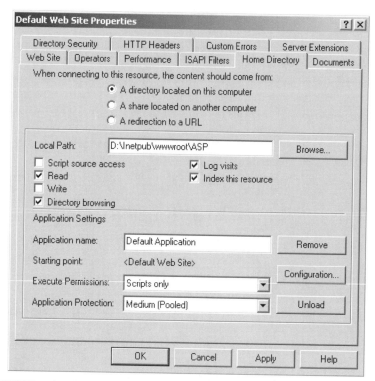

Figure A-21   *The directory where your ASP files reside must grant Execute permission to scripts.*

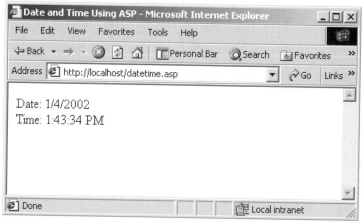

Figure A-22   *Displaying an ASP page where script called built-in functions.*

The big difference between the ASP and CGI examples is in how the functions got invoked. With CGI there was an HTML page that contained a button the user pressed. An HTTP request went to the server, which called a script using CGI. The script, running in a separate process, wrote data which the Web server used to create the HTTP response that went to the client. With ASP the script code is directly on the initial page requested by the client. Recognizing the .asp extension, the Web server called an ISAPI extension DLL asp.dll, which runs in the same process as the Web server. This DLL executed the script, which called the date and time functions. The Web server built the HTTP response and sent it to the client. Here is the ASP file. Notice it is just like HTML, with the addition of the script.

```
<!-- datetime.asp -->
<html>
<head>
<title> Date and Time Using ASP </title>
</head>
<body BGCOLOR=WHITE>
Date: <% = Date %> <br>
Time: <% = Time %> <br>
</body>
</html>
```

The script code is bracketed inside the **<% ... %>** delimiters. This script gets executed on the server, not on the client. You can have both client-side and server-side scripts on the same page. Client-side scripts use different delimiters, the **<SCRIPT>** tag, as we have already seen.

A.4 ASP and COM

The real power of ASP comes from its coupling with COM/COM+. We have seen that ASP files get invoked through an ISAPI DLL and run in-process with the Web server. Thus they are efficient. But once the scripting code starts executing, the efficiency goes out the window. The script code is interpreted and thus runs much more slowly than compiled code.

Scripts are great when they are short and do their processing within compiled functions that they call. The example we looked at fits this case exactly. Each line of script code is only one line long, and all the script does is call a built-in function. There are only a limited number of built-in functions. What makes the whole model extensible is the capability for scripts to invoke any compiled code that you write. This capability is exactly what COM provides, and COM is object-oriented to boot.

Besides providing the ability to call COM components, ASP files themselves are implemented using COM. There is an object model for ASP. Thus programming with ASP is quite seamlessly object-oriented. You invoke the various built-in objects provided by ASP, and you can also invoke your own custom COM objects, sometimes called Active Server Components when used in this context.

ADO is an example of an Active Server Component. You can call ADO directly from an ASP script to do database programming. Even better, however, is to encapsulate your database program into your own COM components, which are the ones that call ADO (or OLE DB directly). These COM components can be imported into COM+ and then enjoy all the power of COM+ applications, such as automatic transactions.

A.4.1 ASP Object Model

There are five built-in objects provided by ASP.

- The **Server** object provides general-purpose utility functions and, through the CreateObject method, the ability to instantiate COM components that are not built-in.
- The **Application** object can be used to share information among all users of an application.
- The **Session** object can be used to store information for a particular user of an application.
- The **Request** object provides all the information associated with a user's request and contains several collection objects, including the **Form** collection.
- The **Response** object can be used to send information to the user and contains the **Cookies** collection.

The workhorse objects are the **Request** and **Response** objects. From the **Request** object you can read information that was submitted when the user filled in an HTML form. The **Response** object is used for writing information that is to be sent to the client. The **Request** object contains five collections:

- The **ClientCertificate** collection retrieves certificate information sent via secure HTTP (URL begins with https).
- With the **Cookies** collection you can retrieve the value of cookies sent in an HTTP request.
- The **Form** collection contains values from HTML form elements.
- With the **QueryString** collection you can retrieve values from the HTTP query string.
- With the **ServerVariables** collection you can retrieve the values of server environment variables (the ones used in CGI programming).

A.4.2 Request and Response Using ASP

We can illustrate use of the **Request** and **Response** objects with a minimal example that echoes back a name submitted by the client. Open up echo.htm in the browser and enter a name. See Figure A-23.

Click the Echo button, and you should see the name echoed back. Here is the HTML code:

```
!-- echo.htm --><HTML>
<HEAD>
<TITLE>Name Input</TITLE>
</HEAD>
<BODY>

<FORM ACTION="echoback.asp" METHOD="POST">
<P>
Name <INPUT NAME="txtName" VALUE="" MAXLENGTH="25" SIZE=25>
<P>
 <INPUT TYPE=SUBMIT VALUE="Submit">
 <INPUT TYPE=RESET VALUE="Reset">
</FORM>

</BODY>
</HTML>
```

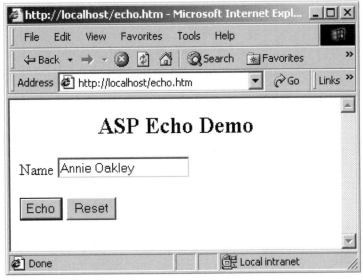

Figure A-23   *A form for entering a name to be echoed back.*

The form's **ACTION** parameter simply specifies an ASP file. That file uses the **Request** object to obtain the name that was submitted. The **Form** collection is used, keying off **txtName**, which was the NAME attribute of the INPUT box. A greeting message is then sent back to the client, incorporating the name that was entered.

```
<!-- echoback.asp -->
<%@ LANGUAGE = VBScript %>
<HTML>
<HEAD>
<TITLE>Echo Back</TITLE>
</HEAD>
<BODY>
<%
name = Request.Form("txtName")
Response.Write("Hello, " & name)
%>
</BODY>
</HTML>
```

Summary

There is a great deal of Web technology that is employed in building and running Web applications. We began with an overview of the classic Web, which consisted of HTML pages displayed in a Web browser, the HTTP communications protocol, Web servers that can service requests received from Web clients and send responses back, typically HTML pages. These HTML pages can be either static or created dynamically. Dynamic Web pages are created on the fly by a Web program. The classic interface to Web programs is CGI, which spawns a separate process for each request.

We then examined Microsoft Web technology. Microsoft's initial emphasis was on the client. VBScript provided a scripting language for HTML pages, and ActiveX controls could provide rich user interface components. Microsoft uses a configurable security system, including the signing of ActiveX controls, in contrast to the Java sandbox.

More important are the server technologies, because they are more widely applicable and do not depend on the client platform. While intranet applications can make assumptions about the client, an Internet application should run on as wide a range of browsers as possible. Microsoft's base server technology is ISAPI, which provides an efficient DLL mechanism for running Web programs that are in process.

We concluded with an introduction to ASP files, which are easy to create and can be scripted using VBScript or JavaScript (like the client).

If you have not done Web programming before, you have more to learn, but it is very worthwhile. Web applications have the tremendous advantage of ease of deployment. All that is needed on the part of a client is a Web browser, and clients can reach the application from anywhere in the world.

New Features of VB.NET

*W*ith .NET Framework comes into being a brand new version Visual Basic, VB.NET. Different from the earlier versions of the language, VB.NET has become a real object-oriented language. The mechanism of namespaces and assemblies has made VB.NET programming modularized. As we know, some casual features and constructs have made Visual Basic programs hard to understand and difficult to debug. Many of these things have been corrected in VB.NET. Working with the CLR, Visual Basic has become safer and more powerful while the programs in VB.NET run with improved performance.

B.1 More Object-Oriented

The object-oriented facility was first introduced to Visual Basic in Version 4.0. Unfortunately, some important object-oriented features have been missing since then. Up to Version 6, the most notably lacking is inheritance capability, which is regarded as the key defining criteria for any object-oriented language. Moreover, essential features, such as method overloading and overriding, are also not supported.

With VB.NET, Visual Basic has finally completed its transition to a fully object-oriented language. Therefore, object-oriented capabilities are some of the most important new features that VB.NET has brought into being. We consider these features in this section.

B.1.1 Inheritance

Inheritance is the idea that a new class is created based on an existing class and gains its property and behavior. Not only is inheritance the key concept to minimizing redundancy in class definition, but it also plays a critical role in the reuse of software components.

VB.NET is the first version of Visual Basic to support inheritance. In the programming environment of .NET Framework, cross-language interoperability allows inheritance, which breaks the barriers between languages. That is a class implemented in VB.NET that may be derived from a base class in other languages, and vice versa.

In Section 3.4, for example, a base class **HelloBase** is first implemented in C#.

```
using System;
namespace CompBase {
public abstract class Hello {
        private String lang = "Unknown";
        public abstract String Greeting(String name);
        public String GetLang() {
            return lang;
        }
        public void SetLang(String l) {
            lang = l;
        }
    }
}
```

Components are then built in various languages, including VB.NET, that are all derived from **HelloBase**. The following program, **CompBase.vb**, was developed in Section 3.4, and defined a subclass **HelloVB** that is derived from **HelloBase**.

```
Imports System
Imports CompBase
Namespace CompVB
    Public Class HelloVB
    Inherits CompBase.Hello

        Public Sub New()
            MyBase.New
            MyBase.SetLang("Visual Basic")
        End Sub
        Overrides Function Greeting(name As String) ⇓
            As String
            Greeting = String.Concat("Hello, ", ⇓
                name, "!!")
        End Function
    End Class
End Namespace
```

In an instance of subclass **HelloVB**, method **SetLang** may be invoked because it has already been implemented in the base class **HelloBase**. Method **Greeting**, however, is an abstract one and not implemented in the base class. It is implemented, or overridden, in the subclass. This issue is addressed in the following section.

B.1.2 Method Overriding and Polymorphism

A subclass may also override the behavior that it gained from the base class. In the example of subclass **HelloVB**, method **Greeting** was overridden to provide an implementation specific to the subclass. When multiple subclasses of a base class override the method, each of them has its own implementation for the specific behavior of the method. This polymorphism allows the designated overridden method to be invoked from a generalized program so as to provide expected services. This mechanism makes for a highly flexible, scalable, and maintainable software development paradigm.

Let us revisit such a program, which we developed in Section 3.5.2, using VB.NET.

```
Imports System
Imports CompBase
Imports CompCS
Imports CompVB
Imports CompCPP
Public Module modmain
    Private name As String
    Sub Main()
        Dim Count As Integer
        Console.Write("Your name, please: ")
        name = Console.ReadLine()
        Dim MyHello(3) As CompBase.Hello
        MyHello(0) = New CompCS.HelloCS
        MyHello(1) = New CompVB.HelloVB
        MyHello(2) = New CompCPP.HelloCpp
        ' loop over the array of objects
        For Count = 0 To 2
            Console.WriteLine()
            Console.WriteLine( _
                myHello(Count).Greeting(name))
            Console.WriteLine(String.Concat( _
                "This is a greeting from a program ⇓
                    written in ", _
                myHello(Count).GetLang(), _
                    ".") _
            )
        Next
    End Sub
End Module
```

In this program, an array of references to the base class **HelloBase** is created and populated with instances of its subclasses, namely **HelloCS**, **HelloVB**, and **HelloCPP**. Then we loop over the array and invoke the **Greeting** method of each element object. That is allowed because each of the subclass has an "*is a*" relationship to its base class. Due to polymorphism, however, the overridden version of the method is actually invoked for the object of the desired subclasses so that the designated behavior can be realized.

More specifically, even though array **myHello** is of type **HelloBase**,

- Statement **myHello(0).Greeting** has method **HelloCS.Greeting** method invoked.
- Statement **myHello(1).Greeting** has method **HelloVB.Greeting** invoked.
- Statement **myHello(2).Greeting** has method **HelloCPP.Greeting** invoked.

It is also important to note that this mechanism with cross-language interoperability is supported in the programming environment of .NET Framework. In the preceding program the subclasses **HelloCS**, **HelloVB**, and **HelloCPP** work together seamlessly, even though they have been implemented in different languages.

B.1.3 Method Overloading

One of the exciting object-oriented features that are new to VB.NET is the ability to overload a method. Overloading means that methods may be declared with the same name but a different parameter list.

The method name implies the functionality of the method and the same function may apply to various objects. For example, both Social Security number and combination of first name and last name can be used as search criteria. In the previous versions of Visual Basic, two functions, such as **SearchByName** and **SearchBySSN**, needed to be defined. In VB.NET, we may have two overloaded methods with the same name **Search**. These are

- Search by name:

```
Public Overloads Function Search( _
    FirstName As String, _
    LastName As String) As ArrayList
```

- Search by Social Security number:

```
Public Overloads Function Search( _
    SocialSecurityNumber As String) As ArrayList
```

With method overloading capability, some old features of Visual Basic that have made the VB program difficult to write and read, as well as error prone, can be eliminated. Here are some examples:

- **As Any** parameters in declarations. Overloaded methods may cover all the acceptable combinations of the parameter types for a function or subroutine. Therefore, eliminating **As Any** parameters in declarations prevents a method from being invoked with data types other than those that have been explicitly defined for acceptance.
- **IsMissing** function. Overloaded methods may cover all the acceptable combinations of the parameter types for a function or subroutine. In addition, VB.NET requires that a default value be specified for all optional parameters. Therefore, there is no need to test to see whether a parameter is missing.

B.1.4 Constructor

In Visual Basic Version 6, an optional subroutine **Sub Main** runs as the component is initially loaded, before the object of the given component is created, and subroutine **Class_Initialize** runs when the object is created. Therefore, debugging **Sub Main** could be very difficult, as it would run even before the error-handling facility is in place.

In VB.NET, on the other hand, there is no concept of component level initialization and a constructor **New** runs when the object is created. That happens before any other code in the object can run, including **Sub Main** as the entry point of a program.

Object construction is triggered each time a new instance of a class is created. **New** method is not automatically carried from base class to a subclass like normal methods. Each subclass must define its own constructors, though it may explicitly invoke that of the base class by using **MyBase** keyword.

Program **CompVB.vb**, which is developed in Section 3.5.2 (also listed in Section B.2.1) creates class **HelloVB**, which is derived from **HelloBase**. In this program, we can see such a constructor.

```
Public Sub New()
    MyBase.New
    MyBase.SetLang("Visual Basic")
End Sub
```

B.1.5 Termination of Objects and Garbage Collection

In Visual Basic Version 6, the run time maintains a reference count for each object and destroys the object when the last reference to it has been removed. In addition, subroutine **Class_Terminate** runs after any other code in an object; it is called as the object is destroyed. Included in this subroutine can be the code for housekeeping, such as making sure that expensive or limited resources are released. This clear termination scheme is known as deterministic finalization.

It is nice to know when an object is destroyed, and a subroutine is called at that time that takes care of what needs to done. However, it is liable that a circular reference between two objects prevents the objects from being destroyed; they stay in the memory forever. That has been a common way of creating memory leak and is a terrible headache for the VB programmers.

In VB.NET, Common Language Runtime does not maintain a reference count. Instead, objects are destroyed through a garbage collection mechanism. Based on some rules, a task runs periodically through all the objects, looks for those no longer having references, and destroys them; in other words, the garbage is collected. In this case, we no longer know exactly when an object will be gone. That is because an object without any references may stay in memory until it is actually destroyed by the garbage collection task. This termination scheme is known as nondeterministic finalization.

Even though the termination of objects becomes unclear, the problem with circular references has been resolved because the garbage collection task can discover and destroy them.

It is also possible to manually trigger the garbage collection process through code:

```
System.GC.Collect()
```

The garbage collection mechanism does provide something that is equivalent to subroutine **Class_Terminate** in VB6. When an object is being terminated, the garbage collection task calls its **Finalize** method, allowing for housekeeping tasks:

```
Protected Overrides Sub Finalize()
    ' Housekeeping work
End Sub
```

The nondeterministic nature of garbage collection may make the **Finalize** behavior unacceptable. In this case, a method may be implemented in the class that will be called explicitly by the client to perform the housekeeping work. Such a method is usually named **Dispose**:

```
Public Sub Dispose ()
    ' Housekeeping work
End Sub
```

The Windows program that we developed in Section 3.5.4 has such a subroutine.

B.1.6 Interface

For some time, Visual Basic has been allowing objects that implement interfaces to be created. VB.NET preserves this facility and enhances it. First of all, interfaces in VB.NET are formally declared. In Section 8.5.2, we developed an interface **IHello** in C#. This interface may also be declared in VB:

```
Public Interface IHello
    Function Greeting(Name As String) As String
End Interface
```

When a class implements an interface, it must implement all its methods, including subroutines and functions. The Hello server program can also be implemented in VB.NET:

```
Imports System
Imports System.Runtime.Remoting
Imports System.Runtime.Remoting.Channels.TCP

Public Class HelloServer
    Inherits MarshalByRefObject
    Implements IHello

    Public Shared Sub Main
        Dim c As TCPChannel
        c = new TCPChannel(8765)
        ChannelServices.RegisterChannel(c)
        RemotingServices.RegisterWellKnownType( _
            "HelloServer", _
            "HelloServer", _
            "SayHello", _
            WellKnownObjectMode.Singleton _
        )
        Console.WriteLine("Press [Enter] to quit ...")
        Console.ReadLine()
    End Sub

    Public Sub New
        MyBase.New
        Console.WriteLine("HelloServer: Activated.")
    End Sub

    Public Function Greeting(Name As String) As String
        Implements IHello.Greeting
        Console.WriteLine( _
            "HelloServer: Method Greeting called with ⇓
                {0}.", _
            Name _
        )
        Greeting = String.Concat( _
```

```
                            "Hello, ", _
                            Name _
                    )
            End Function
        End Class
```

In this program, class **HelloServer** implements interface **IHello**, and its method **Greeting** is implemented:

```
Public Function Greeting(Name As String) As String
    Implements IHello.Greeting
    Console.WriteLine( _
        "HelloServer: Method Greeting called with ⇓
            {0}.", _
        Name _
    )
    Greeting = String.Concat( _
        "Hello, ", _
        Name _
    )
```

As an exercise in VB.NET, you may implement a client object **HelloClient** that also implements interface **IHello** and is able to access the service provided by the server object we developed here.

B.1.7 Delegates

A delegate in .NET Framework is similar to a function pointer in C/C++. It allows a reference to a method to be encapsulated inside a delegate object. The delegate object can then be passed over to another object that may invoke the referenced method without having to know at compile time which method will be called. Using this feature, we implemented programs that access remote services asynchronously in Chapters 6 and 8. The syntax for declaring a delegate is

```
Public Delegate Function HelloDelegate(Name As String) ⇓
As String
```

Then a delegate instance may be created in the following way:

```
Dim MyHelloDelegate As HelloDelegate = ⇓
new HelloDelegate(AddressOf WebHello.Greeting)
```

When a procedure name appears in an argument list, usually the procedure is evaluated and the address of the procedure's return value is passed. The **AddressOf** operator supplies a reference to its operand, either a function or a subroutine. The **AddressOf** operator can also be used within a delegate statement, which also produces a reference to its operand but allows the user more flexibility in where they can place the **AddressOf** operator in the code.

Here is a simple example that shows how to use a delegate statement:

```
Imports System
Public Class Test
    Shared Sub Main
        Dim MyTest As Test = New Test
        Console.WriteLine("4 + 3 = {0}", _
            MyTest.ResultOf(4, 3, New Calculate(_
                AddressOf MyTest.Add)))
        Console.WriteLine("4 - 3 = {0}", _
            MyTest.ResultOf(4, 3, New Calculate(_
                AddressOf MyTest.Subtract)))
    End Sub

    Public Delegate Function Calculate(_
        Operand1 As Integer, Operand2 As Integer) _
            As Integer

    Public Function ResultOf(_
        Operand1 As Integer, Operand2 As Integer, _
            Operator As Calculate) As Integer
        ResultOf = Operator(Operand1, Operand2)
    End Function

    Public Function Add(_
        Operand1 As Integer, Operand2 As Integer) _
            As Integer
        Return Operand1 + Operand2
    End Function

    Public Function Subtract(_
        Operand1 As Integer, Operand2 As Integer) _
            As Integer
        Return Operand1 - Operand2
    End Function

End Class
```

In class **Test**, private methods **Add** and **Subtract** calculate the sum and difference of their operands. Users of this class, such as **Sub Main**, use the service of class **Test** by invoking public method **ResultOf**. This pubic method requires three arguments, such as two operands and a delegate **Calculate**, that reference to either **Add** or **Subtract**. Delegate **Calculate** is defined as

```
Public Delegate Function Calculate(_
    Operand1 As Integer, Operand2 As Integer) _
        As Integer
```

As can be seen, it represents the signatures of both **Add** and **Subtract**.

In **Sub Main**, method **ResultOf** is called twice to calculate **4 + 3** and **4 − 3**:

```
Console.WriteLine("4 + 3 = {0}", _
    MyTest.ResultOf(4, 3, New Calculate(_
        AddressOf MyTest.Add)))
Console.WriteLine("4 - 3 = {0}", _
    MyTest.ResultOf(4, 3, New Calculate(_
        AddressOf MyTest.Subtract)))
```

Note that **AddressOf** is used to construct new instances of **Calculate**. This program will generate the following result:

```
>TestDelegate
4 + 3 = 7
4 - 3 = 1

>
```

B.1.8 Shared Methods and Class Members

A method or class member declared with the **shared** modifier means that the method or class member is shared by all the instances of the class. No matter how many instances of a type are created, there is only ever one copy of a shared method or class member. A shared member comes into existence when a program begins executing and ceases to exist when the program terminates. A shared data member is initialized to the default value of its type. A shared method may be invoked without an instance of the object needing to be created.

A method or class member declared without the **shared** modifier is called an instance member. Every instance of a class contains a separate copy of all instance members of the class. An instance data member is initialized to the default value of its type. An instance data member of a reference type comes into existence when a new instance of that type is created, and ceases to exist when there are no references to that instance and the **Finalize** method has executed. An instance data member of a value type has exactly the same lifetime as the variable to which it belongs. In other words, when a variable of a value type comes into existence or ceases to exist, so do the instance data members of the value type. An instance method may not be invoked without referring to a particular instance of the class. As you may have noticed, an instance is created in order to invoke its methods.

B.1.9 Properties

Properties are a natural extension of data members—both are named members with associated types. Unlike data members, however, a property does not have a stored location. Instead, a property has associated procedures that specify the statements to execute in order to read or write its values. For example, class **Person** may have a property **Name** through which a private member **TheName** might be accessed:

```
Imports System

Public Class Person
    Private TheName As String

    Shared Sub Main
        Console.Write("Your name, please: ")
        Dim p As Person = New Person
        p.Name = Console.ReadLine()
        Console.WriteLine("Hello, {0}!", p.Name)
    End Sub

    Public Property Name() As String
        Get
            Return TheName
        End Get
        Set
            TheName = Value
        End Set
    End Property

End Class
```

B.1.10 Structured Exception Handling

Structured exception handling is done through a **Try-Catch-Finally** statement. When an error occurs, an exception is thrown and caught in a **Try-Catch-Finally** statement. The syntax of the **Try-Catch-Finally** statement is

```
Try
    tryStatements
[Catch₁ [exception [As type]] [When expression]
    catchStatements₁
[Exit Try]
Catch₂ [exception [As type]] [When expression]
    catchStatements₂
[Exit Try]
…
Catchₙ [exception [As type]] [When expression]
    catchStatementsₙ]
[Exit Try]
[Finally
    finallyStatements]
End Try
```

Here is an example with structured exception handling:

```
Imports System
Public Module modmain
    Dim s As String
    Dim n As Integer
    Dim f As Boolean = false
    Sub Main()
        Console.Write("An integer, please: ")
        s = Console.ReadLine()
        Try
            n = CType(s, Integer)
        Catch e As Exception
            f = true
            Console.WriteLine(e.ToString)
        Finally
            If f Then
                Console.WriteLine(_
                    "Conversion Failed.")
            Else
                Console.WriteLine(_
                    "Conversion was successful; ⇓
                        the integer is {0}", n)
            End If
        End Try
    End Sub
End Module
```

This program first prompts the user for an integer. Then it tries to convert the string typed into an integer. If the user typed a proper integer, it is shown on the screen.

```
>TestExceptionHandling
An integer, please: 123
Conversion was successful; the integer is 123

>
```

However, if the string that the user typed cannot be converted into an integer, an exception is thrown and caught:

```
>TestExceptionHandling
An integer, please: abc
System.FormatException: The input string was not in a ⇓
    correct format.
        at System.Number.ParseDouble(String s, NumberStyles ⇓
            style, NumberFormatInfo info)
        at System.Double.Parse(String s, NumberStyles style, ⇓
            NumberFormatInfo info)
        at Microsoft.VisualBasic. ⇓
            Helpers.DoubleType.FromString(String Value)
```

```
    at Microsoft.VisualBasic. ⇓
        Helpers.IntegerType.FromString(String Value)
    at modmain.Main()
Conversion Failed.
```

```
>
```

B.2 More Modularized

Modularity is the property of a system that has been decomposed into a set of cohesive and loosely coupled modules. As Myers observes, "The act of partitioning a program into individual components can reduce its complexity to some degree. . . . Although partitioning a program is helpful for this reason, a more powerful justification for partitioning a program is that it creates a number of well-defined, documented boundaries within the program. These boundaries, or interfaces, are invaluable in the comprehension of the program." (B. Myers, 1987, *Programming as Contracting*, Report TR-EI-12/CO. Goleta, CA: Interactive Software Engineering.)

.NET Framework supports a highly modularized programming paradigm. Not only does it allow for the effectiveness and efficiency of software development, but it also enhances the readability of the programs to a great extent, especially for client-server and Web applications. Visual Basic has experienced structural changes so as to fit in to the paradigm.

In VB.NET, the essential building blocks are classes. A flexible framework is supplied so that the classes are organized in a much more modularized way than in the earlier versions of Visual Basic. Namespaces provide the builders of the classes with the boundaries for logical grouping of the software components, while assemblies serve as functional units for sharing and reuse them. An import and reference mechanism, on the other hand, allows the consumers of the classes to access those components flexibly. In comparison to the previous versions of Visual Basic, VB.NET is a much more reliable way to build complex and large-scale software systems.

B.2.1 Namespaces

VB.NET programs are organized using namespaces. Namespaces serve as an internal organization system for logical grouping of the classes and as an external organization system for presenting program elements that are exposed to other programs. Namespace **TheNamespace** is defined in the following block structure. Within this block, a public class **TheClass** is declared.

```
Namespace TheNamespace
    Public Class TheClass
       ...
    End Class
End Namespace
```

Unlike the other entities, namespaces may be declared multiple times within the same program and may be declared across many programs, with each declaration contributing members to the same namespace. If the preceding namespace block is saved in a source file, we may declare the following namespace block in another source file. Within this block, another public class, **TheOtherClass**, is declared. This public class belongs to namespace **TheNamespace** as well.

```
Namespace TheNamespace
    Public Class TheOtherClass
       ...
    End Class
End Namespace
```

If two programs define an entity with the same name in the same namespace, attempting to resolve the name in the namespace causes an ambiguity error.

B.2.2 Assemblies

An assembly is the functional unit of sharing and reuse in Common Language Runtime (CLR). It provides the run time with the information it needs to be aware of type implementations. To the run time, a type does not exist outside the context of an assembly. Assemblies are a fundamental part of the run time.

In physical terms, an assembly is a collection of physical files that are owned by the assembly. These assemblies, called static assemblies, can include .NET Framework types (interfaces and classes) as well as resources for the assembly (bitmaps, JPEG files, resource files, etc.). In addition, Common Language Runtime (CLR) provides APIs that script engines used to create dynamic assemblies when executing scripts. These assemblies are run directly and are never saved to disk, although you can save them to disk if you so choose.

It is important to understand what an assembly is not. An assembly is not a unit of application deployment. It is a unit of class deployment, much like a DLL. An application is built from assemblies, and these assemblies can be packaged for deployment in several ways.

The important characteristics of assemblies are as follows.

- An assembly contains code that the run time will execute. A program will not be executed if it does not have an assembly manifest associated with it. Note too that each assembly can have only one entry point.

- An assembly forms a security boundary. It is the unit at which permissions are requested and granted. The run time examines the set of permissions in an assembly when granting access privileges. When an assembly is built, the developer can specify a minimum set of permissions that the assembly requires to run. Additional permissions can be granted by the security policy set on the machine on which the assembly will run. At load time, the assembly's permission request is used as input to the security policy. Security policy is established by the administrator and is used to determine the set of permissions that is granted to all managed code when executed.

- An assembly forms a type boundary. Every type has as part of its identity the assembly in which it resides. Therefore, a type **TheType** loaded in the scope of one assembly is not the same as type **TheType** loaded in the scope of another assembly. Assemblies are the construct used by the run time to locate and load types. The assembly manifest contains the information that the run time uses to resolve all type references made within the scope of the assembly. Assemblies provide consistency between the scope of names seen by the developer and the scope of names seen by the run-time system. Developers write types in the context of an assembly. The contents of the assembly that a developer is building establish the scope of names that will be available at run time.

- An assembly forms a reference scope boundary. Its manifest contains the rules for resolving types and resources. It specifies what types and resources are exposed outside the assembly. The manifest also enumerates other assemblies on which it is dependent. An assembly forms a version boundary. It is the smallest versionable unit in the Common Language Runtime (CLR); all types and resources in the same assembly are versioned as a unit. All versioning of assemblies that use Common Language Runtime is done at the assembly level. The specific version of an assembly and the versions of dependent assemblies are recorded in the assembly's manifest. Configuration files define the version policy, including the assembly manifest, the optional application configuration file, and the machine's administrator configuration file. These files provide the means for expressing version and version policy, and the run time then enforces this policy at run time.

- An assembly forms a deployment unit. An application, when launched, only requires those assemblies it initially calls. All assemblies of an application do not have to be present at run time; other assemblies, such as localization resources, can be retrieved on demand. This allows downloaded applications to be kept simple and thin. Because the assemblies are self-describing and define the relationships of their components, application installation and deployment is greatly simplified. Run-time applications do not require any registry entries; deploying a run-time application can be as simple as copying the assemblies that constitute an application to a directory structure on disk. The run time can then launch the application and resolve all references directly from the file system. Because each assembly describes where to locate the classes it contains, there is no need to make registry entries of any kind.

● An assembly is the unit at which side-by-side execution is supported. Side-by-side execution is the ability to run multiple versions of the same assembly simultaneously. Common Language Runtime (CLR) provides the infrastructure to allow multiple versions of the same assembly to be run on the same machine or even in the same process. Code that is side-by-side compatible has more flexibility in terms of providing compatibility with previous versions. Components that can run side-by-side do not have to maintain strict backward compatibility.

B.2.3 Decisions on Modularization

In modularizing VB.NET programs, the developer should balance two technical concerns: the desire to encapsulate abstractions and the need to make certain abstractions visible to other modules. Generally speaking, the system details that are likely to change independently should be hidden from other modules. Implementation of a software component is usually regarded as such a detail. In Chapter 10, we discussed an initiative for deployment of a remote server class without its implementation. On the other hand, the only assumptions that should be presented to other modules are those that are considered unlikely to change. Any internal data structures are private to a module and other modules can access them only through a well-defined program interface.

More technical issues may affect modularization decisions. First, classes and objects have to be packaged in order to make their reuse convenient, because modules usually serve as elementary and indivisible units that are reused across applications. Second, the size of a module may also be restricted by the maximum size of code segment that a compiler can generate.

Moreover, several competing nontechnical needs affect modularization decisions as well. Typically, work assignments in a development team are given on a module-by-module basis, so module boundaries might be established to minimize the interface among groups in the team. On a larger scale, this consideration may also apply to subcontractor relationships. Finally, security issues have also to be considered; classified or secret codes should be packaged in separate modules.

These rules in modularization serve as guidelines for design namespaces and assemblies for VB.NET programs. Even though there are many issues that we have to take into account, the most important rule is always to separate an application into largely independent modules.

B.2.4 Imports Directive

The **Imports** directive is provided to facilitate the use of namespaces. It imports namespaces from referenced assemblies. The syntax of the **Imports** directive is

```
Imports [ <alias_name> = ] <namespace>
```

While **<namespace>** is required, **<alias_name>** is optional; it provides a name that **the <namespace>** is also known as or referred to. When the **Imports** statement does not include **<alias_name>**, the elements defined within the specified **<namespace>** can be accessed within the module without qualification. When **<alias_name>** is specified, it must be used as a qualifier for the names contained in the namespace.

A program may contain any number of **Imports** statements. **Imports** statements must occur in a module before any references to identifiers within the module. Since an alias name is specified within a module, it shadows any names that are defined outside of the module, including imported names. Defining a member at module level with the same name as an import alias is not permitted.

Imports statements in a program should include all the namespaces that contain the classes that the program needs to reference. The program in Section B.1.2, for example, has the following **Imports** statements:

```
Imports System
Imports CompBase
Imports CompCS
Imports CompVB
Imports CompCPP
```

In addition, the libraries or executable files of which the related assemblies are composed need to be supplied when the program is compiled. Library **mscorlib.dll**, which supports namespace **System** is an exception; it is included automatically.

The following command compiles the program in Section B.1.2:

```
vbc ClientVB.vb /r:CompBase.dll /r:CompCS.dll ⇓
    /r:CompVB.dll /r:CompCPP.dll /out:ClientVB.exe ⇓
    /t:exe
```

B.3 More Formal, Less Casual

In its earlier versions, Visual Basic has been very casual. That is one of the reasons why it is attractive to beginners. It does not complain too much when you work with it. Large and complex VB programs would become error-prone, hard to understand, and difficult to debug.

VB.NET is based on .NET Framework. As discussed earlier, it has become a true object-oriented language and taken advantage of .NET cross-language interoperability. Changes have been made to several aspects of the language to deliver these features, making it more formal and less casual. These changes have improved the readability and maintainability of Visual Basic.

Such examples were presented earlier in this appendix. With method-overloading capability, some old features of Visual Basic that have made the VB programs difficult to write and read, as well as error-prone, including **As Any** parameters in declarations and the **IsMissing** function, have been eliminated.

In this section, we do not cover all these changes, only a few significant ones that make the Visual Basic language more formal and less casual.

B.3.1 Variant Type

In VB Version 6, **Variant** is a special, universal data type that can contain any kind of data except fixed-length strings. An **Object** variable is used as a pointer to an object. **Variant** is the default data type.

.NET Framework uses **Object** as the universal data type. VB.NET no longer uses **Variant** in order to avoid confusion in cross-language development. The type system is simplified by having only a single universal data type, **Object**.

B.3.2 Type Statement

In VB Version 6, the **Type** statement is used to define user-defined data. In the object-oriented programming environment of VB.NET, however, the **Type** statement becomes confusing because **Class** is the construct for user-defined types. In .NET Framework, name **Type** is used in a broad sense to include all data types.

However, .NET Framework provides a replacement for the **Type** statement for conversion purposes, **Structure**. For example, a **Type** statement in the VB Version 6 program,

```
Type MyType
    MyVariable As Integer
End Type.
```

can be converted to a **Structure** statement in VB.NET:

```
Structure MyType
    MyVariable As Short
End Structure
```

B.3.3 Def<Type> Statements

Def<Type> statements, such as **DefBool**, **DefByte**, **DefInt**, and **DefObj** statements, are used at the module level to set the default data type for variables, parameters, and procedure return types whose values start with the specified characters. Allowing implicit types, these statements have caused Visual Basic programs to be confusing to read and error-prone. Therefore, VB.NET no longer supports them.

B.3.4 Assignment

In VB Version 6, there are two forms of assignment: the **Let** assignment as the default and the **Set** assignment for assignment of object references only. The rules for **Let** assignments are rather complex:

- If the expression on the right-hand site of the **Let** statement evaluates to an object, then the default property of the instance is automatically retrieved and the result of that call is the value that is to be assigned.
- If the expression on the left-hand side of the **Let** statement evaluates to an object, the default **Let** property of the object is called with the result of evaluating the right-hand side. An exception to this rule applies if the left-hand expression is a variant containing an object, in which case the content of the variant is overwritten.

In VB.NET, the assignment rule has been simplified. There is only one form of assignment x = y, meaning that the value of variable or property y should be assigned to variable or property x. Here, the value of an object type variable is the reference to the object instance. Therefore, if x and y are reference type variables, then a reference assignment is carried out. Meanwhile, **Set** and **Let** statements are removed. This reduces the complexity of the language and makes for much more readable code.

B.3.5 Calling Procedures

In VB Version 6, two forms of procedure calls are supported, one using the **Call** statement, which requires parentheses around the list of arguments, and one without the **Call** statement, which requires that parentheses around the arguments not be used.

In VB.NET, parentheses are now required around argument lists in all cases and the **Call** keyword is no longer needed. This makes for a simple and consistent assignment scheme.

B.3.6 ByVal versus ByRef

In VB Version 6, if you fail to make a parameter explicitly **ByRef** or **ByVal**, whether it becomes **ByRef** or **ByVal** depends on what type the parameter is. If it's an intrinsic type, such as Integer, Long, or String, then it is **ByRef** by default. Otherwise, it is **ByVal**. By default, a variable can be changed by the underlying routine while it is passed as a parameter of a subroutine or a function. This behavior often makes Visual Basic programs hard to understand, error-prone, and very difficult to debug.

In VB.NET, all parameters are **ByVal** by default. You must explicitly declare it if you want to make a parameter **ByRef**. Moreover, it is also recommended that you explicitly declare the **ByVal** parameters.

B.3.7 While Block

In VB Version 6, **While** blocks are ended with **WEnd**. In VB.NET, **While** blocks end with **End While**, to be consistent with other blocks in the language. This improves consistency and readability of Visual Basic.

B.3.8 Nonstructured Programming Constructs

There are a lot of nonstructured programming constructs in VB Version 6, such as **On ... GoTo**, **On ... GoSub**, and **GoSub ... Return**. They have been eliminated from VB.NET.

B.3.9 VarPtr, StrPtr, and ObjPtr

In VB Version 6, **VarPtr**, **StrPtr**, and **ObjPtr** return the addresses of variables, strings, or objects. They make the program difficult to write and read and are no longer available in VB.NET.

B.3.10 Property

In VB Version 6, the **Get**, **Let**, and **Set** functions for a property can be declared with different levels of accessibility. In VB.NET, however, the **Get** and **Set** functions for a property must have the same level of accessibility. This allows programs in VB.NET to be incorporated with those in other .NET languages.

B.3.11 Default Property

In VB Version 6, any member may be marked as default for a class. In VB.NET, only the properties with parameters can be marked as default. A reference to an object variable without a member always refers to the object itself, rather than referring to the object in some context and to the default property in other contexts.

Removing this ambiguity eliminates the need for multiple forms of assignment. An assignment x = y always means to assign the content of variable y to variable x, rather than to assign the default property of the object that y references to the default property of the object that x references. Furthermore, it might be time that you stopped using the default property.

B.3.12 Object Creation

In VB Version 6, an object variable declared with **As New** is initialized to **Nothing**, meaning that no object has yet been created. Each time the variable is encountered during execution, it is evaluated before the code executes. If the variable contains **Nothing**, an object of the appropriate class is created.

In VB.NET, there is no implicit object creation. That is, if an object variable containing **Nothing** is encountered, it is left unchanged and no instance is automatically created. Therefore, an object must be created explicitly.

```
Dim c As TCPChannel
c = new TCPChannel(8765)
```

This can also be done in the statement that declares the object variable:

```
Dim c As TCPChannel = new TCPChannel(8765)
```

or

```
Dim c As New TCPChannel(8765)
```

B.3.13 Optional Parameters

In VB Version 6, you can declare a procedure parameter as **Optional** without specifying a default value. If an optional parameter is of the **Variant** type, the procedure code can use the **IsMissing** function to determine whether the parameter is present.

In VB.NET, every optional parameter must declare a default value, which is passed to the procedure if the calling program does not supply that parameter. The **IsMissing** function is not needed to detect a missing parameter, and it is not supported. The following example shows an optional parameter declaration:

```
Sub Calculate(Optional ByVal Switch As Boolean = False)
```

B.3.14 Static Local Variables

In VB6, you can declare a procedure with the **Static** modifier. This causes every local variable within the procedure to be static and to retain its value between calls.

In VB.NET, the **Static** modifier is not supported in a **Function** or **Sub** statement. You must individually declare each local variable you want to be static.

B.4 Safer, More Powerful, and Improved Performance

As an integral part of .NET Framework, VB.NET takes advantage of CLR. It therefore becomes safer and more powerful, and programs in VB.NET have better performance.

B.4.1 Cross-Language Interoperability

In Chapter 4, we discussed in detail the cross-language interoperability supported by .NET Framework. In the programming environment of .NET Framework, application and components developed in different languages can communicate and interact with each other, and their behaviors can be tightly integrated. You may define a class in one language and then, using a different language, derive a class from the original one or call a method on it. You may also pass an instance of a class to a method on another class that is written in a different language. In addition, a cross-language debugger is supplied whereby you may step into components written in various languages. In this environment, programmers with Visual Basic skills can join a team developing a large-scale distributed system or Web application. On the other hand, Visual Basic programs may also reuse software components written in other languages. Web Services and Object Remoting have provided convenient ways for reuse.

B.4.2 JIT Compilation

Under CLR, the compiler translates VB.NET code into Microsoft Intermediate Language (MSIL), which is a CPU-independent set of instructions that can be efficiently converted to native code. Before the MSIL code can be executed, the .NET Framework JIT compiler converts it to native code that runs at the underlying hardware platform. For each hardware platform on which Common Language Runtime (CLR) runs, a JIT compiler is supplied. Therefore, a program that was developed in one platform can be executed on another. The code in MSIL is portable to any platform where it is supported; it is called a portable executable (PE).

B.4.3 Type-Safe

As a part of JIT compilation, verification processes are carried out whereby the MSIL codes are examined against metadata in order to make sure they are type-safe. The verifications include the following:

- A reference to a type is strictly compatible with the definition of the type.
- Only appropriately defined operations may be invoked on an object.
- Identities are what they claim to be.
- Memory locations and methods can be accessed only through properly defined types.
- MSIL codes have been correctly generated.

B.4.4 Execution

The idea of JIT compilation lies in recognition of the fact that some code may never get executed; thus, rather than waste time and memory converting all the MSIL in a PE into native code, it makes sense to convert the MSIL as it is needed during execution and store the resulting native code so that it is accessible for subsequent calls. The loader creates and attaches a stub to each of the type's methods when the type is loaded; on the initial call of a method, the stub passes control to the JIT compiler that converts the MSIL of the method into native code and modifies the stub to direct execution to the native code it has created. The following calls of the JIT-compiled method proceed directly to the native code that was previously generated so as to reduce the execution time.

B.4.5 Free Threading

VB.NET allows you to write applications that can perform multiple tasks independently. Tasks that could hold up other tasks can execute on a separate thread, a process known as free threading. Free threading allows you to write applications that are more scalable and more responsive to user input because you can cause complicated tasks to run on threads that are separate from your user interface. As an example, the asynchronous invocation of Web Services discussed in Chapter 6 is based on threading and improves the overall performance of distributed applications.

B.4.6 Garbage Collection

Garbage collection is a mechanism that allows the computer to detect when an object can no longer be accessed. It then automatically releases the memory used by that object, as well as calls a clean up routine written by the user and responsible for housekeeping. The garbage collector of Common

Language Runtime (CLR) also compacts memory and therefore decreases the program's working set. Therefore, reference counters need not be maintained and memory leaking can be avoided.

B.4.7 Versioning

DLL Hell refers to the set of problems caused when multiple applications attempt to share a common component like DLL or a COM class. In the most typical case, one application will install a new version of the shared component that is not backward compatible with the version already on the machine. Although the application that has just been installed works fine, existing applications that depended on a previous version of the shared component might no longer work. .NET Framework provides the following features so that DLL Hell can be avoided.

- The software components are now self-describing so as to remove their dependency on the registry. Therefore, their installations have become zero-impact and their deinstallations have been simplified.
- The versioning information has been enforced. That is, information on versions, as well as their interdependency, has been built into the infrastructure of .NET Framework. At run time, such information is loaded and ensures that components of the right versions be used.
- The platform is now capable of remembering the last-known good. When an application runs successfully, the platform must provide the capability to remember the set of components—including their versions—that worked together.
- Side-by-side components are supported. That is, multiple versions of a component can be installed and run on the machine simultaneously. Therefore, inconsistency in versions can be avoided by using components of the relevant versions. .NET Framework also allows multiple versions of the framework itself to coexist on a single machine. This dramatically simplifies the upgrade of the software components and the framework, because an administrator can choose to run different applications on different versions of .NET Framework if required.

Summary

In this appendix, we examined VB.NET, a new version of Visual Basic that is fully object-oriented, more modularized, and more formal. In some sense,

VB.NET is a new language, not simply another version of Visual Basic. The differences between VB.NET and VB Version 6 could be more significant than those between C and C++. That is because, as an integral part of .NET Framework, VB.NET is much safer and more powerful. VB.NET, together with .NET Framework, will play a more important role in development of large-scale applications, especially under Microsoft's new platform.

C# for C++ or Java Programmers

*W**ith .NET Framework, Microsoft has introduced a new lan-guage, C#, which is simple, object-oriented, and type-safe. C# is derived from C and C++ and incorporates the concepts of Java and various scripting languages. Because it is a sibling of Java and C++, both C++ and Java programmers are able to adopt it with-out difficulty.*

C# combines the high productivity of script languages such as Visual Basic and the powerful programming capability of C++ and Java. Both C++ and Java programmers will enjoy the power of C# and find it very clean and simple.

In this appendix, we pay more attention to the C# features that are different from those of C++ and Java. More details about C# may be found in Microsoft .NET Framework documentation and Introduction to C# Using .NET, *another book in this series.*

C.1 C# for C++ Programmers

First, as usual, let us say hello to the world in C#:

```
//Hello.cs
using System;
    class HelloWorld {
```

```
        // Entry point of the program
        public static void Main() {
            // prompt for input
            Console.Write("Your name, please: ");
        // read the response
          String name = Console.ReadLine();

        // write the greeting and identify myself
            Console.WriteLine("Hello,{0}",name);
            Console.WriteLine("This is a greeting " +
                "from a program " +
                "written in C#."
            );
        }
    }
```

The following command compiles this program.

```
csc /r:System.dll /debug+ Hello.cs /out:HelloCS.exe
```

This C# program looks very much like a piece of a program in C++; a C++ programmer should have no difficulty in understanding it. However, there are some differences between programs in C# and C++:

1. In a C# program, the **using** statement loads the designated name-space—**System** in this case.

2. In a C# program, the class **Console** in **System** namespace is used as standard I/O. Methods **ReadLine**, **Write**, and **WriteLine** of class **Console** are invoked to read from the keyboard and to write to the screen of the monitor.

3. Everything in a C# program has to be defined as an object. The entry point of the program is method **Main** rather than subroutine **main**.

4. No global variables or functions are allowed in a C# program.

It looks like there are more restrictions in programming with C# programming. However, these restrictions make the programming simpler and safer to practice.

Many C++ programmers know that some of the powerful features of C++ are double-edged swords; not only do they allow for better performance and flexibility, but they also make the programs difficult to read and debug. C# is an object-oriented language designed to provide simplicity and flexibility without sacrificing safety in programming.

C.1.1 Simpler and Safer

C# takes care of several things that might cause problems in C++.

C.1.1.1 MEMORY MANAGEMENT

Memory management malpractice is the most common problem in C and C++ programming. Problems can result from any of the following.

- *Memory leakage*. The programmer forgets to release the allocated resource when it becomes unused or out of the scope.
- *Memory overrun*. The programmer tries to access the memory locations beyond the bounds of the allocated block, such as an index beyond the bounds of an array.
- *Illegal access*. A miscalculated pointer may result in an unpredictable disaster, and problems of this kind are hard to detect.

Memory management problems are a big headache for C and C++ programmers because the memory pointer may go wrong in one place and cause trouble in the program in another place later. In C#, the following features resolve these problems:

- *Garbage collection*. Memory resource is automatically released when it is out of scope.
- *Elimination of pointers*. In C#, pointers are generally not employed; restricted use of pointers is, however, permitted within code marked unsafe. Using a reference to replace a pointer in C# makes the C# program much safer than C++ because a reference cannot be modified. In C#, a delegate plays the role of function pointer in C++. In this context, the reference operator '.' is always used; the pointer operator '->' is no longer allowed.
- *Safe bounds*. Arrays and strings have **Length** built in, and their bounds are always checked behind the scene when they are accessed.
- *Initialization*. All variables are required to be initialized before use. The compiler enforces the rule.

C.1.1.2 TYPE-SAFE

C# is a strongly typed language. Every variable or constant in C# has an associated type. Variables and constants of different types cannot be mixed unless strict rules are followed. Data types in C# are different from those in C and C++ in the following ways.

In C and C++, the sizes of the integer data types are not specified in the language; they depend on the implementation of compilers for the particular hardware platforms. The intent was to provide flexibility, allowing the compiler to be easily implemented in various computers.

C#, like Java, has defined the sizes of its numerical data types, as shown in Table C-1.

Table C-1	The Numerical Data Types in C#
Type	**Definition**
sbyte	unsigned 8 bits
byte	signed 8 bits
short	signed 16 bits
ushort	unsigned 16 bits
int	signed 32 bits
uint	unsigned 32 bits
long	signed 64 bits
ulong	unsigned 64 bits
float	32 bits
double	64 bits
decimal	96 bits

Note that the **decimal** data type is new in C#; it is not found in C or C++. Individual characters are represented by the **char** data type, which in C# is 16 bits wide and accommodates a Unicode character:

```
char   16 bits
```

C# also supplies a Boolean data type **bool**, which is used to represent logical values. There is no conversion between the **bool** type and other types, especially **int**, and true/false is no longer related to zero and non-zero numbers:

```
bool   8 bits
```

A bugbear of programming in C and C++ is the double equal operator. If the programmer uses a single equal operator, the compiler will not complain. For example, the following code compiles in C and C++.

```
if (x = y) {
   ...
}
```

When the program runs, x will be assigned to the value y, and the result will be used to evaluate the **if** condition. If the value is not zero, it evaluates to true, otherwise to false. This problem does not arise in C#, because **if** tests and similar constructs apply to a **bool**, and there is no implicit conversion from a numerical data type to a **bool** data type. This classic problem has disappeared in C#.

C.1.1.3 DELEGATES

The purpose of a delegate is to provide callback behavior in an object-oriented, type-safe manner. In C or C++, a function pointer is used for this purpose: In C# you can encapsulate a reference to a method inside a delegate object. You can then pass this delegate object to another program, which can then call that method. The program that calls your method in the delegate does not have to know at compile time which method is being called.

C.1.1.4 SYNTAX IMPROVEMENT

C# has a new convenient loop statement, **foreach**.

```
foreach(Object item in Object[] Items){ … }
```

This construct is equivalent to

```
for(int  i=0;  i<Items.Length;  i++){
    Object item = Items[i];
    …
}
```

Here is a sample program that uses this mechanism:

```
// ForEachLoop.cs
using System;

public class ForEachLoop
{
    public static int Main(string[] args)
    {
        int [] primes = {2, 3, 5, 7, 11, 13};
        Console.WriteLine("Using for loop");
        int sum = 0;
        for(int i=0; i<primes.Length; i++)
        {
            int prime =  primes[i];
            Console.Write("{0} ", prime);
            sum += prime;
        }
        Console.WriteLine();
        Console.WriteLine("sum = {0}", sum);
```

```
Console.WriteLine("Using foreach loop");
sum = 0;
foreach (int prime in primes)
{
   Console.Write("{0} ", prime);
   sum += prime;
}
Console.WriteLine();
Console.WriteLine("sum = {0}", sum);

return 0;
   }
}
```

The program produces the following output:

```
Using for loop
2 3 5 7 11 13
sum = 41
Using foreach loop
2 3 5 7 11 13
sum = 41
```

C# improves the **switch** statement as well. A common programming error with the C-style **switch** statement is a missing **break**. That is not a compiler error, but at run time execution will simply flow to the next case. The C# compiler will catch this problem for you, and if you deliberately want to flow to the next case, you can use a **goto** statement. If two cases are treated the same, you can simply have no code after the first case. In other words, C# treats those cases the same if there is no code between them. Another virtue of the C# **switch** statement is that it allows the switch expression to be of type **string**. The following code segment shows the usage of a switch statement.

```
//
   byte red = 255;
   byte green = 127;
   byte blue = 0;
      ...
   byte returnByte ;
   string ColorName= Console.Readline();

      switch(colorName.ToUpper()){
         case "R":
         case "RED":
            returnByte = red;
            break;
```

```
              case "G":
              case "GREEN":
                 returnByte = green;
                 break;
              case "B":
              case "BLUE":
                 returnByte = blue;
                 break;
              default:
                 returnByte = 0;
                 break;
         }
         return returnByte;
...
```

For cases of the value of the variable **colorName**, the program treats them the same respectively, **R** and **RED**, **G** and **GREEN**, as well as **B** and **BLUE**. The compiler will report an error if any break is missed in this piece of code, even the last one after the default.

C# adds a **finally** block for exception handling after **try ... catch** blocks. It provides a chance for a program to clean up something with or without an exception raised.

C.1.2 Object-Oriented

C# is a purely object-oriented language: Everything is an object and everything belongs to a class. Global variables or global functions are not allowed in C#. No header files are used. All the programs are scoped to packages or assemblies so that circular dependency problems can be avoided and the goals of code reuse and thread safety may be easily reached.

In C#, **System.Object** is the default base class. If a class is declared without its base class specified, it will automatically extend **System.Object**. C# also prohibits multiple inheritance, while the interface provides the similar functionality in a better way. In addition, there is no concept of access level for inheritance. All these features reduce the unnecessary complexity of object-oriented programming in C#.

.NET Framework supports cross-language interoperability so that you may declare a class in your C# program that is derived from a base class written in another language, such as Visual Basic or C++ with managed extensions.

C.2 C# for Java Programmers

C# is considered a sibling of Java by many Java developers. Indeed, C# looks more like Java than C++. C# is designed to achieve goals similar to the goals of Java. Java programmers can understand C# programs without difficulty because both languages share concepts and even syntax.

However, C# is not just a clone of Java. C# provides features that are missing from Java. In addition, it offers more flexibility because it does not have all the restrictions of Java. Like Java, C# is a purely object-oriented programming language. Everything is from an object and must be in a class in C#.

Let's look at the basic data type first.

C.2.1 C# Simple Type versus Java Primitive Type

In Java, primitive types, such as **int**, **boolean**, **long**, **float**, **double**, and **char**, are not derived from objects. Java has a corresponding wrapper class for each of them. In C#, each of the simple data types is just an alias of a class. In addition, C# has an additional basic numerical data type, decimal.

The simple data types are general-purpose value data types including numeric, character, and Boolean. Following are the basic numerical data types in C#.

- The **sbyte** data type is an 8-bit signed integer.
- The **byte** data type is an 8-bit unsigned integer.
- The **short** data type is a 16-bit signed integer.
- The **ushort** data type is a 16-bit unsigned integer.
- The **int** data type is a 32-bit signed integer.
- The **uint** data type is a 32-bit unsigned integer.
- The **long** data type is a 64-bit signed integer.
- The **ulong** data type is a 64-bit unsigned integer.
- The **char** data type is a Unicode character (16 bits).
- The **float** data type is a single-precision floating point.
- The **double** data type is a double-precision floating point.
- The **bool** data type is a Boolean (true or false).
- The **decimal** data type is a decimal type with 28 significant digits (typically used for financial purposes).

Table C-2 shows the types in C# and the **System** namespace.

Table C-2	Types in C# and the System Namespace
C#	**System Namespace**
sbyte	System.SByte
byte	System.Byte
short	System.Int16
ushort	System.UInt16
int	System.Int32
uint	System.UInt32
long	System.Int64
ulong	System.UInt64
char	System.Char
float	System.Single
double	System.Double
bool	System.Boolean
decimal	System.Decimal

C.2.2 C# Namespace and Assembly versus Java Package

In Java, the source file of a class must have exactly the same name as the name of the class. When the source file is compiled, a class file is created for the class. The class file has to be organized in a directory hierarchy that is defined in its package path. It has been a burden for programmers to maintain consistency between the file layout and definition of package paths.

In C#, this burden is eased because the programs are organized in namespaces and assemblies in .NET Framework. Namespaces serve as an internal organization system for logical grouping of the classes, and as an external organization system for presenting program elements that are exposed to other programs. In a C# program, the keyword **using** refers to a namespace, just as the keyword **import** in Java refers to a package.

Assemblies, on the other hand, are the functional units of sharing and reuse in CLR. Assemblies provide CLR with the information it needs to be aware of type implementations. In physical terms, an assembly is a collection of physical files that are owned by the assembly. Assemblies serve as a unit of class deployment. When a program is compiled, all the assemblies that contain the required classes have to be supplied for reference.

C.2.3 Properties

The encapsulation principle typically leads us to store data in private members and to provide access to this data through public accessor methods that allow us to set and get values. A property in a Java class, say XXXX, usually follows the Java Bean convention, with a pair of methods, getXXXX and setXXXX, as public accessors.

    C# provides a special property syntax that simplifies user code. Rather than using methods, the properties can be accessed directly; the public accessors that are defined in the class are actually invoked behind the scene.

    In the following program, data members **Balance**, **Id**, and **Owner** of class **Account** are implemented as properties with public accessors, namely **get** and **put**. The first two properties are read-only without a **put** accessor, and the third one is read and write with **get** and **set** accessors. It is also possible to have a write-only property without a **get** accessor. Note that the keyword **value** in the **put** accessor represents the value to be set to the property.

```csharp
// Account.cs

public class Account
{
    private int id;
    private static int nextid = 1;
    private decimal balance;
    private string owner;
    public Account(decimal balance, string owner)
    {
        this.id = nextid++;
        this.balance = balance;
        this.owner = owner;
    }
    public void Deposit(decimal amount)
    {
        balance += amount;
    }
    public void Withdraw(decimal amount)
    {
        balance -= amount;
    }
    public decimal Balance
    {
        get
        {
            return balance;
        }
    }
    public int Id
    {
```

```
      get
      {
          return id;
      }
   }
   public string Owner
   {
      get
      {
          return owner;
      }
      set
      {
          owner = value;
      }
   }
}
```

Here is a program that tests this defined class.

```
// TestAccount.cs

using System;

public class TestAccount
{
   public static void Main(string[] args)
   {
      Account acc;
      acc = new Account(100, "Bob");
      ShowAccount(acc);
      acc.Deposit(25);
      acc.Withdraw(50);
      ShowAccount(acc);
        acc.Owner = "Carl";
      ShowAccount(acc);
      acc = new Account(200, "Mary");
      ShowAccount(acc);
   }
   private static void ShowAccount(Account acc)
   {
      Console.WriteLine(
          "id: {0} owner: {1} balance: {2:C}",
          acc.Id, acc.Owner, acc.Balance
      );
   }
}
```

Here is the output:

```
id: 1 owner: Bob balance: $100.00
id: 1 owner: Bob balance: $75.00
id: 1 owner: Carl balance: $75.00
id: 2 owner: Mary balance: $200.00
```

C.2.4 Indexers

C# provides various ways to access the encapsulated data. The properties discussed in the previous section provide access to a single piece of data of a class, making it appear like a public field. The indexers provide a similar capability for accessing a group of data items, using an array index notation.

Indexers are used when there is a private array or collection as a data member of a class. However, they may also apply to a group of data members other than an array or collection. In addition, a data element may be indexed by a data type other than an integer, such as a string.

The following program, ColorIndex.cs, shows how an indexer works. Class **ColorIndex** has three private data members of **byte** type, namely red, green, and blue, each holding an intensity value of a basic color. As can be seen, there are two ways in which these values may accessed via the color indexers:

1. Integer: 0 for red, 1 for green, and 2 for blue.
2. String: R or Red for red, G or Green for green, and B or Blue for blue. The string text should be case insensitive.

Here is the program.

```
// ColorIndex.cs
using System;
public class ColorIndex
{
   private byte red = 255;
   private byte green = 127;
   private byte blue = 0;
   public byte this[int index]
   {
      get
      {
         if (index == 0)
            return red;
         else if (index == 1)
            return green;
         else
            return blue;
      }
      set
```

```
        {
            if (index == 0)
                red = value;
            else if (index == 1)
                green = value;
            else
                blue = value;
        }
    }
    public byte this[string colorName]
    {
        get
        {
            byte returnByte ;
            switch(colorName.ToUpper()){
                case "R":
                case "RED":
                    returnByte = red;
                    break;
                case "G":
                case "GREEN":
                    returnByte = green;
                    break;
                case "B":
                case "BLUE":
                    returnByte = blue;
                    break;
                default:
                    returnByte = 0;
                    break;
            }
            return returnByte;
        }
        set
        {
            switch(colorName.ToUpper()){
                case "R":
                case "RED":
                    red = value;
                    break;
                case "G":
                case "GREEN":
                    green = value;
                    break;
                case "B":
                case "BLUE":
                    blue = value;
                    break;
            }
        }
    }
}
```

```
 public string Color
{
   get
   {
      return red + ":" + green + ":" + blue;
   }
}
 public string ColorHex
{
   get
   {
      return ⇓
      String.Format("{0:X}{1:X}{2:X}",red,green,blue);
   }
}
public static void Main(string[] args){
   ColorIndex.UnitTest(args);
}
public static void UnitTest(string[] args)
   {
      ColorIndex ci = new ColorIndex();
      Console.WriteLine(ci.Color);
      Console.WriteLine("red = {0}", ci[0]);
      Console.WriteLine("green = {0}", ci[1]);
      Console.WriteLine("blue = {0}", ci[2]);
      ci[0] = 77;
      ci[1] = 133;
      ci[2] = 199;
      Console.WriteLine(ci.Color);
      Console.WriteLine(ci.ColorHex);

      Console.WriteLine("red = {0}", ci["Red"]);
      Console.WriteLine("green = {0}", ci["Green"]);
      Console.WriteLine("blue = {0}", ci["Blue"]);
      ci["red"] = 78;
      ci["green"] = 134;
      ci["blue"] = 200;
      Console.WriteLine(ci.Color);
      Console.WriteLine(ci.ColorHex);

      Console.WriteLine("red = {0}", ci["r"]);
      Console.WriteLine("green = {0}", ci["g"]);
      Console.WriteLine("blue = {0}", ci["b"]);
      ci["r"] = 79;
      ci["g"] = 135;
      ci["b"] = 201;
      Console.WriteLine(ci.Color);
      Console.WriteLine(ci.ColorHex);
      }
   }
```

Here is the output of the program:

```
255:127:0
red = 255
green = 127
blue = 0
77:133:199
4D85C7
red = 77
green = 133
blue = 199
78:134:200
4E86C8
red = 78
green = 134
blue = 200
79:135:201
4F87C9
```

C.2.5 Statements

C# adds a new statement, **foreach**, for the loop logic and changes the rule to use the **switch** statement.

C.2.5.1 FOREACH

Unlike the C-like syntax, **foreach** is a new loop construct that is convenient to use. The statement

```
foreach(Object item in Object[] Items){
    ...
}
```

is equivalent to

```
for(int  i = 0;  i < Items.Length;  i++){
    Object item = Items[i];
    ...
}
```

C.2.5.2 SWITCH

In C#, the **switch** statement allows a program flow to be switched based on cases of various data types, including **integer**, **string**, and **enum**. In the program ColorIndex.cs you may have already seen that program flow may be switched based on cases of string. Moreover, the C# compiler checks the **switch** statement for any missing **break** so as to avoid unwanted fallthrough.

C.2.6 Method Parameter Passing, ref, and out

In Java, when you pass a primitive type of variable to a method as a parameter, it is always passed by value. Therefore, the change that is made to the variable within the method is not carried back when the program returns from the method. If you want to get the changes that a method makes to its parameters, you must pass the reference of a class with the variables in question as its data members.

In C#, on the other hand, you may force a parameter to be passed by reference, using the **ref** keyword. Furthermore, using the **out** keyword will cause the new value of the parameter to be returned and, in this case, the compiler to make sure the value has been assigned.

C.2.7 struct and enum

The keyword **struct** in C# is not the same as in C/C++. In C#, a **struct** is a lightweight class and may have methods. It also behaves as a class with the following exceptions:

- A **struct** is passed by **value** instead of reference.
- No inheritance is supported for a **struct**.
- A **struct** may not have a constructor with no parameters.
- A **struct** that defines constructors with parameters must explicitly define all of its data members before they return control to the caller.

Another keyword, **enum**, is omitted by Java. C# uses it as a collection that defines a type name for a related group of symbolic constants. Compared to **int**, **enum** is more readable. The .NET debugger nicely shows an **enum** value by its name instead of a number code.

C.2.8 Operator Overloading

Operator overloading is a feature that allows for implementation of some methods in a concise format, such as operators with new meanings regarding the class in question. For example, the concatenation of two strings, say s1 and s2, may be denoted as s1 + s2 if the operator '+' is overloaded with the method for concatenation. While it is excluded from Java, this feature has been included in C#.

C.2.9 Preprocessor

Macros are not allowed in Java and many Java programmers who come from the C and C++ world miss this feature. Currently, C# supports a group of **#if** directives for conditional compilation.

C.2.10 XML Documentation versus JavaDoc

C# has its own document notation similar to JavaDoc. However, C# documentation is in XML.

Summary

C# is a powerful programming language that makes software development much simpler and safer. C# under .NET Framework provides an ideal environment for Web programming. Java programmers and C++ programmers who work in Windows need to prepare themselves for the change. As discussed in this appendix, this migration can be a rather pleasant job for them.

New Features in JScript.NET

*J*Script, a relative of JavaScript, is a scripting language used to bring dynamic features to Web pages written in HTML. From its outset, JScript has been implemented by Web browsers only for Web page use and has always been an interpreted language. Now the .NET implementation of JScript, called JScript.NET (JS.NET), adds a number of features, including being a compiled language, CLR, and browser independence.

The new object-oriented features make JS.NET a full-fledged member of your programming language arsenal. JS.NET is currently in review with ECMA[1] and should be a candidate for both Web page scripting and stand-alone applications. The changes to JScript are much less than the changes made to Visual Basic in the .NET environment.

---

[1] *www.ecma.ch*. The CLI documents that cover JScript are TC39/TG3 and can be found on their Web site. ECMA was chosen as the standards body because Netscape had chosen them for JavaScript.

D.1 Why Use JS.NET?

It can be reasonably argued that with VB.NET and C#.NET there is no need for JScript at all. .NET languages can for the most part be used for not only building applications and server-side scripting but for client-side scripting too. This is one of the innovations of .NET. Microsoft is putting forth an architecture which is open to all languages and this means that languages with limited use like JScript can do more while retaining most of their original character. JScript's only use has been Web page scripting and with some modifications make it a .NET language.

But why do this? Why not leave JScript alone as a scripting language which browsers understand? Microsoft is putting forth an architecture where any language can make use of the CLR and benefit from it. One principle benefit is interoperability with CLR-base code. This means that the .NET version of JScript, JS.NET, can work with other .NET languages, script, and build applications. Legacy code built with JScript should still be usable with little if any modification and build new .NET-based Web pages and applications.

With languages like C#.NET and VB.NET which can perform scripting too, will JS.NET be used? Certainly, for the very reasons that JScript was used. In the case of Web pages, JScript has offered an object model which closely mirrored the browser object model better than other languages, and that continues to be the case. Legacy code is in place and coding modifications in another language is an unattractive prospect. JS.NET offers simple scripting capabilities that are now available for use outside of Web pages, possibly replacing languages like AWK and PERL for some jobs.

D.2 Compiled JScript

JS.NET is still available as a typeless language and may be interpreted in Web pages or compiled into stand-alone EXEs. However, this version may be strongly typed, giving you the best of both worlds. For quick scripting projects, you can use it typeless and produce quick, throwaway projects. For more durable uses, employ the typing capabilities to write more robust code: The choice is now yours. When compiled you can produce console EXEs, Windows EXEs, and DLLs. A console EXE is what we used to call a DOS-box application and what some call "running on the command line." Windows EXE produces more typical applications using the Windows GUI.

DLLs can be built using any CLR language and now by JS.NET too. The one caveat is that while JS.NET is a full Common Language Specification (CLS) consumer, it can use any of the existing by-ref parameters, indexers, delegates, events, operators, and conversions. It is something of an extended consumer, meaning it cannot extend classes with abstract methods or an abstract indexer. You cannot declare new delegate types, events, operators, or conversions. These details are beyond the scope of this book. Overall, being able to compile JScript can open new doors for programmers. Improvements in speed and performance are ready for you when using this language.

D.3 The Two Uses of JS.NET

JS.NET has two uses:

* As a scripting language for Web pages
* As a stand-alone scripting language

The two uses make immediate sense. The first, using it for scripting Web pages, is just as JScript has been used before. As .NET is deployed on client computers and employed by Web site developers, JS.NET's power to make more impressive Web pages will come out and justify its use.

The second use is as a stand-alone application language. People already using JScript for Web page scripting can take their knowledge and be productive on work other than Web pages. The same is true with C#.NET, which starts life as a full-fledged language that may be added to Web pages. It can build stand-alone applications and be used for Web page scripting.

D.4 JScript Tour in Visual Studio.NET

Visual Studio.NET (VS.NET) provides some support for JS.NET but not nearly as much support as it does for C#, C++, and VB. Other .NET languages get editing, compiling, debugging, and project-related tools support, but JS.NET support is limited to editing and some debugging.

D.4.1 Working with JS.NET in VS.NET

VS.NET does not support JS.NET the same way it does C#.NET, C++.NET, and VB.NET. VS.NET does not supply project templates to automate the process of creating, building, and maintaining JS.NET code. JS.NET is now a language that can produce executables, be embedded in Web pages, and provide general scripting service. Without a project to wrap your JS.NET code in, VS.NET makes JS.NET harder to work with than the other .NET languages.

To use JS.NET, you create text files and compile them from a prompt box. This is primitive compared to the other .NET languages and their templates and solutions.

D.4.2 Creating a JS.NET File

There are two kinds of JS.NET files that can be created in VS.NET, stand-alone JS.NET files and stand-alone ASP.NET pages. To create either of these, select File | New | File… from the main menu, then select the category Script. In the templates pane you may choose JScript file and JScript ASP.NET page from a number of files.

JScript file creates a vanilla empty file with no further support from VS.NET. It is as if you created an empty .txt file, except that a new solution will be created too. Using the solution will make it easier to maintain the JS.NET file that you create. This is not a template with supporting files or VS.NET framework, it's an empty solution.

JScript ASP.NET page creates an ASPX page with essential tags in place to use as a starting point for your Web code. JScript ASP.NET creates a solution too.

When solutions are created in VS.NET for JS.NET scripts or pages, the JS.NET file is not added to the solution. If you add the JS.NET file to the solution (as an existing item) you will be alerted that the JS.NET file is open in another project. This is because when your new JS.NET file is open, the solution is open, and it's not automatically done for you.

Note: For the remainder of this appendix, always create JS.NET script files.

D.4.3 Building a JS.NET Executable

To build an executable using JS.NET, run the compiler for JS.NET (JSC). Use the supplied Visual Studio.NET Command Prompt shortcut set up for you. This prompt already has the correct environmental variables set up. To make any Command Prompt box ready to do this, run CORVARS.BAT, buried deep in the Microsoft.NET folder when .NET was installed.

The command line making an executable out of JS.NET file is

```
jsc /t:exe your_JScript_file
```

D.4.4 Running Your JS.NET Executable

From a prompt box or from Windows Explorer you can now run your executable. An executable built with JS.NET runs like any other executable. Type the name and arguments and hit Enter:

```
> your_JScript_file
```

These are the basics of creating source files for your JS.NET projects and then building single files into executables. Later in this appendix we discuss building multiple-source projects.

D.5 Object-Oriented Features

Now that you know how to build and run executables we can look at the new features of JS.NET. JScript always had some object-oriented features, but they were unlike those of more common high-level languages. Now these features have been brought into line with those of other languages.

D.5.1 Classes

Originally JScript had the object-oriented notion of classes that were not easily recognizable as such. Thus JScript had less to offer than other languages that had stronger object-oriented features such as C++. The class mechanism used **Expando** properties to mark functions as being part of a class. **Expando** properties are a feature of JScript providing class-like behavior. Function visibility was not an issue since all functions in JScript were visible. Typing data never existed so typical object-oriented concerns about which functions were public and which were private were of no concern.

This is an example of **Expando** versus class-built code. First the **Expando** version:

```
function Tape( name, length)
{
  this.name = name;
  this.length = length;
}
function Tape.prototype.Name()
{
  return this.name;
}
function Tape.prototype.Length()
{
  return this.length;
}
// Create Tape and get its name and length
var myTape = new Tape("Patton", 115);
print(myTape.Name());
```

JS.NET, on the other hand, has object-oriented class syntax, which means you can implement code that matches your object-oriented design directly. The keyword **class** encapsulates functions and variables into an atomic unit, an object.

```
//ClassEx.js
// A class that models the tape object which a VCR uses

class Tape
{
   var name: String;
   var length: long;

   function Tape(name: String, length: long)
   {
       this.name = name;
       this.length = length;
   }
   function Name() : String
   {
       return name;
   }

   function Length(): long
   {
       return length;
   }
}

// Main
var tape : Tape = new Tape("Patton", 94);
print("Tape name: " + tape.Name());
```

Because functions are grouped together into one package of code, classes provide better visual cues that pieces of code belong together. Classes provide for clearer syntax when you use them too.

If you take this bit of code and put it into a file called ClassEx.js you may build and run it this way. Type what appears after the prompt ">":

```
>jsc /t:exe ClassEx.js
…compiler output appears…
>ClassEx
Tape name: The Shining
```

D.5.2 Unique Names

Because JS.NET is a case-sensitive language, variables and functions are in the same namespace. All names have to be uniquely spelled and are case-sensitive. A variable and a function name that are spelled the same will produce an error message when compiled.

In our naming convention, variables begin with a lowercase letter and functions begin with a capitalized letter. JScript has always been case-sensitive and many mistakes that lead to scripts not working correctly are due to a control name[2] or object model[3] element being correctly spelled but incorrectly cased.

D.5.3 Inheritance

JScript does not have inheritance, while JS.NET has two kinds of inheritance, implementation and interface inheritance. JS.NET implements single implementation inheritance the way other .NET languages do, with a few exceptions. A class may be set up as the specialization of a more general class through the keyword extends, as in **derived_class extends base_class**.

```
class Base
{
    . . . attributes and methods . . .
}

class Derived extends Base
{
    . . . attributes and methods . . .
}
```

All members of a class are public by default. See Section D.5.5 for more information.

A class should have a defined constructor that is a function by the same name as the class with no return type. The constructor function is where initialization code is placed and may have parameters. If two or more constructors exist, they must have unique parameters to distinguish them. Here is a simple example of using two constructors. The purpose of this example is to show the simple form that a JS.NET application takes.

```
class Demo
{
    function Demo()  // constructor A
    {
     print("Demo constructor");
    }
    function Demo( item: String ) // constructor B
    {
     print("Demo string is " + item);
```

---

[2] Every control on a Web page has a name. Names are one of the ways scripts refer to the controls.

[3] Every browser has a way of presenting its internal representation of its objects to scripting languages like JScript. This is called the document object model, often called object model or DOM for short.

```
    }
}

// main

var aDemo1 : Demo = new Demo(); // execute constructor A
                                // execute constructor B
var aDemo2 : Demo = new Demo("the washing machine");
```

Notice that those are two constructors in class **Demo**. You can create as many constructors for a class as there are different sets of parameters. Typically, a single constructor with no parameters will do.

If one class inherits from another class, the immediate base class (called the super class) constructor is called automatically. This is what you would expect since the derived object must be made up of all the ancestors it possesses.

In this next example, all other methods in the ancestor object will be called polymorphically when there is no overriding method in the derived class. We use two classes named **Base** and **Derived** to illustrate this:

```
class Base
{
    function Base()          { }
    function PerformAction() { }
    function ReturnResult()  { }
}

class Derived extends Base
{
    function Derived()          { }
    function Specialization() { }
    function ReturnResult()    { }
}

// Main body of code
obj = new Derived; // Construct the derived object
obj.PerformAction(); // The base class' PerformAction()
obj.Specialization(); // The derived class' Specialization()
obj.ReturnResult(); // The derived class' ReturnResult()

A concise real-world example of this.
// InheritanceTest.JS

class Tape
{
    var name: String;
    var length: long;

    function Tape(name: String, length: long)
```

```
    {
        print ("In Tape constructor");
        this.name = name;
        this.length = length;
    }
    function Name() : String
    {
        return name;
    }

    function Length(): long
    {
        return this.length; // added "this" to select
                            // correct scope
    }
}

class CompressedTape extends Tape
{
  var compressionLevel : int;

  function CompressedTape(name: String, length: long)
    {
        print ("In CompressedTape constructor");
        this.name = name;
        this.length = length;
        compressionLevel = 2;
    }
    function Length(): long
    {
        return this length/compressionLevel;
    }
}

// Main
print ("Running... InheritanceTest");

var tape : Tape;

tape = new Tape("The Shining", 120);
tape = new CompressedTape("The Shining", 120);
```

To build this example:

```
>jsc /t:exe Inheritance.js
```

To run this example:

```
>Inheritance.js
Running... InheritanceTest

In Tape constructor
Tape: _test
Tape: name: The Shining
Tape: len: 120

In Tape constructor      << this is called by CompressedTape
                         << constructor automatically
In CompressedTape constructor
Tape: _test
Tape: name: The Shining
Tape: len: 60
```

A second kind of inheritance is interface inheritance, which you can create by adding the keyword **implements** and adding one or more interface names separated by commas. The base classes are called **interfaces** and are defined without implementation.

Here is an example of interface inheritance where form a VCR object from a MatrixDisplay class and a TapeMechanism class.

```
interface MatrixDisplay
{
    function DisplayDigit(digit : int );
}
interface TapeMechanism
{
    function LoadTape(tape: Tape);
}
class VCR implements MatrixDisplay, TapeMechanism
{
    function DisplayDigit(digit : int ) {…}
    function LoadTape(tape: Tape) {…}
}
```

In this case the two classes, **MatrixDisplay** and **TapeMechanism**, are not providing implementations for their functions to class **VCR** to reuse directly. These classes provide the signatures (function names and arguments only) that **VCR** has to reimplement. When this is done, other technology can be used that normally could not, technology that supplies interfaces only, such as COM. This is how you provide a form of multiple inheritance. Class **VCR** is inheriting its structure from **MatrixDisplay** and **TapeMechanism**.

D.5.4 Strong Typing

In JS.NET you can declare variables using any .NET Framework type as well as types imported through namespaces, user-defined types as classes, and existing JScript types. Explicit typing has this syntax:

```
JScript way…
Var name [= default];

JS.NET way…
Var name : type [=default];
```

The inclusion of **type** in the declaration is the critical difference. By typing the variable you add information the compiler needs to ensure that the variable will be a valid value for that type.

There is potential overlap between .NET Framework types and JScript built-in objects, so JS.NET provides a mapping between the two:

Type	in JScript.NET
Boolean	Boolean
Number	Number
String	String
Object	Object
Date	Date object
array	Array
Function	Function object

The documentation tells us that if the **FAST** option is employed, strict type checking is enabled. This doesn't work! You don't need types even though the documentation says so. Eventually this will be fixed.

D.5.5 Visibility

JS.NET can declare classes or components of classes visible or not visible to other classes. Visibility cannot be applied to global functions or variables. Here is a table showing the various kinds of visibility.

Visibility	Meaning
Public	Classes and all components are made visible everywhere. By default all classes are public.
Protected	Methods, properties, and fields are visible to members of this class and all subclasses.
Private	Methods, properties, and fields are visible to members of this class only.
Internal	Classes, methods, properties, and fields are visible within the package declared only.

A member, variable, or function is by default public and therefore visible to the outside world. Adding the public modifier makes no difference because all JScript members are public by default.

As an illustration of visibility concepts as implemented in JS.NET, we introduce a code sample that mimics a VCR. Class VideoTape has two attributes, tapeLength and tapeName. One is private and the other protected, meaning that class VideoTape is the only class that can access tapeLength, the private member. This code resides in VideoTape.js.

```
Class VideoTape {
    private var tapeLength;   -- We've added 'private' here.
    protected var tapeName = "Godfather Part I";
    function ChangeVideoTape( newTape, newLength) {
      tapeName = newTape;
      tapeLength = newLength;
    }
    // New function to access 'tapeName'
    function TapeName()) : String {
      return tapeName;
    }
}
Class User
{
  Watch( aTape ) {
    print ("I am watching ", aTape.tapeName);
  }
  WatchProperly( aTape ) {
    print ("I am watching ", aTape.TapeName());
  }
}
// Here is the "main" code section in this file.
// Both attributes will not be available to direct
// access by other objects. A VideoTape object however
// will always be able to access these.
```

```
var myTape : VideoTape = new VideoTape;
myTape.ChangeVideoTape("Horatio Hornblower", 90);
print ("Tape name:" + myTape.TapeName());
myTape.ChangeVideoTape("Risky Business", 120);
print ("Tape name:" + myTape.TapeName());
var aPerson : User = new User;
aPerson.Watch (myTape);
// an error occurs here - myTape.tapeName is a protected
// member and aPerson cannot access it directly.
//
// This way works because WatchProperly uses TapeName()
// which is public.
aPerson.WatchProperly (myTape);

> VideoTape

Tape name: Horatio Hornblower
Tape name: Risky Business
```

D.6 Performance Enhancements

The **Option Fast** feature of JS.NET disables a number of features in favor of other features. **Option Fast** tells us the following:

* All variables must be declared.
* You cannot assign values to functions.
* Arguments to functions must be the correct number.
* The **arguments** property in function calls is disavowed.
* Predefined properties in JScript objects must not be assigned or deleted.
* You cannot add **Expando** properties to the built-in objects.

Using this option could result in faster code, but if you apply it to existing JScript programs you may get compiler errors.

Declaring variables with types leads to better coding practice and better code. But those who still don't want to avail themselves of this capability can still leave variables untyped. However, JS.NET has an improvement in store for them. Variables that are not typed are coerced into an approximate correct type for them. Where JScript essentially typed all variables as a variant, JS.NET coerces variables into the .NET Framework types if it can tell what they are through their context. As of this writing these **Option Fast** features do not seem to be working as billed. Expect this to be corrected in the future.

D.7 Packaging and Deployment (EXE, DLLs, and Packaging)

For a general discussion of assemblies see Appendix B. You can build multi-file JS.NET programs by specifying all the JS modules on the JSC command line. Here is an example of this with two modules, one containing a class and the other acting as the main. The command line is

```
jsc /out:Book.exe /t:exe Book.js BookMain.js
```

We produce an output EXE called **Book.exe** (**/out:Book.exe**); it's a console application (**/t:exe**) made of the two JS modules at the end of the line.

```
// Book.js

class Book
{
    private var title : String;
    private var author : String;
    private var ISBN : String;

  function Book( title: String, author: String,
     ISBN: String)
   {
     this.title = title; this.author = author;
     this.ISBN = ISBN;
   }
    function Talk()
   {
       print ("The book, " + title + " was written by "
          + author.);
   }
}


// BookMain.js

// Main
var aBook : Book = new Book("Leaves of Grass","Walt
Whitman","0553211161");
aBook.Talk();

>jsc /t:exe /:out Book.js BookMain.js
>Book

The book Leaves of Grass was written by Walt Whitman.
```

D.7.1 DLLs

You can build JScript code into DLLs that is consistent with other .NET languages. This is new and very useful for all the reasons DLLs have been used. Your JS.NET project can be separated into pieces for easier development by various teams or programmers. It can be delivered in pieces, and maintained and upgraded in pieces.

The compiler switch **/t:library** builds the files on the command line into a library that will typically end in .dll. For example, a file called Tape.js might include the following:

```
// Tape.js

class Tape
{
  var name: String
  function Tape(name: String)
  {
    this.name = name
  }
}
```

Another file called TestTape.js contains the main:

```
// TestTape.js

var myTape = new Tape('The Yakousa")
print (myTape.name)

>jsc /t:library /out:Tape.dll Tape.js
This produces a DLL that contains Tape.js code. The command to
link them is
>jsc /out:TapePkg.exe /r:Tape.dll TestTape.js

>TapePkg
The Yakousa
```

D.7.2 Package and Import Keywords

Namespaces can be used with JS.NET. **Package** and **import** keywords provide the necessary support, as they do in other languages. **Package** surrounds JS.NET classes only. All the symbols for the enclosed class and members are added to the declared namespace.

```
// ImportPackage.JS

Package VHS
{
  class Play
  {
```

```
      function Play(name: String, length: long)
      {
      print ("VHS tape "+name+" running "+length+" minutes);
      }
   }
}

Package DVD
{
  class Play
  {
    function Play(name: String, length: long)
    {
    print ("DVD disk "+name+" running "+length+" minutes);
    }
  }
}

// Main
var play : Play;
import VHS;
play = new Play ("The Shining", 120);
import DVD;
play = new Play ("The Shining", 120);

>jsc /t:exe ImportPackage.js
>ImportPackage
VHS tape The Shining running 120 minutes
DVD disk The Shining running 120 minutes
```

Using packages in DLL and then including them for import with other modules does not work as stated in JScript.NET documentation. This should be fixed eventually.

D.8 Debugging

Debugging JS.NET can be done with two tools, VS.NET and Cordbg. We address VS.NET here, giving you the basic process.

There are two ways to use VS.NET to debug an executable. First, if a solution exists containing your files, use it. Select File | Open Solution... and select the solution. This is the best way to start.

Second, open the project and then create a solution for it. From VS.NET, close your existing solution and open the executable file to be debugged. Select File | Open | Project... and open your executable. You will be asked to save a solution—do so. Then open the JS.NET files that you want to debug that are part of this executable.

The solution file will ultimately carry references to all of your files, which is a real convenience.

Set break points on the lines of code and run the debugger. All features of the debugger work, such as code inspection, variable inspection, watch windows, and call stack.

Debugging JScript in VS.NET is not well integrated yet. First, there is a very primitive error message regarding text editor compatibility. If you direct the output of the JS.NET compiler to the output window, you can double-click on error messages in the output window and that line will be highlighted in VS.NET's text editor.

Second, and more importantly, the executable can be debugged in the IDE. The way that you do this is to open the executable as a project, not a file. If you bring up the Solution Explorer (Figure D-1) you can see the files that you have opened. Then open your JS.NET files.

Once you've done this, you can use all the debugging tools available on the Debug menu. When you are done, select File | Close Solution to close this debugging session.

For stand-alone applications built with JS.NET, two debuggers come with the .NET Software Development Kit (SDK), DbgCLR and Cordbg. The former is targeted to debugging programs where CLR issues are at stake and the latter is a command-line debugger for general use. Use VS.NET when possible to debug your application—it's easier.

As of this writing you debug the executable, not the solution. Using a solution to corral JS.NET files makes sense, but no support beyond this is apparent.

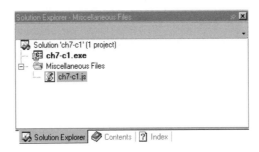

Figure D-1   *Solution Explorer.*

D.9 The Compiler

Compiling JScript code is new and one of the improvements JS.NET offers. As with all other compiled languages, there are various features of the compiler to take advantage of.

D.9.1 Conditional Compilation

Conditional compilation has been in JScript since Version 3. Various variables are predefined for you to use with JS.NET. Conditional compilation is activated by either **@cc_on** directive or **@if/@else/@end** directives. In Web pages **@cc_on** is required before any conditional compiler variable used. In executables this is not so—you can use variables and **@if** and its mates immediately. There are a number of predefined constants that the compiler can take advantage of:

@_win32	True if running on a Win32 system
@_win16	True if running on a Win16 system
@_mac	True if running on an Apple Macintosh system
@_alpha	True if running on a DEC Alpha processor
@_x86	True if running on an Intel processor
@_mc680x0	True if running on a Motorola 680×0 processor
@_PowerPC	True if running on a Motorola PowerPC processor
@_jscript	Always true
@_jscript_build	Contains the build number of the JScript scripting engine
@_jscript_version	Contains the JScript version number in major.minor format

For compiled code conditional compiling is a parameter, **/d[efine]:<symbols>**, added to the command line:

```
>jsc /out: TestTape.exe  /d:@_alpha TestTape.js
```

This produces an alpha processor version of the JS.NET code if the conditional compiler **@if/@end** block is present.

D.9.2 Command Line Arguments

Running the compiler from a command prompt with the help switch **>jsc /?** causes the compiler banner and usage information to be displayed.

```
Microsoft (R) JScript.NET Compiler Version 7.00.9254 [CLR
version 1.00.2914]
Copyright (C) Microsoft Corp 2000-2001. All rights reserved.
```

This banner indicates compiler and CLR version numbers. If you have earlier versions the features described in this appendix may not be available.

The compiler invocation syntax is simple:

```
jsc [options] <source files> [[options] <source files>...]
```

Finally, here are the options for this version of the compiler:

```
JScript.NET Compiler Options:
```

```
                       - OUTPUT FILES -
 /out:<file>
```

You must specify the name of the output file. If it is not specified, the output file will be named for the first file in the list of files on the command line:

```
 >jsc /out:DrawPrj.exe  draw.js, gui.dll
```

```
 /t[arget]:exe
 /t[arget]:winexe
 /t[arget]:library
```

Create an executable, console or windows, or DLL. If not specified, a console executable is the default.

```
                       - INPUT FILES -
 /autoref[+|-] /autoref or /autoref+ is the default and auto-
 matically searches for assemblies for you based on imported
 namespaces and fully qualified names in your code. If /nost-
 dlib is used, then /autoref is turned off.
 /lib:<path>[,<path2>]
```

Specify additional directories to search for libraries.

```
 /r[eference]:<file_list>
```

Specify additional directories to search for references. The directory where the compiler is working is included by default. <file_list> is a comma-separated list of DLL or other assemblies used to link to this job.

```
 /lib: dir1[, dir2]
```

Directories to look for assemblies are specified by /r. The current directory is always included in the search by default.

```
                       - RESOURCES -
 /win32res:<file>
```

Specifies Win32 resource file (.res) to insert into your assembly. Resource files can be created with a resource editor such as Visual Studio.NET. Resources typically contain version information and bitmaps.

```
/res[ource]: <filename> [,<name>[,public|private]]
```

Embeds the specified managed resource into the assembly. <name> is the logical name of the resource. The resource can be public, the default, or private.

```
/linkres[ource]: <filename>[,<name>[,public|private]]
```

Links the specified resource to this assembly rather than embedding it. /resource performs an embed.

```
- CODE GENERATION -
/cls[+|-]
```

This switch ensures the output of JScript is consumable by another CLR-based language. By default it is not enabled.

```
/debug[+|-]
```

The compiler emits debugging information into a .PDB file. By default it is not enabled.

```
/fast[+|-]
```

Disable compiler language features to allow better code generation. These features are as follows:

- All variables must be declared.
- Functions cannot be assigned or redefined dynamically.
- Predefined properties of built-in objects are marked **DontEnum**, **DontDelete**, and **ReadOnly**. They may not be expanded (**Expando**) other than by the **Global** object.
- The **arguments** variable is not available within function bodies.
- Assigments to read-only variables, fields, and methods are not allowed.

By default **fast** is disabled.

```
/warnaserror[+|-]
```

Compiler treats warnings as errors and is enabled by default.

```
/w[arn]:<level>
```

Sets the warning level:

- 0 turns off all warnings; error messages are still available.
- 1 displays errors and severe warnings.

- 2 displays all errors and level 1 warnings, such as class member problems.
- 3 displays all errors, and level 1 and 2 warnings, such as expression evaluations.
- 4 displays all errors and warnings. This is the default.

```
                      - MISCELLANEOUS -
@<filename>
```

Read response file for more options.

```
/?
/help
```

Display help.

```
/d[efine]:<symbols>
```

Define conditional compilation symbol(s).

```
/nologo
```

Do not display compiler copyright banner.

```
/print[+|-]
```

Provide **print()** function and is enabled by default.

```
                        - ADVANCED -
/codepage:<id>
```

Compiler uses the specified code page ID to open source files.

```
/lcid:id
```

Compiler uses the specified code page for printing out messages.

```
/nostdlib[+|-]
```

Compiler does not import standard library (mscorlib.dll) and change the autoref default to off.

```
/utf8output[+|-]
```

Emit compiler output in UTF-8 character encoding.

```
/versionsafe[+|-]
```

Compiler forces user to write version-safe code.

Summary

JS.NET builds on JScript's feature set, making it a .NET language. JS.NET includes features that allow it to work with other .NET languages as well as the CLR and compile code into executables. It provides object-oriented capabilities, moving it away from its scripting-only roots into application programming. All of the JS.NET features have not been implemented, but most seem to be on their way as of this writing.

Visual Studio.NET

Although it is possible to program .NET using only the command line compiler, it is much easier and more enjoyable to use Visual Studio.NET. In this appendix we cover the basics of using Visual Studio to edit, compile, run, and debug programs. You will then be equipped to use Visual Studio in what you have learned in the book. This appendix covers the basics to get you up and running using Visual Studio. Visual Studio is a very elaborate Windows application that is highly configurable, and you may encounter variations in the exact layout of windows, what is shown by default, and so on. As you work with Visual Studio, a good attitude is to see yourself as an explorer discovering a rich and varied new country.

E.1 Overview of Visual Studio.NET

Open up Microsoft Visual Studio.NET 7.0 (VS.NET) and you will see a starting window similar to what is shown in Figure E-1.

What you see on default startup is the main window with an HTML page that can help you navigate among various resources, open or create projects, and change your profile information. (If you close the start page, you can get it back anytime from the menu Help | Show Start Page.) Click

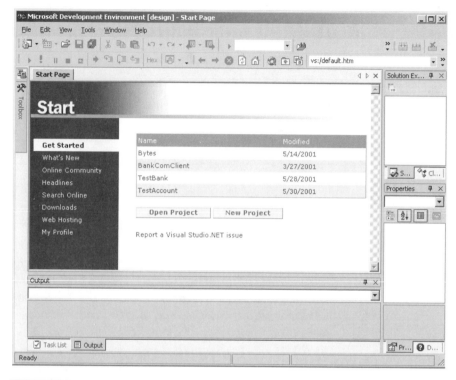

Figure E-1   *VS.NET main window.*

on My Profile to bring up a profile page on which you can change various settings. There is a standard profile for typical work in Visual Studio (Visual Studio Developer profile), and special ones for various languages. Since VS.NET is the unification of many development environments, programmers used to one particular previous environment may prefer a particular keyboard scheme, window layout, and so on. For example, if you choose the profile Visual Basic Developer, you will get the Visual Basic Version 6 keyboard scheme. In this book we will use all the defaults, so go back to the Visual Studio Developer profile if you made any changes. See Figure E-2.

To gain an appreciation of some of the diverse features in VS.NET, open up the Bank console solution in the AppE directory for this appendix (File | Open Solution..., navigate to the Bank directory, and open the file Bank.sln). You will see quite an elaborate set of windows. See Figure E-3.

Starting from the left are icons for the Server Explorer and the Toolbox, followed by the main window area, which currently is just a gray area.

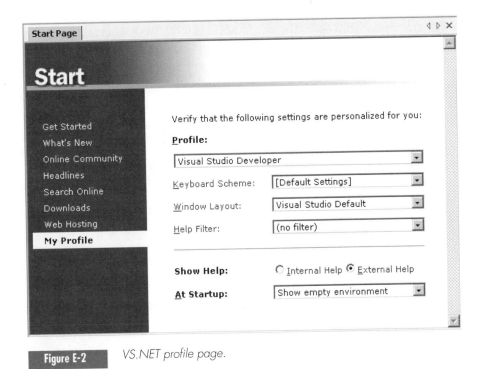

Figure E-2   *VS.NET profile page.*

Underneath the main window is the Output window, which shows the results of builds and so on. Continuing our tour, on the top right is the Solution Explorer, which enables you to conveniently see all the files in a solution, which may consist of several projects. On the bottom right is the Properties window, which lets you conveniently edit properties on forms for Windows applications. The Properties window is very similar to the Properties window in Visual Basic.

From the Solution Explorer you can navigate to files in the projects. In turn, double-click on each of Account.cs and Bank.cs, the two source files in the Bank project. Text editor windows will be brought up in the main window area. Across the top of the main window are horizontal tabs you can use to select any of the open windows. VS.NET allows you to select which window to show from the Windows menu. Figure E-4 shows the open source files with the horizontal tabs.

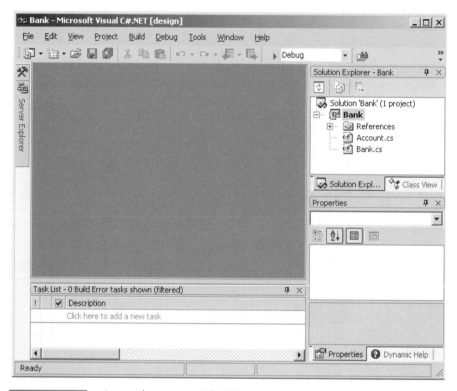

A console project in VS.NET.

E.2 Toolbars

VS.NET comes with many different toolbars. You can configure which toolbars you wish displayed, and you can drag toolbars to any position you find convenient. You can also customize toolbars by adding or deleting buttons that correspond to different commands.

To specify which toolbars are displayed, bring up the menu View | Toolbars. You can also right-click in any empty area of a toolbar. There will be a checkmark next to the toolbars that are currently displayed. By clicking on an item on this menu you can make the corresponding toolbar button appear or disappear. For your work in this book add the Build and Debug toolbars.

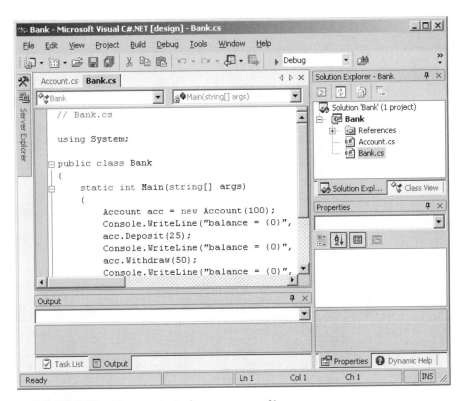

Figure E-4   *Horizontal tabs for open source files.*

We want to make sure that the Start Without Debugging command is available on the Debug toolbar. If it is not already on your Debug toolbar (it is a red exclamation point), you can add it by the following procedure, which can also be used to add other commands to toolbars.

1. Select the menu Tools | Customize... to bring up the Customize dialog.

2. Select the Commands tab.

3. In Categories, select Debug, and in Commands select Start Without Debugging. See Figure E-5.

4. Drag the selected command onto the Debug toolbar, positioning it where you desire. Place it to the immediate right of the wedge-shaped Start button.

5. Close the Customize dialog.

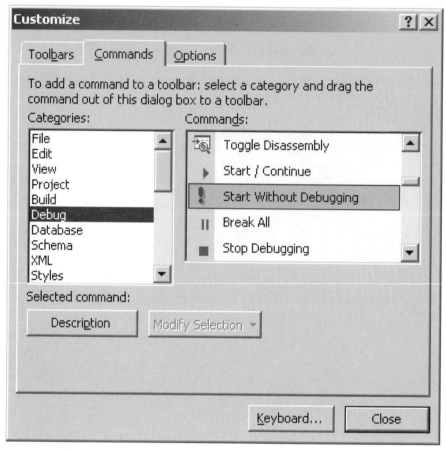

Adding a new command to a toolbar.

E.3 Creating a Console Application

As our first exercise in using Visual Studio, we will create a simple console application. Our program, Bytes, will attempt to calculate how many bytes there are in a kilobyte, a megabyte, a gigabyte, and a terabyte. If you want to follow along on your PC as you read, you can use the Demos directory for this chapter. The first version is in Bytes\Step1. A final version can be found in Bytes\Step3.

E.3.1 Creating a C# Project

1. From the VS.NET main menu choose File | New | Project.... This will bring up the New Project dialog.
2. For Project Types choose Visual C# Projects and for Templates choose Empty Project.
3. Click the Browse button, navigate to Demos, and click Open.
4. In the Name field, type **Bytes**. See Figure E-6. Click OK.

E.3.2 Adding a C# File

At this point you will have an empty C# project. We are now going to add a file, Bytes.cs, which contains the text of our program.

1. In Solution Explorer right-click over Bytes and choose Add | Add New Item.... This will bring up the Add New Item dialog.
2. For Categories choose Local Project Items and for Templates choose Code File.
3. For Name type **Bytes.cs**. See Figure E-7. Click Open.

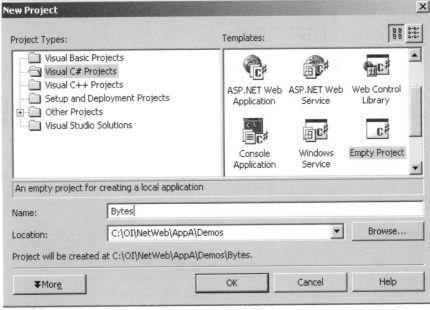

Figure E-6   *Creating an empty C# project.*

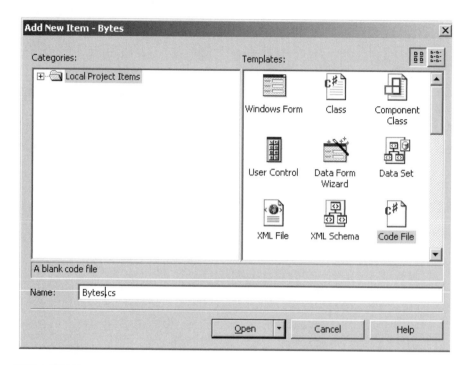

Figure E-7   *Adding an empty C# file to a C# project.*

E.4 Using the VS.NET Text Editor

In the Solution Explorer double-click on Bytes.cs. This will open up the empty file Bytes.cs in the VS.NET text editor. Type in the following program, and notice things like color syntax highlighting, used to indicate reserved words as you type.

```csharp
// Bytes.cs

using System;

public class Bytes
{
   public static int Main(string[] args)
   {
      int bytes = 1024;
      Console.WriteLine("kilo = {0}", bytes);
      bytes = bytes * 1024;
      Console.WriteLine("mega = {0}", bytes);
      bytes = bytes * 1024;
      Console.WriteLine("giga = {0}", bytes);
      bytes = bytes * 1024;
```

```
        Console.WriteLine("tera = {0}", bytes);
        return 0;
    }
}
```

Besides the color syntax highlighting, other features include automatic indenting. All in all, you should find the VS.NET editor friendly and easy to use.

E.4.1 Building the Project

You can build the project by using one of the following:

- Menu Build | Build
- Toolbar Build button
- Keyboard shortcut Ctrl + Shift + B

E.4.2 Running the Program

You can run the program by using one of the following:

- Menu Debug | Start Without Debugging
- Toolbar Start Without Debugging button
- Keyboard shortcut Ctrl + F5

You will see the following output in a console window that opens up:

```
kilo = 1024
mega = 1048576
giga = 1073741824
tera = 0
Press any key to continue
```

We will investigate the reason for this strange output later. If you press any key, as indicated, the console window will close.

E.4.3 Running the Program in the Debugger

You can run the program in the debugger by using one of the following:

- Menu Debug | Start
- Toolbar Start button
- Keyboard shortcut F5

A console window will briefly open up and then immediately close. If you want the window to stay open, you must explicitly program for it, for example, by asking for input. You can set a break point to stop execution before the program exits. We outline features of the debugger later in this appendix.

E.5 Project Configurations

A project configuration specifies build settings for a project. You can have several different configurations, and each configuration will be built in its own directory, so you can exercise the different configurations independently. Every project in a VS.NET solution has two default configurations, Debug and Release. As the names suggest, the Debug configuration will build a debug version of the project, where you can do source-level debugging by setting break points, and so on. The bin\Debug directory will then contain a program database file with a .pdb extension that holds debugging and project state information.

You can choose the configuration from the main toolbar. You can also choose the configuration using the menu Build | Configuration Manager..., which will bring up the Configuration Manager dialog. From the Active Solution Configuration drop-down menu, choose Release. See Figure E-8.

Build the project again. Now a second version of the IL language file Bytes.exe is created, this time in the bin\Release directory. There will be no .pdb file in this directory.

E.5.1 Creating a New Configuration

Sometimes it is useful to create additional configurations, which can save alternate build settings. As an example, let's create a configuration for a checked build. If you build with the /checked compiler switch, the compiler will generate IL code to check for integer underflow and overflow. In VS.NET you set compiler options through dialog boxes. The following steps

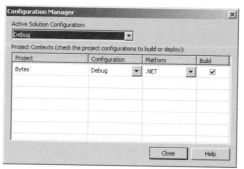

Figure E-8   *Choosing Release in the Configuration Manager.*

will guide you through creating a new configuration, called CheckedDebug, that will build a checked version of the program.

1. Bring up the Configuration Manager dialog.

2. From the Active Solution Configuration drop-down menu, choose <New...>. The New Solution Configuration dialog will come up.

3. Type **CheckedDebug** as the configuration name. Choose Copy Settings from **Debug**. Check "Also create new project configuration(s)." See Figure E-9. Click OK.

E.5.2 Setting Build Settings for a Configuration

Next we set the build settings for the new configuration. (You could also set build settings for one of the standard configurations, if you wanted to make any changes from the defaults provided.) Check the toolbar to verify that the new CheckedDebug is the currently active configuration.

1. Right-click over Bytes in the Solution Explorer and choose Properties. The Bytes Property Pages dialog comes up.

2. In Configuration Properties, select Build. Change the setting for "Check for overflow underflow" to True (see Figure E-10). Click OK.

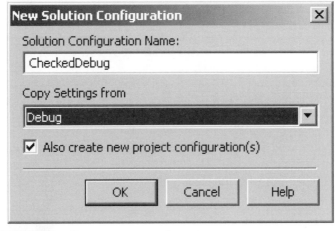

Figure E-9   *Creating a new configuration.*

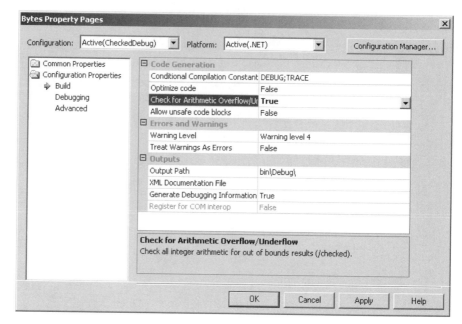

Figure E-10   *Changing the build settings for a configuration.*

E.6 Debugging

In this section we discuss some of the debugging facilities in VS.NET. To be able to benefit from debugging at the source code level, you should have built your executable using a Debug configuration, as discussed previously. There are two ways to enter the debugger:

- *Just-in-Time Debugging.* You run normally, and if an exception occurs you will be allowed to enter the debugger. The program has crashed, so you may not be able to run further from here to single step, set break points, and so on. But you will be able to see the value of variables, and you will see the point at which the program failed.
- *Standard Debugging.* You start the program under the debugger. You may set break points, single step, and so on.

E.6.1 Just-in-Time Debugging

Build and run (without debugging) the Bytes program from the previous section, using the CheckedDebug configuration. This time the program will not run through smoothly to completion, but an exception will be thrown. A Just-In-Time Debugging dialog will be shown (see Figure E-11). Click Yes to debug.

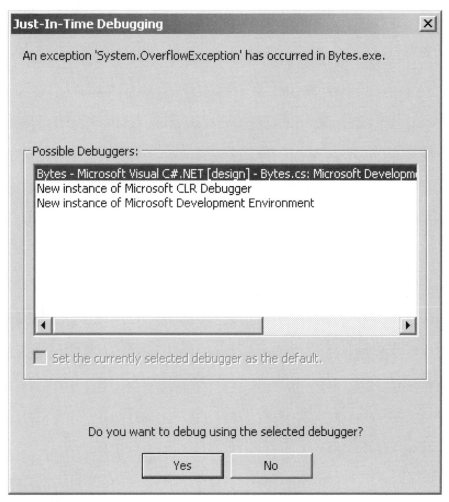

Figure E-11   *Just-in-Time Debugging dialog is displayed in response to an exception.*

Click OK in the Attach to Process dialog and then click Break in the Microsoft Development Environment dialog. You will now be brought into a window showing the source code where the problem arose, with an arrow pinpointing the location.

To stop debugging you can use the Stop Debugging toolbar button or the menu Debug | Stop Debugging.

E.6.2 Standard Debugging

E.6.2.1 BREAK POINTS

The way you typically do standard debugging is to set a break point and then run the code using the debugger. As an example, set a break point at the first line:

```
bytes = bytes * 1024;
```

The easiest way to set a break point is by clicking in the gray bar to the left of the source code window. You can also set the cursor on the desired line and click the hand toolbar button to toggle a break point (set if not set, and remove if a break point is set). Now you can run under the debugger, and the break point should be hit. A yellow arrow over the red dot of the break point shows where the break point has been hit. See Figure E-12.

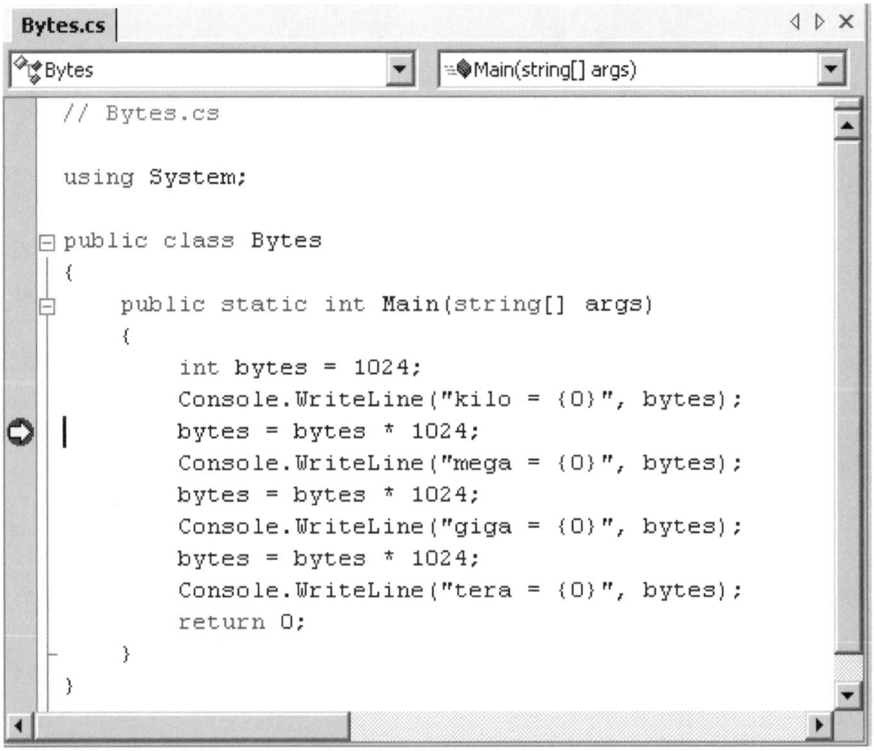
Bytes.cs
Bytes
Main(string[] args)
// Bytes.cs
using System;
public class Bytes
{
public static int Main(string[] args)
{
int bytes = 1024;
Console.WriteLine("kilo = {0}", bytes);
bytes = bytes * 1024;
Console.WriteLine("mega = {0}", bytes);
bytes = bytes * 1024;
Console.WriteLine("giga = {0}", bytes);
bytes = bytes * 1024;
Console.WriteLine("tera = {0}", bytes);
return 0;
}
}

Figure E-12 *A break point has been hit.*

When you are done with a break point, you can remove it by clicking again in the gray bar or by toggling with the hand toolbar button. If you want to remove all break points, you can use the menu Debug | Clear All Breakpoints, or you can use the toolbar button.

E.6.2.2 WATCHING VARIABLES

At this point you can inspect variables. The easiest way is to slide the mouse over the variable you are interested in, and the value will be shown as a yellow tool tip. You can also right-click over a variable and choose Quick Watch (or use the eyeglasses toolbar button). Figure E-13 shows a typical QuickWatch window. You can also change the value of a variable from this window.

When you are stopped in the debugger, you can add a variable to the Watch window by right-clicking over it and choosing Add Watch. The Watch window can show a number of variables, and the Watch window stays open as the program executes. When a variable changes value, the new value is shown in red. Figure E-14 shows the Watch window (note that the display has been changed to hexadecimal, as described in the next section).

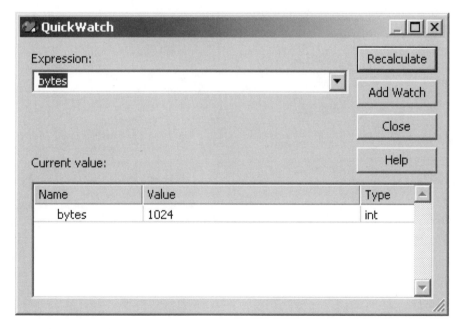

Figure E-13   *Quick Watch window shows variable, which you can change.*

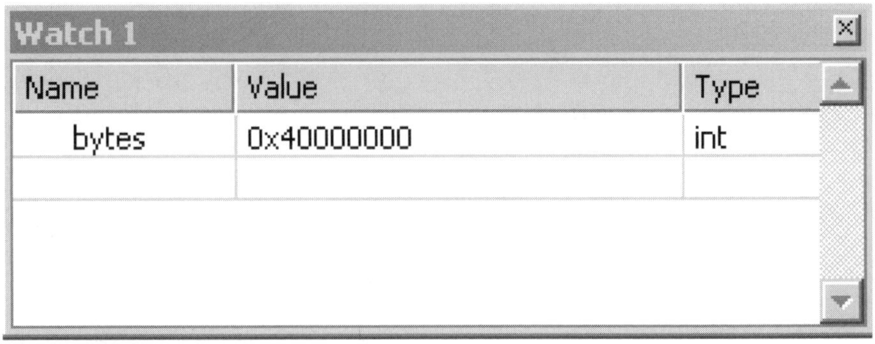

Name	Value	Type
bytes	0x40000000	int

Figure E-14   *Visual Studio Watch window.*

E.6.2.3 DEBUGGER OPTIONS

You can change debugger options from the menu Tools | Options selecting Debugging from the list. Figure E-15 illustrates setting a hexadecimal display. If you then go back to a Watch window, you will see a hexadecimal value, such as 0×400, displayed.

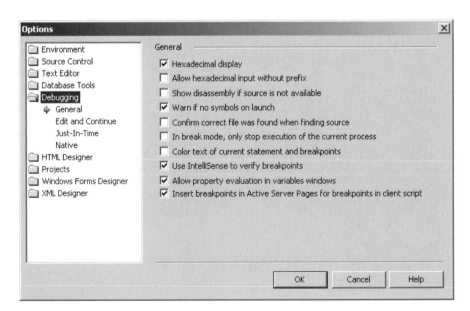

Figure E-15   *Setting a hexadecimal display in Debugging Options.*

E.6.2.4 SINGLE STEPPING

When you are stopped in the debugger, you can single step. You can also begin execution by single stepping. There are a number of single-step buttons. The most common are (in the order shown on the toolbar):

- Step Into
- Step Over
- Step Out

There is also a Run to Cursor button.

With Step Into you step into a function if the cursor is positioned on a call to a function. With Step Over you step to the next line (or statement or instruction, depending on the selection in the drop-down menu next to the step buttons). To see how Step Into works, build the Bytes\Step2 project, where the multiplication by 1,024 has been replaced by a function call to the static method OneK. Set a break point at the first function call, then click Step Into. The result is illustrated in Figure E-16. Note the red dot at the break point and the yellow arrow in the function.

During debugging, VS.NET maintains a call stack. In our simple example the call stack is just two deep. See Figure E-17.

Summary

VS.NET is a very rich, integrated development environment (IDE), with many features that make programming more enjoyable. In this appendix we covered the basics of using VS.NET to edit, compile, run, and debug programs, so that you will be equipped to use VS.NET in what you have learned in the book. Nonetheless, it is worth spending time to become familiar with many more of the VS.NET features, because understanding how to use them will make your development work much easier. A project can be built in different configurations, such as Debug and Release. VS.NET has a vast array of features for building database applications, Web applications, components, and many other kinds of projects. We discuss some of these additional features in the chapters where they are pertinent.

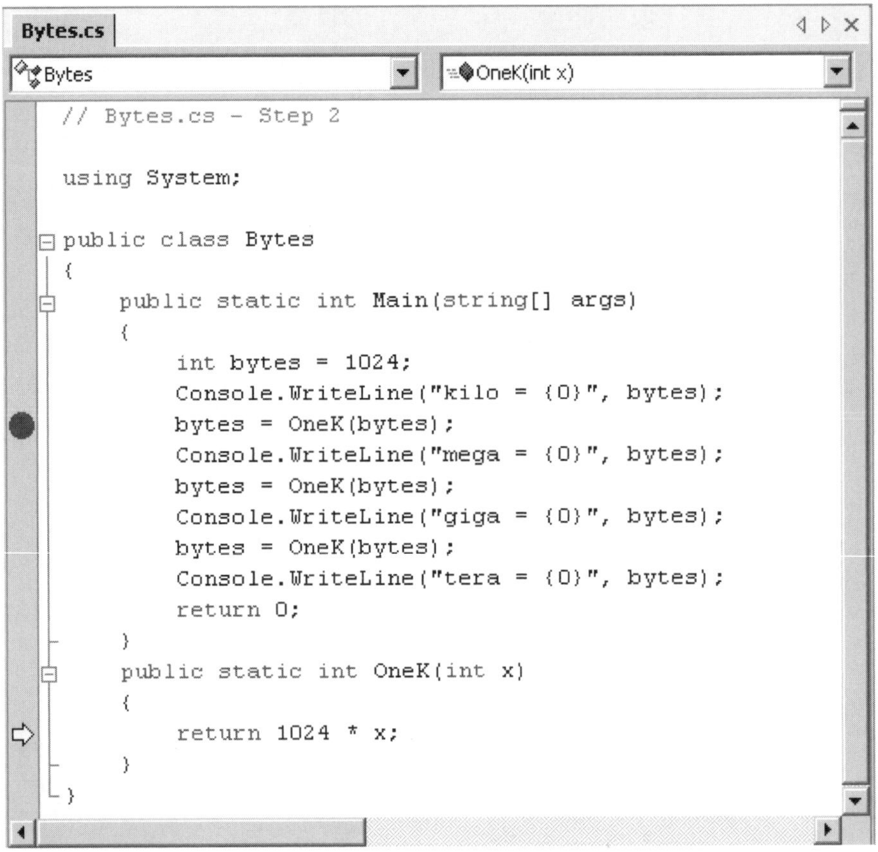

Bytes.cs
Bytes
OneK(int x)
// Bytes.cs - Step 2
using System;
public class Bytes
{
public static int Main(string[] args)
{
int bytes = 1024;
Console.WriteLine("kilo = {0}", bytes);
bytes = OneK(bytes);
Console.WriteLine("mega = {0}", bytes);
bytes = OneK(bytes);
Console.WriteLine("giga = {0}", bytes);
bytes = OneK(bytes);
Console.WriteLine("tera = {0}", bytes);
return 0;
}
public static int OneK(int x)
{
return 1024 * x;
}
}

Figure E-16 *Stepping into a function.*

Call Stack
Name
Language
Bytes.exe!Bytes.OneK(int x = 0x400) Line 21
C#
Bytes.exe!Bytes.Main(string[] args = {Length=0x0}) Line 11 + 0x8 bytes
C#
Call Stack
Breakpoints
Command Window
Output

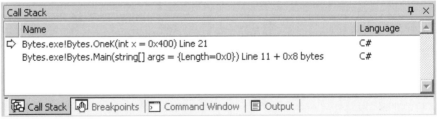

Figure E-17 *The call stack.*

INDEX

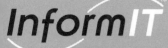

DEVELOPER TRAINING

OBJECT INNOVATIONS offers training course materials in fundamental software technologies used in developing applications in modern computing environments. We emphasize object-oriented techniques, with a focus on Microsoft® technologies, XML, Java™, and Linux™. Our courses have been used by businesses, training companies, and universities throughout North America. End clients include IBM®, HP®, Dell®, Compaq®, FedEx®, UPS®, AOL®, U.S. Bank®, Mellon Bank®, and NASA. Our courses are frequently updated to reflect feedback from classroom use. We aggressively track new technologies and endeavor to keep our courseware up-to-date.

Founded in 1993, Object Innovations has a long record of firsts in courseware. Our Visual C++ course was released before Microsoft's, we introduced one of the first courses in JavaServer Pages, and our Linux Internals 2.4 kernel course came out several months before Red Hat's course. Now we are leading the development of comprehensive developer training in Microsoft's .NET technology.

.NET DEVELOPER TRAINING

Object Innovations is writing the premier book series on .NET for Prentice Hall PTR. These authoritative books are the foundation of our curriculum. Each book matches a corresponding course, and the student materials come bundled with the book, so students have comprehensive reference materials after the course. Each core course is five days in length and is very rich in content, containing well over five days worth of material. The courses are modularized, so background information or special topics not needed for a particular class can be cleanly omitted. On the other hand, the courses can be lengthened as required. Thus each course can be easily customized to meet the particular needs and interests of the students. We also have shorter courses.

The first group consists of shorter, overview courses:

- 401 Introduction to .NET for Developers (1 day)
- 412 .NET Framework Essentials Using C# (3 days)
- 422 .NET Framework Essentials Using VB.NET (3 days)
- 452 Introduction to ASP.NET (3 days)

The second group constitutes the full-length courses that correspond to the books in The Integrated .NET Series form Object Innovations and Prentice Hall PTR:

- 410 Introduction to C# Using .NET (5 days)
- 414 Application Development Using C# and .NET (5 days)
- 420 Introduction to Visual Basic Using .NET (5 days)
- 424 Application Development Using Visual Basic.NET (5 days)
- 434 .NET Architecture and Programming Using Visual C++ (5 days)
- 440 Programming Perl in the .NET Environment (5 days)
- 454 Fundamentals of Web Applications Using .NET and XML (5 days)

MICROSOFT DEVELOPER TRAINING

Our Microsoft curriculum is very extensive, with introductory and advanced courses on C++, Visual C++, MFC, COM/DCOM, OLE, COM+, and advanced topics in Visual Basic™. Selected courses include:

123 Programming COM and DCOM Using ATL (5 days)
127 Programming COM and OLE Using MFC (5 days)
149 Distributed COM+ Programming (5 days)
133 Distributed COM+ Programming Using Visual Basic (5 days)
142 Visual C++ Windows Programming for C Programmers (5 days)
145 MFC Windows Programming for C++ Programmers (5 days)
146 Advanced Windows Programming Using Visual C++ (5 days)
157 Advanced C++ Programming (5 days)

XML DEVELOPER TRAINING

Our XML curriculum covers the broad range of XML technology. We offer courses in "pure" XML – all discussion and exercises based entirely in W3C-recommended standards – as well as training in use of XML through today's dominant enterprise platforms, Java and .NET. Selected courses include:

501 XML for the Enterprise (5 days)
504 Powering Websites with XML (4 days)
506 XML Transformations (3 days)
173 XML and Java (5 days)
454 Fundamentals of Web Applications Using .NET and XML

JAVA DEVELOPER TRAINING

Java training courses span the spectrum from beginning to advanced and provide extensive coverage of both client-side and server-side technologies. Selected courses include:

103 Java Programming (5 days)
105 Using and Developing JavaBeans (4 days)
106 Advanced Java Programming (5 days)
107 CORBA Architecture and Programming Using Java (4 days)
109 Java Server Pages (2 days)
110 Java Servlet Programming (2 days)
111 Introduction to Java RMI (1 day)
163 Enterprise JavaBeans (5 days)
172 Java Foundation Classes (5 days)

LINUX COURSES

Linux courses range from fundamentals and system administration to advanced courses in internals, device drivers and networking. Selected courses include:

135 Fundamentals of Linux (4 days)
310 Linux Internals (5 days)
314 Linux Network Drivers Development (3 days)
320 Linux Network Administration (5 days)

See our .NET website for complete course listings: www.objectinnovations.com/dotnet.htm

OBJECT INNOVATIONS' .NET TRAINING PARTNERS

For information about .NET training using OBJECT INNOVATIONS courseware,
please check with our .NET Training Partners.

ANEW TECHNOLOGY CORPORATION   www.Anew.net

Specialized in IT consulting, training, mentoring, and development, Anew Technology has been serving many satisfied clients. Our business mission is threefold: to stay at the forefront of IT technologies, to satisfy client needs by applying these technologies, and to provide the best service in our industry. Anew Technology is a business partner with Object Innovations in operations and courseware development.

COMPUTER HORIZONS EDUCATION DIVISION   www.ComputerHorizons.com/Training

For over seventeen years Computer Horizons Education Division (CHED) has been providing on-site, instructor-led IT training and customized workshops for organizations nationwide. We have developed extensive curriculum offerings in Web Technologies, Relational Databases, Reporting Tools, Process Improvement, UNIX™ and LINUX™, Client/Server, Mainframe & Legacy Systems, Windows® 2000, and much more. CHED will design, develop and deliver a training solution tailored to each client's training requirements.

COMPUWORKS SYSTEMS, INC.   www.CompuWorks.com

CompuWorks Systems, Inc. is an IT solutions company whose aim is to provide our clients with customized training, support and development services. We are committed to building long term partnerships with our clients in an effort to meet their individual needs. Cutting-edge solutions are our specialty.

CUSTOM TRAINING INSTITUTE   www.4CustomTraining.com

Custom Training Institute is a provider of high quality IT training since 1989. Along with our full line of "off-the-shelf" classes, we excel at providing customized solutions - from technical needs assessment through course development and delivery. We specialize in Legacy Skills Transformation (i.e., COBOL to Java), Oracle (DBA, Developer, Discoverer and Applications), UNIX, C++ and Java for computer professionals.

DB BASICS   www.DBBasics.com

DBBasics, founded in 1988 as a Microsoft® solution development company, has developed and delivered Microsoft technology training since its inception. DBBasics specializes in delivering database and developer technology training to corporate customers. Our vast development experience, coupled with the requirement for instructors to consistently provide hands-on consulting to our customers, enables DBBasics to provide best of breed instruction in the classroom as well as customized eLearning solutions and database technology consulting.

DEVCOM   www.dev-cominc.com

Devcom Corporation offers a full line of courses and seminars for software developers and engineers. Currently Devcom provides technical courses and seminars around the country for Hewlett® Packard, Compaq® Computer, Informix® Software, Silicon Graphics®, Quantum/Maxtor® and Gateway® Inc. Our senior .NET/C# instructor is currently working in conjunction with Microsoft to provide .NET training to their internal technical staff.

FOCAL POINT   www.FocalPoint-Inc.com

Focal Point specializes in providing optimum instructor-led Information Technology technical training for our corporate clients on either an onsite basis, or in regional public course events. All of our course curricula is either developed by our staff of "World Class Instructors" or upon careful evaluation and scrutiny is adopted and acquired from our training partners who are similarly focussed. Our course offerings pay special attention to Real World issues. Our classes are targeted toward topical areas that will ensure immediate productivity upon course completion.

I/SRG   www.isrg.com

The I/S RESOURCE GROUP helps organizations to understand, plan for and implement emerging I/S technologies and methodologies. By combining education, training, briefings and consulting, we assist our clients to effectively apply I/S technologies to achieve business benefits. Our eBusiness Application Bootcamp is an integrated set of courses that prepares learners to utilize XML, OOAD, Java™, JSP, EJB, ASP, CORBA and .NET to build eBusiness applications. Our eBusiness Briefings pinpoint emerging technologies and methodologies.

OBJECT INNOVATIONS' .NET TRAINING PARTNERS

For information about .NET training using OBJECT INNOVATIONS courseware,
please check with our .NET Training Partners.

RELIABLE SOFTWARE   www.ReliableSoftware.com

Reliable Software, Inc. uses Microsoft technology to quickly develop cost-effective software solutions for the small to mid-size business or business unit. We use state-of-the-art techniques to allow business rules, database models and the user interface to evolve as your business needs evolve. We can provide design and implementation consulting, or training.

SKILLBRIDGE TRAINING   www.SkillBridgeTraining.com

SkillBridge is a leading provider of blended technical training solutions. The company's service offerings are designed to meet a wide variety of client requirements. Offering an integration of instructor-led training, e-learning and mentoring programs, SkillBridge delivers high value solutions in a cost-effective manner. SkillBridge's technology focus includes, among others, programming languages, operating systems, databases, and internet and web technologies.

/TRAINING/ETC INC.   www.trainingetc.com

A training company dedicated to delivering quality technical training, courseware development, and consulting in a variety of subject matter areas, including Programming Languages and Design (including C, C++, OOAD/UML, Perl, and Java), a complete UNIX curriculum (from UNIX Fundamentals to System Administration), the Internet (including HTML/CGI, XML and JavaScript Programming) and RDBMS (including Oracle and Sybase).

WATERMARK LEARNING   www.WatermarkLearning.com

Watermark Learning provides a wide range of IT skill development training and mentoring services to a variety of industries, software / consulting firms and government. We provide flexible options for delivery: onsite, consortium and public classes in three major areas: project management, requirements analysis and software development, including e-Commerce. Our instructors are seasoned, knowledgeable practitioners, who use their industry experience along with our highly-rated courseware to effectively build technical skills relevant to your business need.

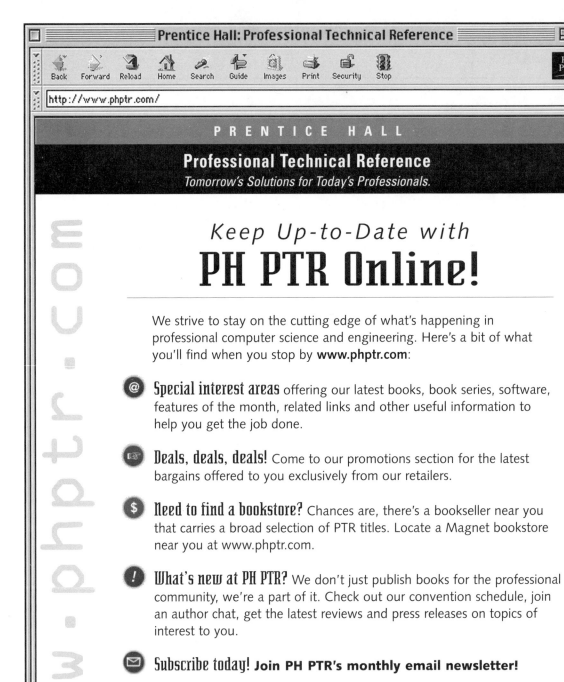